Hans Christian Andersen
and
Community

Hans Christian Andersen and Community

Edited by
Anne Klara Bom, Jacob Bøggild, and
Johs. Nørregaard Frandsen

University Press of Southern Denmark 2019

Publications from the Hans Christian Andersen Center
Volume 7: Hans Christian Andersen and Community
©The authors and University Press of Southern Denmark 2019
Printed by Narayana Press
Cover by Dorthe Møller, Unisats Aps
Cover Illustration: Papercut made by Hans Christian Andersen in 1867. Published with permission from the Hans Christian Andersen Museum.

ISBN 978-87-408-3220-4

University Press of Southern Denmark
55 Campusvej
DK-5230 Odense M
www.universitypress.dk

Distribution in the United States and Canada:
International Specialized Book Services
5804 NE Hassalo Street
Portland, OR 97213-3644 USA
www.isbs.com

Distribution in the United Kingdom:
Gazelle
White Cross Mills
Hightown
Lancaster
LA1 4 XS
U.K.
www.gazellebookservices.co.uk

Table of contents

Hans Christian Andersen and Community   9
An introduction
Anne Klara Bom and Jacob Bøggild

Introductory lecture: The Age of Fairy Tales   23
Hans Christian Andersen and Community
Johs. Nørregaard Frandsen

COMMUNICATION AND DISCOURSE

A Community Incommunicado
On Troubled Communication in Hans Christian Andersen's Fairy Tales   35
Helena Březinová

Toy Stories   57
On Toys and Childhood in "The Steadfast Tin Soldier"
Frederike Felcht

The Problem of "The Red Shoes"   77
Jacob Bøggild

Random Communities, Cross-readings   95
Hans Christian Andersen in between Universality and Historicity
Dan Ringgaard

CONCRETE AND IMAGINARY COMMUNITIES

Hans Christian Andersen, Friend of the Rich and Defender of the Poor   117
Michel Forget

Temporary Communities   133
A Theme in Hans Christian Andersen's Travel Accounts
Lars Handesten

The Grimms as the Elephant in the Danish Fairy Tale Room   149
An Interpretation of Hans Christian Andersen's Concept of a
Future Community of Fairy Tale Readers
Mads Sohl Jessen

Word and Image in Hans Christian Andersen's Papercuts   165
Ejnar Stig Askgaard

Hans Christian Andersen's Discovery of the Poet as   191
National Icon
The Public Memorial as Urban Phantasmagoria
Jakob Stougaard-Nielsen

ETHICS AND VALUES

Ethics of the Discarded: Empathy with the Inorganic   209
Hans Christian Andersen's use of waste, rubbish, and other stuff
Karin Sanders

Hans Christian Andersen between community and commons   223
"The Ugly Duckling" and "The Fir Tree" revisited
Anne Klara Bom

Funen means Fine   243
Andersen the Anti-nationalist
Torsten Bøgh Thomsen

Underground Andersen   259
Political Allegory and the Fairy Tale
Marianne Stecher

Communal Uses

(De-)Constructing Community in Twenty-First Century Literary Transformations of Andersen's "The Little Mermaid" and "The Snow Queen" — 279
Julie K. Allen

Hans Christian Andersen and the Comic Art Community — 301
The Strange Case of the Little Mermaid's New Clothes
Camilla Storskog

War Veterans and Communal Guilt — 319
Hans Christian Andersen's "The Tinder Box" and "The Steadfast Tin Soldier" in Contemporary Scandinavian Cinema and TV
Elisabeth Oxfeldt

"I'll sing about those who are gay, and those who are sorrowful" — 341
The Use of Hans Christian Andersen's Fairy Tales in Narrative Medicine
Anders Juhl Rasmussen and Anne-Marie Mai

Hans Christian Andersen's Literary Imagination Interpreted and Reconstructed in China — 359
A Semiotic Reading
Ye Rulan

Performing Fairy Tales — 375
Possibilities of Practicing Difference in the Museum
Henrik Lübker

Hans Christian Andersen and Community
An introduction

Anne Klara Bom and Jacob Bøggild
University of Southern Denmark, Odense

If no man is an island, then every man belongs to a community – or a number of communities. In fact, we are all inevitably born into a social context consisting of more than one community. We are born into a family and a local community of this or that kind as well as larger communities such as regions or nations. Our profession will often make us a part of yet other communities. Communities are formed on the basis of political agendas, hobbies and a host of other social and cultural phenomena. Modern technology means that some communities can become global – with all the factors of estrangement this involves.

This is one among many reasons why the theme of community has perhaps never been of a more vital significance than in our present day and age. The process we refer to as modernity has been synonymous with the gradual fragmentation and disintegration of traditional communities on various levels of our societies. Today, we might be facing the culmination of this process. The spectres of nationalism are undermining various national and international communities. Inequality is on the rise. If people unite it is too often in the mistrust and sometimes hatred of other people. Hans Christian Andersen lived at a time when this process was at its early stages, and he was acutely aware of its potential perils. We see this in as early a tale as "The Tinderbox" where friends are of the fair-weather kind, where it is an execution that makes people rally together, and where the 'joyous' ending is in fact synonymous with the foundation of a regime of terror.

The theme of community is in fact a major one in Andersen's fairy tales and stories; often in ways which have to do with struggles for recognition in a social arena. As an obvious example, "The Ugly Duckling" is constantly on the move from community to community, and in each community, it is confronted with the narrowmindedness of the inhabitants, who are incapable of recognising it for what it is and turn their backs on it. Many of Andersen's tales and stories about communities are based on acts of exclusion. It can be argued that he, by highlighting the dynamics of social exclusion, establishes a secret community of the desolate, the lonely and the marginalised. This community is for example expressed in his writings when diverging characters isolated from the majority are given the opportunity to speak. We, Andersen's readers, are confronted with life conditions and feelings at the bottom of society in "The Little Match Girl," and we are invited to identify with the little girl in "Heartache," who did not have the one button that could give her access to the pug's grave and thereby to the spontaneously formed community inside the gates.

Across borders, an important part of cultural heritage is the literary canon, and as the battles of modernity are fought on one level, the gatherings around literature unfold on other levels. Heritage is on political agendas worldwide and on school curricula as never before, centered on the question of how we can make sense of ourselves in our brave new world: What materials, beliefs and narratives are valuable enough to be passed on to the next generation? How do they encapsulate the story of 'us' and who are 'the others'? Following geographer and anthropologist David Harvey (2001), these cultural processes are examples of how heritage is never static, but always dynamically in motion, and that heritage is always already about power. Thus, political handlings and instrumentalisations of heritage contain re-workings and adjustments that enable us to see how identity, power and authority is produced throughout societies. Here, it will also be of interest how people engage with heritage on an everyday level; how they perceive it, contest it and use it. When people, individually and collectively, mirror themselves in what they understand as their heritage, other communities seem to appear alongside the transformations of traditional communities. A recurring element in these culturally specific communities is literature, and Hans Christian Andersen is a key figure here, as his literary and cultural legacy has a magnetic effect on people around the globe. A vivid example of this effect was the conference *Hans Christian Andersen and Community*. The conference was held at the University of Southern Denmark to celebrate the 150th anniversary of Hans Christian Andersen's status as honourary citizen in Odense. Twenty countries were represented at the conference, and in a total of 69 papers, scholars presented their thoughts on how Andersen's works can be of use when we try to make sense of ourselves and others in today's world. Many of these papers have later been transformed into articles, and in this book, we introduce 19 of these articles that in various ways activate the concept of community in relation to Andersen as an author and as a citizen of the world he lived in – as well as the cultural icon which he has become. Following our introduction, the book begins with Head of the Hans Christian Andersen Centre, Johs. Nørregaard Frandsen's, introductory lecture from the conference, "The Age of Fairy Tales: Hans Christian Andersen and Community," where he presents his notes and thoughts on the conference theme. We then proceed to present the 19 contributions organized in four sections. The first concentrates on language and discourse in Andersen's tales.

Communication and Discourse

As the fundamental sign system of human beings, language makes communication and thus the formation of communities possible. All human beings are united by the ability to communicate by means of language. There is even an eroticism and sensualism of language, of sounds and cadences, which may originate from the way we are all initiated into the community of human communicators in our very early childhood. But at the same time our tongues are confused and translation from one language into another is often necessary in order to communicate across borders. Language can also be used as a means of division and exclusion. It can be used as a shibboleth in order to exclude those who are not accepted or tolerated within a given community. At the same time as language has the potential of connecting us with each other, it estranges us from ourselves and the world around us. This has been the foundational insight of much thinking about language in the twentieth century in the wake of Saussure's discovery of the arbitrary nature of the linguistic sign. This sign enables us to handle and manipulate the thing abstractly – in its absence – but the prize we pay for this is a fundamental estrangement. Moreover, what Saussure discovered was something many authors and thinkers through the ages had been aware of or sensed. Andersen is one such author to whom the question of language is never simple and straightforward and to whom communication can always break down. The first section of our book is focused on this aspect of Andersen.

Helena Březinová opens the section with her chapter "A Community Incommunicado: On Troubled Communication in Hans Christian Andersen's Fairy Tales." She argues that Andersen's art of storytelling is in fact the exact opposite of *hyggelig* oral delivery. He is not the original or 'organic' storyteller rooted in a comfortable community some would like him to be and communication between his characters does often fail. Březinová begins with a discussion of the basic level of miscommunication between characters in Andersen's fairy tales (in "The Steadfast Tin Soldier" and "The Shepherdess and the Chimney Sweep"). She then addresses a metatextual level where miscommunication is also a misunderstanding between the artist and his or her audience (exemplified by "The Fir Tree" and "The Little Mermaid"). Finally, the chapter attempts to place Andersen's work on and with language (as in "The Shadow" and the various object tales) in the context of the growing general scepticism towards conventional literary expression and language around the year 1900 with the *Lord Chandos Letter* (1902) by Hofmannsthal as a pivotal text.

Frederike Felcht's "Toy Stories: On Toys and Childhood in 'The Steadfast Tin Soldier'" follows up by investigating the role of toys in "The Steadfast Tin Soldier" and other of Andersen's object tales. Her starting point is Georg Brandes as a critic who simultaneously understood and misunderstood what is communicated by Andersen's tales. Brandes perceived that scenes of childhood and play are central in Andersen's tales. But, according to Felcht, he missed the subversive character of such scenes and instead projected into them a childish innocence and naivety which is in fact alien to them. Andersen's poetics of toys is rather one which has the playroom haunted by phenomena connected to the darker sides of the adult world like capitalism and militarism, as Felcht demonstrates in her reading of "The Steadfast Tin Soldier" and other object tales of toys. She shows how Andersen's object tales connect things to their materiality and thereby discursively question gender and power relations, which were believed to be aspects of the natural order of things in his time (and still are in certain ideological constellations of this day and age).

Jacob Bøggild's "The Problem of 'The Red Shoes'" is a discussion of what is communicated by this apparently horrid tale. According to Bøggild, the tale operates at several discursive and generic levels which are not able to communicate with or shed light upon each other. On one level it is a story of everyday life about an orphaned young girl who is kept in the margins of the community that should have embraced her. At this level the story also analyses how desire is the desire of the other instigated by the ban or taboo. On another level "The Red Shoes" is a fairy tale which mimics the Grimm brothers at their gruesome best. On yet another level, the story is a Christian legend about the sin of vanity and ultimate redemption. But the voice of the Law and the ban and the voice of Mercy do not seem to be able to speak the same language at this level of the tale – as if communication between the Old and the New Testament suffered a breakdown. The way Andersen weaves these levels into one single tale while maintaining their inability to comprehend and shed light on each other is a testament to his dizzying mastery in apprehending and mixing various genres.

Dan Ringgaard's "Random Communities, Cross-readings: Hans Christian Andersen in between Universality and Historicity" also situates Andersen in a discursive plurality. Ringgaard investigates how Andersen's tales communicate and translate across temporal and spatial distances in spite of the fact that they are often poorly translated. An investigation, in other words, of how these tales are able to connect to and to create global communities and thereby aspire to become universal literary commons liberated from the constraints of historical study. In order to do this, Ringgaard cross-reads first "Little Ida's Flowers" with Hélène Cixous' *Three Steps on the Ladder of Writing* (1993) and then "Clumsy Hans" with an article about creativity and improvisation by Tim Ingold and Elizabeth Hallam. In the cross-reading with Cixous, Ringgaard shows how what he calls the differential power of language does not lead the reader to an essence shared by the two texts, but to a common ground in the sense of a clearing where thoughts about death, writing and what it means to be human can be exchanged. The cross-reading with Ingold and Hallam is about a different kind of opening, an opening of the text of "Clumsy Hans" to other ideas of improvisation contrary to those of the time of the text. Here the text itself becomes a meeting place where ideas separated by time and space can cross-fertilize.

Concrete and Imaginary Communities

As Ringgaard points out, there is a connective power in and of Andersen's tales which can communicate and translate across temporal and spatial borders. They are commons which can be shared by a global or universal community of readers as well as by reading communities of a more local kind. Different kinds of real, in the sense of non-fictional, communities, some of them communities of readers, are also represented in or implied by the works of Andersen as an author and a visual artist. A number of these communities, a diverse group or assemblage, are discussed in the chapters which make up this section.

Michel Forget writes about how Andersen was split, as it were, between two communities, two societal groups, in his chapter "Hans Christian Andersen, Friend of the Rich and Defender of the Poor." He became recognised and accepted among the cultural elite, nationally and internationally. This elite consisted, to a large extent, of the aristocracy and the rich bourgeoisie. Without the support of this group of people, Andersen would not have survived as an artist. At the same time, Andersen remained faithful to the much humbler community of people which he originated from. He did not forget his poor background and when he could get away with it he acted as a spokesman for the deprived. This was a balancing act, because liberal views were considered to be suspect in the era of absolute monarchy. Forget explores some of the literary strategies Andersen, 'the cautious rebel' in the terms of Elias Bredsdorff (1989), employed in order to maintain this balancing act.

In "Temporary Communities: A Theme in Hans Christian Andersen's Travel Accounts," Lars Handesten focuses on the many intermediate and fleeting communities of fellow travellers Andersen met and was a part of during his many travels abroad by different means of transportation. He wrote about them in his travelogues and in his memoirs and diaries. Handesten pays special attention to the pronoun of "we," which Andersen used to refer to himself and his fellow travellers. Who does this "we" really refer to and include? How does the first-person plural function in various contexts? The chapter thus examines the narrative character of different travel experiences and travelling communities, national as well as cosmopolitan, in Andersen's oeuvre. But Handesten also addresses how large-scale political issues might affect the fleeting communities of travelling companions, something Andersen experienced several times.

In the following chapter, "The Grimms as the Elephant in the Danish Fairy Tale Room," Mads Sohl Jessen writes about the fact that there are very few references to the collection of fairy tales of the Grimm brothers in Andersen's early writings, even if this collection had succeeded in shaping a transnational community of readers of fairy tales and was also popular in Denmark. The success of the collection of tales by the Grimm brothers might even be one source of inspiration to Andersen when he decided to write his own tales, thereby plunging himself into the same market while shaping his own community of readers. The chapter investigates the stylistic inventions, irony and phantasmagoria, which Andersen employed when writing his own tales; the devices, in other words, which make them unique and set them apart from the Grimms' tales. Jessen further debates whether alleged collectors of tales, like the Grimm brothers, did invent much more of their material themselves than we usually think is the case.

Next, in "Word and Image in Hans Christian Andersen's Papercuts," Ejnar Stig Askgaard asks whether it is possible to compare the verbal art of Andersen to his visual art, even if the former did appear and made an impact in the public sphere while the latter remained a private affair in Andersen's own life time. As Askgaard points out, Andersen worked in both media from the very beginning of his career. However, the scholarly focus has been almost exclusively on Andersen's literary production. Askgaard uses Andersen's papercuts to demonstrate that words and images are indeed closely connected in Andersen's artistic oeuvre. This link can be understood in the light of traditions which belong to the kind of folk community Andersen was born into, while, at the same time, it is in unison with the intermediality that was an ideal of the Romantic movement. The folk traditions Andersen was familiar with in his childhood, had to do with puns and riddles and, indeed, letters in the shape of artful papercuts.

Jakob Stougaard-Nielsen concludes this section with the chapter "Hans Christian Andersen's Discovery of the Poet as National Icon: The Public Memorial as Urban Phantasmagoria," which is about the role poets and authors came to play in what we refer to as nation building, the construction of a specific kind of imaginary community. Stougaard-Nielsen's starting point is the travelogue *A Visit to Portugal* from 1866, where Andersen as a literary tourist experiences the modernization and restoration of urban, national spaces in Lisbon and in this context considers a monument to Camões. Stougaard-Nielsen then turns his attention to the tale "The Dryad," an ambivalent celebration of the World Exhibition in Paris in 1867, which Andersen attended, a tale about the turbulent, modern experience of urbanity as display and stagecraft. It is considered how such experiences and impressions had an impact on the canonization of Andersen as they affected the way he made plans for his statue to be erected in Copenhagen. This is then linked to a wider wave of commemorations that passed over Europe in the nineteenth century in which famous authors played an important role in the formation of modern nations – also as communities imagined to be based on certain sets of values.

Ethics and Values

In a globalised world where 'value' is an omnipresent buzzword, both in regressive political discourses (let's go back to the traditional values) and in neoliberal discourses (let's co-create social value), it is pivotal that scholars direct attention to cultural processes that reflect how globalisation in general and neoliberalism in particular have affected an on-going transformation of people's values (Held and Moore 2008). This includes a focus on how a cultural icon like Hans Christian Andersen can avoid being reduced to texts we are required to understand as elements in literary canons. One way to avoid such a reduction is to conceptualise Andersen as a communicator of values: as a potential medium through which new narratives about values can be told (Bom and Thomsen 2018).

The on-going expansion of capitalism through language has as one result that the concept of 'value' and what is termed as 'valuable' is rather foggy, because the fear of an "erosion of values" (Held and Moore 2008, 1) is communicated concurrently with institutional articulations of economic value as the only desirable and valuable form of the concept. A possible scholarly response is to connect the concept of value to something other than economy (Bom and Thomsen 2018). Within such a framework, values can be defined as "guiding principles in life" that affect our perceptions of attitudes, beliefs, norms and traits (Schwartz 2012, 16), and ethics as "secondary reflections on moral values, beliefs and practices" (Zylinska 2006, 76). The four chapters in this section can all be read as suggestions to how Hans

Christian Andersen's work communicates values and triggers ethical reflections, and how his writings can be of present and future use in these contexts, where the main focus is on how people relate to the world.

Hans Christian Andersen's fairy tales and stories are ambiguous and composite, full of paradoxes and grotesque fates. In such chaotic settings it could be tempting for an author to act as a compass that presents implicit and explicit directions to his readers. But Andersen never does that. He always refrains from moralising, and that is probably one of the reasons why Andersen's works still appeal to people across time and space: The fairy tales present and question standards, norms, attitudes and behaviours in open-ended ways that invite us as readers to use our imagination and activate our own moral compasses when we try to make sense of them. The following chapters are examples of the ambiguous complexity that follows if we attempt to identify ethics and values in Andersen's works. But simultaneously, they can be seen as examples of how the fairy tales seem to insist on present-day relevance: They incite us to be skeptical and critical of common-sense perceptions, ideologies and convictions, and to never stop questioning our own motives, history and political agendas.

In the chapter, "Ethics of the Discarded: Empathy with the Inorganic: Hans Christian Andersen's Use of Waste, Rubbish, and Other Stuff," Karin Sanders directs attention to some of the most divergent and marginalised objects in Andersen's fairy tales as she focuses on the agency of rubbish and waste. Through this focus on Andersen's investment with the discarded, Sanders argues, a *material poetics* is created, and the act of adding value to "the ostensibly valueless" contains an ethical claim: When Andersen "picks up the trash" and equips it with voice, affect and agency, processes of discarding, overlooking and alienating are brought to light. In the nineteenth century as well as today, such processes are embedded in social and aesthetic value systems, and in the chapter, Sanders demonstrates how Andersen's use of rubbish in the object tales prod us to consider or reconsider both the world we share with material stuff of all sorts, and how we decide who and what is so shameful that it should be discarded.

In a similar vein, Anne Klara Bom deals with a culturally specific present-day process of alienation in the chapter "Hans Christian Andersen Between Community and Commons: 'The Ugly Duckling' and 'The Fir Tree' Revisited," as she focuses on the use of Hans Christian

Andersen in the Danish citizenship tests that must be passed by newcomers who want to become citizens in Denmark. Bom argues that the tests and their associated learning material positions Andersen as a 'frozen' gatekeeper for an already completed nation: a closed, exclusive community. This makes her revisit two of Andersen's fairy tales and suggest that they hold the potential to be reframed as 'cultural commons' in future more democratic meetings with newcomers, meetings that can contain ethical dialogues and debates about the contents, effects and functions of the term community in Denmark.

Torsten Bøgh Thomsen is also interested in possible alternative interpretations of Andersen that challenge the static, hegemonic images and uses of him. In "Funen Means Fine: Andersen the Anti-nationalist" Thomsen questions the common-sense perception of Andersen as a proponent of a sentimental and national romanticism with reference to Andersen's specific use of irony, which challenges the legitimacy of the so-called Danish Golden Age's nationalist agendas. In his analysis, Thomsen shows examples of how Andersen's work can be said to carry a political and anti-nationalistic undertone that comes across as a discrete critique of the time's dominant propagandistic uses of art and literature, he is frequently associated with. This undertone, Thomsen argues, can be of productive use in future critical analyses of how nationalistic values and images were presented in the Golden Age.

In Marianne Stecher's chapter, "Underground Andersen: Political Allegory and the Fairy Tale," which concludes this section of the book, the focus is also on what lies beneath the polished surface in Andersen's works: Stecher directs attention to the 'underground' Andersen and asks what is at stake when elements from the passive Andersen-archives are suddenly reactivated in cultural memory. In her analysis, she focuses on two "halfway forgotten fairy tales" with the purpose of illuminating the potential of them as political allegories. Stecher argues that this function is a significant element in the sustainability of Andersen's fairy tales across borders: Even if they are currently placed in the archive of cultural memories, the dark and ironic elements they hold appeal to different historical contexts and, thus, they have the potential to be excavated from the underground and revived as aesthetic and relevant reflections of present-day politics.

Communal Uses

The third section's arguments of how Hans Christian Andersen's works hold potential to be of use in current contexts is followed up in this concluding section where different examples are presented of how Andersen is put to use as a cultural icon in different situations, on varying platforms and for diverse purposes. The first three chapters in this section focus on examples of how Andersen is currently (re-)presented in popular culture. Cultural studies scholar Lawrence Grossberg has argued that people primarily invest themselves affectively in popular culture, as they here find the space to mirror themselves and thereby relate to their own identity (Grossberg 1992, 85). Thus, even though popular cultural elements tend to be overlooked or underestimated, they can be considered as pivotal for the sustainability of a cultural icon as Andersen: When Andersen's works are continuously transformed into different popular cultural products and narratives, he is simultaneously supplied with culturally specific meaning that reflects the world view and values where he is put to use (Bom 2014).

Julie K. Allen's focus in her chapter, "(De-)Constructing Community in Twenty-First Century Literary Transformations of Andersen's 'The Little Mermaid' and 'The Snow Queen,'" is on how the global resonance and the sensitivity to community dynamics in Andersen's fairy tales make them continuously relevant to literary adaptations. Allen presents examples of adaptations of "The Little Mermaid" and "The Snow Queen" and argues that it is Andersen's framing and use of communities as threatened and fragmented that appeals to adapters who use the tales to discuss current challenges that face communities across borders. Allen argues that while the processes where adapters engage in a dialogue with the original fairy tales' thematisations of community take place within recognizably derivative frames, they simultaneously reflect distinct sociocultural contexts in which each text was created. Thus, the interconnectedness of Andersen's stories and their adaptations can be seen as examples of how deeply Andersen's stories have integrated themselves into the global community.

In her chapter, "Hans Christian Andersen and the Comic Art Community: The Strange Case of the Little Mermaid's New Clothes," Camilla Storskog is also interested in how Andersen's fairy tales are adapted by other genres. She focuses specifically on the graphic novel. Storskog presents as a case a graphic novel that has adapted central elements from "The Little Mermaid," but unlike most adaptations, this gothic graphic novel reuses the uncanny, dark elements of the fairy tale, which results in an appeal to the "adult readership so often ignored in processes of adaptation." Storskog argues that while the case can be seen as a welcome counter-narrative to other adaptations' tendency towards a taming and sanitising of Andersen's fairy tales, the subtle terror in the original fairy tale is at risk of drowning in the conventions of the genre it is adapted to, which in this case involves the horror and gore of the gothic graphic novel.

Elisabeth Oxfeldt shows in her chapter, "War Veterans and Communal Guilt: Hans Christian Andersen's 'The Tinder Box' and 'The Steadfast Tin Soldier' in Contemporary Scandinavian Cinema and TV," examples of how soldier figures from Andersen's fairy tales are reused in two examples of Scandinavian cinema. She identifies two different war veteran figures in the soldier from "The Tinder Box" and in "The Steadfast Tin Soldier" and illustrates how these figures are reinterpreted in two Scandinavian audio-visual narratives that are concerned with present-day war veterans. In this setting, the fairy tales function as modern narratives that negotiate communal anxiety, guilt and discomfort surrounding the homecoming of psychologically and physically injured soldiers. Thus, Oxfeldt's main argument is that Andersen's two soldiers still serve as stereotypical archetypes in Scandinavian perceptions of the challenging reintegration of veterans into their respective communities in the new millennium.

The appealing qualities of Hans Christian Andersen's fairy tales are of course also recognised on other platforms than the ones belonging to popular culture. In the chapter, "'I'll sing about those who are gay, and those who are sorrowful': The Use of Hans Christian Andersen's Fairy Tales in Narrative Medicine," Anders Juhl Rasmussen and Anne-Marie Mai present an example from an educational context where they show how Andersen is used as a bridge builder between the Humanities and Medicine when he figures as subject matter in the course Narrative Medicine at the University of Southern Denmark. Based on the argument that the competence of reading a fictional narrative is similar to the competence of listening to an authentic patient narrative, they present examples from Andersen's fairy tales that can be of use for today's upcoming doctors. In this context, the fairy tales can serve as means to accomplish Narrative Medicine's goals of improving the ability to listen and communicate with empathy to all persons in the community of health care.

All processes where Hans Christian Andersen is located in new contexts involve interpretation, translation and adjustment. Ye Rulan's chapter, "Hans Christian Andersen's Literary Imagination Interpreted and Reconstructed in China: A Semiotic Reading," presents examples of processes where Andersen is located in past and present Chinese contexts. In a semiotic analysis, she shows how signs and symbols in Andersen's fairy tales are perceived, re-worked and appropriated by Chinese audiences to ensure a positive empowerment of the Chinese readers. Thus, Ye Rulan illustrates how the Chinese gaze works in the translational and interpretational processes as her examples show how texts are read, understood and interpreted based on the involvement of the readers' personal experiences and base of knowledge in the specific cultural context. Ye Rulan's main argument is that Andersen's fairy tales are continuously renewed in these processes, where traces of past practice engage in a dialogic process with the here and now in China – a 'now' that is dynamically in motion.

The severe challenge of capturing and locating Andersen in a solid, justifiable and appealing way in a practical context is the focus of the last chapter in this section, "Performing Fairy Tales: Possibilities of Practicing Difference in the Museum." Henrik Lübker's case is the upcoming international tourist attraction that will transform the original Hans Christian Andersen Museum into a new and innovative 'house of fairy tales.' Obviously, this process involves academic considerations on how to present the fairy tales that "are not willingly reduced to traditional static museum objects," as Lübker puts it. In the analysis, he argues that the performative strategies of Andersen's fairy tales have potential to be of productive use in the inclusion and staging of difference, as both the fairy tales and the new museum are places of disorientation that ask visitors and readers to consider, yet again, what it means to be in a world full of others.

We believe the four sections outlined above provide a comprehensive and in-depth discussion of the theme of Andersen and Community.[1] But of course, there is so much more to be said on this topic and room for further studies. We hope that *Hans Christian*

Andersen and Community will be an inspiration for further conversations and studies among the expanding global community of readers of Hans Christian Andersen.

References

Bom, Anne Klara. 2014. "H.C. Andersen – et kulturfænomen i teori og praksis." In *H.C. Andersen i det moderne samfund*, edited by Anne Klara Bom, Jacob Bøggild and Johs. Nørregaard Frandsen, 185-206. Odense: University Press of Southern Denmark.

Bom, Anne Klara, and Torsten Bøgh Thomsen. 2018. "'La sensazione di una melanconica positività!' Valuations of the Popular Hans Christian Andersen in Italy." *Studi Germanici* 12: 195–216.

Bredsdorff, Elias. 1989: "H.C. Andersen – den forsigtige rebel." In *Udsyn over H.C. Andersen*, edited by Johan de Mylius, 5–14. Odense: H.C. Andersen-Centret, Odense Universitet.

Grossberg, Lawrence 1992. *We Gotta Get Out of the Place: Popular Conservatism and Postmodern Culture*. New York, NY/London, UK: Routledge.

Harvey, David C. 2001. "Heritage Pasts and Heritage Presents: temporality, meaning and the scope of heritage studies." *International Journal of Heritage Studies* 7(4): 319–338.

Held, David, and Henrietta L. Moore. 2008. *Cultural Politics in a Global Age: Uncertainty, Solidarity and Innovation*. Oxford: Oneworld.

Schwartz, Shalom H. 2012. "An Overview of the Schwartz Theory of Basic Values." *Online Readings in Psychology and Culture* 2(1). doi:10.9707/2307-0919.1116

Zylinska, Joanna. 2006. "Cultural Studies and Ethics." In *New Cultural Studies: Adventures in Theory*, edited by Gary Hall and Clare Birchall, 71–87. Edinburgh: Edinburgh University Press.

Notes

1   If nothing else is mentioned in the articles, all translations of fairy tales in this book are Jean Hersholt's that can be found on the Hans Christian Andersen Centre's homepage: http://andersen.sdu.dk/vaerk/hersholt/

Introductory lecture:
The Age of Fairy Tales
Hans Christian Andersen and Community[1]

Johs. Nørregaard Frandsen
University of Southern Denmark, Odense

"Our time is indeed a time of fairy tales." That is how Hans Christian Andersen's story "The Dryad" ("Dryaden," 1868) starts. The dryad is a small spirit or fairy that lives in – and is bound to – life in a tree outside Paris. She can glimpse the light of the great city and wishes to experience it. Just once! Her wish is fulfilled, she gets to Paris, experiences the lights, life and drive of the capital. She gets her wish fulfilled in the urban, modern world, but at the cost of her life. The small spirit cannot live away from her tree. Andersen concludes his story about the dryad in this way: "All this has happened and been experienced. We ourselves have seen it, at the Paris Exposition in 1867, in our time, the great and wonderful time of fairy tales." Hans Christian Andersen regarded his authorship and his fairy tales in particular as a way of understanding his life and his own age. Most of his fairy tales and stories portray transformations: the lovely story, for example, of being changed from a mermaid into a beautiful young woman, but also the profound pain and inevitable price that must be paid. The fantastic story of becoming a beautiful swan, but also the path of suffering the ugly duckling has to take to reach this apotheosis.

*

"Now let's play human beings; that's always something!" So says the old, worn-out doll whose neck has been repaired in the story "The Money Pig" ("Pengegrisen," 1854), which is an amusing and grotesque story about the fall of the piggy bank and the dance macabre of the toys in the children's nursery and in a world of 'as-if-we-were-humans':

> Everybody sat and watched, and the audience had been asked to applaud, crack, and stamp as they were pleased. But the Riding Whip said he never cracked for old folks, only for young ones who weren't yet married. "I crack for everybody," said the Cracker. "One must, of course, be in the proper place!" thought the Spittoon. And such were their thoughts as the play went on.

The money pig has the form of a pig and is so crammed full that he can no longer rattle at all, which is described as "the highest honour a Money Pig can attain." He stands there high above all the other toys, but in the tumult, he crashes down and lies smashed to smithereens on the floor: "while the pennies hopped and danced about. The smallest spun like tops, and the bigger ones rolled away, particularly one big silver dollar who wanted to go out and see the world. And so he did, and so did all the rest." The coins roll on out into the world where they can create new plays, so that more old dolls can pretend to be humans. The tale ends with a new piggy bank arriving and, like its predecessor, it is also unable to rattle, but that is because it is empty. There are fluctuations on the financial markets in Andersen's stories!

In less than three pages, Andersen, in a grotesque and ironic allegory, tells us of the modern forces that are prevalent in his own age. And it is a truly sublime touch to make the setting that of the children's nursery and the universe of toys. This amusing story may on the surface look like a little fairy tale for children, but it is far from just that. "The Money Pig" is a story about the forces – silver coins and human games – that change the world.

Andersen's main theme is often precisely this: How can we become human beings in the centrifuge of time? What constitutes human nature? And what is required to remain a human being when conditions are constantly changing? In "The Galoshes of Fortune" ("Lykkens Kalosker," 1838) Andersen plays with a pair of overshoes that bring the protagonists into strange situations – and he often makes use of footwear as artefacts and symbols in his tales. And if he does not use shoes or other kinds of footwear, there are walks, journeys, ascents into chimneys, voyages down rivers on a water-lily leaf or through scary street gutters in a paper hat.

Andersen's fairy tales and the rest of his art depict transformation and, in particular, the necessity to transform oneself if one is to become a true human being. In such iconic fairy tales as "The Little Mermaid" ("Den lille Havfrue," 1837), "The Snow Queen" ("Sneedronningen," 1845), "The Nightingale" ("Nattergalen," 1844) and "The Shepherdess and the Chimney-Sweep" ("Hyrdinden og Skorsteensfeieren," 1845) it is the desire to transform oneself from an object or a demon into a human being that unfolds in love and in a loving community. This community can be found in faith, in the bosom of the family, it can be the love of a mother or of parents for a child or the bond that can come into being between two people who love each other.

*

The modern societies in which we now live call for constant mobility, ability to adapt and a high level of flexibility in the single individual. Here the silver coins have been rolling a long time, as in "The Money Pig," and we who play humans roll along with them. One could claim that the modern individual has a greater need for boots than roots. It is motion, the feet, that constitute the modern and creates the modern. That motion at the same time creates an eye for the traditional and its values, well, that is another matter and another aspect of the conditions of the modern world.

Hans Christian Andersen lived in a different time. The society and environment he was born into and grew up in as a poor child is far removed from modern welfare societies. Or is it? In the course of Andersen's lifetime, from 1805 to 1875, a society saw the light of day which, in a way, we are still living in. It is a society that is based on common values such as the rights of the individual, trust, humanity towards others, freedom of expression and respect. It is a society that is based on fundamental values that we at present have to ask ourselves: Are these eternal values?

In the traditional, class-divided and privilege-ridden societies of Andersen's time, breaking with social patterns was unusual. But that was precisely what Andersen did. He sort of jumped from one community form to another, from traditionalism to a kind of modernity and individualism. He extracted himself from the soil of his roots. He exchanged his roots for boots and strove towards the sun, the light, fame and the top of the social ladder. Hans Christian Andersen moved up in society and out into society as a free artist and an individual in search of happiness. In the movement he undertook as a human being and as an artist he portrays, one might perhaps say, the formation of the modern. For that reason, Andersen is still topical and modern.

His experiences from this breaking-out process are present everywhere in his writing, perhaps as a motif, theme or figure, but mostly as an enormous productivity, imaginativeness and creativity which may spring from the mental or existential unrest and desire for recognition that could never be completely satisfied in him. In that sense, Andersen is an extremely modern writer. Or rather, his fairy tales and stories possess a nerve and a creative urge that are modern, because they point towards forms of identity that the modern both demands and creates, and that include anxiety, ambivalence, agitation and restlessness.

Many social, work-related, family-related and emotionally determined communities changed considerably during Andersen's lifetime. A number of traditionally determined communities collapsed. Hans Christian Andersen registers and portrays this incessantly in his art, sometimes with pleasure, at other times with horror, but always with an artistic intuitive sense of the tensions in the ambivalence that comes with the beginnings of modernity. He not only describes the new prerequisites for human communities but, to a great degree and with personal pain, how social exclusion results from the formation of modern communities. "The Little Match Girl" ("Den lille Pige med Svovlstikkerne," 1848) depicts the results of social exclusion in the story of the working-class girl who experiences hunger-induced fantasies about vast quantities of food.

*

Andersen registered the new, was enthusiastic but frightened at the same time to see how the old norms and old, solid culture were being undermined and were disintegrating. This ambivalence is everywhere in Andersen, who himself had to break out of difficult circumstances to gain high social status through his art and his genius. There is ambivalence in experiences that make him a 'mould-breaker' both socially and as an artist. He has to develop a new genre in order to express himself. This he does in his fairy tales and stories. In his fairy tales, then, Andersen is capable of speaking with many voices and thus to many different realities: that of the child, the dreams of the young person, the voice of those in love, the experiences of the adult, the retrospective gaze of the old person.

It is interesting to see how, in his early works, Andersen is bound by such traditional genres as, for example, the classical folk tale. But in 1835, he breaks out and publishes *Eventyr, fortalte for Børn* (Tales, Told for Children). This marked the birth of a completely new, worldwide literary genre.

The German cultural scientist Walter Benjamin ([1936] 1977) has argued that the folk tale belongs to the people and not to an individual artist. The folk tale contains common experience, it passes from mouth to mouth, is adapted and altered in the course of time. The *Kunstmärchen*, the novel and the novella, on the other hand, belong to a single personality, that of a writer and his or her ability to transmute experiences into artistic form. Hans Christian Andersen takes the common genres, such as the folk tale, as his point of departure, but makes them personal and lends them his own artistic expression. This enables his stories and fairy tales to include the deep experiences, pains, sorrows, humiliation, social climbing, love and loss of love of the poor man, the child and the little man in society.

*

In his memoir *The Fairy Tale of My Life* (*Mit Livs Eventyr*, 1855), Andersen transforms his life into a fairy tale. At the same time, he describes the journey through his own age as one towards the light, although typified by anxiety and at great personal cost. He became what is now often called a 'mould-breaker.' The age Andersen travelled through in his lifetime and in which he wrote his legacy was 'The Time of the Fairy Tales,' characterised by rapid leaps forward within social, political and technological development.

In the European countries and elsewhere, the ideas of the Enlightenment regarding the transference of sovereignty from an absolute monarch to the people and the nation made their mark. The European nation states were formed as new, national communities that are held together by conceptions of a common ethnic base, history, literature, art and culture. This transformed the political culture and the political communities.

Denmark also moved from an absolute monarchy to a democratic system, with the approval of the Constitution in 1849 as a concrete result of this. But in addition, the traditional communities that tied everyday life together for the most part were also transformed. Out in the country, where 85 percent of the population lived at the time, the old village communities were dissolved. The so-called 'enclosure movement' and reorganization of land ownership changed the traditional concept of community. In the towns, crafts and trade underwent major changes and the old guilds and privileges came under siege from a freer market economy and the beginnings of industrialisation. At the same time, new ideas of the family became widespread, with the individual being increasingly viewed as the center of things.

*

Politically speaking, Denmark was hardly fortunate. In the year 1800, the dual monarchy of Denmark-Norway still included the duchies of Schleswig, Holstein and Lauenborg as well as a number of overseas colonies. This kingdom had a powerful international position as well as a strong navy. Between then and 1870, however, the country underwent a succession of disastrous events. Denmark chose an unfortunate alliance with the French emperor, Napoleon, which led to the superior British navy fighting and defeating the Danish navy at so-called Battles of Copenhagen in 1801 and 1807. This led to Denmark losing its position as a naval power and subsequent chaos and national bankruptcy in 1813, followed by the loss of Norway in 1814. In the latter half of the 19th century, in 1864, Denmark lost yet another fatal war against Germany, and lost Schleswig, Holstein and Lauenborg. From that point onward, Denmark has been considered one of the small countries of Europe.

One of the reasons why Denmark got involved in this fatal war against Germany in 1864 can be found in the strong nationalist sentiment that was flourishing in Europe, including Denmark. The 19th century was a period of 'nation-building' in Europe, when national sentiment and culture were strong and expressive. In Denmark, the period of the 1830s and 1840s has subsequently been referred to as the Danish Golden Age, because it was characterised by a great upsurge within culture, art and science. This was when the philosopher Søren Kierkegaard lived and wrote his works. Andersen published, as mentioned, his first tales in this period: *Eventyr, fortalte for Børn* (Tales, Told for Children) in 1835. The sculptor Bertel Thorvaldsen and the greatest Danish painters, Christen Købke and C.W. Eckersberg, are active at this time too, as is the writer and educationalist N.F.S. Grundtvig. Science flourished, with Hans Christian Ørsted discovering electromagnetism, which was a prerequisite for the later electrification of industry.

Andersen was fascinated by the developments within technology and natural science. The British instrument-maker James Watt had managed to get the first steam engine to work in 1774. It was the prerequisite for industrialisation and for new, revolutionary forms of transport, such as the steamship and the steam locomotive. Andersen enthusiastically described the potential of the steam locomotive in his travel account *A Poet's Bazaar* (*En Digters Bazar*, 1842), where speed and power are a fairy tale. In other stories, such as "Thousands of Years from Now" ("Om Aartusinder," 1853), he fantasises about how it might be possible for people to "fly on wings of steam through the air, across the ocean." Electromagnetism created a technological revolution, both to power electromotors and as a basis for the development of the telegraph, which became the first global communications technology when in the 1860s and 1870s cable links were established between Europe and China and between Europe and North America.

Hans Christian Andersen was enthusiastic about and fascinated by the potential that lay in technical advances. At the same time, he was scared by the changes they brought about. In the tales "The New Century's Goddess" ("Det nye Aarhundredes Musa," 1861) and "The Dryad" he refers to the steam engine as "Master Bloodless," which implies that steam and its power lacked soul and the values that best served humanity.

From the beginning of the 19th century onwards, Europe was characterised by new currents of ideas. The so-called romantic period begins in Europe around 1800 and it is first seen in literature, philosophy and art. The codex of reason is gradually replaced in Romanticism by the freer cultivation of feelings, individual imagination and the connection between spirit and nature. The individual, with his or her rich emotional life, existence and development become the aim for 'Bildung' and the shaping of the personality. Later, the romantic idea is to a great extent linked to notions of the national and the popular as cohesive forces in communities. The poetry, tales, novels and plays of Romanticism deal with such subjects as the past, history and that which is particularly national. In addition, there are the depictions of love and of the role of the artist and of imagination. A particular angle is linked to the 'discovery' of the child and childhood. Writers such as B.S. Ingemann, N.F.S. Grundtvig and of course Hans Christian Andersen do not only write *about* the child but *for* the child – and not least perhaps about the child within the adult.

*

Grundtvig said that no one had ever lived who had made out something without first having loved it. This became one of the basic assumptions of a Danish pedagogy that was based on the experiences and prequalifications of the individual pupil. The heart, love, emotions, tales and imagination were given higher priority. As was the individual. For Grundtvig this was the idea of how children learn and how young people acquire knowledge via narration and making their own experiences. The same inspiration is to be found in Hans Christian Andersen, who developed his own literary genre. In both Andersen and Grundtvig it is the heart, desire and love that are to fuel the exploratory process. Andersen said about his fairy tales and Stories that they were 'Told for Children.' This does not mean that they are children's stories, but that they are told for the child in all human beings. The child and the child's fantasy, the child's ability to imagine things become important categories for understanding what learning and artistic awareness are. The person who does not love his or her material like a child will never acquire it. It is learning and values that are basically more important today than back then.

And so that time – that of Hans Christian Andersen – was indeed the time of fairy tales. The modernity which Andersen sensed, and which broke down traditional communities has since developed and forms the prerequisite for our own age and its communities. Have the modern characteristics that Andersen saw and sensed perhaps now reached a point from where other possible forms will take over? Perhaps we have to find new ways of playing human beings. Hans Christian Andersen's art is still there at our disposal by its insistence on the fact that a human being is basically a human being. It is his great work that made him honourary citizen in Odense on the 6th of December 1867 and his ground-breaking thoughts with universal potential that still talk to us now, in Andersen's prosperity. With these words, I leave the scene to 19 great examples of how we can make sense of Hans Christian Andersen and Community today.[2]

References
Benjamin, Walter. (1936) 1977. "Der Erzähler. Betrachtungen zum Werk Nikolai Lesskows." In *Gesammelte Schriften*, vol. II, 2, 438–465. Frankfurt am Main.

Note
1 This introductory lecture has also been published in the special issue *Hans Christian Andersen in communities* of the online journal *Aktualitet* (2019), edited by Anne Klara Bom, Torsten Bøgh Thomsen, and Johs. Nørregaard Frandsen.
2 This essay has not been peer reviewed.

COMMUNICATION AND DISCOURSE

A Community Incommunicado
On Troubled Communication in Hans Christian Andersen's Fairy Tales

Helena Březinová
Karlova University, Prague

Hans Christian Andersen's choice of the fairy-tale genre provides clear evidence of his efforts to reach a whole community of readers and listeners. He installs a typical storyteller in his stories and he plays on the ultimately connective appeal of the fairy tale. It is noteworthy, however, that Andersen's fairy tales often exhibit a loss of confidence in the communicative power of language. The protagonists' particular communication codes frequently seem to be mutually incompatible and the communication is abortive or nonsensical: the porcelain ballerina, for example, does not comprehend the tin soldier and there is but infinitesimal understanding between the shepherdess and the chimney sweep. What's more, in "The Little Mermaid" the storyteller thematises his cultural discourse as being incongruous with the shared codes of his audience. My chapter examines the failing communication in Andersen's object tales and views his work on language as a precursor to the fin de siècle "language crisis," by showing affinities between Andersen's object tales and Hugo von Hofmannsthal's famous Lord Chandos Letter (1902). Besides, the loss of the connective power of communication signals the erosion of community in which, according to Lewis A. Friedland, communication is "the central system of action that binds together many different types of social actors and groups."

Surely almost everyone would agree that Hans Christian Andersen makes his language in the fairy tales simple in a hitherto unseen way.[1]

His fairy tales reveal a clear tendency to talk clearly. The oral nature of Andersen's fairy tales is obviously referring back to the classic storytelling tradition in which the performer and her or, in this case, his audience have reached unconditional mutual understanding. The language is fluent and familiar evoking the shared memory and experience of both the storyteller and his audience.

Klaus P. Mortensen ascribes to Andersen's old-fashioned storyteller the same qualities which Walter Benjamin attributes to the classic narrator in his famous essay "The Storyteller: Reflections on the Works of Nikolai Leskov" ("Der Erzähler: Betrachtungen zum Werk Nikolaj Lesskows," 1936). In this essay Benjamin laments the loss of traditional community with its foremost cohesive power: the power of storytelling. Concerning this, Mortensen insightfully remarks:

> If you apply the viewpoint of Walter Benjamin to Andersen's fairy tales, you might consider them as a series of attempts to break through the undesirable isolation of the individual. In other words, repeated attempts to return from the individual exile to the storytelling which reinforces the community. Perhaps fruitless attempts? (2000, 23, my translation)

The form of Andersen's fairy tales undeniably recalls the ancient community and deludes us into thinking that we are dealing with straightforward narration. Nothing could, however, be further from the truth. The stories are refined, the complete opposite of the seemingly *hyggelig* oral delivery.

But what is extremely self-contradictory in this argument is that the orality and straightforwardness contrast strikingly with the fact that the communication between the characters often fails. But in fact, these elementary communication breakdowns are a mirror of a much greater miscommunication – the profound misunderstanding between the artist and his audience. The artist seems to speak a different language; indeed, sometimes, as in "The Little Mermaid" ("Den lille Havfrue," 1837), the protagonist has literally lost her tongue (by amputation). Other examples of tongue trouble appear in "The Fir Tree" ("Grantræet," 1845), "The Steadfast Tin Soldier" ("Den standhaftige Tinsoldat," 1838), and "The Shepherdess and the Chimney Sweep" (1845). This chapter begins with a discussion of the basic level of miscommunication between the main characters in the fairy tales, and then moves to a higher, metatextual level, where we can see the misunderstanding between the artist and his audience, and, finally, it closes with an attempt to place Andersen's work on and with language in the context of the growing general scepticism towards conventional literary expression and language in about 1900. In the conclusion, I employ key findings of sociologists on the function of communication in community.

Now, let's recall a scene in "Ole Lukoie" ("Ole Lukøie," 1842), which illustrates a total communication breakdown. This time the isolation of the characters is not caused by a language deficiency, but, on the contrary, by an overabundance of language accompanied by a total absence of listening comprehension:

> As soon as Hjalmar was in bed, Ole Lukoie touched all the furniture in the room with his little magic sprinkler, and immediately everything began to talk. Everything talked about itself except the spittoon, which kept silent. It was annoyed that they should be so conceited as to talk only about themselves, and think only about themselves, without paying the least attention to it, sitting so humbly in the corner and letting everyone spit at it.

Here everybody talks and nobody listens. Another famous hero of Andersen's fairy tales, the tin soldier, by contrast, is deprived of his voice because of his material substance. Actually, it is not clear whether he cannot speak at all or simply keeps his mouth shut because in his position talking would seem inappropriate. At any rate, he remains mute till he ends up being burned. For our purposes, it is significant that prior to the final cremation scene, the storyteller strikingly often mentions the non-communication of the soldier.

"The Steadfast Tin Soldier:" The Most Silent Hero in World Literature

The one-legged protagonist of this fairy tale absurdly mistakes the ballerina character to be one-legged as well, but the situation becomes increasingly absurd because of the soldier's steadfast silence. At the end of the story the soldier reunites with his beloved dancer after a dangerous voyage in the gutter and after being swallowed by a fish in the canal, ultimately experiencing a rare state of harmony. But despite being moved to tears, he still doesn't say a word:

> That touched the soldier so deeply that he would have cried tin tears, only soldiers never cry. He looked at her, and she looked at him, and never a word was said. Just as things were going so nicely for them, one of the little boys snatched up the tin soldier and threw him into the stove.

The irony of the narrator whose statement about the established idyll becomes clear if we take into consideration that the ballerina expresses no feelings towards the silent soldier. That is not surprising, since the soldier's only attempt to approach the ballerina is an act of voyeurism, at the beginning of the story: "Still as stiff as when he stood at attention, he lay down on the table behind a snuffbox, where he could admire the dainty little dancer who kept standing on one leg without ever losing her balance." In fact, the storyteller is as silent as his eponymous character: neither he nor the soldier can tell whether the tin hero is consumed by the fire or by his own unexpressed love in the grand finale:

> He felt a terrible heat, but whether it came from the flames or from his love he didn't know. He'd lost his splendid colours, maybe from his hard journey, maybe from grief, nobody can say. He looked at the little lady, and she looked at him, and he felt himself melting. But still he stood steadfast, with his musket held trim on his shoulder.

The soldier dies without ever uttering a word to his beloved dancer or for that matter to anyone else. He is silent even in situations where his life is at stake, as in his encounter with a frightening rat which lives under the gutter plank and demands the soldier's passport: "The soldier kept quiet and held his musket tighter."

Of course, one can object that the substance the soldier is made of prevents him from talking, but in that same fairy tale a rat is able to speak, so the soldier's silence is of a much greater significance – it denotes tragic isolation.

Dialogues Gone Astray:
"The Shepherdess and Chimney Sweep"

Interestingly enough, we find the same miscommunication in fairy tales where the characters *are* granted the gift of speech – regardless of their inanimate nature. The shepherdess and the chimney sweep are porcelain figurines, but they can talk, although their dialogues don't make much sense. Or rather, they make sense in the course of the narration because they contribute to the feeling of isolation and despair in the finely furnished room in which the fairy tale is set. The conversations are so nonsensical that it is fair to say that the communication becomes one of the themes of this fairy tale.

The shepherdess and the chimney sweep are in love and would like to marry, but there is an obstacle. A strange man fancies the shepherdess and asks the Old Chinaman doll for her hand in marriage. The Old Chinaman is himself a dubious character because he is supposed to be the grandfather of the shepherdess, yet the storyteller makes it clear that there is no evidence for such a kinship. The wooden man has got goat legs, so it's not surprising that he has married eleven wives already and they are kept in his chest. Naturally, the shepherdess wants to flee the room because of the threat represented by the goat-man and the Old Chinaman. She convinces her beloved chimney sweep to run away with her, and the reader is confronted with the immense pressure the shepherdess puts on the chimney sweep:

> "Please let's run away into the big, wide world," she begged him, "for we can't stay here."
> "I'll do just what you want me to," the little chimney sweep told her. "Let's run away right now. I feel sure I can support you by chimney-sweeping."
> "I wish we were safely down off this table," she said. "I'll never be happy until we are out in the big, wide world."

After his first experience on the run with the shepherdess, the chimney sweep becomes somewhat hesitant.

> "Are you really so brave that you'd go into the big wide world with me?" asked the chimney sweep. "Have you thought about how big it is, and that we can never come back here?"
> "I have," she said.

The narrator leaves no doubt that it is the shepherdess who is the instigator of running away to the "big wide world." The chivalrous chimney sweep definitely would be fine with staying home. On that account, the reaction of the shepherdess is shocking when – after a distressful journey up the chimney they reach the top and the panorama of the big wide world finally unfolds in front of them. From this very moment the absurdity of their direct speech is enhanced markedly, as we see in the next passage:

> "This is too much," she said. "I can't bear it. The wide world is too big. Oh! If I only were back on my table under the mirror. I'll never be happy until I stand there again, just as before. I followed you faithfully out into the world, and if you love me the least bit you'll take me right home."

The shepherdess presents an extremely creative version of the truth about their escape. The couple then climbs down the chimney again and, in the meantime, they exchange meaningless lines like these:

> "Oh, dear," said the little shepherdess, "poor old grandfather is all broken up, and it's entirely our fault. I shall never live through it." She wrung her delicate hands.
> "He can be patched," said the chimney-sweep. "He can be riveted. Don't be so upset about him. A little glue for his back and a strong rivet in his neck, and he will be just as good as new, and just as disagreeable as he was before."
> "Will he, really?" she asked, as they climbed back to their old place on the table.
> "Here we are," said the chimney-sweep. "Back where we started from. We could have saved ourselves a lot of trouble."
> "Now if only old grandfather were mended," said the little shepherdess. "Is mending terribly expensive?"

Yes, one can say this dialogue sounds perfectly naturalistic: a couple's subtle disagreements and lack of understanding. In any case, the two characters are not having a conversation; they are merely performing monologues. The shepherdess in particular. Her question "Will he, really?" following the chimney sweep's biting remark that the Old Chinaman will be "just as disagreeable as he was before" clearly shows her total lack of ability to communicate. The characters in this fairy tale remain locked up in their monologues and failing communication becomes one of the main themes of the tale.

These conversations cast a long dark shadow on the ending which, in my view, is far from happy: "So the little porcelain people remained together. They thanked goodness for the rivet in grandfather's neck, and they kept on loving each other until the day they broke." Considering their dialogues, their relationship fell apart no later than during their unconvincing escape. The lines in their conversation run obliquely, the communication collapses. A similar communication breakdown appears in "The Fir Tree," in which the protagonist is similarly estranged and isolated.

"The Fir Tree:" An Unacknowledged Storyteller

"The Fir Tree" is a story of a never satisfied tree longing for the time to come. It is unable to seize the moment; the tree realises only in retrospect that the peak moments of its life are gone. It serves as a Christmas tree, is beautifully decorated, yet it doesn't enjoy itself even on Christmas Day. It ends up being burned and the storyteller assures the reader that everybody and everything, including the storytelling, will meet the same fate.

The isolation of the fir tree is only briefly interrupted when the tree is stored in the attic after it has served as a Christmas tree. The tree begins to chat with some mice, hence, it becomes a storyteller. Yet the communication is invalid from the beginning. The mice repeatedly address the tree jovially, trying to please the tree and rewarding it for its storytelling:

> "It is fearfully cold," one of them said. "Except for that, it would be very nice here, wouldn't it, you old fir tree?"
>
> "I'm not at all old," said the fir tree. "Many trees are much older than I am."

We can see that the communicative functions of language are undermined. Seen from the perspective of Karl Bühler's *Organon model*, the address of the mice serves the appellative or conative function of language, but the tree understands it in its representational function describing the actual state of the tree. In his *Handbook of Semiotics*, Winfried Nöth explains the two relevant functions of communication according to Bühler's Organon model as follows: "The function of representation dominates whenever the focus of the message is on the referential objects. [...] The function of appeal dominates when the message focuses on the hearer 'whose outer or inner behaviour it directs just as other traffic signs do'." (Nöth 1995, 185). In our context this means that the tree takes the address of the mice literally, but the mice use the address in order to bond with the tree. The very same misunderstanding is repeated in the next passage:

> And he went on to tell them about Christmas Eve, when it was decked out with candies and candles.
> "Oh," said the little mice, "how lucky you have been, you old fir tree!"
> "I am not at all old," it insisted. "I came out of the woods just this winter, and I'm really in the prime of life, though at the moment my growth is suspended."
> "How nicely you put things," said the mice. The next night they came with four other mice to hear what the tree had to say.

The source of the mice's shouts of joy is hard to comprehend; they are either grateful for every word the tree says without paying attention to the content or they find the fact that the tree is "sat i Væxten" that is, its "growth is suspended," of a great entertainment value. The tree is basically scolding the mice and they praise it for wonderful storytelling. The mice happily listen to the stories of the tree until a couple of rats join them one day and start criticising the tree's stories. Instantly, the mice too lose their interest. This situation has been reasonably interpreted as Andersen's satire on a prototypical situation between the artist and his reviewers – personified by rats (de Mylius 2004, 110). But even in the happy times of his storytelling, we can observe alarming signs of miscommunication between the tree and its audience. Hence, in this fairy tale the miscomprehension is not reserved to a couple, as in the "The Shepherdess and the Chimney Sweep," in "The Fir Tree" it applies to the relationship between the artist and his world.

"The Little Mermaid:" Elevated into Oblivion

One of the most prominent examples of this motif is, of course, to be found in "The Little Mermaid." As Pernille Heegaard and Jacob Bøggild (1993) concluded, there can, indeed, be little doubt that the mermaid is to be interpreted as an artist. The human love for the mermaid is a mere vehicle to obtain an immortal soul, whereas the mermaid's instrument in her quest for eternity is her singing and dancing. In other words, the fairy tale can plausibly and usefully be interpreted as a story concerned with the role and position of art and the artist.

The little mermaid's journey passes through three elements: water, earth and air. In all three, she is a performing artist. In the ocean she sings, on dry land she dances, and, finally, in the air she regains her amputated tongue and, besides, she produces a fragrance that consoles the people, encounters and relieves them. What is particularly striking, however, is that in all three of her elements the little mermaid is separated from her audience. By her origin she is a siren, no matter how domesticated and harmless she seems, and sirens allure sailors by something they themselves consider beautiful singing, though the sailors hear the horrifying voice of the storm – which means her singing signifies death to the sailors. In essence, the mermaid's art is tragically incompatible with her desired audience, as we can see in the following passage:

> They had beautiful voices, more charming than those of any mortal beings. When a storm was brewing, and they anticipated a shipwreck, they would swim before the ship and sing most seductively of how beautiful it was at the bottom of the ocean, trying to overcome the prejudice that the sailors had against coming down to them. But people could not understand their song and mistook it for the voice of the storm. Nor was it for them to see the glories of the deep. When their ship went down they were drowned, and it was as dead men that they reached the sea king's palace.

The little mermaid has to sacrifice her tongue in order to gain human love, which means that on dry land she cannot sing. Instead, she communicates by means of her newly obtained legs – she becomes a dancer. Every one of her steps aches immensely, but the prince as her prime audience can only appreciate her art to a very limited degree. He is unaware of her pain or that art is of existential importance to the mermaid. His reward to her is utterly degrading: he treats the mermaid like a dog:

> She charmed everyone, and especially the Prince, who called her his dear little foundling. She danced time and again, though every time she touched the floor she felt as if she were treading on sharp-edged steel. The Prince said he would keep her with him always, and that she was to have a velvet pillow to sleep on outside his door.

Hence, on dry land the little mermaid is separated from her audience as she was in the water, and the same situation is repeated in the air. At the end of the fairy tale the mermaid can save her life killing the prince, she refuses but is saved anyway. She is elevated into the air where she joins the "daughters of the air," and in our context, it is significant that the little mermaid's voice "sounded so spiritual that no music on earth could match it." In the air the little mermaid is clearly reincarnated as an artist. The activity of the daughters of the air is depicted as follows:

> "We are the daughters of the air," they answered. "A mermaid has no immortal soul and can never get one unless she wins the love of a human being. Her eternal life must depend upon a power outside herself. The daughters of the air do not have an immortal soul either, but they can earn one by their good deeds. We fly to the south, where the hot poisonous air kills human beings unless we bring cool breezes. We carry the scent of flowers through the air, bringing freshness and healing balm wherever we go."

If we take a closer look at this passage, we see that the narrator stresses that the mermaid's singing is not only beautiful, but also healing and generally beneficial. This description basically corresponds with the famous doctrine "aut prodesse aut delectare', that is, *to instruct and delight* which, according to Horace, is the aim of all good art. The audience which the little mermaid is separated from bears a striking similarity to the prototypical audience of Andersen's fairy tales: children. In order to acquire an immortal soul, the mermaid needs the children to be well behaved, but she can have no influence whatsoever on their behaviour since human beings cannot hear or see her. She, once again, is totally deprived of the possibility of communicating her spherical music to the coveted audience:

> In the bright sunlight overhead, she saw hundreds of fair ethereal beings. They were so transparent that through them she could see the ship's white sails and the red clouds in the sky. Their voices were sheer music, but so spirit-like that no human ear could detect the sound, just as no eye on earth could see their forms.

Manifestly, the little mermaid as an artist cannot communicate with the human world in any of the three elements. She is always outside, deprived of the language to communicate her message.

An interesting commentary on the art theme of the fairy tale is provided by the journey of the protagonist. The trajectory of the little mermaid is ascending, she rises from the sea, after which comes her earthbound stage until, finally, she is elevated to the air. In fact, we see a transition in which a substance is transformed from a solid into a gas. Obviously, I am hinting at sublimation, that is, Freud's famous mature type of defence mechanism whereby socially unacceptable impulses such as sexual instincts are unconsciously transformed into higher activities such as art.[2] The little mermaid evaporates or, rather, sublimates into sheer music; her tragic terrestrial love is transformed into something higher, useful, healing and delightful.

In fact, Andersen's friend, the writer B.S. Ingemann, recommended to Andersen, in a letter from January 20, 1831, that he embark on the same journey of sublimation. Ingemann tried to console his heartbroken young friend with this metaphor of ascension:

> The passion behind that idea is of worldly and final nature; it has to be stoically suppressed, and through the pain of self-denial a higher joy necessarily evolves. The deeper and higher our love is, the closer it is to merge with the highest and most unconditional submission to the will of God and to the eternal divine source of all love.
>
> I hope as well that your passion for poetry and your urge to be part of the life of the mind and art will become your guardian angel who will lead you safely over the abyss. God bless you! (Andersen 1831, my translation)

As we can see, in Ingemann's letter the spatial metaphor is pervasive; Andersen is in the depths of despair and must, he is advised, surmount it by means of art. The process of sublimation in "The Little Mermaid" is yet more evidence of the eponymous protagonist being an artist, and though she successfully elevates herself into the higher spheres there is a fly in the ointment – she can be neither seen nor heard.

What actually is Ingemann's advice to Andersen? He advises him to get into the higher regions on the wings of art, the only way for him to become cultivated – *dannet*, to use the Danish expression. *Dannelse* is the Danish version of the German noun *Bildung*, which refers to the tradition of self-cultivation leading to personal and cultural maturation as described, for instance, in the paradigm novel establishing this ideal, Goethe's *Wilhelm Meister's Apprenticeship* (*Wilhelm Meisters Lehrjahre*, 1785–86), the classic Bildungsroman. Within the process of cultivation, the lower, carnal energies have to be transformed and the main vehicle for cultivation is considered to be the art. The problem is, however, that the little mermaid clearly does not speak the language of the community dominated by this idea. This means that we have good reason to assume that in "The Little Mermaid" the idealised world of cultivation, *dannelse*, is being mocked. Being an artist in this particular fairy tale means the same as not being heard or seen at all.

Andersen is certainly not the first writer to oppose what is known as *dannelseskultur*, the culture of cultivation. One thinks, for instance, of E.T.A. Hoffmann's biting satirical assault on the Bildungsroman in *The Life and Opinions of the Tomcat Murr together with a fragmentary Biography of Kapellmeister Johannes Kreisler on Random Sheets of Waste Paper* (*Lebens-Ansichten des Katers Murr nebst fragmentarischer Biographie des Kapellmeisters Johannes Kreisler in zufälligen Makulaturblättern*) from 1819 and 1821, or the fierce fight against the 'Bildung' concept as a whole, fought by the philosopher Søren Kierkegaard. But there is a revolutionary novelty to be found in Andersen's fairy tales. Andersen's criticism begins at the very beginning – with language as a means of communication. Andersen is experimenting with showing its limits, and on that account, we strikingly often see the sheer impossibility of individual discourse connecting with others.

Andersen and the Language Crisis

Andersen's ultrasensitive awareness of the communication gaps, indeed abysses, in everyday conversations is subsequently mirrored in the profound misunderstanding or even complete blocking of the communication channel between the artist and his audience. Neither his characters nor the artist and his audience speak the same language with each other, in other words, at both the textual and metatextual level we observe a collapse of communication.

It is fair even to go as far as to call Andersen's work with language in his fairy tales pioneering in relation to the looming *Sprachschock* or *Sprachskepsis*, that is, the language crisis arising in about 1900. The fin de siècle crisis centred on doubts about the efficacy of language to express not only abstract concepts but even thought in general. The philosopher Fritz Mauthner pointed out the abstract and unreal character of language in his *Beiträge zu einer Kritik der Sprache* (Contributions to the Critique of Language, 1901). He maintained that language is a suitable medium for communication in a social or artistic context but not for communicating truth and reality, since all language is metaphorical. This was almost exactly the same as what Friedrich Nietzsche had written in his "On Truth and Lying in an Extra-Moral Sense" ("Über Wahrheit und Lüge im Aussermoralischen Sinne," 1873). For Nietzsche, language is based on metaphors and as such utterly unable to adequately express the real state of things. On the contrary, language, due to its merely metaphorical nature, is, he argued, here to create an illusion, or rather a deception, and hide the real state of things.[3] Ideas like those of Mauthner and Nietzsche led, in about 1900, to a general mistrust of the representational capacity of language.

Emblematic of that crisis is an idea of Ludwig Wittgenstein's, who, developing Mauthner's theories, argued that "language is the limit of our world." I will, however, refer in greater detail, rather, to Hugo von Hofmannsthal's famous letter written in the voice of Lord Chandos because in it Hofmannsthal expresses the view that language makes things go mouldy and concentrates on things as they appear instead of language. In the *The Lord Chandos Letter* (*Chandos-Brief*, 1902) the narrator laments the loss of words; the words have, as Lord Chandos puts it, "crumbled in my mouth like mouldy fungi" ([1902] 2018, n.p.). In particular, Lord Chandos has a distaste for abstract terms: "I experienced an inexplicable distaste for so much as uttering the words *spirit, soul,* or *body.*" Finally, Lord Chandos becomes speechless, deprived of the natural flow of language, yet this does not mean that he does not experience ecstatic moments of comprehension – comprehension beyond language. He enjoys concrete, tangible things, and in this respect, we find a great deal of affinity with the fairy tales of Hans Christian Andersen.

I would illustrate the affinity between Andersen's style and Hofmannsthal's renouncing of abstract terms on the Platonic triad from Andersen's famous tale "The Shadow" ("Skyggen, 1847"). The triad consists of the true, the good and the beautiful, and these three categories are the watchwords of the scholar in "The Shadow." In this story, Andersen radically replaces the motto of the cultivated hero. The abstract terms beauty, goodness and truth are substituted by the physical or even carnal reality of being "under the skirts of a cake-woman." Here, the shadow of the scholar seeks refuge, which in the narrative means that the good and beautiful are replaced by an extremely concrete and rather uncultivated truth. It is as if the storyteller had the urge to misbehave and shout aloud all the nasty words the *dannelseskultur* tries to avoid. At the same time, the passage taking place under the skirts of the cake-woman reveals a striking turn towards concrete objects; truth, beauty and goodness are being swapped for the skirts of the cake-woman; the abstract ideas are being replaced with the physical world. It is significant that the point of view of the shadow prevails over the cultivated hero in the end of the story.

What is remarkable, in this respect, is Andersen's keen interest in trivial and destroyed things. He dedicates a story to a bottleneck, another to a broken darning needle, aphids or plant lice, an old house, an old street lamp, old rags, a shirt collar cut to pieces, and a tin soldier without a leg who experiences being thrown away twice. Frequently, the things in Andersen's fairy tales make an equally abandoned impression as the harrow depicted by Lord Chandos in his letter:

> A pitcher, a harrow abandoned in a field, a dog in the sun, a neglected cemetery, a cripple, a peasant's hut – all these can become the vessel of my revelation. Each of these objects and a thousand others similar, over which the eye usually glides with a natural indifference, can suddenly, at any moment (which I am utterly powerless to evoke), assume for me a character so exalted and moving that words seem too poor to describe it. (von Hofmannsthal [1902] 2018, n.p.)

Klaus Müller-Wille (2009) appositely labels Andersen an object theorist, and he explores Andersen's preoccupation with inanimate objects from various perspectives. For example, he anchors Andersen's dealing with broken and used things in the theories of commodity fetishism. In general, the recent research in Andersen's fairy tales is fervently focused on the character and function of object protagonists in *tingseventyr*, object tales or (fairy) tales about things. Two articles, Brigid Gaffikin's "Material Witnesses: Hans Christian Andersen's *Tingseventyr* and the Memories of Things" (2004) and Jette Lundbo Levy's "Om ting der går i stykker: Ekelöf og Andersen" (1998), are widely considered ground-breaking on this subject. In them, both scholars concentrate on the broken items in fairy tales, and although their focus is different each scholar argues that Andersen rehabilitates broken and omitted things in his narratives. I do not intend to go into object and materiality theories, so I will restrict myself to conclude that the poetic devices in Andersen's fairy tales are based on a hitherto unseen interest for concrete nouns and in fact this does not apply to things only. His fairy tales have a wide range of petty protagonists, such as aphids and all kinds of insects, snails, plants and bushes. For my current purposes, I will answer in the negative Finn Hauberg Mortensen's question from his article "Ting og relation" whether things differ substantially from other types of agents in the tales, such as children, animals or plants (2006, 47). From the structural point of view, there is no difference between the living nightingale and the imitated one in the fairy tale of that name, and in respect to my topic, it is equally irrelevant whether the role of the neglected or ostracized protagonist is assigned to aphids or a broken wine bottle. What is important in our context is that Andersen's protagonists, be they parasites, things or animals, are strikingly often deprived of language and excommunicated from polite society, and from literature. Yet they demonstratively exist anyway – in the stories of Hans Christian Andersen.

In this new literary style things take the place of abstract terms, and sometimes the language or narrative goes silent, as in the scrapbook full of withered flowers and leaves in Andersen's "The Silent Book." In this tale, the narrator does not even bother to go into details, or in fact he does not tell the story at all: the whole life of an unfortunate drunkard is compressed into a herbarium of withered flowers. The end of the story goes like this:

> The faded oak leaf in that silent book is the memento of a friend, the school friend who was to remain a friend for life. He himself had fastened that leaf in the student's cap in the green forest long ago, when that lifelong bond of friendship was made. Where is that friend now? The leaf is kept; the bond – broken.
>
> Here is a foreign hothouse plant, far too tender for the gardens of the North; its fresh odor seems to cling to it still. The daughter of a noble house gave it to him out of her own garden.
>
> Here is a water lily that he himself plucked, and watered with his bitter tears, a water lily of sweet waters. And what do the leaves of this nettle tell us? What were his thoughts when he plucked it and laid it away?

> Here are lilies of the valley from the dark solitudes of the forest, honeysuckle from the taproom flowerpot, and here the sharp, bare grass blade.
>
> Gently the blooming lilac bends its fresh and fragrant clusters over the dead man's head; the swallow darts by again – "Quivit! Quivit!" Now the men come with nails and hammer; the lid is laid over the dead, who rests his head silently on the silent book.

The storyteller admits that memories are connected to every single leaf or plant, yet the herbarium is growing more and more silent and the storyteller himself becomes equally taciturn. As Thomas Seiler incisively puts it: the story makes the motif of falling silent its own chief poetic strategy (2009, 112). Müller-Wille views the "The Silent Book" as a text which in retrospect tries to provide things with a story based on words, but this attempt is according to Müller-Wille contradicted with the silence of the book mentioned in the title (2009, 152). In this particular story, I would definitely stress Müller-Wille's latter observation, and prefer to read the fairy tale as a story about falling silent, thus becoming a story about renunciation of a narrative based on words that seem to be "too poor to describe" – as Lord Chandos puts it in his despairing letter:

> Each of these objects and a thousand others similar, over which the eye usually glides with a natural indifference, can suddenly, at any moment (which I am utterly powerless to evoke), assume for me a character so exalted and moving that words seem too poor to describe it. (von Hofmannsthal [1902] 2018, n.p.)

Instead, the agents seizing control of the narrative and putting a brisk end to the story are utterly concrete items: the nails, the hammer and the lid: "Now the men come with nails and hammer; the lid is laid over the dead, who rests his head silently on the silent book. Hidden – forgotten!"

In general, however, I agree with Müller-Wille that Andersen's object tales are a continuous series of attempts to give voice to things. In his essay "Der Mensch und die Dinge: Die Revolution der deutschen Prosa," Walter Jens pronounces Hofmannsthal's *Chandos Letter* a literary revolution since things for the first time claim their own independence from the writing subject and cease to confirm each other as straightforward parables. Jens calls Lord Chandos the "mystic without mysticism" because the possibility of limitless communication with things is only momentary since a language of things has yet to be invented; that is, "the diction of the object is still missing completely" (1957, 321). Actually, Hans Christian Andersen may reasonably be considered one of the first alchemists in the field of inventing a language of things. Jens further concludes that in the *Chandos Letter* "things became partners and from partners they became enemies," which is even more evident in the later works of Hofmannsthal and, particularly, Rainer Maria Rilke's novel *The Notebooks of Malte Laurids Brigge* (*Die Aufzeichnungen des Malte Laurids Brigge*, 1910) where the meticulously depicted things in the brutal urban reality appear frightening and sinister. The reader of Andersen's object tales is familiar with the fact that things in these texts often stay in the role of a partner, but we do encounter the hostility of things in the object tales as well, for instance the "The Shepherdess and the Chimney Sweep" where all things inhabiting the bourgeois room radiate anxiety.

Finn Hauberg Mortensen aptly notes that Andersen's fairy tales have an affinity with the poetic devices of two Danish modernist lyricists, Johannes V. Jensen and Klaus Rifbjerg. Hauberg Mortensen's argument is based on the fact that all three writers stage humourous collisions between highly existential problems and the most profound words (2006, 43–44). In fact, it is a poetic device in which things somehow replace words, and this rhetorical strategy seems to be profoundly connected with the scepticism towards language which is the essential building material of a writer. Owing to their turn towards the language of concrete things both Hofmannsthal and Andersen can reasonably be labelled pioneers for some of the literary isms of the twentieth century such as imagism, the Scandinavian "nyenkelhet" from the 1960s, or the particular version of modernism the reader is confronted with in Rifbjerg's collection of poems *Konfrontation* (1960). All these isms have one important strategy in common: there is a clear tendency to free literary expression from abstract terms, and a major impulse for the poetical renewal of that kind rests in the mistrust of conventional (literary) language.

This brings us back to our problem. Many of Andersen's fairy tales play with the arbitrariness of language and depict a kind of *Sprachschock*. The failing of language as a means of communication is often not merely a motif; rather, it becomes the very theme of a considerable number of his tales. We find examples of this both in two of his *object tales* ("The Steadfast Tin Soldier" and "The Shepherdess and the Chimney Sweep"), but it is also present in his other fairy tales of a different type, such as "The Little Mermaid." It is fair to say that the communication theme is discussed in different types of Andersen's short prose works and can reasonably be regarded as a leitmotif in his fairy tales; one only has to think of the solipsistic communication of the flowers in the garden scene of "The Snow Queen" ("Sneedronningen," 1845). Language (or tongue) is significantly often not at the disposal of the characters, and the communicative capacity of the protagonists is depicted in its negation. In some instances, language is radically replaced by a direct confrontation with things. If language cannot be trusted, all that remains is things.

Conclusion: Language as an Eroding Factor in the Community

The community in sociology may in general be defined territorially, especially in the traditional rural sense, or as a community one belongs to despite geographical distance. According to Seymour Sarason's classic sociological definition, community is based on "the perception of similarity to others, an acknowledged interdependence with others, a willingness to maintain this interdependence by giving to or doing for others what one expects from them, and the feeling that one is part of a larger dependable and stable structure" (1974, 157). In the Andersen fairy tales I discuss here we could see the willingness to be part of the community, yet communication or language as a means of achieving this goal of belonging failed. Another important aspect of community is emphasised by David W. McMillan and David M. Chavis who elaborate on the concept of "sense of community" as follows: "a feeling that members have of belonging, a feeling that members matter to one another and to the group, and a shared faith that members' needs will be met through their commitment to be together" (1986, 9). If we apply the "sense of community" category to the Andersen fairy tales we have looked at, it must be concluded that it is this feeling that is so often absent from the lives of the protagonists.

The terms communication and community, however, are not only etymologically connected. The sociologist Lewis A. Friedland has keenly observed that communication is the essential component constituting a community: "communication is the central system of action that binds together many different types of social actors and groups" (2001, 361). He bases his argument on Jürgen Habermas' conception of the *Lebenswelt* (lifeworld) which is linguistically organized and in which communication is an utterly essential factor. Habermas lifeworld is, actually, nearly identical with the concept of community (in German, *Gemeinschaft*), as has been insightfully demonstrated by Michael Opielka in "Kommunikation als Gemeinschaft: Habermas' Diskursmoral" (2006). Habermas views the lifeworld as consisting of socially and culturally sedimented linguistic meanings and as something thoroughly constituted by language and culture or, as he puts it: the lifeworld is a "culturally transmitted and linguistically organized stock of interpretive patterns" (1987, 124). Hence, it is clear that communication, or language, is an essential component of any community according to sociologists, yet for Andersen in his fairy tales this component is defective.

As mentioned in the beginning of this chapter, Klaus P. Mortensen characterises Hans Christian Andersen's fairy tale production as attempts to break through the undesirable isolation of the individual, in fact, as repeated attempts to return from the individual exile to the storytelling which reinforces the community. And he suggests that these attempts might be labelled fruitless. Well, not really. Were Andersen's efforts fruitless, we would not read his fairy tales today. Andersen reached his community then and still manages to collect a vast number of readers all over the world. Nevertheless, a number of his fairy tales thematically illustrate the sheer impossibility of escaping an individual exile. Many a character in his fairy tales remains excommunicated – and one of the culprits to blame seems to be language itself. In the fairy tales of Hans Christian Andersen we are conspicuously often caught in worlds where communication with others is impossible. Simply, we are confronted with outsiders caught in communities incommunicado.

Acknowledgment

The work was supported by the European Regional Development Fund-Project "Creativity and Adaptability as Conditions of the Success of Europe in an Interrelated World" (No. CZ.02.1.01/0.0/0.0/16_019/0000734).

References

Andersen, Hans Christian. 1831. Letter from Bernhard Severin Ingemann to Hans Christian Andersen, January 20. http://andersen.sdu.dk/brevbase/brev.html?bid=16267 (the letter is kept at The Royal Danish Library).

Bøggild, Jacob, and Pernille Heegaard. 1993. "H.C. Andersens 'Den lille Havfrue' – om tvistigheder og tvetydigheder." In *Andersen og Verden. Indlæg fra den Første Internationale H.C. Andersen-Konference 25.-31. august 1991*, edited by Johan de Mylius, Aage Jørgensen, and Viggo Hjørnager Pedersen, 311–320. Odense: H.C. Andersen-Centret/Odense Universitetsforlag.

Freud, Sigmund. 1961. "Civilization and its Discontents." In *The Complete Psychological Works of Sigmund Freud, Vol. XXI: The Future of an Illusion, Civilization and its Discontents, and Other Works*, 64–145. Translated by James Strachey. London: Hogarth Press, 1953–66.

Friedland, Lewis A. 2001. "Communication, Community, and Democracy: Toward a Theory of the Communicatively Integrated Community." *Communication Research* 28 (4): 358–391.

Gaffikin, Brigid. 2004. "Material Witnesses: Hans Christian Andersen's *Object tales* and the Memories of Things." *Edda* 2004 (3): 186–200.

Habermas, Jürgen. 1987. *Lifeworld and System: A Critique of Functionalist Reason*. Vol. 2 of *The Theory of Communicative Action*. Translated by Thomas McCarthy. Boston: Beacon Press.

Hofmannsthal, Hugo von (1902) 2018. "The Letter of Lord Chandos" (*Chandos-Brief*). http://depts.washington.edu/vienna/documents/Hofmannsthal/Hofmannsthal_Chandos.htm.

Jens, Walter. 1957. "Der Mensch und die Dinge. Die Revolution der deutschen Prosa." *Akzente*, no. 4: 319–34.

Kofoed, Niels. 1967. *Studier i H.C. Andersens fortællekunst*. København: Munksgaard.

Levy, Jette Lundbo. 1998. "Om ting der går i stykker: Ekelöf og Andersen." *Edda* 1998 (3): 259–268.

McMillan, David W., and David M. Chavis. 1986. "Sense of Community: A Definition and Theory." *Journal of Community Psychology* 14 (1): 6–23.

Mortensen, Finn Hauberg. 2006. "Ting og relation." In *H.C. Andersen. Modernitet & Modernisme*, edited by Aage Jørgensen and Henk van der Liet, 41–67. Amsterdam: Universiteit van Amsterdam.

Mortensen, Klaus P. 2000. "Den sande prins: Om 'Den lille Havfrue'." In *Ud af det moderne. Den kritiske tanke anno 2000*, edited by Erik Svendsen and Henrik Ljungberg, 16–24. København: Forlaget Spring.

Mauthner, Fritz. 1901. *Beiträge zu einer Kritik der Sprache*. 2 vols. Stuttgart/Berlin: J. G. Cotta'sche Buchhandlung Nachfolger.

Müller-Wille, Klaus. 2009. "Hans Christian Andersen und die Dinge." In *Hans Christian Andersen und die Heterogenität der Moderne*, edited by Klaus Müller-Wille, 132–161. Tübingen and Basle: A. Francke Verlag.

Mylius, Johan de. 2005. *Forvandlingens pris. H.C. Andersen og hans eventyr.* København: Høst & Søn.
Nöth, Winfried. 1995. *Handbook of Semiotics.* Bloomington/Indianapolis: Indiana University Press.
Nietzsche, Friedrich. 1989. "On Truth and Lying in an Extra-Moral Sense." In *Friedrich Nietzsche on Rhetoric and Language*, edited by Sander L. Gilman, Carole Blair, and David J. Parent and translated by David J. Parent, 246-257. New York/Oxford: Oxford University Press.
Opielka, Michael. 2006. "Kommunikation als Gemeinschaft. Habermas' Diskursmoral." In *Gemeinschaft in Gesellschaft. Soziologie nach Hegel und Parsons*, 311-352. Wiesbaden: Verlag für Sozialwissenschaften.
Sandersen, Vibeke. 2005. "Om sprog og stil i H.C. Andersens eventyr." *Nyt fra Sprognævnet*, no. 4: 1-8.
Sarason, Seymour B. 1974. *The Psychological Sense of Community: Prospects for a Community Psychology.* San Francisco: Jossey-Bass.
Seiler, Thomas. 2009. "'Aber ich habe die Erinnerung, die kann mir keiner nehmen'. Figurationen der Erinnerung in H.C. Andersens Dingmärchen." In *Hans Christian Andersen und die Heterogenität der Moderne*, edited by Klaus Müller-Wille, 95-117. Tübingen and Basle: A. Francke Verlag.

Notes

1. Vibeke Sandersen (2005) documents the process of simplification comparing two Andersen fairy tales, "Dødningen, et fyensk Folke-Eventyr" ("The Spectre, A Funen Folktale," 1830) and "The Traveling Companion" ("Rejsekammeraten," 1835). Concentrating on linguistic devices, she reaches the same conclusion as Niels Kofoed (1967), who, in his comparison of the same material, focuses on Andersen's shifts in poetic devices.
2. Sigmund Freud suggests in his "Das Unbehagen in der Kultur" (1930) that it was by diverting sexual instincts into acts of higher social valuation that humankind actually made progress. He writes that sublimation is "an especially conspicuous feature of cultural development; it is what makes it possible for higher psychical activities, scientific, artistic or ideological, to play such an 'important' part in civilised life." (1961, 79-80).
3. Nietzsche maintains: "When we speak of trees, colours, snow, and flowers, we believe we know something about the things themselves, although what we have are just metaphors of things, which do not correspond at all to the original entities. Like sound in the sand-figure, so the mysterious X of the thing appears first as a nerve stimulus, then as an image, and finally as a sound. In any case, the origin of language is not a logical process, and the whole material in and with which the man of truth, the scientist, the philosopher, works and builds, stems, if not from a never-never land, in any case not from the essence of things." (1989, 249).

Toy Stories
On Toys and Childhood in "The Steadfast Tin Soldier"

Frederike Felcht
Goethe University, Frankfurt

This chapter explores representations of toys in Hans Christian Andersen's fairy tales, focusing on "The Steadfast Tin Soldier" from 1838. It presents several interpretations from recent research that deal with the relationship between subjectivity and material culture and thus underlines the complexity of Andersen's texts. Furthermore, it argues that "The Steadfast Tin Soldier" subverts the notion of the sheltered bourgeois childhood that dominated the nineteenth century, by revealing how the text deals with problems related to militarism, capitalism, and patriarchism. The fairy tale also criticises a lack of community that the lonely main character experiences. Yet Andersen's fairy tales show, on the other hand, the interrelatedness of human and non-human beings – a community of modern material culture.

In his famous essay about Hans Christian Andersen, the literary critic Georg Brandes explained:

> *The starting point* of his [Andersen's] art is the playing of children that transforms anything into anything. That is why Andersen's playful mood makes toys become natural creatures, supernatural beings (trolls), heroes, and why it uses, vice versa, the entirety of nature and the supernatural – heroes, trolls, and fairies – as toys, that is, as artistic means. *The nerve* in this art is the child's imagination that animates and personifies everything; [...]. Even a jumping goose becomes a living whole, a thinking, desiring being. *The model* of such a poetry is the child's dream [...]. ([1869] 1899, 94–95)[1]

The literary scholar Klaus Müller-Wille has stated that Brandes was the first critic who understood that Hans Christian Andersen's fairy tales resulted from an aesthetic strategy (2009, 133). However, Müller-Wille adds, the idea that this aesthetic strategy is based on childlike imagination is a projection. According to Müller-Wille, Brandes projects the idea of wholeness onto Andersen's texts when they actually call this idea into question. Müller-Wille argues that Andersen's *object tales*, his fairy tales about things, critically explore the relationship between subjects and things. I agree with Müller-Wille that Andersen's texts question the dominant concept of subjectivity in the nineteenth century that emphasised the autonomy, rationality, and superiority of the human. However, the aspects of play and childhood that are central to Brandes' thoughts are not relevant in Müller-Wille's argument. Brandes' observation that Andersen's texts include a particular relationship to play and childhood is correct, but Andersen's writings are rarely naïve. Brandes missed the subversive aspects of Andersen's fairy tales. In Brandes' statement, toys and artistic means are interchangeable. The following reflections about Andersen's poetics of toys show that Andersen indeed used toys as artistic means – with a subversive effect. In my contribution to this book, I will investigate how Andersen's fairy tale "The Steadfast Tin Soldier" ("Den standhaftige Tinsoldat," 1838) deals with questions of subjectivity in modern culture and with the social role of things by focusing on a specific category of things, namely toys. In my reading, "The Steadfast Tin Soldier" subverts the notion dominant in the nineteenth century of the bourgeois childhood as a sheltered space.

My reflections are embedded in a wider theoretical context. The literary scholars Finn Barlby and Jacob Bøggild consider "The Steadfast Tin Soldier" to be the first real ("egentlige") *tingseventyr*; that is, according to a more general definition, a fairy tale in which things come to life ("er levendegjorte" [2015, 17]). Several definitions of object tales exist. Recent research challenges some of the anthropocentric assumptions of older approaches, such as literary scholars Paul Vilhelm Rubow's ([1927] 1967) and Polonca Kovač' (1993) reflections on the role of things in Hans Christian Andersen's fairy tales. Newer concepts of object tales interpret active things no longer solely as projections of human qualities onto things, but rather acknowledge that things have agency in themselves (for an overview of these approaches see Felcht 2013, 50–65).

This development in how the genre is conceptualised responds to changes in cultural theory. Since the 1990s, cultural theories have increasingly reflected on the role of things in modern life, for example Bruno Latour's (1995, 2005) actor network theory, Bill Brown's (2001) thing theory, or Hartmut Böhme's (2006) history of fetishism and culture. These approaches emphasise the interrelatedness of humans and non-humans and locate agency in both humans and non-humans, thus creating a hybrid concept of action and questioning the traditional distinction between active human subjects and passive non-human objects. Referring to the double sense of "ting" in Scandinavian languages, designating material objects and places of political assemblies, Bruno Latour (2005, 119) points to the fact that material structures produce and stabilise societies. My approach to toys in Hans Christian Andersen's fairy tales is based on these assumptions.

"The Steadfast Tin Soldier" also criticises a lack of community caused by social exclusion and aggression. The representation of toys in "The Steadfast Tin Soldier" shows how material culture shapes human experience. As I have argued elsewhere, Andersen's fairy tales point to a concept of the social as an assembly of humans and non-humans – a form of modern material community (Felcht 2013, 38–50, 65–75). This is valid for the representation of toys in his texts, too. Instead of opposing active human subjects to passive objects, Hans Christian Andersen's texts reveal the interdependence between things and human identities.

Toys: Instruments of Projection

"The Steadfast Tin Soldier" is not the only one of Hans Christian Andersen's fairy tales in which toys play a central role. For example, in "The Sweethearts"; or, "The Top and the Ball" ("Kjærestefolkene," 1844; known also as "Toppen og Bolden"), a top (he) falls into love with a ball (she), who, however, rejects his advances, thinking that she belongs to a superior class and will get engaged to a swallow. Jumping as high as she can, she gets lost. Years later, the top and the ball meet again in the dustbin. The ball, who had been lying in the gutter for a long time before she entered the dustbin, has lost her former appearance. She is now very interested in talking to the top, but the top does not answer, recognising that his love for her has vanished.

"The Sweethearts" could be read as a grown-up and disillusioned variation of the romantic love story in "The Steadfast Tin Soldier," showing what happens when the admirer does not unite with the admired (although, in "The Steadfast Tin Soldier," this union is only for a single moment, which is immediately followed by death), but meets her again after years of longing. The literary scholar Jette Lundbo Levy has shown how "The Sweethearts" uses the ambiguity and materiality of the playthings top and ball as a poetic principle and argues that the fairy tale melancholically denies the discovery of the world that is the privilege of children's play (1998, 263). "The fairy tale takes its point of departure in the children's world and in the playroom; however, one hopes that the children do not understand it" (263).[2] Müller-Wille states that the fairy tale can, on the one hand, be read as a simple parable of the proverb "pride goes before a fall" (2009, 143), but that it, on the other hand, tackles the more complex problems of lack and desire. "The Sweethearts" is rich in puns, comic elements, and lively passages of dialogue that children can enjoy, whereas its melancholic reflection on the structure of desire is more accessible for adults. This form of double address is typical of Andersen's fairy tales (see for example Andersen 2003, 16–35; Anz 2005, 37–39; Baggesen 1993).

Another fairy tale with toys as main characters, "The Money Pig" ("Pengegrisen," 1855), depicts a playroom at night in which the toys play, observed by the piggy bank. All the toys' thoughts are directed towards the contents of the piggy bank – capitalism rules even the playroom (Felcht 2013, 239–244). This fairy tale underlines the close connection between the new model of childhood that developed from the late eighteenth century and modern consumer culture. The literary scholar Dennis Denisoff emphasises the development of this relationship: "To establish and maintain its position as a broad social ideology, consumer culture had to develop not simply in step with the new model of childhood, but *through* it" (2008, 6).

Toys have not always been associated with childhood. In the eighteenth century, toys could be "any small, cheap object [...] sold by a traveling peddler or 'toyman' to both children and adults" as literary scholar Teresa Michals states with reference to an eighteenth-century dictionary (2008, 32). Prior to this period, as philosopher Giorgio Agamben reminds us in his reflections on toys, "[t]hings that to us appear as toys were originally objects of such seriousness that they were placed in the tomb to accompany the deceased during the otherworldly sojourn" ([1977] 1993, 58). However, "by the nineteenth century, 'toy' was well on its way to becoming a synecdoche for childhood" (Michals 2008, 32). Andersen's fairy tales reflect this association of toys and childhood. At the same time, they subvert the bourgeois concept of childhood as a sphere of innocence that is separated from the adult world, by showing how gender roles, class differences, or other power relations shape the experience and environment of children. In addition to the fairy tales mentioned above, "The Shepherdess and the Chimney Sweep" ("Hyrdinden og Skorsteensfeieren," 1845) is a good example of this quality of Andersen's *Eventyr og Historier* (Fairy Tales and Stories) (see also Felcht 2013, 244–249). By sending the tin soldier into the darkness of the gutter and the stomach of a fish, "The Steadfast Tin Soldier" even relates the plaything with the transitional function of toy-shaped figures mentioned by Agamben: during these events, the tin soldier is on the edge of earthly existence and the other-worldly sojourn. The tin soldier, however, does not accompany a human, but travels alone, sent by two boys who thus exercise power over him.

"The Steadfast Tin Soldier" plays with the assumption of a separated domestic sphere by placing the soldier in a playroom or in part of another room that is full of toys. Playrooms or separate indoor spaces for playing are characteristic of the bourgeois concept of childhood in the nineteenth century: they constituted a sheltered space for growing up by excluding the outside world (Felcht 2013, 239) – and they promoted consumption. However, the tin soldier leaves this sheltered space: he is blown out of the window, placed in a paper boat, and eaten by a fish. The children's space is no longer secluded. The literary scholar Kirsten Møllegaard describes the ambivalent function of the tin soldier's trip in the fairy tale:

> Through the ages, the sanctuary of the home shines a bright beacon in children's literature about animated toys. Separation from home is conceived as one of the most dreadful things that can happen to a toy (and by extension, to a child). Andersen's toy heroes typically face formidable challenges when they get lost or leave the safe, though typically oppressive, world of home and go out into the world. Nevertheless, for the tin soldier to go AWOL does represent an unexpected occasion to earn valor and prove his manliness. (2017, 36)

The trip oscillates between the neglect of military duties and a heroic journey. The tin soldier, however, is not destroyed on his journey; he first melts when back home. In her reading, Møllegaard emphasises how the fairy tale criticises dominant social values of its time:

> [The tin soldier] is a unique individual entrapped in a strict social world where he is allowed neither voice nor gaze, and where he has internalised the very values that oppress him.
>
> Andersen criticises Biedermeier values such as sentimental piety and domestic security by situating the one-legged tin soldier in a social world of totalitarian rule, social injustice and ultimate death. (2017, 41)

Her inspiring interpretation leads to results that are similar to my impression of "The Steadfast Tin Soldier." However, she conceives of the soldier as a mere "*Sinnbild*, or symbolic allegory" (41), and thus neglects the complex effects of the aesthetic representation of toys in the text. This complexity is based on Andersen's use of materiality, the motif of projection, and on his playing with the functioning of toy culture in the nineteenth century.

Although the tin soldier is originally produced as a toy that is usually used for a defined purpose (war games [Kollbrunner 1979, 8–9]), in the story of the fairy tale, the children do not play with him according to this function. He does not fight in a combat unit; rather he is isolated, lost, and destroyed without any reason by the boys in the fairy tale. He and the dancer he is looking at also do not play when the rest of the toys in the room begin "to play among themselves at visits, and battles, and at giving balls" as soon as the humans are gone. Thus, the behaviour of the tin soldier also differs from that of the other toys, who enter a game of human role-playing whenever possible. However, from his internal perspective, he stays faithful to expectations of his behaviour when he keeps his composure, stays quiet, and avoids attracting attention whatever the situation. According to Møllegaard, the story "explores the duality between inner and outer worlds, which much Romantic literature focuses on" (2017, 32).

According to whose expectations does the tin soldier act (or, rather, not act)? In his review entitled "Spielzeug und Spielen" ("Toys and Play"), the philosopher Walter Benjamin states: "Toys are, even where they do not imitate adults' utensils, a form of occupation; not so much the child's occupation with the adult, as the adult's occupation with the child. Who gives the child a toy at the beginning if not them?"

([1928] 1972, 128).³ Based on Walter Benjamin's observation, the cultural theorist Knut Ebeling has elaborated on the projective character of toys, stating: "Toys aren't objects of insight – but of knowledge. You cannot see anything in toys (namely the nature of playing or the child's wishes), but only decipher (namely the parents' wishes and projections)." (2008, [10]).⁴ From this perspective, toys are the result of adult's projections on children.

In "The Steadfast Tin Soldier," the tin soldier thus incorporates, on the one hand, the adult concept of soldiery that is closely related to a concept of manliness (Møllegaard 2017, 29) and nationhood. The philosopher Roland Barthes' critique of toys that "prefigure the world of adult functions" in order to "prepare the child to accept them all" (Barthes [1957] 1972, 53) applies also to tin soldiers in general, and Møllegaard states that the tin soldier in "The Steadfast Tin Soldier" has internalised ideals about bravery and honour that lead to his passive behaviour (2017, 41). Thus, we can say that in the narrative of the fairy tale, it appears that the tin soldier tries to act according to the expectations of the adult world, a world that produces, buys and sells tin soldiers. The narrative portrays this striving by presenting an inner perspective that interprets the immutability of the tin soldier as a decision rather than the effect of his existence as a tin soldier. On the other hand, his striving to fulfil this role is ironically deconstructed throughout the fairy tale. For the narrative not only depicts the striving of the tin soldier, but also combines his inner perspective with an external perspective that questions this striving. The fairy tale oscillates between attributing agency to the thing and subjecting it to the whimsical powers of children and the wind.

In his philosophical article "Towards a Theory of Toys and Toy-Play," Alan Levinovitz has discussed the difficulties of defining toys (2017, 274–78, 281). He states that smallness is a quality of most toys, that toys are often insignificant (they do not have a telos) and do not prescribe rules (in contrast to a game) and, focusing on the changing "relationship between subject, object, and context," that "*a toy is an invitation to play with its identity*" (278). "The Steadfast Tin Soldier" develops this form of playing on a poetic level. For example, "The Steadfast Tin Soldier" deals with the problematic relationship between individuality and collectivity in modern culture.

The Military Collective

The fairy tale introduces twenty-five tin soldiers that are brothers, since they are born from the same old tin spoon. They all carry a gun, have the same posture and wear uniforms. The first word they hear in this world is "Tinsoldater!" (Andersen 2003, 188) – tin soldiers. Thus, their perception and self-perception as a collective is established: instead of giving them individual names, they are addressed as a group. However, perceptions reveal themselves to be projections in this text. The tin soldier is not really part of a combat unit.

Levy explains that "The Steadfast Tin Soldier" belongs to the category of object tales, that involve toys that copy the figure and the roles of humans (1998, 261–63). According to Levy, these fairy tales describe gender and power relations. But tin soldiers do not only *copy* a specific role – as toys they also serve a purpose in the *learning* of a role. Thus, not only does the role shape the toy; the toy also shapes the role. Boys practice the role of the soldier – a role which was becoming increasingly associated with the nation as a whole during the nineteenth century – by playing with tin soldiers. Furthermore, a central feature of the soldier, his uniformity or non-individuality, depends on his uniform, and the distinctive accessory that identifies him as a soldier is his gun. Obviously, the functioning of social roles is inseparable from material culture.

Levy mentions that tin soldiers have their origin in the early context of industrialisation, the Nuremberg toy industry (262). Thus, "The Steadfast Tin Soldier" deals not only with the collective in the form of a military unit, but also in relation to seriality and mass production. Møllegaard explains that in Denmark, "tin soldiers' uniformity and lack of individual expression gave rise to colloquial sayings about the human condition" (2017, 30) and that according to the Danish language dictionary *Ordbog over det danske Sprog* (1946), Andersen's contemporary Søren Kierkegaard compared commonplace and unremarkable people with tin soldiers. Tin soldiers thus were uniform and mass produced and represented uniformity and a lack of identity.

Seriality and mass production often provoke a longing for authenticity and originality. "The Steadfast Tin Soldier" reflects this longing by letting its main figure deviate from the other soldiers by his one-leggedness – and marking him as "remarkable," "mærkværdig." As Møllegaard points out, "mærkværdig" can also mean "strange" or "odd" (2017, 35). The scholars in disability studies David Mitchell and

Sharon Snyder – who refer to a retelling of "The Steadfast Tin Soldier" by Katie Campbell, obviously without knowing the original source of the fairy tale – assume that the "imperfection" is the starting point of the narrative: "Narrative interest solidifies only in the identification and pursuit of an anomaly that inaugurates the exceptional tale or the tale of exception" (2000, 54). Møllegaard, in contrast, asks: "Is it the missing leg that makes him remarkable, or is it his romantic sentiments and tragic fate?" (2017, 36). The question remains open. The one-leggedness, we can nevertheless declare, provides the tin soldier with an individual appearance.

In comparison with the other soldiers, however, it is also a lack. The text explains this lack as resulting from the insufficient amount of tin derived from the tin spoon – thus the lack is linked to the production of the tin soldier. The tin soldier's lack is converted into desire when he falls in love with a dancer who seems to have only one leg too in his eyes – a conversion that is typical of Marxian commodities (see Xenos 1989, 1–54).

The Soldier and the Dancer: Things, Lack and Desire

On the table where the soldiers are placed there are many playthings, including a paper castle. The castle is surrounded by a mirror that is meant to look like a moat filled with water. (This detail is the first indicator of the problematic role of self-reflection in the text: the mirror stands for something other than a mirror.) In the open door of the castle, a young lady or maiden, "Jomfru," is standing (Andersen 2003, 188). She is made of paper too, but wears a skirt made of lawn, and a blue ribbon with a shiny sequin. "The little lady held out both her arms, as a ballet dancer does, and one leg was lifted so high behind her that the tin soldier couldn't see it at all, and he supposed she must have only one leg, as he did. / 'That would be a wife for me,' he thought."

The text explains the opened arms and thus the apparently inviting gesture with reference to the profession of the figure; and the impression of a single leg is a misperception. Obviously, the tin soldier projects his own interests and features onto the lady. Levy emphasises the different meaning of the single leg: whereas the tin soldier's missing leg is the result of a deficiency, in the dancer, it is a sign of perfection and artistry (1998, 262). The literary scholar Vivian Yenika-Agbaw reads the romantic interest of the tin soldier as an "attempt to link up with someone who shares his physical disability" (2011, 96). The tin soldier, however, never explicitly conceives of his one-leggedness as a disability. This interpretation results from a specific reading perspective.

The literary scholar Peer E. Sørensen explains that the fairy tale presents a romantic love narrative of postponed desire, since the soldier and the dancer meet only in death, when they end in the same fire (1973, 172). However, things are the protagonists in this story of unfulfilled desire. There are several possible reasons for this artistic decision. The literary scholar Karin Sanders states that Andersen's "use of non-humans (things, animals) is important precisely because they allow him freedom to articulate the follies of human vanity and expose humankind's fraught social behaviours." (2012, 30). In "The Steadfast Tin Soldier," this form of representation also permits sexual allusions that would have been impossible in other forms. For example, while he rushes, in a paper boat, under a gutter plank into the darkness, the tin soldier thinks: "'[...] Ah! if only I had the little lady with me, it could be twice as dark here for all that I would care'." The literary scholar Mads Sohl Jessen's interpretation focuses on the representation of male sexual desire in "The Steadfast Tin Soldier" (2015, 89–93). In his reading, the tin soldier represents a single bourgeois male in the nineteenth century who does not want to go to war, but rather wants to have a woman.

However, the sole focus on sexuality neglects other aspects. In his comparative study of the motif of the tin soldier in literature, Karsten Essen emphasises that the tin soldier in Andersen's fairy tale is aware of the class difference between the paper dancer and himself (2007, 31–32). For example, when the tin soldier dreams of marrying the paper dancer, he says to himself: "But maybe she's too grand. She lives in a castle. I have only a box, with four-and-twenty roommates to share it. That's no place for her." The soldier's thoughts reflect not only on the problem of how to meet a girl alone when you have twenty-four roommates, but also the supposed social difference between him and the dancer.

This social difference, though, may be a projection, too. In the nineteenth century, the audience suspected actors and ballet dancers of doubtful morality and they usually had no access to higher social circles (Engberg 1995, 1:161; Kvam, Risum, and Wiingaard 1992–93, 1:194–196; Andersen 2005, 83–84); but the same audience admired them and paid them for showing their bodies. If ballet dancers (and, we could add, unmarried women in general) fulfilled male sexual desire, they ran the risk of being socially ruined – a risk that is reflected in the conclusion of the fairy tale, where the dancer burns instantly when she meets the soldier. Thus, the fairy tale negotiates the problematic attitude towards female sexuality that requires both virginity or purity (she is a "Jomfru," a virgin) and seductiveness from women.

Sørensen argues that transferring a love story into the sphere of things depicts humans as passive objects rather than active subjects (1973, 172). The tin soldier is indeed characterised by passivity. The narrator reinterprets this passivity as steadfastness or appropriate behaviour, but this interpretation is strongly ironic. As the literary scholar Joan Haar states: "[T]he narrative questions the very decorum it praises." (2000, 497).

However, there are more aspects involved in taking the perspective of things than just representing human problems in another form. Levy shows not only for "The Sweethearts," but also for "The Steadfast Tin Soldier" how the materiality of the figures shapes the course of the story (1998, 262). For example, the steadfastness of the tin soldier is part and parcel of the material of which he is made. The paper boat, on the other hand, dissolves, thus pointing to the unstable nature of paper. At the end of the story, the tin soldier melts slowly in the fire and becomes a heart of tin, whereas the dancer blazes like a flash, leaving behind only a sequin that is black as coal. In Levy's interpretation, the inflammability of the material of the figure also applies in a figurative sense to her love for the soldier. In a course on literature and material culture, my students have suggested an interpretation of the sequin as a sign of luxury and superficiality and remarked that its blackness puts an end to the dancer's role as an object of projections: nothing can be seen on her surface any longer. In "The Steadfast Tin Soldier," the ballet dancer's internal perspective is never shown, and the tin soldier never talks with her. Her association with the mirror and the sequin reminds the readers of her quality as an object of projection and associates this quality with modern consumer culture.

Müller-Wille reads the postponement of desire for things – in contrast to people – that are out of reach as an indirect reflection of commodity fetishism (2009, 144–145). In his introduction to commodity fetishism in the first chapter of *Capital*, Karl Marx sets out how capitalism neglects use value in favour of exchange value ([1867] 1962, 85–91). A process of abstraction takes place when goods enter the market as commodities, whereby relationships between people, as well as relationships between people and things, are mediated by money. This process of abstraction makes us forget the processes by which the commodity was produced and thus the fact that every exchange on the market expresses social relationships. This is the starting point of a never-ending desire – as soon as humans and things no longer have individual, concrete relationships with each other, you will never have enough money and things. Agamben ([1977] 1993, 31–60) refers to Marx's concept and combines it with observations on the fetishistic character of art and erotic desire in modern culture – taking the form of commodities and fetish objects – and on the emotional ambiguity of toys which are "distant and beyond our grasp" and "an inexhaustible object of our desire and our fantasies" (58), as well as sources of infantile disappointment or frustration. Müller-Wille bases his interpretation of "The Steadfast Tin Soldier" on Agamben's reflections and considers the tin soldier's desire as a reflection of desire in modern consumer culture. Although the fairy tale does not address explicitly the issue of commodification, Müller-Wille's reference to the new ambivalent mechanisms of desire that unfold in a modern consumer culture helps us to understand the passive and visual attraction experienced by the tin soldier. Müller-Wille supposes that the dancer's leg is the soldier's object of desire and reminds him of his own lack. I suggest a different reading.

The One-legged Soldier

As we already have seen, the missing leg is an important feature of the tin soldier. Yenika-Agbaw (2011) and Mitchell and Snyder (2000, 54–56) base their interpretation of the story on the assumption that it deals with dis/ability. However, I think that the fairy tale has a different meaning than these critical readings assume. In contrast to these interpretations, I do not think that the missing leg simply stands for a human dis/abilty. In my reading, it is significant that the missing leg is the result of a production fault that is, however, not presented in the text as a fault – on the contrary, the narrator always emphasises that the one-legged tin soldier stands as firm as tin soldiers with two legs: "there he stood, as steady on one leg as any of the other soldiers on their two". Together with the representation of military virtues in the text, this representation of the missing leg allows for a subversive interpretation of "The Steadfast Tin Soldier."

The first time the tin soldier is explicitly characterised as steadfast, he is "just as steadfast on his one leg" as the dancer is on her tiptoe. The second time, he is standing on a whirling paper boat: "The paper boat pitched, and tossed, and sometimes it whirled about so rapidly that it made the soldier's head spin. But he stood as steady as ever" – the original wording of the last sentence is "men han blev standhaftig" (Andersen 2003, 189), that is "but he stayed steadfast." The third time, he lies inside the stomach of a fish: "My! how dark it was inside that fish. It was darker than under the gutter-plank and it was so cramped, but the tin soldier still was staunch. He lay there full length, soldier fashion, with musket to shoulder" – the original wording of "but the tin soldier still was staunch" is "men Tinsoldaten var standhaftig" (Andersen 2003, 190). These pictures undermine his supposed steadfastness, since they repeatedly indicate the concrete absence of a firm position. However, this absence is not related to the missing leg, but to the prevailing circumstances of the situation.

Furthermore, the military bearing of the soldier is an illusion. After he has fallen out of the window, the boy who owns him and the housemaid look for him, and, "though they nearly stepped on the tin soldier, they walked right past without seeing him. If the soldier had called, 'Here I am!' they would surely have found him, but he thought it contemptible to raise an uproar while he was wearing his uniform." However, he has "landed cap first, with his bayonet buried between the paving stones and his one leg stuck straight in the air," thus he already finds himself in a situation far removed from the military discipline he still strives to act in accordance with. The fall seems to have impaired his ability to understand his own situation. His self-control is an obstacle in his way to the ballet dancer. Møllegaard comments on his steadfastness in the paper boat: "Of course, the irony is that since he really is a tin soldier he can't change his expression even if he wanted to. He is literally cast in a mould, meaning a social gender role, from which he cannot escape." (2017, 39). The soldier tries to preserve a military identity, whereas his surroundings undermine the possibility of giving meaning to this identity.

In fact, he is not even part of a military collective, since he does not communicate with his fellow soldiers. Andersen had already used the comic motif of the lonely soldier who still behaves like a part of a combat unit in the opening sequence of his first fairy tale collection, in the fairy tale "The Tinder Box" ("Fyrtøjet," 1835): "There came a soldier marching down the high road – *one, two! one, two!* He had his knapsack on his back and his sword at his side as he came home from the wars." Even before the soldier of "The Tinder Box" meets the witch, the adult reader knows that this is no realistic text: a single soldier who returns from war would never march.

While the soldier in "The Steadfast Tin Soldier" is travelling in the paper boat, a strange episode takes place: a rat asks for his passport and follows him, gnashing its teeth, trying to stop him since he did not pay the toll. These details undermine the social role of the soldier, the role that should be learned by playing with tin soldiers: the steadfastness, the military bearing and control are only illusions. Comradeship does not exist. The border – that is, the zone that was the reason for most wars during the nineteenth century when the territorial national state developed – is guarded by a rat that demands money.

In the end of the story, the boy throws the tin soldier into the fire without any reason. We note that the child is socialised by military toys. His behaviour could be the result of the aggressions stimulated by war toys. But it also relates to the anomaly of the soldier: as a one-legged soldier, he is the element of war that must not appear in play that upholds the military ideal. The injured, the wounded, the invalids are, of course, excluded when tin toys are produced. Møllegaard points to the fact that after the Napoleonic wars, large numbers of wounded veterans, many of them amputees, returned from the wars: "The tin soldier's missing leg alerts us to consider the implication of warfare on the human body." (2017, 41). However, as her argument continues, it deviates from my reading, since she states that the tin soldier was "'born that way'" (41). But the fairy tale explicitly explains the missing leg as a result of the production process, not birth. In this explanation there is an ironic twist, since the real production fault – with regard to practicing warfare – is not the missing leg, but the integrity or completeness of the other soldiers who are consequently neglected by the narrator of the fairy tale. They give an illusionary impression of warfare.

"The Steadfast Tin Soldier" is a fairy tale that explores the difficulties of how to make love, not war. Including the missing leg in our analysis, instead of excluding it, reveals what is usually missing in the representations of war that adults produce for children.

In "The Old House" ("Det gamle Huus") – which was first published in an English translation in 1847 before the Danish original appeared in 1848 (Andersen 2003, 533) – Andersen depicted a very different portrait of a tin soldier (Kuznets 1994, 82). Here, the tin soldier is given by a little boy to an elderly man who lives alone in an old house on the opposite site of the street, because the boy feels sorry for his lonely neighbour. As soon as the little boy visits his neighbour, the tin soldier complains that he cannot bear the lonesome and boring life at the old house. The boy encourages the tin soldier to keep his spirits up and to see the good sides of his new situation, the interesting memories that visit the old man. The second time the little boy visits the elderly man, the tin soldier wails: "I've been shedding tin tears." This is in contrast to the steadfast tin soldier who is touched so deeply when he sees the paper dancer after his return home that "he would have cried tin tears, only soldiers never cry." The tin soldier in "The Old House" also exclaims: "[I]t's too sad here! I'd rather go to the wars and lose arms and legs; at least that would be a change! I just can't stand it!" Obviously, the soldier's concept of war and suffering is naïve. Whereas the steadfast tin soldier tries to embody military ideals in a mutilated body, the tin soldier in "The Old House" has no ideals and wants to risk his intact body purely for entertainment. The little boy refuses to take the tin soldier away with him and reminds him that he was a present and must stay. The tin soldier's reaction is like that of a small child who is far from any self-control. "'I'm going to the wars! I tell you I'm going to the wars!' the tin soldier shouted as loudly as he could, then he threw himself off the chest right down to the floor." Going to war, in this story, is no heroic act, but the result of selfishness and boredom. Although the tin soldier "had fallen into one of the many cracks in the floor and lay there as if in an open grave" and is thus symbolically buried, he is found many years later by the wife of the now grown-up boy and woken up from his trance. The plot of "The Old House" is more merciful towards the tin soldier than in "The Steadfast Tin Soldier," but the portrait of his character is not. When the tin soldier in "The Old House" finally exclaims: "But it's wonderful not to be forgotten!," the narrator adds a strange commentary from a scrap of pigskin which agrees with the tin soldier and gives its opinion: "*Gilding fades fast; / But pigskin will last!* / But the tin soldier didn't really believe it." Without its gilding, the pigskin "looked like a piece of wet clay," and it is most likely that it will not last, but pass away. The final scene thus points to the transient nature of existence and associates it with the tin soldier who does not believe the pigskin. It is indeed the tin soldier of "The Old House" who is forgotten today, whereas the steadfast tin soldier is still well-known. Love wins.

Conclusion

Hans Christian Andersen's object tales do not only make reference to a childlike imagination as Brandes thought. Rather, they are multidimensional. They use toys as artistic means. They connect characters to their materiality and use this technique to question gender and power relations, as Levy has shown. Thus, the texts associate toys with specific aesthetic strategies. Toys shape and reflect social roles. "The Steadfast Tin Soldier" highlights this social function of toys. In modern consumer culture, identity is produced through the convergence of humans and things, as the text shows. Furthermore, "The Steadfast Tin Soldier" ironically deconstructs the military ideals of heroic strength and comradeship. The fairy tale instead associates the military collective with the normalising effects of industrialised mass production. The individual longing of the tin soldier becomes a symptom of the emotional economy of capitalism, where desire and loneliness become constant feelings. The text thus also criticises a lack of emotional community.

Andersen's texts also call into question a particular bourgeois concept of childhood. This chapter has shown how "The Steadfast Tin Soldier" is one example of this questioning; however, "The Money Pig" and "The Shepherdess and the Chimney Sweep" further support this reading (Felcht 2013, 239–249). These object tales incorporate spaces and things that are typical of childhood in the nineteenth century, but they break with the phantasmagoria of a childhood that is separate from the world of adults and thus can be entirely controlled by them. Rather they show that this understanding of childhood is a projection, whereas the world of childhood is pervaded by problems and contradictions stemming from militarism, patriarchism, and capitalism – even in the playroom.

References

Agamben, Giorgio. (1977) 1993. *Stanzas: Word and Phantasm in Western Culture*. Translated by Ronald L. Martinez. Minneapolis: University of Minnesota Press.
Andersen, Dorthe Sondrup. 2005. *Kanøflet i København. H.C. Andersen og Det Kongelige Teater*. København: People's Press.
Andersen, Hans Christian. 2003. *Eventyr og Historier I: 1830-1850*, edited by Laurids Kristian Fahl, Esther Kielberg, Klaus P. Mortensen, and Jesper Gehlert Nielsen. Vol. 1 of *Andersen. H.C. Andersens samlede værker*, edited by Klaus P. Mortensen. København: Det Danske Sprog- og Litteraturselskab/Gyldendal. 2003-07.
Anz, Heinrich. 2005. "'Aber das ist ja gar kein Märchen!' Überlegungen zu Hans Christian Andersens Märchenpoetik." In *Hans Christian Andersen zum 200. Geburtstag: "Mein Leben ist ein schönes Märchen so reich und glücklich!,"* edited by Svenja Blume and Sebastian Kürschner, 35-55. Hamburg: Verlag Dr. Kovač.
Baggesen, Søren. 1993. "Dobbeltartikulationen i H.C. Andersens eventyr." In *Andersen og Verden. Indlæg fra den Første Internationale H.C. Andersen-Konference 25.-31. august 1991*, edited by Johan de Mylius, Aage Jørgensen, and Viggo Hjørnager Pedersen, 15-29. Odense: Odense Universitetsforlag.
Barthes, Roland. (1957) 1972. "Toys." In *Mythologies*, selected and translated by Annette Lavers, 53-55. New York: Hill and Wang.
Barlby, Finn, and Jacob Bøggild. 2015. "Det euforiske spejl. Om H.C. Andersens tingseventyr, genren, det essentielle tingseventyr og bogens tilblivelse." In *Det euforiske spejl. Dialoger om H.C. Andersens tingseventyr*, 15-21. Charlottenlund: Dråben.
Benjamin, Walter. (1928) 1972. "Spielzeug und Spielen." In *Kritiken und Rezensionen*, edited by Hella Tiedemann-Bartels, 127-132. Vol. 3 of *Gesammelte Schriften*, edited by Rolf Tiedemann and Hermann Schweppenhäuser. Frankfurt am Main: Suhrkamp.
Böhme, Hartmut. 2006. *Fetischismus und Kultur. Eine andere Theorie der Moderne*. 2nd ed. Reinbek bei Hamburg: Rowohlt.
Brandes, Georg. (1869) 1899. "H.C. Andersen som Æventyrdigter (Juli 1869)." In vol. 2 of *Samlede skrifter*, 91-132. København: Gyldendalske Boghandels Forlag. 1899-1906.
Brown, Bill. 2001. "Thing Theory." *Critical Inquiry* 28 (1): 1-22. http://www.jstor.org/stable/1344258.
Denisoff, Dennis. 2008. "Introduction. Small Change: The Consumerist Designs of the Nineteenth-Century Child." In *The Nineteenth Century Child and Consumer Culture*, edited by Dennis Denisoff, 1-25. Aldershot: Ashgate.
Ebeling, Knut. 2008. "Spiel/Zeug. Eine Archäologie des homo ludens." Accessed 24 April 2018. www.dgae.de/wp-content/uploads/2008/09/Knut_Ebeling.pdf.

Engberg, Jens. 1995. *Til hver mands nytte. Historien om Det Kongelige Teater 1722–1995*. 2 vols. København: Frydenlund.
Essen, Karsten. 2007. *Standhafte Zinnsoldaten. Motivstudien zu Andersen, Wagner, Thomas Mann und Tomasi di Lampedusa*. Würzburg: Königshausen & Neumann.
Felcht, Frederike. 2013. *Grenzüberschreitende Geschichten. H.C. Andersens Texte aus globaler Perspektive*. Tübingen: A. Francke Verlag
Haar, Joan G. 2000. "The Steadfast Tin Soldier." In *The Oxford Companion to Fairy Tales*, edited by Jack Zipes, 496–497. Oxford: Oxford University Press.
Jessen, Mads Sohl. 2015. "Ubehaget i tingene – Andersens satire over det hoffmannsk uhyggelige i 'Den standhaftige Tinsoldat' og 'Hyrdinden og Skorsteensfeieren'." In *H.C. Andersen og det uhyggelige*, edited by Jacob Bøggild, Ane Grum-Schwensen, and Torsten Bøgh Thomsen, 85–101. Odense: Syddansk Universitetsforlag.
Kierkegaard, Søren. 2007. *Journals AA–DD*. Vol. 1 of *Kierkegaard's Journals and Notebooks*, edited by Niels Jørgen Cappelørn, Alastair Hannay, David Kangas, Bruce H. Kirmmse, George Pattison, Vanessa Rumble, and K. Brian Söderquist. 8 vols. Princeton/Oxford: Princeton University Press. 2007–15.
Kollbrunner, Curt F. 1979. "Einführung." In *Zinnfiguren, Zinnsoldaten, Zinngeschichte*, edited by Curt F. Kollbrunner, 7–10. München: Hirmer Verlag.
Kovač, Poloncа. 1993. "Die lebendige Welt der leblosen Gegenstände." In *Andersen og verden. Indlæg fra den Første Internationale H.C. Andersen-Konference 25.-31. august 1991*, edited by Johan de Mylius, Aage Jørgensen, and Viggo Hjørnager Pedersen, 295–302. Odense: Odense Universitetsforlag.
Kuznets, Lois Rostow. 1994. *When Toys Come Alive: Narratives of Animation, Metamorphosis, and Development*. New Haven: Yale University Press.
Kvam, Kela, Janne Risum, and Jytte Wiingaard. 1992–93. *Dansk Teaterhistorie*. 2 vols. København: Gyldendal.
Latour, Bruno. 1995. *Wir sind nie modern gewesen. Versuch einer symmetrischen Anthropologie*. Translated by Gustav Roßler. Berlin: Akademie Verlag.
Latour, Bruno. 2005. *Reassembling the Social: An Introduction to Actor-Network-Theory*. Oxford: Oxford University Press.
Levinovitz, Alan. 2017. "Towards a Theory of Toys and Toy-Play." *Human Studies: A Journal for Philosophy and the Social Sciences* 40 (2): 267–284. https://doi.org/10.1007/s10746-016-9418-0.
Levy, Jette Lundbo. 1998. "Om ting der går i stykker. Ekelöf og Andersen." *Edda: Scandinavian Journal of Literary Research* 1998 (3): 259–268.
Marx, Karl. (1867) 1962. *Das Kapital. Kritik der politischen Ökonomie*. 3 vols. Vol. 1: "Der Produktionsprozeß des Kapitals." Berlin: Dietz.
Michals, Teresa. 2008. "Experiments before Breakfast: Toys, Education and Middle-Class Childhood." In *The Nineteenth Century Child and Consumer*

Culture, edited by Dennis Denisoff, 29–42. Aldershot: Ashgate.

Mitchell, David T., and Sharon L. Snyder. 2000. *Narrative Prosthesis: Disability and the Dependencies of Discourse*. Ann Arbor: The University of Michigan Press.

Müller-Wille, Klaus. 2009. "Hans Christian Andersen und die Dinge." In *Hans Christian Andersen und die Heterogenität der Moderne*, edited by Klaus Müller-Wille, 132–158. Tübingen: A. Francke Verlag.

Møllegaard, Kirsten. 2017. "'The Steadfast Tin Soldier' as Romantic Hero and Tragic Lover." In *Toy Stories: The Toy as Hero in Literature, Comics and Film*, edited by Tanya Jones, 27–44. Jefferson, NC: Mc Farland & Company.

Ordbog over det danske Sprog. 1946. "Tinsoldat." Vol. 23. Det Danske Sprog- og Litteraturselskab. Accessed 15 May 2018. https://ordnet.dk/ods/ordbog?query=tinsoldat.

Rubow, Paul V. (1927) 1967. *H.C. Andersens Eventyr. Forhistorien – Idé og Form, Sprog og Stil*. København: Gyldendal.

Sanders, Karin. 2012. "'Let's be human!'" – On the Politics of the Inanimate. *Romantik* 1 (1): 29–47. https://tidsskrift.dk/rom/article/view/15849/13720.

Sørensen, Peer E. 1973. *H.C. Andersen & Herskabet. Studier i borgerlig krisebevidsthed*. Grenaa: GMT.

Xenos, Nicholas. 1989. *Scarcity and Modernity*. London: Routledge.

Yenika-Agbaw, Vivian. 2011. "Reading Disabilities in Children's Literature. Hans Christian Andersen's Tales." *Journal of Literary and Cultural Disability Studies* 5 (1): 91–108. https://doi.org/10.3828/jlcds.2011.6.

Notes

1 "*Udgangspunktet* for hans Kunst er Barnets Leg, der gør Alt til Alt. Derfør gør Andersens spillende Lune Legetøjsstykker til naturlige Skabninger, til overnaturlige Væsener (Trolden), til Helte, og bruger omvendt hele Naturen og alt det Overnaturlige, Helte, Trolder og Feer som Legetøj, det vil sige som kunstneriske Midler. *Nerven* i denne Kunst er Barnets Indbildningskraft, der besjæler og personliggør Alt; [...] Selv en Springgaas bliver da for Barnet et levende Hele, et tænkende, villende Væsen. *Forbilledet* for en saadan Poesi er Barnets Drøm [...]." (Italics in the original. My translation)
A "Springgaas" or "jumping goose" is a toy made from the breast bone of a goose which can be set into flight with a spring. See Kierkegaard 2007–15, 1:551.

2 "[N]ok tager eventyret udgangspunkt i børnenes verden og i barnekammeret, men man beder til, at børnene ikke forstår det." (My translation)

3 "Das Spielzeug ist, auch wo es dem Gerät der Erwachsenen nicht nachgeahmt ist, Auseinandersetzung, und zwar weniger des Kindes mit dem Erwachsenen, als des Erwachsenen mit ihm. Wer liefert denn zum Anfang dem Kinde sein Spielgerät wenn nicht sie?" (My translation)

4 "Das Spielzeug ist kein Gegenstand der Erkenntnis – sondern des Wissens. In ihm kann man nichts schauen (nämlich das Wesen des Spielens oder die Wünsche des Kindes), sondern nur entschlüsseln (nämlich die Wünsche und Projektionen der Eltern)." (My translation)

The Problem of "The Red Shoes"

Jacob Bøggild
University of Southern Denmark, Odense

"The Red Shoes" is rarely commented on in the scholarly reception of Andersen. And the comments are either neutral or negative. It thus appears that the tale is considered to be a problem – if not even a scandal. The argument of this chapter is that the problem of the tale is basically a problem of reading. This is the case because the tale consists of several tales, so to speak, which have trouble reading each other – understanding and shedding light on each other. It is a tale about the vanity of an orphaned girl, Karen, who is not successfully integrated in a narrow-minded community. This community is even shown to be implicated in the formation of Karen's vanity. It is also a gruesome fairy tale in the mode of the brothers Grimm. And it is a tale about vanity considered as a sin in religious terms and in this respect the tale is both a tale about punishment and a tale about mercy and redemption. The tale thus balances between a literal and a figurative understanding of Karen's suffering and in this way, it addresses a key question of Christian religion and Dogmatics: in what way can the Old and the New Testament read each other – understand, comprehend and shed light on each other? This is why this tale of Andersen's is indeed a profound one.

"The Red Shoes" ("De røde Skoe," 1845) is a serious problem – or even a scandal – it appears. The tale does not fit in with the popular image of Andersen as the avuncular teller of fairy tales for children. In fact, it does not fit in with any preconceived ideas about what kind of an author Hans Christian Andersen is. Thus, it is rarely commented upon in the scholarly reception of Andersen. It is usually passed over in silence or only briefly mentioned. Niels Kofoed devotes a couple of lines to it in *Studier i H.C. Andersens fortællekunst*. He dismisses it as "a harsh, moralistic tale." (1967, 256). Peer E. Sørensen writes a couple of pages about it in *H.C. Andersen og herskabet*, but also more or less dismisses it as "a regular pietistic story about conversion." (1973, 195). According to Paul Binding in *Hans Christian Andersen: European Witness*, it is a "troubled" tale (2014, 226). Johan de Mylius does not pass any moral judgement on it in *Livet og skriften* but characterises it as: "[...] a strange mixture of a socio-moral story about everyday life, a gruesome fairy tale in the mode of the Grimm brothers and a pious, Christian legend." (2016, 647).

This is a good platform from which to begin to address the problem of "The Red Shoes." One thing is for sure: The tale is strange, and it does mix several genres or modalities. I will add that it is one of Andersen's most interesting and profound tales and for that reason very disturbing indeed. Not because of the apparent moral condemnation of the vanity of the hapless protagonist, or anti-protagonist, Karen. Not because of the violent and grotesque image of the red shoes' dancing away with her chopped-off feet. The tale is disturbing because of the way it demonstrates that desire is always the desire of the other[1] and that this has to do with the Law or the Commandment in a Christian sense. Desire is communal and a result of the ban or prohibition, the "Thou shalt not." Time to begin.

Red Shoes are Not a Problem

And let us begin with "The Snow Queen" ("Sneedronningen," 1845), Andersen's grand, arabesque, Christian allegory which was written earlier the same year as "The Red Shoes." The two tales appear to be diametrical opposites. The protagonist of "The Snow Queen," Gerda, seems to be the incarnation of innocence and pure faith. She completes her mission of rescuing Kay from the Snow Queen thanks to these qualities. Karen in "The Red Shoes" is on no mission at all – this is why you might say she is an anti-protagonist – but is the victim of her own vain desire for red shoes which in the story connote sin and sexuality – or so it seems. There is a common denominator between the two tales, however: the motif of red shoes.

When Gerda sets off on her mission she first goes down to the river. Before she goes she puts on a pair of new red shoes which Kay has never seen. Thus, she might be just a little bit vain. She has no idea about where to start looking for Kay, so she hopes that the river can give her some advice. Once she is down by the river, she proposes it a deal. Her idea is that the river has taken Kay and she offers it her red shoes in return for him. She then throws the shoes into the river. But the waves carry them up on the bank again immediately. Her offer or sacrifice is not accepted. Gerda thinks she did not throw the shoes far enough and enters a boat lying in the rushes by the bank. She throws the shoes again, but this makes the rushes lose their hold on the boat and it starts floating down the river with the barefoot Gerda on board. Her quest proper begins in this accidental way. And no one asks about red shoes in the rest of the tale. There is no indication that red shoes are a problem.

Gerda seems to be quite like Karen at this point in the story. Her pair of red shoes is her dearest possession and she wants the person she cares most about, Kay, to see her wearing them. Her willingness to sacrifice the shoes demonstrates how much she will do to find Kay again, of course. However, nothing indicates that her offer is accepted. As just mentioned, she embarks – or is embarked – on her quest as a result of pure chance or coincidence.

In "The Red Shoes" Karen's first pair of red shoes are not a problem either. She is so poor that she has to walk barefoot in summer and wear clogs in winter. An old woman who is a cobbler takes pity on her and sews a pair of red shoes for her. They are kind of clumsy, we are told, but they are still red. On the day Karen receives them her mother dies, and she has to wear them at her funeral. When she walks in the procession following her mother's coffin she is spotted by an old lady driving by in a carriage. The old lady takes pity on the orphaned child and promises to take care of her. Until this point in the story red shoes have not been an issue or a problem in any serious way.

Red Shoes become a Problem

According to the childish logic of the little girl it is thanks to her new red shoes that the old lady takes pity on her. But she is then taught a harsh lesson indeed. The old lady states that the red shoes are appalling and has them burned. This is how scandalous a pair of clumsy red shoes sown from rags is to the old lady. They must be done away with in the most dramatic fashion conceivable. This will of course teach the little girl a lesson. The old lady's reaction to the shoes and her subsequent action must be entirely enigmatic to the little girl. But she is not quite as innocent as she was before. She has learned that red shoes represent or stand for something which is dangerous and mysterious and therefore alluring. Her imagination will be occupied with the enigma of what this dangerous and mysterious sphere or zone which red shoes represent is like or consists of.

Burning the shoes is of course a psychological assault on the little girl. But a fairy tale does not deal with such psychological matters in any everyday sense. The old lady rather represents the Law and the Commandment, the 'thou shalt not': "thou shalt not wear red shoes!" The Commandment, the ban on red shoes, is of course what makes them not only desirable but irresistible to Karen. The seed of desire and vanity has been sown in Karen as a consequence of the burning of the shoes. Red shoes have now become a serious problem.

According to the apparent logic of the tale, the next misfortune of Karen is that she is good-looking. This makes people feed her awakened vanity. They say that she is "nydelig" (Andersen 2003, 349): "nice-looking." This seed of vanity is then inflated by "the mirror" (349) – we are not told whose mirror or what kind of mirror this is – which says that Karen is much more than nice-looking, that she is "deilig" (349): "lovely" or "very attractive indeed" (my translations).[2] One should definitely compare to "Snow White" as regards this. In "Snow White" the queen has got a magic mirror which does not flatter her, but which has to tell her the truth: That Snow White is the prettiest one in the country. The unspecified mirror in "The Red Shoes" is obviously a much more metaphorical one. It magnifies or intensifies the verdict of the gazes of the others of the community which Karen has internalised. Karen sees herself through the eyes of the Other, she mirrors herself in the Other's gaze. And her imagination transforms the verdict of this gaze, the one that she is good-looking, into the one that she is lovely and very attractive indeed. The origin of her vanity is therefore not in the deep and dark recesses of her originally sinful soul. The origin of her desire is in the gaze of the Other which is constituted by the community which surrounds her but does not fully integrate her.

Her vanity is further intensified by the encounter with another Other who represents the possibility of a social climb to the uppermost sphere of society. Karen sees the little daughter of the queen who is travelling through the country. This princess is wearing a fine, white dress and dashing red shoes when she poses in order to be admired. We are informed that she wears this instead of a train and a golden crown. As Andersen scholar Torsten Bøgh Thomsen has pointed out in an unpublished study, this means that she is not cast as a folk or fairy tale princess in the text. She is cast as a modern one who is not dressed according to the code of power but according to the code of fashion. This already hints at the complexity of the question of the genre of "The Red Shoes." The result of the encounter with the princess is that Karen is now assured that "nothing compares to red shoes."

When the time comes for Karen's confirmation the old lady wants to buy her a pair of new shoes which will fit the occasion. The old lady cannot see very well so when Karen chooses a pair of red shoes she is not aware of it. In this way Karen obtains her second pair of red shoes, the pair which proves to be well and truly problematic. We can rest assured that this second pair of red shoes is not clumsy but dashing. She wears this pair when she is confirmed, and she can think of nothing else during the ceremony:

> Everyone was looking at her feet, and when she went up the floor of the church to the door of the choir, she thought that the old funereal images, these portraits of vicars and wives of vicars with stiff collars and long, black dresses, fixed their eyes on her red shoes, and she would only think of them when the vicar put his hand on her head and spoke of the sacred baptism, about the Covenant with God and that she would now become a grown-up Christian person. (Andersen 2003, 350, my translation)[3]

The ban or Commandment of the Law and the internalised gaze of the other is working in communion here, you might say. Karen imagines the gazes of the images of the deceased others – the vicars and wives of vicars – fix upon the red shoes which the prohibition has fixed on her. Karen has been trapped in a trap which is not of her own making.

The Problem of Red Shoes becomes Intolerable

After the ceremony everybody tells the old lady about the scandal of Karen wearing red shoes for her confirmation. The old lady has perhaps softened a bit, since she does not have this second pair burned. She tells Karen that her behaviour was awful and inappropriate and that she henceforth, when going to church, shall wear black shoes. Yet when they go to church the next Sunday in order to take communion Karen has not put on black shoes but is again wearing the red ones. An old soldier with a crutch and a strange beard which is "more red than white, since it was red" (Andersen 2003, 350) is sitting outside the church. He hits or taps the red shoes with his hand and says: "Look, what lovely shoes for dancing! [...] stick when you dance!" (350). When Karen and the old lady leave the church after communion the old soldier again says "look, what lovely shoes for dancing!" (351) as they enter the old lady's carriage. Karen then involuntarily starts to dance having no power over her legs which seem to be governed by the shoes. Only when the old lady and the coachman manage to force the shoes off her feet do Karen's legs relax.

The old soldier is perhaps the most enigmatic element of the tale. He is sitting outside the church. This indicates that he does not belong to the Christian community. He offers to dust people's shoes in exchange for alms. Presumably, he sits beside the church door because everybody in the community will pass by him. But the old soldier not only does not belong to the Christian community. He is also the first folk or fairy tale element proper to enter the tale. He casts a spell of a kind and it appears to have an effect. At his second "look, what lovely shoes for dancing!" the shoes seem to stick to Karen's feet and make her dance involuntarily.

As a folk or fairy tale element, the old soldier would essentially belong to a pagan culture. If we understand him in this way, it makes good sense that he is situated outside the church, advancing no further than its threshold. However, it is more complicated than that to situate the soldier. His spell is activated again when the old lady is mortally ill. Instead of caring for her, Karen goes off to a ball wearing the red shoes. This time she begins to dance involuntarily and uncontrollably again. Eventually the shoes have her dance into the dark forest. What Karen takes to be the moon visible between the trees proves to be the face of the soldier. He again repeats his "look, what lovely shoes for dancing!" (Andersen 2003, 351). This terrifies Karen, but when she tries to remove the shoes she finds them to have grown together with her feet. The spell is now effective indeed. And when the shoes dance her into the graveyard by the church an angel is standing in a white dress at the open church door holding a shining sword. The angel repeats and intensifies the spell of the soldier in a way which turns it into a proper curse:

"Dance you shall!" he [the angel] said, "dance on your red shoes until you turn pale and cold! until your skin shrinks like that of a skeleton! You shall dance from door to door and where proud, vain children live you shall knock at the door in order that they hear you and fear you! Dance you shall, dance – –!" (352)

The angel is thus situated at the threshold of the church too and as mentioned it amplifies the spell of the soldier and turns it into a regular curse. Thereby, the angel appears to be in league with the soldier and this is why the latter is such an ambiguous figure. He might seem to be a pagan figure, but he appears to be on the side of the angel at the same time. The strange comment about his beard by the narrator perhaps emphasises this ambiguity: As quoted, the beard is "more red than white, since it was red." Red and white seem to be the two dichotomous colours of the tale. The angel is clad in a white dress. The shoes of sin and desire are red. But the princess who wears red shoes is also clad in a white dress. And when the angel appears a second time – this time as an angel not of cursing and damnation but as one of Mercy – it does not hold a sword in its hand but a green branch with roses the colour of which we are not told. They *might* be red, then. At any rate, the dichotomy between white and red is by no means clear. The white dress of the princess wearing the red shoes is enough to unsettle it. The beard of the soldier might signal that this is the case. It is red, and this would position him at the side of paganism, sin and desire if the dichotomy in the tale between red and white was simple and clear. But paganism cannot just be associated with sin and evil. What goes before the advent of Christ can of course not actively deny or turn away from either Christ or Christianity. It is, in a way, 'before' or 'prior to good and evil'. The 'fact' that the beard of the soldier is more red than white, because it is red, could well hint at this complicated or even paradoxical state of affairs.

The angel is no less complicated. The first time it is an angel of cursing and damnation. It is an angel of the Law who punishes transgression – the transgression made possible by the Law – without mercy. According to Kierkegaard in *Works of Love* (*Kjerlighedens Gjerninger*) the Law famishes you, literally it "hungrer ud:" "hungers you out:"

> It is as if the Law hungers you out; with its help one never reaches fulfilment, since its purpose is to take away, to demand, to impoverish to the

utmost (...). With every demand the Law requires something and yet there is no limit to the number of demands. The Law is therefore the very opposite of life, but life is the fulfilment. The Law is like death." (Kierkegaard 1995, 105-106, translation modified by me)[4]

The angel's curse very much literalises this statement as it condemns Karen to dance until her "skin shrinks like that of a skeleton." The law which hungers you out is the Law of the Old Testament. In order to keep skin and flesh on our bones we are therefore in dire need of the Gospel, the Mercy announced by the New Testament. Karen cries for Mercy after the angel has cursed her, but she does not hear any reply because the shoes have already danced off with her. The angel is thus very much one of the Old Testament. Its sword could have been burning.

The Radical Solution to the Problem of Red Shoes

When Karen later dances past a door only too well known to her and she sees a coffin decorated with flowers being carried out, she realises that the old lady is dead. She now feels truly forlorn and cursed by the angel of God. She is then taken by the shoes to a lonely house on a heath where the executioner lives. He threatens to cut off her head with his axe, but she begs him to sever off her feet with the shoes instead in order that she can repent her sin. We are told that she confesses her sin before the executioner does what she asked him to do. Off dance the shoes with her feet into the deep forest. The problem of red shoes appears to have been solved in this radical way.

This is another extremely ambiguous part of the tale. The image of the shoes dancing on with the feet after they have been severed from the legs is worthy of a horror movie – or of the brothers Grimm at their gruesome best. So much for the element of horror. The fact that Karen confesses her sin to the executioner is uncanny. The executioner is an instrument of the merciless Law. The executioner knows no mercy. "I chop the heads off evil people" (Andersen 2003, 352), he says, and he feels his axe quivering at the sight of Karen. Sinners get their just reward in the executioner's opinion, we cannot understand him otherwise. It makes no sense to confess your sin to such an instrument of the merciless Law.

Could we anyhow understand the executioner as a paradoxical instrument of Mercy? Does he do what is necessary in order that Karen's process of genuine repentance can begin? This is certainly one way one could understand the tale. But mercy then only comes at a prize which risks turning its name into a misnomer if we understand the tale literally. We might also understand the tale more figuratively. We might take it – or this part of it – as an allusion to a statement made by Jesus as a part of the Sermon on the Mount:

> And if thy right eie offend thee, plucke it out, and cast it from thee. For it is profitable for thee that one of thy members should perish, and not that thy whole body should be cast into hell.
> And if thy right hand offend thee, cut it off, and cast it from thee. For it is profitable for thee that one of thy members should perish, and not that thy whole body should be cast into hell. (Matthew, 5:29-30)

One cannot be offended – tempted to sin – by one's eye or one's hand. Such members of the body do not possess any agency of such a kind. This part of Jesus' statement must obviously be figurative. And it seems apparent that it is literalised in Andersen's tale. Karen is offended – tempted to sin – by both her feet wearing the cursed shoes. She duly has the executioner cut both her feet off.

This part of "The Red Shoes" can then be understood as a kind of parable. The statement of Jesus is apparently literalised and turned into a story. If we understand this story literally it is of course quite outrageous. But we might understand the story figuratively: While turning Jesus' statement into a story it still retains its figurative dimension – thus precisely being a parable. Such an understanding will to some extent get us off the hook. But not quite.

One cannot ignore the second part of Jesus' statement. The alternative to getting rid of the offending member is being cast into hell. There is no indication that this part of the statement is figurative. Jesus rarely speaks like a hell preacher. But he indeed seems to speak like such a preacher here. This further complicates matters. From what we know, Andersen completely rejected the idea of eternal damnation and everlasting fire. It was totally incompatible with his idea of what the Christian religion is about. But he cannot turn the statement of Jesus into a parable without importing the literal idea of hell, of eternal damnation and everlasting fire, so to speak.

We are thus suspended between a literal and a figurative understanding of this part of the tale. Or perhaps more precisely: A complete escape from the literal understanding of it is not possible. Reading this part of the tale "properly" is impossible. This indicates that there must be a more fundamental mistake in or impossibility of reading at work somewhere in the equation. The tale about Karen as a victim of circumstances and woeful pedagogical measures (the burning of the first pair of red shoes) and the tale about Karen as a selfish sinner who must repent to the very core of her being before the Law's curse on her will be lifted seem unable to "read" – understand and shed light on – each other. And this might have to do with the fundamental problem of understanding how the Law of the Old Testament and the fulfilment of it in the New Testament relate to each other.

The Problem of Red Shoes Continues

The executioner fashions wooden legs and crutches for Karen and teaches her a hymn always sung by sinners. She leaves his place and walks over the heath. She believes she is now ready to go to church:

> "Now I have suffered enough because of the red shoes!" she said, "now I will go to Church in order that they can see me!" and she went swiftly towards the church door, but when she got there the red shoes danced before her and she got terrified and turned around. (Andersen 2003, 352)

According to Karen she has now suffered enough. One would tend to agree. But it is of course not up to a sinner to decide when enough suffering has taken place. One could take this statement as an indication that Karen is still errant in her spiritual ways – even if it appears very cruel to do so. She wants to go to church in order that the others – the community, the congregation – should see her. Does she want to be admired because of the visible proof of all that she has suffered: the crutches and the wooden legs? In that case she still sees herself through the eyes of others in her imagination.

At any rate, her severed feet wearing the red shoes block the entrance to the church and bar her from entering. First of all, this is more horror in the mode of the brothers Grimm at their gruesome best. But the motif is very disturbing at another level too. The shoes block Karen's way into the church much like the angels who guard the entrance to the Garden of Eden after Adam and Eve were expelled. These are indeed angels with swords, burning ones. The shoes appear to be somehow in the service of the angel with the sword who cursed Karen to dance until the flesh drops from her bones. The shoes seem to embody the offence – the temptation to sin – and the punishment for sinning at one and the same time.

After weeping and grieving for a week, Karen the next Sunday thinks that she has now suffered and striven enough. She believes that she is "quite as good a person as many of those who sit upright inside the church" (Andersen 2003, 353) and therefore walks confidently towards the church door again. One would presume that Karen is quite as a good a person as many of those sitting inside the church. But she also imagines those persons sitting upright, sitting in a proud manner. Of course, sitting proudly upright in the house of God is not proper conduct. A much humbler attitude would be more fitting when inside this very house. This might be yet an indication that Karen is still errant in her spiritual ways. She is still vain and projects her vanity onto those people she imagines inside the church and whom she compares herself to. And again, she is barred from entering the church by her severed feet wearing the red shoes dancing before her. Once more, she turns around and, we are informed, in her heart repents her sin.

But should we believe this statement from the narrator that she now, finally, after being barred from entering the church by the shoes a second time, is truly repentant in her heart? One wonders. When has one suffered enough? When has one repented deeply enough? The case of Karen tempts one to ask whether one can ever have suffered enough and whether one can ever have repented deeply or truthfully enough? If the Law does not "hunger you out," it appears to be the case that the work of repentance will do the same job. Will Karen have to repent until her skin shrinks like that of a skeleton?

Karen now humbly asks to be taken into the household of the vicar in order to serve as a maid of sorts. She does not care whether she is paid for her work or not. Having a roof over her head is all that she asks for. The vicar's wife takes pity on Karen, we are told, and her offer is accepted. We do not learn whether Karen is paid anything or not. She lives in a room so small that there is only room for a bed and a chair. She is diligent and thoughtful. The little ones like her. When the vicar reads from the Bible in the evening, she listens in. There is no sign that Karen becomes a member of the Vicar's household in any profound sense. Only the little ones interact with her. Otherwise she is someone who is "there," someone somewhere in the periphery. She is no nearer being welcomed and fully integrated in the community.

The next Sunday everyone in the household is going to church. They ask Karen if she would like to come along. With tears in her eyes she looks at her crutches. Then the others leave in order to go and listen to the Word of God. What has taken place is highly ambiguous because of the little we are told. Did Karen not believe that the others would help her get to the church on time in her maimed state? Would the others in fact do nothing of the sort? Or is Karen afraid that the red shoes will again appear and bar her from entering through the church door – this time for everyone in the community to witness her disgrace? We cannot tell.

The Problem of Red Shoes is Forgotten

Karen goes to her small room and sits down in the single chair with a hymn book. As she reads the wind carries the sound of the organ from the church to her. She lifts her tearstained face to the heavens and says: "Oh God, help me!" (Andersen 2003, 353). The second version of the angel now appears, still dressed in a white dress but with a green branch with roses in its hand instead of a sword. It touches the roof and it rises towards the sky where a star is shining. It touches the walls and they widen so that she can see the organ in the church. And she can see:

> [...] the old pictures with vicars and the wives of vicars, the congregation sat in the ornamented chairs and sang from their hymn book. – Because the church itself had come home to the poor girl in the little, narrow room or else she had gone there; she sat in the chair with the other people of the Vicar and when they had stopped singing the hymn and looked up, they nodded and said: "It was Right that you came, *Karen*!"
> "It was Grace!" she said. (353)

The tale ends with one of the religiously charged but also highly ambiguous death scenes which we know from Andersen – from "The Ice Maiden" and "A Story from the Sand Dunes" for example. Karen's heart bursts as the sun shines through the church windows and the organ plays and the choir sings. Her soul flies on the sunshine to God where, with the final words of the text, "no one asked about *the red shoes*." (353).

For whatever reason, Karen gives up on going to church. She goes to her small room. She sits alone there like the single individual she is instead of going to the official institution of the church. When she hears the sound of the organ she looks up towards the heavens and addresses God. This is the first time in the tale we hear that she does this. She opens herself to God, lets him in. And this turns the tables completely. The answer to her predicament is not to be found in the official institution. When she opens herself to God in true humility and as a single individual the answer presents itself.

The institution then comes to her or she comes to it. This complicates matters once more. We have to ask whether this is something which actually happens or whether it is some kind of vision or dream. Anyhow, the congregation is present, and Karen sits among the members of it. The members of the congregation finish singing a hymn and then they look up. They appear to sit very much upright. They then pronounce that it was "Right" that Karen came. It was just and fair. Who are they to judge about that? Who are they to judge about what only God can judge about: the ways of his Grace and Mercy? These people are not so much people of God as they, as they are referred to, are "the people of the vicar:" a tight community who never really welcomed or integrated Karen in their midst. Who fuelled her vanity and then scorned her for being vain.[5] Who represented or embodied the gaze of the Other which led her further astray. And, as far as we can judge, they have not even begun repenting any of these or other of their sins. They are not even aware of them.[6]

The tale leaves the self-righteous congregation in this state or situation of being completely unaware of their own sins and judging about what they should certainly not judge about. Karen's soul flies home to God on rays of sunshine. And there, we are told, no one asked about *the red shoes*. We might conclude that in heaven everything is forgotten and forgiven, and Karen is allowed to leave her issue with red shoes well and truly behind. But the last three words are in italics. This means that Andersen, as he is prone to do, repeats the title of a tale with its final words. He thus establishes a frame which frames the text as a self-conscious work of art and piece of fiction. And it is this work of art, this piece of fiction, "The Red Shoes," which no one in heaven asks about if we read the final sentence to the letter. What is going on?

The Genre of the Problem of "The Red Shoes"

Of course, Andersen is very much capable of reading what he writes. But why does he stage this tale in a way that it appears to consist of parts which are unable to understand and shed light on each other? One way of tentatively answering this question might be to give the question of the genre of the tale some extra thoughts. The already mentioned remark about the question of the genre by de Mylius will serve as an excellent point of departure: "[...] a strange mixture of a socio-moral story about everyday life, a gruesome fairy tale in the mode of the Grimm brothers and a pious, Christian legend." (2016, 647). Let us consider each part of this tri-part definition of the genre carefully.

"a social-moral story about everyday life"

"The Red Shoes" is in some ways a story about everyday life, there is no denying that. And it very much focuses on the social sphere. Karen is born to a poor and single mother. She is born on the edge of the community. When her mother dies there is no one who will immediately take care of her. She is spotted by the old lady who decides to care for her. This might to some extent be due to a selfish motive. The old lady might be lonely and therefore want some company and perhaps someone to look after her in her old age.[7] She then becomes the cause of Karen's fascination with and fixation on red shoes by having the first pair burned. The community further fuels Karen's vanity. The tale thus diagnoses how desire is not a private but a communal or societal phenomenon in a way which would be recognised by psychoanalysis. But there is no apparent moral in the story which fits this kind of tale about everyday life. Karen has to follow the wayward path – dictated by the shoes – of her very private *via dolorosa* and her ultimate salvation – if such a thing indeed takes place – is of course also a private affair.

"a gruesome fairy tale in the mode of the Grimm brothers"

The tale is violent in the same way as some of the fairy tales you find in the brothers Grimm, there is no denying that either. But considered as a fairy tale, "The Red Shoes" is a strange one indeed. Karen is a victim of circumstances she cannot control in any way. In this sense, she is not really a protagonist. While being a victim she also acts in a selfish manner which is untypical of a fairy tale heroine. She tricks the old lady into buying the second pair of red shoes. And she goes off to a ball when she should have cared for the mortally ill old lady. This might be compared to *failing* a qualifying test. But from the perspective of a story about everyday life, Karen merely acts selfishly and recklessly in a way many teenagers do.

Moreover, the number three does not play a significant part in the tale. The number two does. There are two pairs of red shoes. The old soldier appears twice. The angel appears twice. Karen is barred from entering church twice. This aspect of the tale might be connected to the fact that it is governed by dichotomies to an extent which is alien to the folk tale proper. Red shoes are opposed to black shoes. Karen as a single individual is opposed to the community which never really embraces or integrates her. The old soldier is opposed to the angel while at the same time seeming strangely in league with it. And the first appearance of the angel is opposed to the second appearance of it. The latter is the strongest dichotomy and the starkest contrast in the story. The angel in its first appearance is one of damnation and of the Law of the Old Testament which will hunger you out. The angel in its second appearance is one of Mercy or Grace and maybe of the fulfilment of the Law in the New Testament. Such a dichotomy is indeed absolutely alien to the universe of the folk tale.

"a pious, Christian legend"

If this is a pious story it must be in the sense in which it depicts Karen's *via dolorosa*. From such a perspective, Karen has to follow the path of a gruesome Grimm brothers' tale because she does not look for God where God can be found. Her failure is not that she has sinned and transgressed and that her repentance is not profound enough. Her failure is that she still compares herself to others ("I have now suffered enough. I will go to church so they can see me"; "I am as good a person as those people sitting upright in the church"; 352, 353) and is therefore still occupied with herself (as Other). Her failure is that she does not completely abandon herself and make it possible for God to reach her. She only makes it possible for God to reach her towards the end when she looks up to the heavens and cries for help. Then God's Mercy or Grace can reach her. Such an understanding of the pious aspect of the tale would be in perfect accordance with the theology of Kierkegaard, of course, and so would the mistrust of the official institution of the church and the good people of the vicar which is evident in the tale.

Due to the depiction of Karen's *via dolorosa* she is in a way a much more powerful heroine of a Christian legend than Gerda of "The Snow Queen" (who had no qualms sacrificing her red shoes) – and even than Elisa of "The Wild Swans" ("De vilde Svaner," 1838) (who is from the outset quite as innocent and good as Gerda and never changes in this respect). The story about everyday life and the gruesome tale in the mode of the Grimm brothers in fact both assist in giving Karen her power as such a heroine. But this is not a Christian legend without some very unsettling elements. As mentioned, it is unclear whether any actual salvation takes place at the end or whether what Karen experiences is some kind of dream or vision. And there is the further complication that Andersen ends the story in the way he does. If the tale had ended with the statement that in the realm of God "no one asked about red shoes" we could understand this as an indication that this realm is one of complete and absolute forgetting of sin and thus a realm of absolute forgiveness. But when it is stated that no one asked about "*the red shoes*" in italics, this, as mentioned, is in effect a repetition of the title of the story. A Christian legend does not end in such a way. A *Kunstmärchen* by Andersen, as also mentioned, often does.

Andersen in this way undermines the possibility that the Christian legend somehow synthesises the mixture of genres and in doing this well and truly integrates and suspends the story about everyday life and the gruesome tale in the mode of the brothers Grimm. Therefore, de Mylius might in fact have assisted us in realising that "The Red Shoes" specifically consists of *three* stories – the story about everyday life, the gruesome folk tale and the Christian legend – which are ultimately unable to read, to understand and shed light on, each other. This is how it should be. This is how a tale about the *modern* (in the widest sense) human condition should be. Our culture is very much a culture of the impossibility of three such stories reading each other and achieving a synthesis which will allow us to sleep soundly at night.[8]

The old soldier with his beard "more red than white, since it was red" might well be understood as an emblem of this situation of an impossibility of reading. He belongs to the story of everyday life. He might be a war veteran abandoned by society and left to survive by begging for alms. Like Karen, he does and does not belong to the community. Like her, he is situated somewhere in its periphery. But he also belongs to the pagan realm of the folk tale, remaining outside the church door (accordingly, his "Look, what lovely shoes for dancing!" is repeated *three* times). He can even cast a spell. But in so doing he becomes a kind of instrument of the angel of the Law of the Old Testament who will turn his spell into a regular curse. The Old Testament, one might add, is not just the book of the Law and the Covenant, but also a collection of myths and folk tales, some of them gruesome.

References

Andersen, Hans Christian. 2003. "De røde Skoe" ["The Red Shoes"]. In vol. 1 of *Andersen. H.C. Andersens samlede værker* [The Collected Works of Hans Christian Andersen], edited by Klaus P. Mortensen, 349–353. København: Det Danske Sprog- og Litteraturselskab/Gyldendal, 2003–07.

Binding, Paul. 2014. *Hans Christian Andersen. European Witness*. New Haven/London: Yale University Press.

Felcht, Frederike. 2013. *Grenzüberschreitende Geschichten. H.C. Andersens Texte aus globaler Perspektive*. Tübingen: A. Francke Verlag.

Kierkegaard, Søren. 2004. *Kjerlighedens Gjerninger*. Vol. 9 of *Søren Kierkegaards Skrifter*, edited by Niels Jørgen Cappelørn et al. København: Gads Forlag, 1997–2012.

Kierkegaard, Søren. 1995. *Works of Love*, edited and translated by Howard V. Hong and Edna H. Hong. New Jersey: Princeton University Press.

Kofoed, Niels. 1967. *Studier i H.C. Andersens fortællekunst*. København: Munksgaard.

Lacan, Jacques. (1979, 1991) 1994. *The Four Fundamental Concepts of Psycho-Analysis*. Translated by Alan Sheridan. London: Penguin Books.

Mackie, Erin. 2001. "Red Shoes and Bloody Stumps." In *Footnotes: On Shoes*, edited by Shari Benstock and Suzanne Ferriss, 233–247. New Brunswick, NJ/London, UK: Rutgers University Press.

Mortensen, Finn Hauberg. 2005. "Little Ida's Red Shoes." *Scandinavian Studies* 77 (4): 423–438.

Mylius, Johan de. 2016. *Livet og skriften. En bog om H.C. Andersen*. København: Gads Forlag.

Sørensen, Peer E. 1973. *H.C. Andersen og herskabet. Studier i borgerlig krisebevidsthed*. Grenå: GMT.

Notes

1. As formulated by Lacan in The Four Fundamental Concepts of Psycho-Analysis: "Man's desire is the desire of the Other." ([1979, 1991] 1994, 235).
2. In a quite mysterious article, "Little Ida's Red Shoes" (no red shoes of Little Ida are mentioned in "Little Ida's Flowers"), Finn Hauberg Mortensen delivers a sketch of about two pages for a reading of "The Red Shoes" (2005, 435–436). According to Hauberg Mortensen the story is about "pride and thus about one of the seven mortal sins" (435) of Catholicism. This is an odd idea, since Andersen was not a Catholic and there are no indications in the story that it takes place in a Catholic setting.
3. All subsequent quotes from the tale will be translated by me. I have chosen not to use Hersholt's translation of the story because it is too imprecise when it comes to passages on which I base central arguments.
4. The translation has been modified because it has omitted the "ligesom" of Kierkegaards original formulation: "Loven hungrer ligesom ud."
5. As Frederike Felcht also observes in Grenzüberschreitende Geschichten: "Not just Karen but also her surroundings are fixated upon red shoes. The anti-fetishism of the community is not less compulsive than the kind of fetishism which was promoted by new modes of consumerism." (2013, 197, my translation). Or, in the words of Erin Mackie (also quoted by Felcht): "the censure of Karen's fetishism itself works through fetish supernaturalism." (2001, 234).
6. Moreover, the Danish word for "Right" used by Andersen, "Ret," is a part of the Danish word he uses for the executioner: "skarpretter" (the verb "rette" in Danish could formerly not only mean "correct" but also "execute"). This distances the congregation even further from any realm of mercy and grace.
7. As suggested by Frederike Felcht: "What appears to be an act of mercy has the other aspect that Karen must subject herself to strict rules and that the old lady at a later time will need care. Therefore, the mercifulness of the old lady is also an investment in her own future." (2013, 191, my translation).
8. I can therefore totally subscribe to Finn Hauberg Mortensen's emphatic conclusion to his otherwise strange sketch for a reading of "The Red Shoes:" "Andersen did not leave the dining room as a nihilistic vacuum; instead he positioned the vacuum as a question in the lap of the educated family." (2005, 436). And he goes on to write about the tale that it "tells us about our fragile epistemological foundation." (437).

Random Communities, Cross-Readings
Hans Christian Andersen in between Universality and Historicity

Dan Ringgaard
Aarhus University

The chapter takes as its point of departure the discrepancy between a common appreciation of Hans Christian Andersen's fairy tales and stories resting on universal acclaim, and a scholarly one enforcing historical research. The question becomes how to read Andersen in a way that reaches beyond the confines of historical context without relapsing into a general notion of universal humanism. An answer is attempted by way of two cross-readings, one of "Little Ida's Flowers" and Hélène Cixous' writing manual Three Steps on the Ladder of Writing, *and another one of "Clumsy Hans" and Tim Ingold and Elizabeth Hallam's article "Creativity and Cultural Improvisation." By connecting texts across time, space and genre, the cross-readings investigate the texts of Andersen as what is termed literary 'commons.' With the help of Alain Badiou's* Handbook of Inaesthetics *and Rita Felski's* The Limits of Critique *two types of literary commons are articulated: With Badiou the commons is interpreted as a clearing, an emergence of a mutual ground to some extent unchained by cultural explications; with Felski (and her use of Bruno Latour) the commons is construed as a meeting place for all, a nodal point in a time-space network. Read like this Andersen's texts become places where communities across time and space are either made possible or continually recreated; and the notion of the universal appeal of Andersen is, hopefully, qualified.*

> Sometimes I find that, for a moment anyway, my favourite Andersen story is "The Collar," an apparent trifle of just two pages, but these are as rammed with life and meaning as a fragment or parable of Kafka's, like "The Bucket Rider" or 'The Hunter Gracchus." (Harold Bloom 2005, 403)

When we speak of Hans Christian Andersen's "unique connective power" we speak about his fairy tales and stories. They in particular "have made an impact across cultures around the world."[1] Although often subject to poor translations, they still translate and thrive as sources of imaginative, intellectual and childish pleasures. Despite their universal appeal, modern scholarly approaches to Andersen's writings remain primarily historical. The uniqueness of each particular fairy tale or story can only be fully comprehended by way of its historical context, it seems. We witness a split in two types of appreciation: a common one resting on universal acclaim, and a scholarly one enforcing historical research.

From a historical and by expansion linguistic and cultural point of view Andersen's fairy tales and stories are untranslatable. Yet they translate brilliantly. What they lose in historical, linguistic and cultural accuracy, they apparently gain by offering unique structures for a more random production of meaning and presence in whatever time or space they are thrown into. One might ask what are the intrinsic qualities of the texts that make this possible. I shall refrain from this and instead pose a theoretical question about the texts' ability to connect to and to create global communities, their aptitude to speak across time and space. In spatial terms the fairy tales and stories may be regarded as places to meet, as a common ground, or – with the recurrent metaphor of these pages – as literary commons. How do we qualify this ability without regressing into simplified notions of universality and – that goes without saying – without overruling history?

I will suggest two theoretical approaches each accompanied by what I will call a cross-reading. Both readings share an interest in Andersen and the subject of creativity. They ask what we can learn from Andersen about writing and improvisation. The first cross-reading is of "Little Ida's Flowers" from 1835 ("Den lille Idas Blomster") and French-Algerian author Hélène Cixous' 1993 writing manual *Three Steps on the Ladder of Writing*. Here Cixous points any writer in the direction of three schools: those of death, dreams and roots. In doing so she makes the claim that good writing goes deep, and, by way of the differential power of language, it goes to what we have in common. On the basis of this reading the concluding part of the first part of the chapter will address the issue of universality, historicity and community in Andersen with reference to Alain Badiou's *Petit manuel d'inesthetique* (*Handbook of Inaesthetics* 2004) and Emily Apter's discussion of Badiou in *The Translation Zone* (2006).

In the second part of the chapter I will cross-read "Clumsy Hans" ("Klods-Hans") first published in 1855 with Tim Ingold and Elizabeth Hallam's theory of improvisation as it is put forward in their 2007 article "Creativity and Cultural Improvisation." My claim is that Clumsy Hans is an improviser and that by cross-reading the fairy tale with the theoretical text it becomes apparent that his improvisation skills go beyond a romantic idea of improvisation. Our understanding of the protagonist in Andersen's fairy tale is in other words broadened by loosening the ties to its historical context and connecting it to a text that is remote in time, space and genre. To explain why, and to justify this type of reading, I take recourse in the post-critique of Rita Felski and her suggestion that we can transgress "the historical box," as she calls it in *The Limits of Critique* from 2015, by way of Bruno Latour's Actor Network Theory. In this second theoretical framing it is a matter of continually establishing communities by making connections of all sorts regardless of time and space.

Cross-Reading "Little Ida's Flowers"

Writing is telling the truth and telling the truth is exposing the lie. The lie is what we live by because we cannot stomach the fact that we must die. It is the purpose of literature to insist on the fact that we all must die. This is the credo of the first of three schools that you, according to Hélène Cixous, must attend if you want to become a writer: The School of the Dead, The School of Dreams and The School of Roots. The writing school of Cixous thrives on surrealism, modernism, psychoanalysis, feminism and deconstruction. It is not rhetorical as the majority of American writer's schools counselling the would-be writer in detail on how to do this and that. Instead it is about seeking out and surrendering to certain states of mind and language. She does so by way of examples taken from a western canon of modern texts that reflect each other across time and space. Thus, Cixous asserts a certain universality of literature.

The School of the Dead: "Philosophizing is learning to die" Michel de Montaigne writes (Cixous 1993, 10). In a letter to his friend Oskar Pollak the young Franz Kafka writes "a book must be the axe for the frozen sea inside us" (Cixous 1993, 17). Like Kafka, Cixous insists that we read the most uncompromising writers when it comes to death and truth although we know that on the flip side of any truth there is a lie. Thomas Bernhard's road to school became his initiation to writing. It took him past a butcher's shop:

> Open doors, axes, knives, cleavers, tidily arranged, slaughter ring instruments some bloody, others shining and clean, slaughtering pistols, then the noise of the horses collapsing, those huge open bellies vomiting bones, pus, blood. Then past the butcher's, a few steps leading to the cemetery, to the morgue, to the tomb. (Cixous 1993, 8)

Cixous tells the story of a woman that for a long time brought food to her husband in jail not knowing that he was already dead. That is what we do. Live our lives ignoring the fact that we must die. Writing is to peel off layers of lies knowing that it may never end. I'm reminded of Gunnar Ekelöf's poem "Xoanon" in *Sagan om Fatumeh* from 1966 (Ekelöf 1991–93, 3:71–72) where he removes each part of an icon, lifts away the Jesus-child, takes off the clothes of the Madonna piece by piece, takes her eyes away until in the end there is only the black board left that the icon was painted on and a knot in the tree that stares back on him. It is like writing a confession without God, Cixous writes. There is no mercy, just one's own humanity. That is what stares back at you from The School of the Dead. It is not about making it new. It is simply about not lying.

Andersen's "Little Ida's Flowers" targets death head on. The story begins: "'My poor flowers are quite dead,' said little Ida." Klaus P. Mortensen has written about how Ida cannot understand why living things must die (2007, 231–232). It is the student's task to explain it to her. You can't, of course, so he tells her a fairy tale instead: "'They were at the ball last night, that's why they can scarcely hold up their heads.'" "'How can anyone stuff a child's head with such nonsense – such stupid fantasy?'" says the councillor. He bans any talk of death, the student on the contrary makes death graspable by telling a story. Ida goes along with the game: "'Can the flowers who live in the botanical gardens visit the castle? [...] Can the professor understand their signs?'" Ida and the student indulge in the excess. In the evening she goes on playing the game by herself and in the night, she dreams on. In the morning Ida has accepted the idea that all living things must die, and she buries her flowers. The fairy tale about the dancing flowers were not a white lie but a way to let the living pass into the night, the dream, the fatigue in order to finally let it rest.

The School of Dreams: You can't decide that you want to go there; it takes luck to be admitted. And even then, there is no guarantee that we can come back the next morning. It is however easier to gain entrance to the dreams than to the dead. In the school of dreams, you "rediscover the night hidden within the day" (Cixous 1993, 104). Here you are facing the soul. The school road resembles the fairy tale about the daughters that wear down their shoes because each night they disappear through a trapdoor underneath their bed to go dancing. The original dream is that of Jacob, and the special thing about it is that the angels don't climb upwards but downwards. It is the "*descending* angels" that you must learn to follow (68). Down there we discover the "impossible innocence" and a whole lot more (71). The dreams have no beginning, middle or end, instead they have speed and they take semantic short cuts. Kafka's dreams are "angels without wings," Cixous writes, and quotes one that seems to run quickly in many directions (105):

> Who is it? Who walks under the trees of the quay? Who is quite lost? Who is past saving? Over whose grave does the grass grow? Dreams have arrived, upstream they came. They came, they climb up the wall of the quay on a ladder. One stops, makes conversation with them, they know a number of things, but what they don't know is where they come from. It is quite warm this autumn evening. They turn toward the river and raise their arms. Why do you raise your arms instead of clasping us in them? (105)

The flowers' ball in "Little Ida's Flowers" is perhaps also a dream: "When the time came to say good night, little Ida sneaked back to bed too, where she dreamed of all she had seen." The flowers and Ida leave their beds at night in order to experience a world where a wax figure all of a sudden can grow big and long, twist itself around paper flowers and yell like the councillor, where the councillor in the shape of the wax figure are whipped by a birch wand, where the court and all things respectable are transformed into a comical flowers' parade, and where Ida's doll live through moments of social anguish and sexual bliss, first by being ignored by the party, later as it dances with the moon. The ball is the place of excess, cruelty, laughter, anxiety and rapture, a distorted pantomime of the courtly world. A carnival. A metamorphosis.

The School of the Roots: This one is also about what we don't see; it is about what is covered up or rejected. It is the impure, whatever is kept out of the world, forbidden by an unfounded 'because'. According to Cixous this is often women, birds and writing. Sex is banned because it dissolves identity into anonymity. It is yet another movement downwards but this time towards the non-human and organic. Roots in this sense do not mean source but the organic life in the dark. Cixous quotes Água Viva, Clarice Lispector's novel from 1973, a piece of free jazz that improvises its way into the wild:

> What does this improvised jazz bespeak? It bespeaks arms entangled in legs and flames rising and l passive like a piece of flesh that's devoured by that sharp hooked beak of an eagle that stops its blind flight. I express to myself and to you my most secret desires and with the words achieve a confused, orgiastic beauty. I shiver with pleasure in the midst of the innovation of using words that form intense underbrush! [...] I surround myself with carnivorous plants and legendary creatures (animals), all bathed in the coarse, awkward light of a mythical sex. I go ahead intuitively, and without looking for an idea: I'm organic. And I don't question myself about motives. I immerse myself in the near pain of an intense happiness (joy) – and to adorn me leaves and branches are born out of my hair. (1993, 134)

"Everything ends with flowers," Cixous concludes (1993, 151). We slide through the animal towards the vegetable. It ends with flowers for Lispector as well as for the dying Kafka: "In this condition I am in, recuperating from it, if it is possible at all, will take me weeks. Please look and see that the peonies don't touch the bottom of the vase. This is why they have to be kept in bowls" (152). The flowers are the last that we see of Ophelia. They float on the water over and around her body, a phantasmagoria of femininity.

Little Ida's flowers are removed from the human to an extent that makes it bearable to watch them die, and they are sufficiently close to the human for Ida to identify with them and feel grief. In the story the human is entangled in the vegetable kingdom. Like all metaphors the anthropomorphism of the flowers works both ways: It is not just that the flowers become human, the humans also become flower-like. The roots intertwine the human with birch wands, paper flowers and not least dolls – this inorganic half way human state of life. Man, plants and things are all twisted vibrant matter (Bennett 2010). Given the ambiguous nature of dreams and roots, the comfort of telling stories in order to deal with death becomes equally dubious. Even more so if we read the burial by the end of the fairy tale alongside the similar mock burial of a dog in the thoroughly ironic anti-narrative "Heartache" from 1852 ("Hjertesorg"). You cannot bury your dead, both texts seem to conclude. Nor can you restore innocence. Facing death by way of a narrated diversion is apparently by no means calming yet alone comforting; it seems to take you into even shadier realms.

Universalism as Singularity

In *Handbook of Inaesthetics* Badiou writes: "I do not have much faith in comparative literature. But I believe in the universality of great poems, even when they are represented in the almost disastrous approximation that translation represents. 'Comparison' can serve as a sort of experimental verification of this universality" (2004, 46). In other words: If two texts can be compared meaningfully despite their apparent incompatibility there must be a universality of literature. He goes on to compare French poet Stéphane Mallarmé's *Coup de dés* from 1897 with a pre-Islamic ode from the 7th century by the Arabic poet Labîd ben Rabi'a. What they share is not a common truth. There is no truth to single out, yet alone a common one. Instead they both stage the event of truth, Badiou writes. This coming-toward-truth can only occur in so far as the two poems withdraw from all common notions and pretence of mastery and insist on the inexplicable singularity of the void. So, universality to Badiou, as Emily Apter explains it in her discussion of his reading in *The Translation Zone*, is not a question of transcending cultural norms in order to find or (worse) impose a common denominator, but a question of ridding the texts of cultural explications, leaving them free to exchange singularities.

In this mind frame history is a sense-making that may differentiate a text from other texts but never the less runs the risk of neutralising, diminishing and confining it by way of context. Historical readings are tales of origins and original environments. For this reason, the further apart the two texts that you compare are, the more freely they may enter into an exchange with one another. "Singular universalism" Apter calls it and adds that a

[...] comparison between two wildly divergent authors – one a nomad writing in classic Arabic in the pre-Islamic period, the other a bourgeois saloniste of Second Empire France – has just as much credence for Badiou as a comparison between authors hailing from a shared tradition. Indeed, it would often seem that the greater the arc of radical dissimilitude and incomparability, the truer the proof of poetic universalism. (2006, 86)

As in the translation theories of Friedrich Schleiermacher and Walter Benjamin, good translations are those that do not erase differences between languages but expose them. By boldly comparing the incomparable, by a "*comparatisme quand même*" as Apter puts it, we get to consider the convergences of otherwise inconvertible texts (2006, 86). What Badiou offers is a philosophical as opposed to a philological comparatism. One that does not constrain itself to historical explication and origination but asks questions across the entire cosmopolitan realm of literature. By this I obviously don't mean to devaluate the virtues of a philological comparatism – the need to read the original language, to know about the cultural environment etcetera – nor do I want to exclude the apparent middle ground, the fact that you can do both at the same time, I just want to point to what we then might call a philosophical comparatism as another route of inquiry and one that may have some bearing on the issue of Andersen as a writer whose texts partake in and create communities.

You might say that I have made use of Andersen's fairy tale in order to better understand and explain Cixous' ideas on writing, and in doing so have shed some light on Andersen's text as a text that is not just about death but also about dreams, roots and writing. I'm not saying: Look, Andersen is saying the same thing as Cixous, I'm rephrasing the one with the help from the other, reciprocally developing ideas of writing, dying and what we might with Giorgio Agamben (2002) call "the open:" the no longer modern field where what it means to be human is renegotiated. Neither do I use the theoretical text to frame the literary text. For one, Cixous' text is just as literary as it is theoretical, secondly, I begin from the other side using the literary text to narrate, rewrite or allegorise the not-entirely-theoretical text. In doing so I point to a common ground because the texts both point to the continual re-expression of truths about writing, dying and the open.

Looking closer at what the two texts are in fact saying about writing, dying and the open it becomes clear that they don't. Cixous doesn't tell us how to write, because it cannot be told, instead she leads us down the first steps of writing. She is clearing the way for writing. Likewise, Andersen doesn't explain why all living things must die, because there is no explanation, instead he tells a story about death that is also a story about writing and various ways of human entanglement and disruption. Cixous as well as Andersen deals with basic human issues but they do so without a shared truth. In the parlance of Badiou they don't tell the truth, they don't master truth, instead they clear the way for the event of truth. Here the metaphor of literary commons comes to mean a clearing, an opening of a mutual ground.[2]

The Post-critical Network

A phrase such as 'clearing the way for the event of truth' is, no matter how seductive or convincing we may find it, a general statement. Any text as well as any meeting between texts tends to come to a standstill, each event singular, but nevertheless somehow the same, leaving no room for further interpretation or distinction. It appears to be a reduction of meaning to the point of an ever-recurring Other named truth. A different way of going about the issue of connecting texts across time and place points in the opposite direction: to the continual production of presence as well as meaning. I am referring to Rita Felski's use of Bruno Latour's Actor Network Theory in her book *The Limits of Critique*.

Felski's so-called post-critical theory points to the gap that I started out with between the use of literature and the critical reading of literature. The idea of the 'post' in post-critical is not to erase or overcome the critical, but to criticise its sometimes unacknowledged dogmas from the point of view of a more pragmatic and pluralistic politics of reading. More specifically post-criticism criticises the pathology of the too critical and too predictable discursive reading, replacing it with affective or temperately hermeneutical readings, surface readings or Actor Network Theory-readings (Felski 2008, 2015; Anker and Felski 2017; Macé 2011; Moi 2017). Given that we in the case of Andersen are facing a similar divide between uses of literature and critical reading, one might suggest that in this case the post-critique should direct itself towards the rarely questioned authority of history: Do we really have to read exclusively historical? Not according to Felski.

In fact, "Context Stinks!" she writes in the title of the fifth chapter in her book: "We cannot close our eyes to the historicity of art works, and yet we sorely need alternatives to seeing them as transcendentally timeless on the one hand and imprisoned in their moment of origin on the other" (Felski 2015, 154). The challenge is to overcome the text-as-object and context-as-container model. New Historicism managed to level this foreground-background model by what Felski calls a "slice-of-time approach" (157). However, the thick description of New Historicism limited itself to the historical period of the text. It didn't manage to escape the idea of history as a "box" (154). It is here that Bruno Latour's idea of the social as an assemblage of associations, a flat network of human as well as non-human actors offers itself as an alternative to, for instance, the social as a Foucauldian epistemic superstructure of periods. The art work, according to Latour in "Why Has Critique Run out of Steam? From Matters of Fact to Matters of Concern" (2004), is an actor and an arena. As an actor it comes into being by way of the relations it is involved in. As an arena it offers itself as a meeting place for all sorts of relations. This gives a different meaning to the metaphor of literary commons: not so much a clearing or a condition of possibility, as a mutual ground of activity, a meeting place for all. Viewed as a relational being, the art work is, in Latour's terms, among matters of concern as opposed to matters of fact. It cannot be separated from its impact in time and space, and especially it cannot, following Felski, be separated from the attachments and affects of the reader. Felski emphasises that an ANT-inspired reading "would require us to treat texts not as objects to be investigated but as co-actors that make things happen, not as matters of fact but as matters of concern" (2015, 180).

As matters of concern texts are involved in time in a special way. Seeing somebody reading a copy of *Pride and Prejudice* in the subway confirms, according to Felski, everyday intuition: "Art works may not be timeless, but they are indisputably – in their potential to resonate through time – time-full" (2015, 161). Felski's idea of the art work as full of time relates to theories of an all-encompassing and heterogeneous present such as Hans Ulrich Gumbrecht's "broad present" or the concept of the "comtemporary" in, among others, Lionel Ruffel (Gumbrecht 2014; Ruffel 2017). Felski dates these theories back to Walter Benjamin, while Ruffel points to the spatial turn and Michel Foucault's posthumous "Of Other Spaces" (Felski 2015, 155; Ruffel 2017, 181). Whether it is the eternally recurring potentiality of the past in the present in Benjamin's "Theses on the Philosophy of History," or the substitution of temporal succession with spatial networks in Foucault's "Of Other Spaces" – the latter perhaps challenging his own history writing with this idea – the present becomes the whirlpool of history as opposed to linear history being the cause of the present. In the words of Felski paraphrasing Latour:

> Time is not a tidy sequence of partitioned units but a profusion of whirlpools and rapids, eddies and flows, as objects, ideas, images, and texts from different moments swirl, tumble, and collide in everchanging combinations and constellations. (2015, 158)

Neither Felski nor Latour shows us how to read in this manner. What they offer is an argument for why it may be rewarding to read across time, and how such a reading might be an escape from the box of historical periodisation without taking recourse in universalities. Following Felski's layout, an ANT-inspired reading would be something like a thick description beyond the limits of the historical period and with the attachments and the affects of the reader as the power center of the whirlpool. I will not attempt such a reading. It may be too broad in scope and too abstract in its conception ever to be performed in full. Nor will I elaborate on the risk of losing sight of the art work in the network immanent in most aesthetic adaptions of Latour's theory. Instead I will use the idea of the art work as an arena and do a second cross-reading, leading a text into the arena of an Andersen-story, one that, again, is foreign to it in time, space and genre. One might hope for a meaningful exchange of ideas between the two, and more specifically to display aspects of Andersen's story that would have gone unnoticed had it not been for the untimely interruption of the foreign text.

Cross-Reading "Clumsy Hans"

Let me begin with what might be a historical interpretation of the story "Clumsy Hans." The subtitle of "Clumsy Hans" is "An old story told once again." In the artful retelling of the folk tale Clumsy Hans becomes a romantic character. Or more precisely: His character is the expression of qualities that the romantics held in high esteem and that may be assembled in his ability to improvise. Clumsy Hans is an improviser, and the improviser is the epitome of free creation.

From a romantic point of view the improviser is spontaneous. To him action follows directly behind thought, or action and thought are in fact one. Contrary to his brothers who know all beforehand and have prepared everything in detail. Once they face the princess and she defines the scene differently than they had expected, they are lost. Clumsy Hans is whole in the sense that he doesn't suffer from this divide between thought and action. He lives in a full present. Furthermore, when he speaks you hear exactly that, a speaker, because there is no gap between word and thought either. No rhetoric as in the case of the brothers. The princess has challenged the boys in the art of eloquence. The smoothest talker takes the prize, but the proper eloquence, it turns out, is spontaneous, it comes straight from the mouth, it has the rhythm of the body and the breath, as if it where the direct expression of life.[3] Andersen is, right from the sweeping opening of "The Tinderbox," his first fairy tale, the creator of oral prose in Danish literature.

From a romantic point of view the improviser is also a virtuoso. He manages to grab whatever comes his way, even without knowing exactly what to use it for, and to put it into use when it is opportune. The crow may fry with the cockerels in the old wooden shoe, and the mud may serve as sauce. The improviser shapes the vicissitudes of life in a way that doesn't force them in line or into rank (as the suitors who can barely move their arms in the courtyard), but instead bends and gives way to the movement of life itself.

Finally, and still from a romantic point of view, the improviser is inspired. Reading Hans Christian Andersen's debut novel from 1838, *The Improvisatore* (*Improvisatoren*), you understand that to improvise you need to be in a vital relation to memory and childhood. Without that connection, no words will come, no improvisation only groans and growls. "Bah!," says the first brother, "What-what did you-uh-what?" says the other. Clumsy Hans is not a character in a novel, as Antonio in *The Improvisatore*. Antonio is a round and searching character, the fairy tale-character Clumsy Hans is flat and ruthless. Antonio had a childhood, Clumsy Hans *is* childhood. The child has a ruthless side. Like the soldier in "The Tinderbox" nothing is allowed to stand in his way. However, Clumsy Hans' vile nature is never violent. Contrary to the soldier he doesn't slaughter whatever comes in his way. Instead he improvises. He manages to bend and give way. He is alert to his surroundings. He listens and replies. As when he, by the end of the story, abandons his solos, and jams with the princess: "'Terribly hot in here,' he said. 'I'm roasting young chickens,' replied the Princess. 'Why, that's fine!' said Clumsy Hans. 'Then I suppose I can get my crow roasted?'"

This is one way to look at Clumsy Hans. One that corresponds with his times. But Clumsy Hans' range as an improviser goes beyond romanticism. You realise that once you cross-read him with the contemporary improvisation theory of Tim Ingold and Elizabeth Hallam (2007; also Ingold 2010). From that point of reference Clumsy Hans is no genius, in fact he is quite ordinary. Improvisation, they claim in their article, "Creativity and Cultural Improvisation," is a basic cultural ability – and as such if not universal at least shared across time and space – that can be divided into four aspects.

Improvisation is generative. It is something that is developed, it is actions and solutions along the way. Therefore, improvisation cannot be judged on the final result, but must be assessed on how skilfully the improviser finds solutions to whatever problem that might occur. As life itself, improvisation is experienced forwards, not backwards. Improvisation then, is not innovation, if innovation presupposes a final product or art work. Hence, the opposition between creativity and imitation is false. It is not about making it new, it is about finding solutions. Good improvisations bring something into light by way of a number of choices, and it never really stops. As opposed to the judgement of taste that distances itself from the movement itself to consider the final result, improvisation *is* that movement.

Clumsy Hans not only has a talent for finding solutions, literally along the way, he is also a headstrong copycat, the little brother aping whatever his brothers do. Like them he sets out to marry the princess, he finds something to ride on, and he prepares as he proceeds. He is playing an adult game, he is just too simple-minded to play it by the book. What he does, he doesn't do without reason, he does what he thinks he is supposed to do. He is a naïve imitator, not a stupid one, which is to say that he is without prejudice, ready for whatever may turn up. In his comical attempt to do what he thinks he is supposed to, he stumbles upon opportunities to reach his goal, but paradoxically, by forgetting all about it. The crow, the old wooden shoe and the mud make him forget. Instead he slips into the process of living, he is led astray as he moves along in ways that end up clearing his track.

Improvisation is relational. It is related to things and other persons.

The improviser is not the exceptional human being that breaks the rules, but one who navigates imaginatively within a framework. As the pedestrian of Michel de Certeau, Ingold and Hallam suggest, who finds a path through traffic by choosing the right solutions, manipulating the ever-changing structures by making choices, we cannot plan a walk beforehand, things always turn up because the fabric of traffic is constantly changing. For that reason, the pedestrian can have no strategy, instead – and still with reference to de Certeau – the pedestrian is a tactician.

Clumsy Hans is doing his best to deal with the structure. He is neither lucky nor a genius, instead he challenges the framework that is laid out for him. His creativity doesn't come out of nothing, it is a result of the obstacles that he either creates for himself or is presented with. And because he has a talent for dialogue, for creating relations, he is successful. He doesn't think ahead, as would the strategist, his tactics is to relate to circumstance and happenstance and turn things to his advantage.

Improvisation is temporal. If modernity is the break with time in order to create a new present (de Man 1986, 148; Jauß 2005, 332; Latour 1993, 10), then improvisation is not modern. Its time is a twisted line, irreversible and without a goal. Improvisation is rhythmical, not metrical, if we understand rhythm with Henri Lefebvre as "movement and variation within repetition" (Ingold and Hallam 2007, 10). Also with rhythm it is a matter of freedom within structure. The time of improvisation is, with Henri Bergson, a *durée*, a continuous present, that is a present not yet separated from the past and always already attached to the future. The past is not the cause of the future, but its condition of possibility.

The spontaneity of Clumsy Hans, what I earlier roughly named a full present, is his ability to inhabit this *durée*. He uses what he has brought with him (from past to present), and he brings it along (from present to future) without knowing what use he is going to make of it. Contrary to the brothers his forward movement is unpredictable, in other words rhythmical, not metrical. The other suitors are ruled by metrics. "Each suitor was given a numbered ticket, and as fast as they arrived they were arranged in rows, six to a row." Clumsy Hans on the other hand has rhythm. He keeps falling behind only to catch up with his brothers again who, on their side, keep a steady pace until they escape him. The princess too is caught up in metrics, forced to repeat her "No good [...] Out with him."⁴ Right up until Clumsy Hans arrives and they begin jamming in a structure of exclamations that all begin with the indefinite pronoun 'it' ('det' in Danish). And the narrator jams along beating the rhythm with 'he said' 'she said.' Unfortunately, the English translation by Jean Hersholt is not as repetitive as the Danish, so here it is in Danish:

> "*Det* var da en gloende hede!" *sagde* han.
> "*Det* er fordi jeg steger Hanekyllinger"! *sagde* Kongedatteren.
> "*Det* var jo rart det!" *sagde* Klods-Hans [...].
> "*Det* kan De meget godt!" *sagde* Kongedatteren [...].
> "Men *det* har jeg" *sagde* Klods-Hans. [...]
> "*Det* er jo et helt Maaltid!" *sagde* Kongedatteren [...].
> "*Den* har jeg i Lommen!" *sagde* Klods-Hans. [...]
> "*Det* kan jeg lide!" *sagde* Kongedatteren [...].
> "*Det* er nok Herskabet!" *sagde* Klods-Hans [...].
> "*Det* var fiint gjort!" *sagde* Kongedatteren [...]."
> (Andersen 1964, 293–294, my italics).⁵

Improvisation, finally, is a kind of work. It belongs to the daily life of actions. Improvisation is not inspired, not touched by spirit, instead it is based on experience and habit. The ability to react appropriately and to keep things going depends on the proficiency of perception and action, and it depends on our experience with things and people, operations and systems. These practises – Ingold and Hallam refers to Pierre Bourdieu's concept habitus – is just as far from innovation as it is from mechanical reproduction. Improvisation is unsurprising since it cannot deviate from a plan that it doesn't have. It is unending to the extent that its purpose is to move along.

Clumsy Hans does what he always does and reacts quickly and with precision to the challenges presented to him because he knows his own world, a world where he acts straight away. That is just what he does. His world is a world of habits and without a script. The brothers, on the other hand, have a script that they have rehearsed. When they lose their bearings, it is because something unprecedented happens. Nothing unprecedented can happen to Clumsy Hans since he doesn't predict anything. Faithful to the world of its protagonist who lives in a world without a date of expiry, the story postpones the traditional fairy tale-ending: "And Clumsy Hans was made king, with a wife and a crown, and sat on a throne. And we have this story straight from the alderman's newspaper – but that is one you can't always depend on." This ending appears itself to be an improvisation as the rhymes in the original Danish version take control, and the story at the same time is held within the continual movement of life as the narrator poses the question whether it is true or not.[6]

Ingold and Hallam are preoccupied with the creativity of the everyday, however, the artistic improvisation of Andersen's story goes beyond that. Clumsy Hans incarnates the turn-around of the carnival, which is a blind spot to Ingold and Hallam. With him comes billy goats, crows and clerks that spurt blots of ink, mud in the trousers and a gigantic feast. He and the princess take to each other straight away: "ferociously hot in here!," the seducer says as he repeats the suitors, but he turns up the heat saying "ferociously hot" instead of "very warm" and "terribly hot." And she replies defiantly as is her nature, although this time without mentioning her father and saying "I" instead of "we:" "'I'm roasting young chickens'." Improvisation means blindness of what to come. As such it surrenders control and at the same time takes control of its surroundings, sexually and socially. In this way the theoretical text is not merely adding a perspective to the story, the story points out the limitations of the theoretical text.

Two Kinds of Literary Commons

I started out with an obvious dilemma especially acute with regard to Hans Christian Andersen's fairy tales and stories: on the one hand a global fame resting on universal reach, and on the other a scholarly appreciation enforcing historical research. This dilemma is not necessarily a problem. We can allow for a split between general admiration of a work and the professional scrutiny of it. However, if we are to take Andersen's worldwide success seriously we must concede that it has come about in ways that have been somewhat, if not completely, ignorant of his historical environment. It follows from this that there must be qualities in his work that are cast into the shadows by a historical approach, that connections have been made, and are constantly being made, that may open the texts to other horizons and help them escape what Rita Felski calls the "box" of history.

I have proposed two escape routes. One of singular universality where the meeting with remote texts may liberate the art work from contextual restraints and preconceptions and open a discussion across time and space, and another where the art work is part of a literal contemporary (a coexistence of times) in which connections across time and space are going on all the time because that is, quite simply, how we use literature, it is our way of attaching to it. In both scenarios the inclusion of knowledge of the historical period of the texts in question are by no means excluded. In his reading of Mallarmé and Labîd ben Rabi'a Badiou makes use of the historical differences as a base of knowledge and distinction, and since nothing is excluded from or subordinated in Latour's network, the historical circumstances of any given text are of course also part of the system.

In the Cixous cross-reading what I to begin with called the differential power of language did not lead the reader to a concept or an essence shared by the two texts, but to a common ground, a common in the sense of a *clearing*, where thoughts about death, writing and what it means to be human could begin to be exchanged. In the Ingold and Hallam cross-reading another kind of opening was at stake, an opening of the text to other ideas of improvisation contrary to those of the time of the text. Here the text itself was an arena – or to rephrase Latour – a common in the sense of a *meeting place* where ideas separated by time and space could cross-fertilize. Andersen's fairy tales and stories have long since proven themselves to be uniquely qualified participants of the literary community, and extraordinary examples of literary commons. Why this is the case is still an open question. All I have tried to do is reintroduce them to the broadest community possible: that of any time and any space.

References

Agamben, Giogio. 2002. *The Open: Man and Animal*. Stanford: Stanford University Press.
Andersen, Hans Christian. 1963. "Den lille Idas Blomster." In vol. 1 of *H.C. Andersens eventyr*, edited by Erik Dal, 43–49. København: Det Danske Sprog- og Litteraturselskab/Reitzel, 1963–90.
Andersen, Hans Christian. 1964. "Hjertesorg" and "Klods Hans." In vol. 2 of *H.C. Andersens eventyr*, edited by Erik Dal, 291–294 and 245–246. København: Det Danske Sprog- og Litteraturselskab/Reitzel, 1963–90.
Andersen, Hans Christian. 1987. *Improvisatoren*. København: Det Danske Sprog- og Litteraturselskab/Borgen.
Anker, Elisabeth S., and Rita Felski, eds. 2017. *Critique and Postcritique*, Durham: Duke U. P.

Apter, Emily. 2006. *The Translation Zone.* Princeton: Princeton University Press.
Badiou, Alain. 2004. *Handbook of Inaesthetics.* Stanford: Stanford University Press.
Benjamin, Walter. 1999. "Theses on the Philosophy of History" in *Illuminations: Essays and Reflections*, 245-255. London: Pimlico.
Bennett, Jane. 2010. *Vibrant Matter: A Political Ecology of Things.* Durham, NC: Duke University Press.
Bloom, Harold. 2005. "'Trust the Tale, Not the Teller': Hans Christian Andersen." *Orbis litterarum* 60 (6): 397–413.
Cixous, Hélène. 1993. *Three Steps on the Ladder of Writing.* New York: Columbia University Press.
Damrosch, David. 2003. *What is World Literature?* Princeton, NJ: Princeton University Press.
D'haen, Theo, César Dominguez, Mads Rosendahl Thomsen. 2013. *World Literature: A Reader.* London/New York: Routledge.
Dimock, Wai Chee. 2006. *Through Other Continents: American Literature Across Deep Time.* Princeton, NJ: Princeton University Press.
Ekelöf, Gunnar. 1991-93. *Skrifter.* 8 vols. Stockholm: Bonniers.
Felski, Rita. 2008. *Uses of Literature.* Malden/Oxford: Blackwell Publishers.
Felski, Rita. 2015. *The Limits of Critique.* Chicago/London: The University of Chicago Press.
Foucault, Michel. 1986. "Of Other Spaces." *Diacritics* 16 (1): 22–27.
Gumbrecht, Hans Ulrich. 2014. *Our Broad Present: Time and Contemporary Culture.* New York: Columbia University Press.
Grum-Swensen, Ane. 2014. "Fra strøtanke til værk: En genetisk undersøgelse af de kreative processer i den sene del af H.C. Andersens forfatterskab." PhD diss., University of Southern Denmark.
Heidegger, Martin. 2001. "The Origin of the Work of Art." *Poetry, Language, Thought.* New York: Perennial.
Ingold, Tim. 2010. "The Textility of Making." *Cambridge Journal of Economics* 34 (1): 91–102.
Ingold, Tim, and Elizabeth Hallam. 2007. "Creativity and Cultural Improvisation." In *Creativity and Cultural Improvisation*, edited by Hallam and Ingold, 1–24. Oxford, UK/New York, NY: Berg.
Jauß, Hans Robert. 2005. "Modernity and Literary Tradition." *Critical Inquiry* 31 (2): 329–364.
Latour, Bruno. 1993. *We Have Never Been Modern.* Cambridge, MA: Harvard University Press
Latour, Bruno. 2004. "Why Has Critique Run out of Steam? From Matters of Fact to Matters of Concern." *Critical Inquiry* 30 (2): 225–248.
Macé, Marielle. 2011. *Façons de lire, manières d'etre*, Paris: Gallimard.
Man, Paul de. 1986. "Literary History and Literary Modernity." in *Blindness and Insight*, 142-165. Minneapolis. University of Minnesota Press.

Moi, Toril. 2017. *Revolution of the Ordinary. Literary Studies after Wittgenstein, Austin, and Cavell*. Chicago, IL: University of Chicago Press.
Moretti, Franco. 2000. "Conjectures on World Literature." *New Left Review* 1 (4): 54–68.
Mortensen, Klaus P. 2007. *Tilfældets poesi. H.C. Andersens forfatterskab*. København: Gyldendal.
Müller-Wille, Klaus. 2017. *Sezierte Bücher. Hans Christian Andersens Materialästhetik*. Paderborn: Wilhelm Fink.
Ong, Walter J. 2012. *Orality and Literacy: The Technologizing of the Word*. 3rd ed. London/New York: Routledge.
Ruffel, Lionel. 2017. *Brouhaha: Worlds of the Contemporary*. Minneapolis, London: University of Minnesota Press.

Notes

1. I quote from the call of papers for the conference "Hans Christian Andersen and Community." https://www.sdu.dk/en/om_sdu/institutter_centre/c_hca/hca_and_community/call+for+papers. Accessed 21 May 2018.
2. Using the word 'clearing' is to point Badiou's 'event of truth' in the direction of Martin Heidegger (2001, 38–55).
3. Klaus Müller-Wille points to the opposition in the story between the unnatural violence of written language represented by the brothers and the scribe, and the sabotage performed by the natural spoken language of Clumsy Hans. He argues that since the story itself is a rewrite one may in fact find a critique in it of the romantic idea of the natural spoken language (2017, 234–238). One might say that Andersen fairy tales and stories often, perhaps always, signal that their oral prose is of a secondary orality, to use the term of Walter J. Ong. Since both the cross-readings of this chapter deal with creativity in Andersen it is worth mentioning two recent studies that deal with this subject, one being Müller-Wille's book *Sezierte Bücher. Hans Christian Andersens Materialästhetik* and the other Ane Grum-Swensen's *Fra strøtanke til værk: En genetisk undersøgelse af de kreative processer i den sene del af H.C. Andersens forfatterskab*.
4. In the Danish original, as opposed to the English translation, there is no variation, every time the princess says: "'Duer ikke," sagde Kongedatteren. 'Væk!'" (Andersen 1964, 293).
5. "– Terribly hot in here,' he said. 'I'm roasting young chickens,' replied the Princess. 'Why, that's fine!' said Clumsy Hans [...]. 'That you can,' said the Princess. 'But have you anything to roast it in? [...] But I have,' replied Clumsy Hans [...]. 'Why, that's enough for a whole meal!' said the Princess [...]. 'I have that in my pocket,' replied Clumsy Hans [...]. 'I like that!' said the Princess [...]. 'Oh, so these are the gentlemen!' said Clumsy Hans [...]. 'Cleverly done!' said the Princess."
6. "Og saa blev Klods Hans Konge, fik en Kone og en Krone og sad paa en trone, og det har vi lige fra Oldermandens Avis – og den er ikke til at stole paa!" (Andersen 1964, 294).
7. Again the English translation doesn't come out as precisely as the Danish that moves from "svær Varme" (very warm) to "forfærdelig Hede" (terribly hot) to "gloende Hede" (ferociously hot).
8. A third line of escape from history as a box, one that may be more related to Badiou than Latour is the idea of constellations put forward by David Damrosch in *What is World literature?* (2003). The whole field of world literature, including Moretti 2000, Dimoch 2006, and D'haen, Dominguez, and Thomsen 2013, deals in different ways with problems related to those of the present chapter.

Concrete and Imaginary Communities

Hans Christian Andersen, Friend of the Rich and Defender of the Poor

In memoriam Erik Holst, Odense

Michel Forget
University of Strasbourg

All his life, Andersen felt a sort of fascination for the world of royalty, aristocracy and the rich bourgeoisie. Born and brought up in extreme poverty, he always sought the company of the great and powerful. Without their financial and moral support, despite his wealth of talent, he would never have achieved the literary success he did. Yet he remained faithful to his social background all his life. He never forgot the world he was born into, that of the poor, the outcasts, the humble, and he often acted as the spokesman or advocate of the deprived. However, it was not easy to display liberal views in the era of absolute monarchy, when concern for the poor was soon considered suspect. So, throughout his life he had to face this contradiction between his liberal beliefs and the dominant values of the milieu in which he yearned to live. This chapter sets out to identify some of the literary devices Andersen used in order to cope with this contradiction.

Born poor among the poorest – "a mere marsh plant" (Andersen 1833),[1] Andersen nevertheless spent most of his life among the upper classes of the society of his day: the upper bourgeoisie, the aristocracy and the royal courts of Europe. They welcomed him with pleasure and were even honoured by his presence. Moving thus from obscurity into the limelight, he could easily have forgotten his humble origins. On the contrary, although they caused him pain, he never disowned them, and the author of "The Little Match Girl" ("Den lille Pige med Svovlstikkerne," 1848) never gave up defending the poor and protesting in his own way against the injustice and poverty of his time. This attitude, which we would describe nowadays as "socially aware," was not easy to sustain in the last years of absolute monarchy, in high society, where any stance in favour of the common people could soon become suspect and be viewed as potentially revolutionary, or at least "liberal," the term used at the time to denote supporters of constitutional reform.

How to avoid offending the wealthy to whom he owed everything, without denying his deep-rooted solidarity with the poor and humble: that was one of the many contradictions Andersen had to struggle with in his work. He didn't find a simple solution to it. He used a variety of literary strategies in turn, ranging from conformist to subversive (humour, irony, transposition of situations from the adult's to the child's world) in order to give his thinking an acceptable form. But his position on the social issue always remained somewhat ambivalent.[2]

Andersen and the Poor

When Andersen talks of poverty, he is obviously thinking first and foremost of his own life story. His diary includes countless references to his childhood among the poor. What strikes him most is the long road travelled by the child who used to run in clogs along the streets of Odense and the famous writer he later became. He was fond of counting himself among those renowned artists who were born like him in anonymous poverty, such as Thorvaldsen, Ole Bull, Camões, Schiller, Oehlenschläger or Jenny Lind (Brøndsted 1976).

Andersen never ceased to observe his times, the condition of his contemporaries and particularly the human consequences of the industrial revolution. Here he is in London, for instance:

> I have seen high life and – poverty. [...] Poverty, I saw personified in the form of a pale, hungry young girl in miserable, ragged clothes hiding in a corner in an omnibus. I saw wretchedness, and yet it never uttered a word in all its misery, for that was not allowed. I remember beggars [...] carrying on their breasts a large, stiff piece of paper on which were written the words, I am dying of hunger! Have pity on me! [...] They stop in front of people and [...] stare fixedly at them with such eyes, oh, such eyes as only misery can give! (2013, 293)

Actually, his fellow feeling for the poor was so strong that he was sometimes tempted to idealize them, ascribing sublime qualities to the destitute and contrasting them with the arrogance of the rich. Examples include a poverty-stricken woman setting fire to her own house because she could find no other way of warning a festive, oblivious crowd of the rapidly approaching tornado ("Something"). Elsewhere, he draws a parallel between the poor man and the poet, since they are both capable of seeing and enjoying those little things that the rich man doesn't notice. A simple wild flower which the rich man passes without a glance can fill a sick pauper with joy ("The Angel"). In this sense the pauper is like the poet, who "sees the entire sky where others perceive only a bit of air."

However, in Andersen's eyes the concept of poverty or destitution doesn't boil down to lack of money. To him, extreme poverty is less a matter of material deprivation than of the feeling of exclusion and humiliation it generates. So, his work teems with portraits of poor people, penniless travelling musicians, wanderers (34) and social outcasts (131).

For the same reason, unlike many of his contemporaries, Andersen quite often stood up for Jews and opposed antisemitism, "the evil beast" (2003–07, 5:186), as well as slavery, since he was also a fervent advocate of black people and of the abolition of slavery, as shown by his play *The Mulatto* (*Mulatten*, 1840).

Likewise, ahead of his contemporaries, Andersen was keenly aware of the lower status of women. In Turkey, at the Cemetery at Scutari, he noted that men's gravestones carried the name and social status of the deceased in gold letters, while "where a woman rests, we see only a carved lotus-leaf, ornamented with gold; but not a word is said of her. Even in death, a woman here is veiled and unknown to the stranger." (2010, 153).

This haunting awareness of the feeling of exclusion obviously derives from the memory of his origins; in spite of his later social success and celebrity, Andersen never freed himself entirely from them. In the tale "Heartache" ("Hjertesorg," 1853), he portrays a little girl in rags whose poverty keeps her at a distance from the other children, who are holding their own kind of burial ceremony for a pug. From afar she tries to glimpse the scene as best she can, each time the gate opens. True, it was a very trivial incident. Yet "It was a heartache as great as any grown-up can experience." Poverty excludes and separates, and this state of exclusion condemns the poor to take only a remote part in community life, as mere onlookers "when the door is ajar."

What all these situations have in common is Andersen's acute awareness of a *gap* between two worlds, an insuperable distance. The barrier is sometimes a practical one – a closed gate or door – but this frontier, although real, is usually invisible. In "She Was Good for Nothing" ("Hun duede ikke," 1853), the son of the household has fallen in love with the servant girl. This young gentleman's mother summons her to an interview:

> she looked so grave and yet so kind [...] She pointed out to me the gulf of difference, both mentally and materially, that lay between her son and me. 'Now he is attracted by your good looks, but that will fade in time. You haven't received his education; intellectually you can never rise to his level. I honour the poor [...] and I know that there is many a poor man who will sit in a higher seat in the kingdom of heaven than many a rich man. [...] Left to yourselves, you two would drive your carriage full tilt against obstacles, until it toppled over with you both.

Andersen can also express the same idea on a more humourous note. His story "The Porter's Son" ("Portnerens Søn," 1866) starts like this: "The General's family lived on the first floor, and the Porter's family lived in the cellar. There was a vast distance between them - the whole first floor, as well as all the grades of society."

The backdrop to Andersen's social thinking is thus set with the contrast between two worlds: that of the rich and that of the poor, that of "wheat bread" and that of "black bread" ("Lucky Peer," 1870), the world of Peer, the poverty-stricken child who will owe his glory to his genius alone, and the world of Felix, born in luxury but whose only source of pride will be his wealth. As Andersen sees it, this division of the world into two parts is first and foremost a *fact*, but it is also a *mystery*: "One has to bow, one has to please! [...] because one is born poor, he is placed under obligation and subjection to these richly born people. Are they then better than we? And why were they created better than we?"

All this makes it quite clear that from the social point of view, Andersen was in every sense a "liberal" (de Mylius 1999), as they were conventionally called at the time. That his sympathies lay with the liberal movement is beyond doubt. He sometimes expressed them directly, and at other times more indirectly, by repeated allusions to his friendship for certain prominent supporters of liberalism, such as

But what upset Andersen most was the inequality between people and the consequent differences in treatment. In *A Visit to Spain* (*I Spanien*, 1862) he notes that there are rough paths for ordinary people and the new road being built for the queen's visit (1975, 55–56). Likewise, there are all sorts of bottles. "All had been born from the same furnace, but some had been blown into champagne bottles, some into beer bottles, and that makes a difference" ("The Bottle Neck," 1858). The tale "There is a Difference" ("Der er Forskjel," 1852) focuses entirely on a discussion of this issue. The apple branch has been broken off and because it is so beautiful, placed in a vase to adorn the drawing room in which all sorts of people mingle. They express themselves in different ways according to their social rank. Andersen writes:

> All sorts of people passed through the rooms, and according to their rank expressed their admiration in different ways; some said too much, some said too little, and some said nothing at all. And the apple branch began to realise that there were differences in people as well as in plants. "Some are used for nourishment, some are for ornament, and some you could very well do without," thought the apple branch. From its position at the open window the apple branch could look down over the gardens and meadows below, and consider the differences among the flowers and plants beneath. Some were rich, some were poor, and some were very poor.

Adults are unwilling to talk about these differences between people, but children are aware of them and state them bluntly.[8] A little girl – her father was a Knight of the Royal Bedchamber – tells her friends:

> "I'm a child of the chamber," she said. [...] Then she explained to the other children that she had "birth," and insisted that anyone who didn't have "birth" from the beginning couldn't in any way get it; it did no good to study or be ever so industrious if you didn't have "birth." And as for people whose names ended with "sen," she declared, "They'll never amount to anything. ("Children's Prattle," 1859)

Andersen mocks the pretentious attitudes of the high and mighty. His irony gleefully targets "those in the front row," meaning the spectators who paid the highest price for the puppet show and can therefore sit in front ("The Spectre, A Funen Folktale," "Dødningen, et fyensk Folke-Eventyr" 2003-07, 1:52).[9] In a fragment, "Brudstykke af en udflugt i sommeren 1829" ("An Excursion in Summer-time 1829" [fragment]), when he was 24 years old, he says that the hierarchical structure of the world was brought home to him when he watched a puppet show where "the quality" could set their own price and choose their seats according to the amount paid: "That was where I first realised that we were not all made of the same stuff." (2003–07, 14:63).

That is also the reason for his countless ironic remarks about titles,[10] decorations[11] and precedence, both in his fairy tales and in real life. In *A Poet's Bazar* he writes:

> Towards evening the leading citizens of the good city of Semlin came on board and, one could see, they greeted each other according to rank; some received a low bow – they were the most important; others got a gracious inclination of the head which was laughable to see. In the end I thought I was at home – people are the same the whole world over! (1988, 183–184)

Jack Zipes' theory that Andersen's life was "one based on servility" and that his works, especially his fairy tales, were simply "exercises in the legitimation of a social order to which he subscribed" (2005, 75) is definitely excessive. True, Andersen constantly had to face the question he considered fundamental: *why* are there such differences between people? *Why* are some entitled to an easy, pleasant life while for others, life is a daily struggle against hunger and poverty? But he could never bring himself to choose once and for all between the various possible answers to those questions and his position on that point remained ambivalent.

One simple way of resolving the issue was to view the problem of social inequality and injustice in terms of a certain Christian tradition which held that compensation for the hardship endured on this earth would be provided in the hereafter. Andersen sometimes seems to adopt this theory of compensation, which was formulated in great detail by Jean-Jacques Rousseau, in particular, in *The Creed of a Savoyard Priest* (1762). The good, says the Priest, "have suffered in this life and it will be made up to them in the life to come." (*Emile*, Book IV). Along the same lines, Andersen writes: "Romance and reality are very nearly alike, but romance has its harmonious ending here on earth, while reality more often delays it and leads us to time and eternity." ("The Thorny Road of Honour," 1856)[12]

This "eschatological" concept, which seeks to make the present unjust stem acceptable by stating the compensations expected in the next world, was widely accepted in the circles Andersen moved in. It allayed qualms of conscience by providing a simple explanation for the mystery of inequality in the human condition, and it reassured people by asserting that injustice and poverty were temporary. Poverty and inequality exist. They are parts of life, but the balance will be restored in the afterlife. Andersen used this kind of argument as an easy way out, enabling him to show concern for the poorest without being suspected of subversive intentions.[13]

He cited other arguments less to explain or justify inequality in the human condition than to minimise its seriousness. One of these is that there are admittedly major differences in condition between people on this earth, but that basically "before the Lord we are all children of the poor." (*The Two Baronesses*, 1848/2002, 261). In other words, set against the transcendental dimension of human destiny, inequalities in condition are ultimately of little importance. At the end of the tale "The Bell" ("Klokken," 1845) the prince and the poor boy come together hand in hand, facing the great majestic sea in the midst of nature's and poetry's great church. The argument is endlessly repeated: "the stars overhead shone on all the houses, rich or poor, with the same light, clear and kind." ("The Candles," 1870), and:

> "And that is why she does so many good deeds and remembers all those in the poor homes about her and in the rich homes, too, where there also are afflicted people. Her deeds are done in secret, and kept secret, but they are not forgotten by our Lord." ("Kept Secret but Not Forgotten," 1866).

And: "The girl from the Campagna is as beautiful as your princess in the marble castle. They are both daughters of Eve, and you can't tell them apart." ("The Psyche," 1861) In other words, under the eye of God human inequalities disappear and He makes his sun rise upon all alike (Matthew 5, 45).[14]

Another argument Andersen often brings up to make the difference between rich and poor acceptable is to distinguish between true and false riches or true and false nobility. "I love your heart better than I do your crown," says the Nightingale to the Emperor ("The Nightingale," 1843). The theme of true nobility runs through his entire work, repeating that true nobility is that of the heart or mind, not that of birth or blood.[15] This idea reflects Andersen's deep-seated belief, as several posthumous papers prove beyond doubt. In one of them Andersen writes:

> There is no other true nobility than that of the mind, and in times to come princes will choose their great men from it. [...] Most of those *of noble birth* are no more than the shield-bearers of the nobility of the mind; they are nothing but the show-dish, entirely insipid. (1926, 16)

Andersen and Revolution

A final question needs to be asked. If Andersen really felt that the major issue was inequality in people's conditions, and the unequal distribution of wealth in this world, wasn't the revolutionary option the way to end disorder and social injustice? In the tale "The Gardener and the Noble Family," (1872) the servant who tends the garden is constantly humiliated and reprimanded by his master and mistress. On this point Zipes asks: "Why doesn't the gardener rebel and quit his job? Why does he suffer such humiliation and domination? Why doesn't he emigrate?" (2005, 75).

Clearly, in the period of absolute monarchy in which Andersen lived, it was impossible to imagine resorting to violent revolution in order to solve the problem of social inequality. Does that mean that this convinced liberal never, even in his heart of hearts, visualised revolution as an end to injustice?

Errors or omissions excepted, only two tales suggest the idea of a violent overthrow of the established order. The first, "The Storm Shifts the Signboards" ("Stormen flytter Skilt," 1865) is a burlesque account of a stormy evening when the wind switches round all the shop and office signs in the town, creating some purely funny situations and other thought-provoking ones. There were even people who mistook the church for the theatre, and that was a dreadful error!

The second tale, "Everything in its Proper Place," (1853) dwells at length on the theme of true nobility, that of the heart and mind as opposed to noble blood. Then, at the end, with a sudden twist involving a magic flute that causes a storm wind, Andersen offers a glimpse of the established order being suddenly turned upside down: the master of the mansion, a respectable baron, is carried away and finds himself in the shepherd's cottage, while the shepherd himself is flown to the mansion, "among the haughty lackeys strutting in their silk stockings. The proud servants were almost paralyzed at the very thought that such a common person would dare to sit at table with them!" Only an old count escapes this sweeping overthrow of the social order: he remained seated in his place of honour, because the flute that started this tremendous upheaval "was just, as everyone ought to be!" Notice this unexpected reversal: in this case, the sense of justice doesn't mean redressing social inequalities, but on the contrary, ensuring that the former order is not completely subverted by revolutionary fervour. Changes and reforms are fine, but on condition that the pillars of the former system are kept standing. Of course, such words, and the intervention of the flute that turned the social order upside down without affecting the upper classes, would reassure high society. Talk of revolution is all right as long as it is done in facetious terms, with sound common sense finally taking over and the "natural" hierarchies remaining unchallenged. Thus, Andersen dodges the more radical conclusions to which his beliefs were liable to lead him. A typical example of this attitude is his description of the slave market in Constantinople. Once he has realistically depicted the predicament of these women, who are sold off like cattle, we expect him to voice a strongly worded protest against this human trafficking. Instead, he launches into lyrical praise of the "houris," those divinely beautiful women the Coran promises to faithful male Muslims – a poetic twist that enables him to avoid taking any personal stance on this highly sensitive political and moral issue (2006, 248–250).[16]

Here it is clear that a liberal writer in conservative circles could only go so far. Andersen is extraordinarily good at describing objective reality, including the trivial or substantial shortcomings of an inegalitarian society, and even at highlighting their scandalous or unjustifiable nature, but he refuses to take the next step, which would be to denounce the unacceptable or demand that it be abolished.

Conclusion

To cope with this problem, he used various literary strategies in an effort to make himself clearly understood without either offending the upper classes he depended on or taking the risk of a break with them. Most of the time, his humour and irony proved to be his favourite tools here. Other ways of dealing with the difficulty was either to speak through children – who, indeed would take serious offence at a child's prattle? – or to use analogies with the inanimate world, that of flowers and objects coming to life in a domestic setting. Thus, satire or malicious irony could clearly be perceived by reading between the lines.

Sometimes, however, he couldn't help but endorse the conventional ideas favoured in the circles he moved in: for instance, the idea that inequality on earth will receive compensation in the next world, or the recurrent distinction between true and false nobility.

All his life, Andersen tried to get round this contradiction, without entirely managing to avoid the pitfalls of conformity and the ambivalence of his preconceptions. A 'cautious rebel' (Bredsdorff 1989), he didn't always have the courage to follow his convictions through. Yet he did what he could to make the voice of justice heard in circles little inclined to hear it. His sense of humour remained his best weapon in this struggle. In spite of everything, it enabled the ugly duckling to be the guilty conscience of his time.

Acknowledgment

I would like to express my thanks to my friend Clarissa Barton who has been kind enough to translate this chapter into English and who gave me a large number of helpful comments and suggestions on its first draft.

References

Andersen, Hans Christian. 1833. Letter to Henriette Wulff, February 16. http://andersen.sdu.dk/brevbase/brev.html?bid=499 (the letter is kept at the museum H.C. Andersens Hus).

Andersen, Hans Christian. 1845. *Only a Fiddler! And O.T. or, life in Denmark.* London: Richard Bentley.

Andersen, Hans Christian. 1926. *Optegnelsesbog.* Edited by Julius Clausen. København/Oslo: E. Jespersens Forlag.

Andersen, Hans Christian. 1971–77. *H.C. Andersens Dagbøger 1825-1875.* 12 vols. H. Topsøe-Jensen and K. Olsen (eds.). København: Det Danske Sprog- og Litteraturselskab/Gad.

Andersen, Hans Christian. 1975. *A Visit to Spain and North Africa, 1862.* Translated by Grace Thornton. London: Peter Owen.

Andersen, Hans Christian. (1829) 1986. *Fodreise fra Holmens Canal til Østpynten af Amager i Aarene 1828 og 1829.* København: Det Danske Sprog- og Litteraturselskab/Borgen.

Andersen, Hans Christian. 1988. *A Poet's Bazaar: A Journey to Greece, Turkey and up the Danube*. Translated by Grace Thornton. New York, NY: Michael Kesend Publishing.

Andersen, Hans Christian. (1849) 1997. *De to Baronesser*. Edited by Erik Dal. København: Det Danske Sprog-og Litteraturselskab/Borgen.

Andersen, Hans Christian. 2000. *Samlede digte* [Complete Poems]. Edited by Johan de Mylius. København: Ascheoug.

Andersen, Hans Christian. 2002. *The Two Baronesses*. Amsterdam: Fredonia Books.

Andersen, Hans Christian. (1831) 2003. *Skyggebilleder af en Reise til Harzen, det sachsiske Schweitz etc. etc., i Sommeren 1831*. 2nd ed. Edited by Johan de Mylius. København: Det Danske Sprog-og Litteraturselskab/Borgen.

Andersen, Hans Christian. 2003-07. *Andersen. H.C. Andersens samlede værker* [The Collected Works of Hans Christian Andersen]. Edited by Klaus P. Mortensen. 18 vols. København: Det Danske Sprog- og Litteraturselskab/Gyldendal.

Andersen, Hans Christian. 2006. *En Digters Bazar*. København: Det Danske Sprog- og Litteraturselskab/Borgen.

Andersen, Hans Christian. 2007. *H.C. Andersen Fairy Tales*. Translated by Marte Hvam Hult. London, UK/New York, NY: Barnes and Noble Classics.

Andersen, Hans Christian. 2010. *A Poet's Bazaar*. Reprint. Memphis: General Books LLC.

Andersen, Hans Christian. 2011. *Shadow Pictures, From a Journey to the Harz Mountains, Saxon Switzerland, etc. etc. in the Summer of 1831*. Edited by Sven Hakon Rossel and Monika Wenusch, translated by Anna Halager. Wien: Praesens.

Andersen, Hans Christian. 2013. *My Fairy-Tale Life*. Translated by W. Glyn Jones. Sawtry, UK: Dedalus.

Bredsdorff, Elias. 1989. "H.C. Andersen – den forsigtige rebel" [Andersen, the Cautious Rebel]. In *Udsyn over H.C. Andersen. Tre forelæsninger ved H.C. Andersen-Centrets åbning d. 12. september 1988*, edited by Johan de Mylius, 5–14. Odense: H.C. Andersen-centret, Odense Universitet.

Brøndsted, Mogens. 1976. "H.C. Andersens personlighedsproblem." In *H.C. Andersen og hans kunst i nyt lys*, by Jørgen Breitenstein, Mogens Brøndsted, Bo Hakon Jørgensen, Finn Hauberg Mortensen, and Johan de Mylius, 9–30. Odense: Odense Universitetsforlag.

Mylius, Johan de. 1995. *"Hr. Digter Andersen." Liv, digtning, meninger*. København: Gad.

Mylius, Johan de. 1999. "H.C. Andersen, on the Wave of Liberalism." In *Hans Christian Andersen: A Poet in Time: Papers from the Second International Hans Christian Andersen Conference, 29 July to 2 August 1996*, edited by Johan de Mylius, Åge Jørgensen, and Viggo Hjørnager Pedersen, 109–124. Odense: Odense University Press.

Zipes, Jack. 2005. *Hans Christian Andersen: The Misunderstood Storyteller*. New York, NY/Abingdon, UK: Routledge.

Notes

1. While all translations of the fairy tales and of Lykke-Peer adhere to Hersholt's translations, all other translations are made by Clarissa Barton unless otherwise indicated.
2. Allusions to the social problem can be found everywhere in Andersen's writings, in his fairy tales, travelogues, novels and plays (The Mulatto), as well as in his diaries or his voluminous correspondence. The ubiquity and consistency of these occurrences (and their coherence) clearly show that the social issue remained a major concern for Andersen throughout his life.
3. He also makes very frequent references to The Galley Slaves, a play now forgotten which was nevertheless famous in his time and regarded as a violent denunciation of intolerance.
4. Among them: Ludwig Tieck, Felix Mendelssohn-Bartholdy, Adam Oehlenschläger, the pianists Sigismund Thalberg and Franz Liszt, Fredrika Bremer...
5. Both in his diaries and in his correspondence, Andersen voices his surprise and pleasure at being welcomed on an equal footing in princely circles. For instance: "To think that I, the poor child, son of a shoemaker and a washerwoman, have been kissed by the nephew of the emperor of Russia!" (June 23, 1856; 1971-77, 4:213). Elsewhere he gives a detailed account of a banquet in the royal palace in Copenhagen where he was asked to lead Princess Thyra to the dinner table and relates how the prince and the king drank his health during the meal. "I felt particularly fêted" he notes to himself (March 26, 1871; 1971-77, 9:45).
6. Cf. also: "Inside the fence stood all the stiff, proud flowers, and the less scent they had the more they seemed to strut." ("The Daisy").
7. Elsewhere, we see the courtiers obsequiously repeating the princess' words, when they have just been asserting the opposite ("The Swineherd")
8. And the same is true of animals: "the good things of this world aren't dealt out equally either to dogs or to men." ("The Ice Maiden")
9. This fairy tale was not translated by Jean Hersholt, instead, the translation is made by Clarissa Barton.
10. "General Headquarters-Hindquarters-Gives-Orders-Front-and-Rear-Sergeant-Bill-Goat-Legs" ("The Shepherdess and the Chimney-Sweep")
11. "She [the sea king's mother] was a clever woman, but very proud of her noble birth. Therefore, she flaunted twelve oysters on her tail while the other ladies of the court were only allowed to wear six. [...]." ("The Little Mermaid)
12. Cf. also: "the Thorny Road of Honour - not a path that ends, like a fairy tale, in gladness and triumph here on earth, but one that leads onward and upward, far into time and eternity." ("The Thorny Road of Honour")
13. For example: Jørgen is a gifted young man with great prospects. After a shipwreck in which he has lost his fiancée, he sinks into madness and ekes out a life of wretched poverty. "Could this really be the destiny of a soul created in the image of God - a mere game, battered by the chances of this world? No! The God of love will compensate him in another life for all that he lost and suffered in this." ("A Story from the Sand Dunes")
14. This theme occurs over again in his works. Cf. "The Porter's Son," "There is a Difference," "From the Ramparts of the Citadel" ("Et Billede fra Castelsvolden," 1846), "Kept Secret but not Forgotten" as well as: Fodreise (1829), The Two Baronesses (De to Baronesser, 1849), Lucky Peer, Shadow Pictures (Skyggebilleder, 1831).
15. See, for instance: "No one can respect nobility less than I do - that nobility which is only conferred by birth; it is nothing, and a time will come when this will not be prized at all, when the nobility of the soul will be the only nobility." (Andersen 1845, 118-119)
16. The passage dealing with the 'houris' has been omitted in Grace Thornton's translation of the book (Andersen 1988).

Temporary Communities
A Theme in Hans Christian Andersen's Travel Accounts

Lars Handesten
University of Southern Denmark, Odense

Hans Christian Andersen experienced many different kinds of communities and he made them last in his travel accounts, whether you will find them in his diaries, travelogues, or memoirs. Andersen usually writes "we" in his travel accounts. But who is this "we"? This chapter examines the different kinds of communities Andersen depicts in his travel accounts. They may differ through his life time due to his overall life experience and to specific travel experiences and travel companions, but from a systematic point of view, the communities are of a national, cosmopolitan, and narrative character.

On a journey, you will experience different kinds of communities. They are temporary and fleeting like many of the communities in our everyday lives. But compared to our everyday life experiences, being on a journey highlights the temporary and fleeting nature of these encounters and emphasises some general conditions for our communities. Going on a journey enlarges and clarifies both problems and possibilities of communities. We belong to communities as long as we can benefit from them and as long as we have to follow the same path, and then we go our separate ways. We change carriage, change track, change vehicle and get new travelling companions, and a new community emerges, new attachments are made. On the journey, you are tied together with your fellow travellers for a short while. Nevertheless, these relationships can be intense and have everything that communities usually offer: intimacy, animosity, compassion and idiosyncrasies.

Hans Christian Andersen experienced many of these fleeting communities. During the time when Andersen was young, a journey could last for a long time, and he would be caged inside a stagecoach with a company of pleasant or unbearable people for days. When he arrived at a new place, new companionships and communities emerged, either spontaneously or because of recommendations he had got from important persons at home.

Usually, you will easily forget these fleeting communities because of their very nature: they are transient and ephemeral; but Andersen preserved them by writing them down in his travel accounts.[1] Thus, they are available for our own experience, and we can even study them.

In this chapter, I will examine some of these communities and show how they work, how they develop, and the conditions they emerge in. Andersen's travel accounts depict a wide range of different communities. Some of them are real; some of them are imagined. Some of them are for Andersen only; some of them embrace the reader as well. In short, you can point to a national, an international and a narrative community. On a more symbolic level Andersen himself depicts a community of mankind, and with Elisabeth Oxfeldt (2010) it is possible to point to an ideological community defined by the opposition between European self-consciousness and its picture of the Oriental way of living and thinking. Poul Houe (1996) gives a detailed overview of Andersen's itineraries with a focus on the relationship between being home and away. Andersen can feel at home among foreigners outside Denmark just as well as he may feel himself away among his countrymen in Denmark.

In his travel accounts and diaries, Andersen tends to write "we" when he is telling about his journeys and experiences. But who is this "we"? What kind of communities did he depict and what is their nature? To deal with these questions, I want to point out some passages from his diaries and travel accounts to show how different his relationships appear to be.

The Written Community

In the diary from Andersen's first travels abroad, you can tell that he met a lot of people whom he joined for smaller trips and events. Some of them he visited because of their reputation to initiate an acquaintance, or even a friendship. These short meetings gave him at least two different types of experiences: positive and negative.

The positive kind of experience occurred when he was recognised as the kind of person he really felt he was. In his diary he writes about a meeting he had with a Norwegian. It was a book trader named Hoppe who knew about Andersen and went to his hotel in Leipzig to meet him. Together they went to the theatre and afterwards they went out for dinner. On May 31, 1831, Andersen notes:

> Ate with Hoppe at the Hôtel de Saxe; he recounted to me episodes of his life, and we parted with sincere friendliness [...]. There are some people one can rub shoulders with for many years without feeling close to them; others, one has scarcely looked them in the eye before one has found a heart where one feels at home. – Oh, to travel, to travel, if one could only spend his life fluttering from one place to another! Indeed, I feel as if the world is my home, and I shall, I must, frolic about in this home. (Andersen 1990, 27–28)[2]

Andersen was probably not going to see Hoppe again, and that was precisely the condition for the outcome of this short relationship. It may *seem* superficial and it may *be* superficial, but in the eyes of Hoppe, Andersen was exactly the poet that Andersen actually wanted to be. And that gave Andersen a confidence which made him feel comfortable. There was no time for Hoppe to get tired of Andersen and annoyed by all his oddities. In the eyes of friendly foreigners, Andersen was perfect company. This was quite the same when he visited the famous German poet Ludvig Tieck and got his recognition; he recognised Andersen as a real poet and accepted him as a true member of the poet's society (Andersen 2011, 114–115; de Mylius 1986, 140–141). In Denmark that was not quite obvious – yet.

These positive moments were followed by negative experiences because a short-termed relationship could result in filling Andersen with anxiety and turmoil as well. After a dinner at table d'hôte in a hotel in Berlin, he asked a young Frenchman to join him for a walk. On June 13, 1831, Andersen writes in his diary:

I joined him and now he told me all about his Don Juan life. In the beginning, I was amused but as we entered a street "de Plaisir," and he invited me in for a glass of wine, I became terrified; I was, indeed, ashamed of walking through this street of Sirens as the street narrowed more and more until we escaped. We separated kindly, but the young man who already knew the world so well was not in the best of moods. (1995–96, 1:108, my translation)[3]

Here, the young Frenchman is leading him to his limit, and then Andersen quits. He considers that this is not an acquaintance for him. He is scared to be part of that intimacy and that kind of fellowship that he is offered by the Frenchman.

These two acquaintances indicate that Andersen at this stage of his life was a listener rather than a teller of his own secret life. The openness was one way and Andersen was sucking in all kinds of stories and stored them in his diary and memory for later use.

According to his travel account in his diary, Andersen did not have many moments when he was on his own. He was looking for company all of the time and he got it with a lot of different types of people. In the travelogue *Shadow Pictures* (*Skyggebilleder*, 1831), he writes about some of them. Sometimes the persons are mentioned by their names, sometimes just included in the anonymous "we." Thus, "we" can cover persons you can find by their names in the diary, but not in the travelogue. However, Andersen is establishing a community with the reader of the travelogue as well. He is always trying to let the reader feel like a part of the journey and a fellow traveller. In this way, the "we" is the poet and the confidential reader, who are both embedded in the text itself. They are travelling companions on a more abstract and sophisticated level. This "we," mediated by a very often ironical and satirical narrator, is then offered to the real reader who can join the community while reading about it.

Changing Companions

In *Shadow Pictures* Andersen for the first time wrote about the communities that emerge when you are travelling by a stagecoach. His vivid depiction creates a tableau with interesting figures and small and humourous conflicts. But in *A Poet's Bazaar* (*En Digters Bazar*, 1842), he unfolds the theme in the longer text: "Travelling with the

Vetturino." Here, he gives an impression of the dynamics of a six-day community made on the basis of two square metres in a cold wagon with a single little window. The road and weather is bad, and so are the inns they stay at for nights and meals. The situation is tense from the beginning, but the tension increases during the travel. Conflicts are growing very fast, and Andersen is the involved spectator who can observe how different people react to the situation.

From the beginning of the journey the company described consists of six persons, including Andersen. Right from the first moment a big and fat Englishman stands out and does not belong to the "we." He has a "Nobleman's mind and the attitude of a pork butcher," as Andersen writes with irony and contempt. The others are a monk, an English vicar, a plump Roman woman, and her little and insignificant husband. The two clergymen avoid interaction with the rest by reading their prayer books all of the time. The monk does not talk to anybody and leaves the company without a goodbye to anyone. Meanwhile, the others pay a lot of attention to the Englishman whom they treat with great respect – in the beginning.

The travel companions try to entertain themselves with four-part songs, but soon the Englishman reveals all of his bad manners and his rude and egoistic mind. This becomes evident when Andersen has to share his bed with him for the night due to lack of accommodation. That is tough and he refuses to do so again. Then, there is an open conflict between the two of them. The conflict between the Englishman and the other travellers escalates when he refuses to give two monks money for their sightseeing in Assisi. Then, the Roman woman gets upset about him. In the end, the consequence is that the Englishman is completely isolated from the rest of the company, and they stand together against him and his wishes for the journey.

Thus, a community emerges due to a common enemy. It is "we" against "him." "He" poisons the community and makes life a burden for the others. Andersen concludes:

> Unpleasant company, bad weather, miserable roads, and poor horses; everything was united to make the journey a penitential one. The sun would not shine into my heart, nor would it shine upon the landscape around me; and the extent of country which we have just passed lay in the most charming sunshine when I was last here. But nature doubtless thought

thus: "For that party yonder I need not put on my best [...]." (Andersen 1871, 72)[4]

In *A Poet's Bazaar* you find a variety of communities.[5] On his way to Constantinople, Andersen is on board a steamboat full of Turks. He opens the travel account with a "we," but very soon he is a stranger among the Turks, and for a while he is separated from the travel community because of a language he does not understand. The Turks are gathering around a young man who is telling stories and improvising verses, but Andersen can only watch. The "we" is suspended in his travel account, and he uses the singular instead of the common plural. This continues through the rest of the chapter. However, Andersen tries to be part of the Turks' community, and he uses two children to obtain his goal. Andersen notes: "If a man would be on good terms with parents, he must make friends with the children." (Andersen 1871, 222).[6]

Consequently, he starts to play with a little girl and speaks Danish to her, so she is laughing at all the crazy words. And then he gets her father's attention. The Turkish man invites Andersen to smoke tobacco and to drink a cup of coffee and then Andersen becomes a part of the little family community: "I accepted the coffee, and lay down on the cushion with the friendly husband, whose little daughter's heart I had already won." (Andersen 1871, 223).[7]

It is, however, striking that he does not return to the "we" in his description of the situation. The Turks are friendly to him, but to become a real part of their community is impossible for him. In this case, he cannot write himself into the foreign community because he, after all, is the lonely stranger and not a real family man.

On the following Danube-trip he experiences how his fellow travellers change all the time. In the chapter "We sail!" Andersen exclaims:

> "Here are fresh faces on board; Rustzuk has sent us many guests during the night. What a mixed tribe! The Turk kneels and says his morning prayer; his brow touches the ship's deck; close by him sits a Jew in coat of silver tissue, and purple-coloured turban" (Andersen 1871, 281).[8]

Thus, the community is changing and nobody in particular is distinguished from the crowd. Further up the Danube river, the travellers have to spend a week in quarantine. Andersen writes his account in the first person plural through the whole chapter "Qvarantine," but without mentioning who the "we" is. It is a common "we" pointing to the general experience of the situation and to his anonymous fellow travellers who also have to stay in quarantine. Only two fellow travellers are mentioned by name, but they never come to life in Andersen's depiction; they never get distinguishing features, and remain as just names. Then, "we" is everybody, without any particular features. This "we" is not the memorable community that Andersen sometimes describes in enthusiastic and sentimental terms.

Andersen: A Fellow Traveller

When Andersen grew older and became an experienced traveller, his way of travelling changed as well. He did not travel like he did in Italy by the primitive and uncomfortable Vetturino. Now, he travelled first class and was part of the high society. A lot of people knew him from his books and reputation, so as a special and honoured guest he was invited to many important and noble houses in central Europe.

On several of his later and long journeys, he had a fellow traveller all the way instead of or besides the changing companions. When he went to Spain in 1862, he was accompanied by the young Jonas Collin, born in 1840 and son of his old protector and benefactor Edvard Collin. Andersen was a kind of supervisor for the young man. He had the travel experience, acquaintances in many parts of Europe, and the goodwill to open doors to interesting and important people. In the travelogue *In Spain* (*I Spanien*, 1863), you will find a "we" that refers to Andersen and Collin. But according to the diary, it was a problematic relationship. They were tied together by the fact that they had to follow each other although they sometimes were like cat and dog. Andersen was 35 years older, and yet Collin, it seemed to Andersen, felt superior due to his wealthy and important family. They were both trapped by the circumstances, and there was no way out of their company. They travelled together twice, and each time for over half a year. They were together in Rome on their first journey and went to see the pope in the Lateran church. But it was so crowded that Andersen felt ill and wanted to leave. Collin went on and left Andersen who then had to carry on alone. In the diary on May 9, 1861 he writes: "I was bothered by it all and irritated; Jonas had as refrain: -'You must pull yourself together!' I was not pleased by this. There was no thought of sympathy; he looked cranky and irritated" (Andersen 1990, 275).[9]

A month later, on June 10, it was all wrong again, and Andersen was sorry about the behaviour of Collin. Collin did not show him any respect, and Andersen felt that he had to mobilise a whole lot of patience and love to stand the young man's bad manners.

In the travelogue *In Spain* the "we" refers to this problematic relationship. But in the travelogue the conflicts are not exposed as much as in the diary. The "we" in the travelogue is of a more formal than embracing character. This is stressed by the fact that the travelogue *In Spain* is different from *Shadow Pictures* and *A Poet's Bazaar*. In *In Spain* Andersen is not trying to write the reader into an imagined community. When, for example, he tells about his visit in Alicante, he does not write "we should see Alicante," but "yes, now one should see Alicante" (Andersen [1863] 2004, 467; my translation).[10] The reader is not part of the journey, but a distanced, yet interested spectator to what Andersen is telling and showing. In this late travelogue in Andersen's oeuvre, he's much more of a reporter than a fellow traveller. He is not fraternising with the reader.

Communities Abroad

These last examples first of all show the more negative aspect of Andersen's travel communities. But you may as well point to the positive moments. In *A Poet's Bazaar*, Andersen makes it very clear how communities emerge when you are abroad: "The further the Swede, Norwegian, and Dane travels from home, the louder sings the heart of each when they meet. 'We are one people, we are called Scandinavians!' When I was in Rome, in 1833, the three nations kept their Christmas Eve in company, like one family." (Andersen 1871, 92).[11]

Abroad everybody gathers with his own countrymen, or with those who belong to the same linguistic community. In Rome, Scandinavians established The Scandinavian Society and joined each other in the legendary Café Greco: "There is something naturally heartfelt by the fellow countrymen here," Andersen wrote after his first visit on October 19, 1833 (1995–96, 1:217, my translation).[12] And at Christmas in 1833, the Scandinavians went together to a party in Villa Borghese. For a moment, all the Scandinavian artists, poets and scholars in Rome were in a happy brotherhood. They were linked together in a way that could never happen at home. In this foreign town, the differences among them vanished, as the similarities flourished. Andersen was, for example, together with his former opponent Henrik Hertz who had published a satirical poem at home, called *Gjengangerbreve* (1830), that had made a fool out of Andersen, among others. But in Rome they became friends and even went on a trip together to Naples. Thus, the Scandinavian Society in Rome was a catalyst for new friendships that at least lasted as long as everybody was abroad and on the move. In the foreign land, they all became friends.

Still, Danes could bother him abroad. On his way home from Constantinople in 1841, he is on a boat on the river Elb, and writes in *A Poet's Bazaar*:

> We have a Copenhagener with his daughter on board. "It is delightful!" says she; "but the water is so horribly yellow; here are none of our beech woods!"
>
> "They are terrible mountains!" says the father. "See, what a fellow! I shall not go up it! One can see just as well from below!"
>
> That one cannot! Ascend the rock! Let the fresh mountain breeze whistle round you, and be glad with the great abroad and with – the beautiful at home! (Andersen 1871, 340)[13]

Andersen writes about the Copenhagener and his daughter as if they were not part of the community on board, but only guests. They are not part of the "we." Contrary to his experience in Rome, there is, at this time, no happy community with his fellow countrymen in the foreign countries. He only shows contempt and quiet regret.

As one more contradiction to the happy days in Rome, one can mention the elderly Andersen's stay in Paris during the World Exposition in 1867. He went to Paris twice that year. On the second journey, he had a young travel companion, the English writer Robert Watt, by his side. In Paris, Andersen went to see the exposition several times, and became a part of the visitors' international society for weeks. According to his diary, one day followed the other with endless visits, meetings with friends and acquaintances in cafes and restaurants. The impression of Andersen's stay in Paris is not that he enjoyed it and was enthusiastic about his experiences at the exposition; rather, one may feel his exhaustion of being in this state of perpetual superficiality. All the time people are coming and going, and Andersen only made friends with very few of them. On September 11, 1867, he writes in his diary:

> Wednesday 11. Very hot; slept to 9 o'clock, Callon and Wolfhagen came to visit. Callon offered us his loge in the great opera tonight. Appointment with Wolfhagen to dine with him at the hotel at 6 o'clock, the painter Gertner joins us – beginning to be bored with being here. Went out to the legation where I met Bille and chatted with him. I have caught a terrible cold. He told that the crown prince has been engaged to the Swedish princess. Watt out the whole day. I dined at Table d'hote here in the hotel with chamberlain Wolfhagen and the painter Gertner, then drove to the great opera and Callon's Loge where we listened to le Trovere and saw the ballet La Sourd, which was pretty to look at. In Loge, directly opposite, attaché Bille and his wife and another lady were seated. After 12, I went to Caffe Regence for a beer and went home half past twelve, it was after one, Watt came to see me and it was around two o'clock when I, tired, turned off the light. (1995–96, 7:346, my translation)[14]

Three days later, he is still on the move and is still meeting new people:

> Sunday 15. Watt went to the countryside, I was idling about, I was bored, thought it was all wrong to spend a lot of money, now, when I was satiated. Had trouble getting a seat in the tram to the exhibition. I saw quite a lot that I hadn't seen yet. In the tram home again, I met doctor Bruun from Odense who now lives as a married man in Altona. This morning I met Mr. and Mrs. Warburg from Altona in Caffee Regence. Dinner in Hotel d'Angleterre with Wolfhagen (who offered Champagne) Miss Gertner, Schmidt, Dr. Wrowlsy. Eating and drinking was good, then went to Caffe Regence, I wished I was on my own; I told them stories until 11 and then was at the hotel. (7:348–349, my translation)[15]

Thus, the days went on, until he and his fellow traveller, Robert Watt, finally left Paris and returned to Denmark.

Andersen's journeys also led him into communities of a more lasting character. Over the years he made very good friends in Dresden, Weimar and Augustenburg, and he was visiting them for weeks. He became a part of noble and high society communities that worshiped and supported artists like him.

Through his many journeys and stays in different parts of Europe, Andersen developed the mindset of a European cosmopolitan and celebrity. He felt he had his home everywhere. But his German acquaintances also caused him trouble because of the tension and wars between Denmark and Prussia, and the conflict between Denmark and the dukedoms Schleswig and Holstein. He was forced to choose sides despite the fact that he did not want to. Even some of his best friends, such as the ducal family of Augustenburg, he felt he had to avoid, so he would not get in trouble with his nationalistic Danish countrymen in the period around the war 1848-50. Yet, Andersen still visited the Serre family at their manor in Maxen near Dresden during the 1850s. But after 1864, he had problems with his friends there too. They supported the Prussian side of the conflict while Andersen was committed to the Danish side.

Andersen was upset by the conflict in 1864. He was embarrassed about it, but there was no way out of the dilemma. He was trapped by high policy, and he could not flee away from it. On April 16, 1864, he writes in his diary:

> Today I've really been tormented by the pressure of political events that are carrying me along – I feel each kindness people in Germany have shown me, acknowledge friends there but feel that I, as a Dane, must make a complete break with them all. They have been torn out of my heart; never will we meet again; a beautiful past cannot be renewed. My heart is breaking! (Andersen 1990, p. 308)[16]

The war in 1864 was a trauma for Andersen, as it was for all Danes. But for him it caused extra pain, because the Germans were his good readers and customers, and because he had to abandon many of the good relationships he had made during his journeys and stays in Germany. The Germans were not decent company for him anymore. His further travels through Germany were no longer to the same degree as earlier characterised by the many stays he had with good friends in Dresden and Maxen. After 1864, he was a more infrequent guest there. "We" didn't include as many Germans as before. He was travelling through, rather than to Germany after 1864.

All in the Same Boat

In a symbolic manner, Andersen perceives the journey as a metaphor for our life spans. In *Shadow Pictures* he bursts into this euphorical vision:

I now say: To be a traveller is surely the happiest lot, which we all travel. Everything in the whole universe travels! Even the poorest of men possesses the winged horse of thoughts. If it turns old and feeble, Death will take him on the journey, the great journey, which we all make. The waves roll from coast to coast. The clouds float across the great sky and the bird joins in the journey across fields and meadows. We are all on a journey. Even the dead in their quiet graves move with the earth around the sun. Indeed, "to travel" is a fixed idea for the entire universe. But we human beings are children. We even like to imagine that we are "travelling" in the middle of our own natural journey and that of the universe. (Andersen 2011, 29).[17]

In such a view, all of us are travellers throughout our lives, and we share a common destination: death and the promised afterlife. In that respect we are all travel companions participating in the same community of mankind.

For a more literal perception of Andersen's journeys, you may perceive them as a significant part of a modern life style. Andersen is expressing experiences that have become more and more common to modern people who travel due to their profession, or as tourists. The special thing about Andersen is that he is among the first to render these experiences and to write about them. Nowadays a lot of people travel like Andersen did – as tourists – and they get the experience of travel communities in many ways. One of the most common and popular ways of travelling, and one which differs substantially from Andersen's, is with a group. The journey is arranged in advance, and you buy a whole package with travel, hotels and restaurants, excursions, and a travel leader. You do not make friends and acquaintances with the foreign people you are visiting as much as you participate in a travel community with your fellow travellers and fellow countrymen. The journey does not make you a cosmopolitan, but rather a more committed member of the national community. But it is still an opportunity to mix the nationalities on cruise ships. There, the community could easily be described like Andersen does in his memoir *The Fairy Tale of my Life* (*Mit Livs Eventyr*, 1855), where he tells about his trip to Greece: "[...] on the ship all was gayety. We frolicked, sang, danced, played at cards, and chatted together, – Americans, Italians, and Asiatics; bishops and monks, officers and travellers. A few days of living together at sea make close fellowship. I was as at home, and it was therefore a real grief to me to leave the ship at Syra." (Andersen 2000, 163).[18]

We are all drifting between communities, small and large ones. In this respect we are like Andersen and part of his "we." We form communities across national borders in a globalised world. But as for Andersen, higher politics may interfere with our private communities and relations. The national feeling both initiates and dissolves communities, just like Andersen experienced it in the glorious Christmas days in Rome in 1833, and as it sadly became a fact in his life after the fatal war in 1864. We are still in the dilemma between the national community and the cosmopolitan society; between the concern for our countrymen and our feelings for our personal friends of all nationalities. We are, like Andersen, still negotiating with ourselves and our companions which kind of "we" we belong to, and we are still travelling between communities of all kinds.

References

Andersen, Hans Christian. 1871. *A Poet's Bazaar: Pictures of Travel in Germany, Italy, Greece, and the Orient*. New York: Hurd and Houghton/Cambridge: Riverside Press.

Andersen, Hans Christian. (1859) 1975. *Mit Livs Eventyr*. 2 vols. København: Gyldendal.

Andersen, Hans Christian. (1831) 1986. *Skyggebilleder af en Reise til Harzen, det sachsiske Schweitz etc. etc., i Sommeren 1831*. København: Det Danske Sprog- og Litteraturselskab/Borgen.

Andersen, Hans Christian. 1990. *The Diaries of Hans Christian Andersen*. Selected and translated by Patricia L. Conroy and Sven H. Rossel. Seattle, WA: University of Washington Press.

Andersen, Hans Christian. 1995-96. *H.C. Andersens Dagbøger 1825-1875*. 12 vols. Compiled by Kåre Olsen and H. Topsøe-Jensen and edited by Helga Vang Lauridsen, Tue Gad, and Kirsten Weber. København: Det Danske Sprog- og Litteraturselskab/Gad.

Andersen, Hans Christian. 2000. *The Fairy Tale of my Life*. New York: Cooper Square Press.

Andersen, Hans Christian. (1863) 2004. *I Spanien*. København: Det Danske Sprog- og Litteraturselskab/Borgen.

Andersen, Hans Christian. (1842) 2006. *En Digters Bazar*. København: Det Danske Sprog- og Litteraturselskab/Borgen.

Andersen, Hans Christian. 2011. *Shadow Pictures, From a Journey to the Harz Mountains, Saxon Switzerland, etc. etc. in the Summer of 1831*.

Edited by Sven Hakon Rossel and Monika Wenusch, translated by Anna Halager. Wien: Praesens.

Handesten, Lars. 1992. *Litterære rejser. Poetik og erkendelse i danske digteres rejsebøger*. København: Reitzel.

Handesten, Lars. 2004. "Rejsebogen. En grænseoverskridende genre." In *Genrer på kryds og tværs*, edited by Katja Teilmann, 71–86. Odense: Syddansk Universitetsforlag.

Houe, Poul. 1996. "Going Places: Hans Christian Andersen, the Great European Traveller." In *Hans Christian Andersen: Danish Writer and Citizen of the World*, edited by Sven Hakon Rossel, 126–175. Amsterdam/Atlanta, GA: Rodopi.

Mylius, Johan de. 1986. "Efterskrift." In *Skyggebilleder af en Reise til Harzen, det sachsiske Schweitz etc. etc., i Sommeren 1831*, by Hans Christian Andersen, 133–154. København: Det Danske Sprog- og Litteraturselskab/ Borgen.

Oxfeldt, Elisabeth. 2010. *Journeys from Scandinavia. Travelogues of Africa, Asia, and South America, 1840-2000*. Minneapolis: University of Minnesota Press.

Notes

1. In Handesten (2004) you will find a general introduction to the travelogue genre and in Handesten (1992) an introduction to Hans Christian Andersen's travelogues.
2. "[...] han [Hoppe] fortalte mig Scener af sit Liv, og med inderlig Venlighed skildtes vi ad; [...] – Der gives Mennesker man kan omgaaes flere Aar, uden at faae Fortroelighed til, andre seer man neppe ind [i] Øiet, før man finder et Hjerte, hvor man føler sig hjemme. – 0, reise! reise! hvem der dog, hele sit Liv kunde flagre om! – – ja, jeg føler Verden er mit Hjem og jeg skal, jeg maa, tumle mig i Hjemmet." (Andersen 1995–96, 1:90).
3. "[...] jeg gik med og nu fortalte han sit hele Don Juan Liv, der i Begyndelsen morede mig, men da vi med et stod i en Gade de plaisir, og han i[n]viterede mig ind paa Viin, blev jeg ganske forskrækket; jeg skammede mig ordenlig ved at gaae denne lange Sirene Gade igjennem, der blev mere og mere smal til vi slap ud og jeg skildtes venlig, men ikke med det bedste Sindelag fra det unge Væsen, der alt kjendte Verden saa godt." (Andersen 1995–96, 1:108).
4. "Ubehageligt Selskab, slet Veir, daarlige Veie og usle Heste. Alt var forenet for at gjøre Reisen til en Bods- og Poenitense-Reise. Solen vilde ikke skinne mig ind i Hjertet og heller ikke skinne paa Landskabet uden omkring mig; og just den Strækning, vi nu passerede, laae i det deiligste Sollys, da jeg sidst var her; men Naturen tænkte som saa, for det Selskab der behøver jeg ikke at see godt ud [...]." (Andersen [1842] 2006, 83).
5. Oxfeldt points to different kinds of communities. Some are ideological, e.g. traditional or modern European communities (2010, 10); some are made without words but due to the exchange of objects (14).
6. "Vil man staae sig godt med Forældre, saa skal man give sig af med deres Børn, det er en Visdoms-Regel!" (Andersen [1842] 2006, 239).
7. "[Jeg] lagde mig paa Hyndet hos den venlige Ægtemand, hvis lille Datters Hjerte jeg alt havde vundet." (Andersen [1842] 2006, 240).
8. "Her ere nye Ansigter ombord, Rustzuk har i Nat sendt os mange Gjæster. Hvilket broget Folkefærd! Tyrken knæler og holder sin Morgenbøn, hans Pande berører Skibsdæk-

9 ket; tæt ved sidder en Jøde, i Sølvmors Kjole med purpurfarvet Turban [...]." (Andersen [1842] 2006, 302).
9 "[...] jeg var lidende og ærgerlig, Jonas havde til Refrain: 'De maa tage Dem sammen!' det behagede mig ikke; Tanke om Deltagelse var der ikke, han saae gnaven ud [...]. (Andersen 1995–96, 5:44).
10 "Næste Morgen, – ja nu skulde man see Alicante!" (Andersen [1863] 2004, 46).
11 "Jo længer bort Svensk, Norsk og Dansk kommer fra sit Hjem, des høiere synger Hjertet hos hver, i det de mødes.'Vi er eet Folk, vi kaldes Skandinaver!' Da jeg i 1833 var i Rom holdt de tre Nationer deres Juleaften i Fællesskab, som een Familie." (Andersen [1842] 2006, 103).
12 "[...] der er noget naturligt hjerteligt hos Landmændene her." (Andersen 1995–96, 1:217).
13 "Vi have ombord en Kjøbenhavner med sin Datter! 'det er nysseligt!' siger hun, "men Vandet er saa fælt gult! [...]
   'Det er nogle skrækkelige Bjerge!' siger Faderen, 'see hvilken Karl! jeg skal ikke op paa den! man ser den da ligesaa godt nedenfra!'
   Det gjør man ikke! stig op på Fjeldet! lad den friske Bjergluft omsuse Eder, og vær glad ved det Store ude og ved – det Smukke hjemme!" (Andersen [1842] 2006, 363).
14 "Onsdag 11. Meget varmt; sov til 9, fik da Besøg af Callon og Wolfhagen. Callon bød os i sin Loge i store Opera iaften. Aftalte med Wolfhagen at spise med ham her i Hotellet Klokken 6, Maleren Gertner spiser med. – – Begynder at være træt af at være her. Gik ud i Legationen hvor jeg traf Bille og sladdrede med ham. Jeg er stærkt forkjølet. Han fortalte at Kronprindsen blev nu forlovet med den svenske Prindsesse. Watt hele Dagen ude. Jeg spiiste Table d hote her i Hotellet med Kammerherre Wolfhagen og Maleren Gertner, kjørte saa hen i den store Opera i Callons Loge hvor vi hørte leTrovere og saae Balletten La Sourd, som er nydelig at see. Ligeoverfor i Loge sad Attachee Bille med Fru Bülov og en anden Dame. Efter 12 gik jeg i Caffe Regence drak Øl og kom hjem halv eet, den var over eet da Watt kom at besøge mig og nær to da jeg træt slukkede Lyset." (Andersen 1995–96, 7:346).
15 "Søndag 15. Watt tog paa Landet, jeg drev om, kjedede mig, syntes at det var galt at anvende saa mange Penge da jeg nu var mæt. Havde Nød med at faae Plads i Sporvognen ud til Udstillingen. Der saae jeg en Deel jeg endnu ikke havde seet. I Spoervognen hjem traf jeg Lægen Bruun fra Odense der nu lever gift i Altona. Imorges traf jeg i Caffee Regence Hr og Fru Warburg fra Altona. Middag i Hotel d'Angleterre med Wolfhagen (som gav Champagne) Frøken .... Gertner, Schmidt, Dr. Wrowlesky. Drak og spiiste godt, gik saa til Caffe Regence, jeg [havde] helst været min egen Herre; jeg fortalte Historier for dem til Klokken gik til 11 og var da i Hotellet." (Andersen 1995–96, 7:348–349).
16 "Idag har jeg ret lidt under det politiske Tryk jeg rives med i; jeg føler hver Velvillie man i Tydskland har viist mig, erkjender Venner der og føler som dansk at jeg nu aldeles maa bryde med dem Alle; de ere revne ud af mit Hjerte, aldrig kunne vi oftere mødes, en deilig Fortid vil ikke fornyes. Jeg er bedrøvet til Døden." (Andersen 1995–96, 6:40].
17 "'O reise! reise!' det er dog den lykkeligste Lod! og derfor reise vi ogsaa Alle; Alt reiser i det hele Univers! selv den fattigste Mand eier Tankens vingede Hest, og bliver den svag og gammel, tager Døden ham dog med paa Reisen, den store Reise, vi alle reise. Bølgerne rulle fra Kyst til Kyst; Skyerne seile hen ad den store Himmel og Fuglen flyver med over Mark og Enge. Vi reise Alle, selv de Døde i deres stille Grave, flyve med Jorden rundt om Solen. Ja, 'reise', det er en fix Idee hos det hele Univers, men vi Mennesker ere Børn, vi ville endogsaa lege 'at reise', midt under vores og Tingenes store, naturlige Reise." (Andersen [1831] 1986, 11).
18 "[...] paa Skibet selv var Selskabs- og Salon-Liv, der blev musiceret, sunget, dandset, spillet Kort og livligt ført Conversation; Amerikanere, Italienere, Asiater, mellem

hverandre. Biskopper og Munke, Officerer og Turister. – Faa Dages Samliv paa Havet knytter saaledes hverandre fast; jeg var bleven som hjemme, og det var derfor en heel tung Skilsmisse ved Syra, at forlade dette Fartøi." (Andersen [1859] 1975, 1:238).

The Grimms as the Elephant in the Danish Fairy Tale Room
An Interpretation of Hans Christian Andersen's Concept of a Future Community of Fairy Tale Readers

Mads Sohl Jessen
University of Southern Denmark, Odense

There is a curious lack of references to the Grimm collection of tales in Andersen's early writings. This may lead to the conclusion that the Grimms were of no special importance to Andersen's art of the fairy tales. This is not the case. As Andersen in early 1835 decided to embark on his great career as a fairy tale writer, the Grimms' narrative aesthetics was on the one hand his main model in terms of plot structure and narrative voice. On the other hand Andersen sought to break free from the purist epic style of the Grimms by fusing his narrative art with his own unique blend of irony and phantasmagoria. Andersen's ambition in 1835 was in fact to attain the same transnational community of readers as the Grimms were reaching in Europe in this decade, but Andersen had to produce his own fundamentally new and distinct type of fairy tale to reach his goal.

In his reading of "The Tinderbox" ("Fyrtøiet",1835) the Danish Andersen scholar Helge Topsøe-Jensen declares that there can be no doubt that the fairy tale is "based on an authentic Danish folk fairy tale" (1971,12). Topsøe-Jensen thus argues that Andersen's own statement in regard of the true origin of his first fairy tales is to be taken at face value. In his remarks "To the Older Readers" from 1837 Andersen writes:

> In my childhood I happily listened to fairy tales and stories, several of which are still living in my memory. Some of them seem to me to be originally Danish, completely derived from the people, I have not in any foreign country come across the like. In my way I have told them, allowed myself any change I found suitable, let my fantasy refresh the bleached colours of the pictures. This is how four fairy tales came to be: "The Tinderbox," "Little Claus and Big Claus," "The Princess on the Pea" and "The Travelling Companion." (Andersen 2003–07, 3:vii)[1]

Andersen is clearly participating in the romantic worship of the people in which the Grimm brothers played a particularly important role when it comes to the genre of fairy tales. In Ruth B. Bottigheimer's words the "Grimms believed an individual's knowledge of brief narratives (*Märchen*) proved the existence of a common national folk heritage that had generated those narratives." (2009, 105). Though Andersen emphasises that he has taken the liberty to shape the fairy tales he heard in his childhood according to his own will, he is evidently at this time positioning himself as being in line with the Grimms' belief in the unique qualities of a national fairy tale tradition deriving from the common people.

Bottigheimer is building her case against folkloristic ideas of fairy tale oral origin and transmission on a variety of European book historical studies of the rich fairy tale publications and translations from Straparola's time in the 16th century and onwards to the period of the Grimm brothers. She writes in her *Fairy Tales: A New History* from 2009: "The basic argument of this book replaces an anonymous folk with literate authors who are city-oriented people like ourselves" (113). Following Bottigheimer and inspired by Harold Bloom's agonistic poetics of influence Andersen's Grimm-like national romantic insistence on the oral origin of his first fairy tales will be disregarded in this study. Rather, the argument presented here will be that Andersen knowingly bases two of his first fairy tales, "The Tinderbox" and "Little Claus and Big Claus" ("Lille Claus og store Claus," 1835) on specific tales by the Grimms. Andersen hardly mentions the Grimms in his diaries and letters from the 1830s, but his early fairy tale art form is deeply related to the narrative aesthetics of the German master collectors and stylists.

In the urban and elite circles Andersen was part of in Copenhagen in the 1830s the Grimms were widely regarded as the preeminent tellers of fairy tales. In the first part of this study the early Danish Grimm reception is discussed followed by a presentation of one of the most important proponents of the Grimms in Denmark, Christian Molbech. Molbech also happened to write the first review of Andersen's first published fairy tale from 1830. This review is crucial in understanding Andersen's fairy tale breakthrough in 1835. "Swerve" is perhaps Bloom's most important concept in terms of how his theory has influenced literary readers' psychological understanding of intertextual relationships. The concept was introduced in *The Anxiety of Influence* (1973) where Bloom uses it as a synonym for "clinamen" and places it as a crucial concept for his vision of literary history: "the true history of modern poetry would be the accurate recording of these revisionary swerves" ([1973] 1997, 44). In the first part of this article the underlying theoretical argument is that Bloom's theory of the agonistic struggle of the poet-to-be against great forerunners is relevant to Andersen's relation to the Grimms in 1835. The Grimms' aesthetic and narrative accomplishment simply could not be circumvented by Andersen, but he could stay silent about his forebears. Andersen therefore consciously internalised their epic style in his narrative tonality while swerving from his literary predecessors via irony and phantasmagoria. In the second and final part an interpretation of Andersen's canonical ambitions is offered in which the main title of the article is used as the main analytic metaphor.

On New Year's Day 1835 Andersen writes to his friend Henriette Hanck: "Now I begin [to write] some 'children's fairy tales.' I will seek to win the coming generations, you must know!" (Hanck 1942, 104). Considering the time of writing when Andersen took the most important decision in his career as a poet, he may well have been influenced by the Christmas sales of children's literature. At the time one finds a lot of advertisements in the newspapers like this one from December 23, 1834:

> Library for young people
> With this title the present writer will from the beginning of next year publish a booklet mainly intended for young people. According to the plan this library will admit everything that can serve to ennoble the heart of youth, enlighten its mind and, all in all, achieve a benign and instructive entertainment. The booklet will thus, among other things, contain: moral stories, descriptions of excellent people and important events, ex-

tracts from travelogues, natural historical depictions, remarkable inventions, fairy tales, parables, fables, maxims, riddles. A booklet will be published each month in 144 pages. (Riise 1834, n.p.)

The writer was a certain J. Chr. Riise who had also translated a volume of Straparola's fairy tales in 1818 from a German version from 1817. It was common at Andersen's time to publish booklets as serials so as to increase revenues as well as keeping the reading public interested. So when Andersen in May 1835 published his first serial booklet with four fairy tales including "The Tinderbox" and "Little Claus and Big Claus" he was following a trend in the book market. However, when Andersen writes of winning a future community of readers for himself he is thinking in competitive terms. Who did Andersen see as his main competitors? The answer to this question has to do with Andersen's complex relation to the Grimm brothers and their extremely influential collection of tales. Already in 1835, Andersen was so ambitious that he wanted to win the same pan-European readership that the Grimms were attaining in the 1830s.

The Grimms, Molbech, and Andersen's Debut as a Fairy Tale Writer

In his study on the Danish Grimm reception Cay Dollerup has noted that the "Danish response to the *Tales* was by far the most prompt outside Germany." (1999, 152). Already in 1821 the so-called Lindencrone translation came out in Danish which consisted of a complete translation of the first Grimm volume of 1812 (J. Grimm 1821). Included in the Danish translation was also the Grimm brothers' revised and expanded foreword for their second edition from 1819 in which they express their hope that the collection would not only be enjoyed because of its poetic qualities, but also as a "book of education" (B. Grimm 1819, viii). During the 1830s the Grimm brothers did experience that their collection was conquering the future generations of German and European readers as parents bought their collection and read the tales aloud to their children. Their huge success was mainly due to the so-called small edition which came out in 1825 and which was addressed primarily to parents and their children (Zipes 2015, 33–57). So when Andersen uses this particularly ambitious phrase in his letter to Ms. Hanck he is expressing an ambition on behalf of his art in which only the Grimm brothers had succeeded in his contemporary literary field. Andersen wanted to compete with the producers of the biggest success story in the European world of fairy tale book sales. Indeed, Andersen in early 1835 possibly dreamt of founding a distinctly Danish tradition of fairy tales which could travel across language barriers just like the Grimms' collection was doing at this time in European literature.

Andersen's reliance on the Grimms in many of his first fairy tales has been a neglected field of study in the Danish reception. Arguably the most important scholarly work in this field has been the commentaries written by Flemming Hovmann and Erling Nielsen in volume 7 of the critical edition from 1990. In this study only two fairy tales by Andersen will be discussed, "The Tinderbox and "Little Claus and Big Claus." In regard of "The Tinderbox" Hovmann and Nielsen's commentary states that the fairy tale "matches pretty well" (Andersen 1990, 20) with the Grimms' "The Blue Light" ("Das blaue Licht," 1815) after the soldier returns to the city. This is right. In regard of "Little Claus and Big Claus" Hovmann and Nielsen also point out that Andersen's narrative bears resemblance to certain stories by Straparola and the Grimms (Andersen 1990, 23). This is also correct and something I will elaborate on later. In his new study on the narrative art of Perrault, Grimm, and Andersen, Cyrille François discusses how Andersen's revolution of Danish prose style was "inspired by the Grimms' tales" (2017, 327). This is an important insight and as such this short article is a contribution to a reevaluation of the importance of the Grimms for Andersen which François' study has laid the groundwork for in contemporary Andersen scholarship.

One of the most important Danish proponents of the Grimms also wrote the first piece of criticism on Andersen's first published fairy tale. Christian Molbech was a very productive librarian, historian, professor of literary history at the University of Copenhagen, travel writer, influential critic and taste arbiter. His connection to the Grimm brothers goes back to the late 1810s when he visited them in Kassel. Molbech also corresponded with Jacob Grimm (Clausen 1907). In 1832 Molbech published a primer on which Dollerup has written the following: "This edition was produced for teaching school children Danish in the first classes in grammar school (secondary school); it is therefore the earliest example of the use of the *Tales* for instructional purposes in Denmark. The volume contains 106 fairy tales, legends and sketches from numerous sources, and includes six tales by

Grimm" (Dollerup 1999, 74–75). Molbech's volume shows that the Grimms were succeeding in terms of getting their collection accepted for educative purposes, at least in Denmark.

At the very end of his first major collection of poetry, *Digte* (*Poems*) from 1830 Andersen had included a fairy tale entitled "The Spectre, A Funen Folktale" ("Dødningen, et fyensk Folke-Eventyr"). Andersen's fairy tale is a gothic extravaganza which tells the story of good-hearted Johannes who secures a proper burial for a corpse some evil men want to mutilate. Then the corpse reappears as a living man to befriend and repay Johannes his good deed. Molbech's review published in a scholarly journal in 1830 is crucial to Andersen's debut in 1835. Molbech faults Andersen for narrating the tale in an ironic and self-conscious manner:

> The author has mistaken the epic tone in which such fairy tales must be told. By adorning it with too much colourful finery in his own fantastic manner; and by painting it with an occasionally quite empty copiousness and in a tone wherein lies now way too much subjectivity and oddness now an expressive elegance which is not suited for the language of folk fairy tales. (1830, 171)

Here is one of the passages which Molbech faults for being too extravagant. As the fairy tale begins, Andersen describes a late summer evening in the following manner:

> It was a lovely August evening, the mosquitoes were dancing their airy quadrilles, and the frogs were sitting like tipsy musicians, croaking a merry chorus in their deep-pitched orchestras, the nuns had just concluded their devout evensong and each was on her way to her cell.[2]

Andersen's art is clearly not related to Grimms' narrative tone at this early point in his career as a fairy tale writer. In his essay "On the Nature of Fairy Tales" ("Ueber das Wesen der Märchen") from the first volume of the 1819 edition and also included in the Lindencrone translation, Wilhelm Grimm writes that the narrative art of folk tales is epic: "everything epic stands in a safe circle" (B. Grimm 1819, 1:xxvi). Molbech's critique of Andersen's lack of adherence to the principle of epic narration is completely in line with Grimm, as François has also noted (François 2017, 339).

Then Molbech writes something which is of the utmost importance to Andersen's choice of subtitle in 1835. Molbech writes of himself in the third person: "Never has he as a child heard a folk fairy tale told in such a way; since all irony in the form falls away." (1830, 171). Again, Molbech is following Wilhelm Grimms' lead. In the same essay Grimm writes that there is true humour in their German tales which should not be confused with "the modern narrator's inserted irony" (B. Grimm 1819, 1:xxvi). Wilhelm Grimm is clearly implying that the modern literary tales which often use an explicitly ironic narrator are aesthetically inferior to the folk fairy tale narrator whose epic tone has been perfected throughout numerous generations. When Molbech speaks of his own childhood, he is referring to the short notice by which Andersen introduces the story:

> As a boy it was my greatest joy to listen to fairy tales. A great number are still quite vivid in my recollection and some of these are only little known or not known at all; here, I have retold one and if it is received with applause I will do likewise with more and at some point deliver a cycle of Danish folk tales.

When Andersen chooses the subtitle "Told to Children" in 1835 it contains a subtle allusion to Molbech's negative point of view in his review. The meaning of the allusion is an emphatic rejection of Molbech's (and Wilhelm Grimm's) insistence on the incompatibility of ironic and epic narration. That this is so can be seen by the way Andersen constructs the very opening of "The Tinderbox:" "There came a soldier marching down the high road – *one, two! one, two!*" This very sentence also contains an allusion to Molbech's review.

Molbech faults a particular rhetorical comparison in "Dødningen" by referring to it as Andersen's use of "trivial and low everyday language." (1830, 171). In the story the main character Johannes and his older anonymous friend meet an old lady in the woods who has sore legs. The older man has a magic ointment which immediately cures all physical ailments:

> Scarcely had he smeared the miraculous ointment on her leg before the old woman got up, and assured him that she had never been so light on her feet before, and asked him if he would not smear a little on the other leg too, so that she would not have to start limping but have two healthy legs

to go on; scarcely had he fulfilled her wish before both her pins started to go back and forth like drumsticks, she curtseyed and disappeared into the green wood.

It is the comparison "started to go back and forth like drumsticks" which Molbech points his finger at. Andersen consciously uses what Molbech calls trivial everyday language when he writes "one two one two." In epic terms the addition is unnecessary as it does not do anything for the progress of the story, but it certainly contains ironic value. Johan de Mylius makes a point when he writes: "Andersen's fairy tales and stories are in no way attempts to imitate or preserve an oral tradition. Whatever sources Andersen had for his stories, his tales are literary products, in style and intention submitted to a literary strategy." (2004, 2). When Molbech writes on Andersen's "trivial and low everyday language" he is actually constructing a problematic, but very influential critical stereotype: Andersen's rhetorical style is founded on his imitation of folk oral culture. This is not the case. Around 1835 Andersen was a very capable prose writer, deeply read in the German romantic tradition, and with his own highly original rhetorical agenda. Andersen begins "The Tinderbox" in an epic style very similar to an Grimms' fairy tale tone, but he then interrupts the epic flow by using pseudo-naïve irony "one two, one two." The soldier's feet are also going like drumsticks just like the old woman in "Dødningen" albeit, perhaps, in a somewhat lower tempo. In using irony Andersen is claiming his own narrative freedom from whatever Molbech may think is the right way to tell fairy tale stories to children.

While "Dødningen" hardly has anything to do with the Grimms' narrative aesthetics, "The Tinderbox" is indeed related to a specific story in their collection. Many commentators have noted that "The Tinderbox" fuses a peculiar Danish setting with "oriental" metaphors which Andersen has taken from *Arabian Nights*. The third and biggest dog has eyes the size of the Round Tower which is an iconic building in Copenhagen, but Andersen also recirculates particular motives and comparisons from the stories of Aladdin, Sinbad the Sailor as well as Ali Baba and the Forty Thieves (Andersen 1990, 19-23). Nevertheless, the story to which "The Tinderbox" bears the strongest resemblance is the Grimm story "The Blue Light" as noted by Hovmann and Nielsen.

Andersen has clearly recycled some of the plot structure from this story when writing "The Tinderbox." Indeed, Andersen does not mind copying a particular part almost verbatim. This happens when the soldier enters the city as a rich soldier. Here is the wording of Grimm in Margaret Hunt's translation from 1884: "He went to the best inn, ordered himself handsome clothes, and then bade the landlord furnish him a room as handsomely as possible." (J. Grimm 1884, 2:123). And Andersen in Hersholt's version: "He took the best rooms at the best inn, and ordered all the good things he liked to eat, for he was a rich man now because he had so much money." Once again Andersen produces a difference to the Grimms by knowingly fusing the epic with the ironic. In this case the narrator's irony consists in Andersen's use of a pleonasm. The reader already knows that the soldier is rich, and she certainly also knows that he is rich because he has a lot of money. This pseudo-naïve voice is Andersen's swerve from Wilhelm Grimms' and Molbech's insistence on epic and nothing but epic fairy tale narration.

Marina Warner (2008) has demonstrated that phantasmagorical aesthetics is a prevalent and encompassing phenomenon of modernity. Here I use the concept in a more narrow sense as Oxford English Dictionary designates one of its main meanings (first entry is from 1822): "A shifting and changing scene consisting of many elements, *esp.* one that is startling or extraordinary, or resembling or reminiscent of a dream, hallucination." In contrast to tableaus phantasmagorias are characterised by dynamic movements, but they share a dreamlike quality. Andersen also departs from the Grimms' aesthetics in writing passages that are clearly modelled on their fairy tales, but that are much richer in phantasmagoric energy.

The best example of Andersen's phantasmagorical capability in his debut collection of 1835 is at the end of "Little Claus and Big Claus" where little Claus cheats big Claus who goes on to drown himself. This motive – the good guy cheats the bad guys into drowning themselves based on economic incentives – is first used in Straparola's collection of fairy tales *The Pleasant Nights* from 1550–53 in the story of the rich priest Scarpaccio (first night, third tale) who gets fooled by three thieves, but then he fools them:

> They asked him how he was able to get out of the river. The priest replied to them, "Oh, you madmen, you do not know anything! If you had drowned me deeper, I would have come up with ten times more sheep." Hearing this the three friends said, "Oh sir, would you do us this favour?

> Would you put us into sacks and throw us into the river, so that we will change from thieves into shepherds?" The priest said, "I am prepared to do anything that pleases you and there is nothing in this world that I would not do willingly for you." (Straparola 2015, 72)

With these ironic words Scarpaccio seals their destiny. In Grimms' "The little Peasant" ("Das Bürle," 1819), which Andersen is definitely very indebted to in terms of the plot line for "Little Claus and Big Claus," the imaginary life under water is represented as follows:

> After that the peasants went home, and as they were entering the village, the small peasant also came quietly in, driving a flock of sheep and looking quite contented. Then the peasants were astonished, and said, "Peasant, from whence comest thou? Hast thou come out of the water?" "Yes, truly," replied the peasant, "I sank deep, deep down, until at last I got to the bottom; I pushed the bottom out of the barrel, and crept out, and there were pretty meadows on which a number of lambs were feeding, and from thence I brought this flock away with me." Said the peasants, "Are there any more there?" "Oh, yes," said he, "more than I could do anything with." (J. Grimm 1884, 1:269)

In the Grimms' version the little peasant begins to envision an underwater pastoral paradise, but due to the epic restraints of their tales the imaginary qualities of this world are not explored by the narrator. Andersen expands on the Grimms' so as to turn it into a marvelous piece of phantasmagoria:

> "But when I was in the sack, with the wind whistling in my ears as you dropped me off the bridge into the cold water, I was frightened enough. I went straight to the bottom, but it didn't hurt me because of all the fine soft grass down there. Someone opened the sack and a beautiful maiden took my hand. Her clothes were white as snow, and she had a green wreath in her floating hair. She said, 'So you've come, Little Claus. Here's a herd of cattle for you, but they are just the beginning of my presents. A mile further up the road another herd awaits you.' Then I saw that the river is a great highway for the people who live in the sea. Down on the bottom of the river they walked and drove their cattle straight in from the sea to the land where the rivers end. The flowers down there are fragrant. The grass

is fresh, and fish flit by as birds do up here. The people are fine, and so are the cattle that come grazing along the roadside."

It is one of the first instances of Andersen's perfect and superbly ironic phantasmagorias. Andersen, so to say, taps into the collective Danish folk imaginary landscape here by depicting the underwater world as the main road in Jutland, Hærvejen, where cattle were transported to Germany. Hærvejen was renowned for its liveliness and an atmosphere of 'money' (i.e. cattle) on the move. In addition to his expansion of Grimm Andersen also introduces an erotic motive. The attractive sea girl helps little Claus, so that he can enter into this pastoral paradise where he can have as much cattle as he wants, and he can also easily have a sea maiden for a wife, it seems. Therefore, big Claus quite rationally asks little Claus why he did not stay underwater when life is so good down there. In his reply Andersen breaks away from any debt to the Grimms' version:

> "Well," said Little Claus, "I'm being particularly clever. You remember I said the sea maiden told me to go one mile up the road and I'd find another herd of cattle. By 'road' she meant the river, for that's the only way she travels. But I know how the river turns and twists, and it seemed too roundabout a way of getting there. By coming up on land I took a short cut that saves me half a mile. So I get my cattle that much sooner." "You *are* a lucky man," said Big Claus, "Do you think I would get me some cattle too if I went down to the bottom of the river?"

Andersen is very funny. When big Claus calls little Claus a happy man he is not thinking of the sea maidens, but solely on the amount of cattle he has amassed. Happiness for big Claus is not the prospect of getting to know sea girls with green wreaths in their wet hair, but solely the vast amount of sea cattle down in the water. In "Little Claus and Big Claus" Andersen subtly connects erotic desire with the desire for money and social rise while humourously suggesting that there is no doubt as to which of these forces are the strongest for the two protagonists. In contrast to the minor characters in the story (the farmer's wife and the sexton) little Claus and big Claus are not interested in erotic desire whatsoever, but only in money and social appearance. This is the one thing they have in common. From the beginning of the story little Claus lives in a phantasy world where the whole world is witnessing his cattle wealth. At the end of the story, due to his cunning, little Claus is about to turn his dream scenario into reality. By using phantasmagoria Andersen is evidently producing a literary tale but in contrast to for example E.T.A. Hoffmann Andersen's early phantasmagorias build on Grimm so as to surpass their vision of the great imaginary life of the people.

The Grimms as the Elephant in the Danish Fairy Tale Room

Andersen finds his true voice as a fairy tale writer in "The Tinderbox" and "Little Claus and Big Claus," but the genesis of Andersen's great discovery is hardly understandable if we do not presume that Andersen was deeply read in the Grimms. There is a puzzling lack of references to the Grimms in Andersen's writings in the period leading up to his debut in 1835. This could be interpreted as a lack of interest on Andersen's part, but this is clearly not the case. Andersen's art form in 1835 exhibits deep immersion in the Grimm tales while "Dødningen" from 1830 does not. There may be a number of reasons why Andersen refrains from mentioning the Grimms, but I think there is one important explanation which has to do with canon formation. Andersen wants to carve out a place for his own fairy tale art by suggesting that there is a deep link between his fairy tales, his childhood and the Danish folk imaginary, but in this way Andersen refrains from telling who his true literary fathers were, namely the Grimms. Before this argument is presented let us consider how Mathias Winther tried to produce the foundation of a distinct Danish folk tale tradition by also keeping silent about the Grimms.

Arguably the best case study for discussing how quickly the aesthetics of the Grimms' narrative art became dominant among Danish critics, collectors and poets is an involuntary one. Mathias Winther's *Danish Folk Tales* (*Danske Folkeeventyr*, 1823) has an ambiguous stature in Danish literary history. Erik Dal, a Danish Andersen scholar, writes in his postscript to a collection of Danish folk poetry from 1965 that Winther's collection may contain "silent loans from German poetry and folklore" (Dal 1965, 360), but argues that it is not fair that Winther's work has disappeared from Danish histories of literature. Dal is sympathetic to Winther, but the main reason why Winther has been neglected is most likely this: Some of his so-called Danish fairy tales bear the impression of being rewritings of German textual sources rather than his written records of Danish oral sources, as Winther claims many of them were. Winther is also clearly anticipating critique in his foreword:

> "If you are, dear reader, a book learned man, and take my present in your hand to take apart the single stories with a jealous regard or you wish to speak a word with the publisher, then I must ask you to be lenient" (Winther 1823, xv).

In her article on the early history of the Danish reception of the Grimms Karin Pulmer notices that Winther does not even mention the Grimm collection in his detailed (and book learned) notes at the end of his collection even though, for example, his first tale "Pandekagehuset" ("The Pancake House") is undoubtedly a revision of "Hansel and Gretel" ("Hänsel und Gretel," 1812) as Dal and Pulmer have also stated (Dal 1965, 360; Pulmer 1988, 188). Considering Winther's evident in-depth knowledge of German romantic collectors and literature in general it is highly unlikely that he was not familiar with both the German original as well as the Danish translation from 1821. Winther's narrative tone is also clearly influenced by the Grimms. As Pulmer says, Winther's tales exhibit "unmistakable traces of Grimms' fairy tale tone" (1988, 189).

Pulmer's argument can be extended to its logical conclusion: Winther consciously chose to make no reference to his knowledge of and debt to the Grimms and their collection. But why? Most likely for the obvious reason that this would render Winther's claim that there was a unique Danish folk tale tradition more problematic. This is not to say that there was not a community of oral tale tellers in Denmark in either Andersen's youth or in the 1820's when Winther supposedly gathered his folk tales. I only want to point out that Winther without any doubt used his readings of German collections of tales, and especially the Grimms, when producing his texts. In this particular sense the Grimm collection was the elephant in Winther's Danish folk tale room, but it is also the elephant in Andersen's fairy tale debut from 1835. "The Tinderbox" and "Little Claus and Big Claus" are in my opinion inconceivable without Andersen's study of the Grimm collection.

There is a striking similarity between Winther's lack of acknowledgement of his indebtedness to the Grimms and Andersen's selfsame as he composes his remarks in 1837 on his first fairy tales. In his foreword Winther writes:

> Dear reader! I bring you here quite a few strange fairy tales. But you should not expect to read modern decorated stories that satisfy the taste of the time; since when I walked around in the field or sat at the hearth during a long winter evening in a farmer's room, I heard several of them as an honest farmer or old woman could tell them to me. Then I began to feel soft-hearted and started thinking of my childhood when my wet nurse told me something similar and I thought it may very well be worthwhile to write down what I have heard and collect more. (Winther 1823, xi)

In his intro remark to his first fairy tale from 1830 as well as in his remarks "To the Older Readers" from 1837 Andersen also relates the origin of his fairy tales to his childhood. Both Winther and Andersen use the reference to the stories told in their childhood as a defence against coming clean with their readers of their debt to the Grimms. They were both trying to create an independent Danish tradition of fairy tales. Whereas Winther clearly modelled himself on the German romantic collector, Andersen was of course an independent writer who cared about fairy tales like many of his romantic contemporaries. In fact, Winther and Andersen worked in much the same way, but with extremely different results. Winther rewrote Grimm while carefully avoiding any example of explicit borrowing from the German fairy tales while Andersen also rewrote Grimm, but did not bother to avoid explicit traces of indebtedness. While Winther tried to produce a narrative tone in Danish very close to the Grimms', Andersen wanted to find his own independent voice by using advanced rhetorical strategies, among others phantasmagoria and pseudo-naïve irony. They both wanted to inaugurate their own new Danish canon of fairy tales, but their achievements could not have been further apart in terms of aesthetic merit.

When Andersen wrote that he had begun composing fairy tales in order to win the coming generations for his literary art, his intended community of readers was the same that had fostered the ever-expanding European fan base of Grimms' tales. The most important insight this study has sought to convey is that this dream is embedded in the way Andersen rhetorically swerves from the Grimms. Just like the Grimms witnessed their massive transnational success Andersen lived to see his dream come through. Andersen knew in early 1835 that there was no way of avoiding the Grimms if he was to have a European and even worldwide community of (parent) readers.

References

Andersen, Hans Christian. 1990. *Kommentar*. Edited by Flemming Hovmann and Erling Nielsen. Vol. 7 of *H.C. Andersens Eventyr*, edited by Erik Dal. København: Reitzel, 1963–90.

Andersen, Hans Christian. 2003–07. *Andersen. H.C. Andersens samlede værker*. Edited by Klaus P. Mortensen. 18 vols. København: Det Danske Sprog- og Litteraturselskab/Gyldendal.

Andersen, Hans Christian. (1830) 2015. "The Spectre, A Funen Folktale." ["Dødningen. Et fynsk Folkeeventyr." Translated by John Irons in 2015 for the Hans Christian Andersen Centre at the University of Southern Denmark]. http://andersen.sdu.dk/moocfiles/spectre.pdf

Bloom, Harold. (1973) 1997. *The Anxiety of Influence*. 2nd ed. Oxford: Oxford University Press.

Bottigheimer, Ruth B. 2009. *Fairy Tales: A New History*. Albany: State University of New York Press.

Clausen, Julius. 1907. "Acht Briefe von Jacob Grimm an Chr. Molbech." *Euphorion: Zeitschrift für Literaturgeschichte* 14: 587–595.

Dal, Erik, ed. 1965. *Dansk Folkedigtning*. København: Gyldendal.

Dollerup, Cay. 1999. *Tales and Translation. The Grimm Tales from Pan-Germanic narratives to shared international fairytales*. Amsterdam/Philadelphia: John Benjamins Publishing Company.

François, Cyrille. 2017. *Les Voix des contes: stratégies narratives et projets discursifs des contes de Perrault, Grimm et Andersen*. Mythographies et sociétés 542. Clermont-Ferrand: Presses Universitaires Blaise Pascal.

Grimm, Brüder (Jacob u. Wilhelm). 1819. *Kinder- und Haus-Märchen. Zweite vermehrte und verbesserte Auflage*. 3rd vol., 1822. Berlin: G. Reimer.

Grimm, Jacob. 1821. *FolkeEventyr samlede af Brødrene Grimm*. Translated by Johan Frederik Lindencrone. København: C.H. Nøer.

Grimm, Jacob. 1884. *Grimms' Household Tales*. 2 vols. Translated and edited by Margaret Hunt. London: George Bell.

Hanck, Henriette. 1942. *H.C. Andersens Brevveksling med Henriette Hanck. 1830-1846*. Edited by Svend Larsen. *Anderseniana* X, 2. Published by H.C. Andersen Samfundet. København: Ejnar Munksgaard.

Molbech, Christian (anonymous). 1830. "Review" in the journal *Maanedsskrift for Litteratur* 3: 162–172.

Molbech, Christian. 1832. *Dansk Læsebog i Prosa til Brug ved Sprogundervisning i Modersmaalet, særdeles for Mellemklasser i Skolerne*. København: C. A. Reitzel.

Mylius, Johan de. 2004. "Orality – Reinvented or Invented." Paper presented at the conference *Memory and Mediation. European Narratives of Identity*, SDU, 2004. http://www2.lingue.unibo.it/acume/acumedvd/Essays%20ACUME/DeMylius.pdf

Pulmer, Karin. 1988: "Zur Rezeption der Grimmschen Märchen in Dänemark," in *Brüder Grimm Gedenken. Band 8*, published by Ludwig Denecke, 181–203. Marburg: N.G. Elwert.

Riise, J. Chr. 1834. "Bibliothek for Ungdommen." *Kjøbenhavns kongelig alene privilegerede Adressecomptoirs Efterretninger* 36 (306): unpaginated.

Straparola, Giovan Francesco. 2015. *The Pleasant Nights*. Edited and translated by Suzanne Magnanini. Toronto: Iter Academic Press.

Topsøe-Jensen, Helge. 1971. *Buket til Andersen. Bemærkninger til 25 eventyr*. København: Gad.

Zipes, Jack. 2015. *Grimm Legacies: The magic Spell of the Grimms' Folk and Fairy Tales*. Princeton, NJ: Princeton University Press.

Warner, Marina. 2008. *Phantasmagoria: Spirit Visions, Metaphors, and Media into the Twenty-first Century*. Oxford: Oxford University Press.

Winther, Mathias. 1823. *Danske Folkeeventyr. Samlede af M. Winther*. København: Wahlske Boghandlings Forlag.

Winther, Mathias. 1989. *Danish Folk Tales*. Edited and translated by T. Sands and J. Massengale. Madison, Wisconsin: University of Wisconsin.

Notes

1. If not otherwise stated, I have translated all Danish and German quotes.
2. This particular fairy tale was not translated by Jean Hersholt. By permission of John Irons I have been allowed to use his translation which is as yet unpublished.

Word and Image in Hans Christian Andersen's Papercuts

Ejnar Stig Askgaard
Odense City Museums

Is it possible to compare Hans Christian Andersen's literary works and his visual art in order to find similarities between the two art forms? Since Andersen became an object for studies in the Humanities, the main focus has been on his literary works – even though the author throughout his life and alongside with his writings created numerous works of visual art. This chapter will focus on Andersen's papercuts and show how word and image are closely linked together and based on a tradition popular in folk culture, which Andersen was very familiar with from his childhood.

While Hans Christian Andersen's preserved visual art works evolve in parallel with his authorship from the beginning in 1822 to his death in 1875, several years were to pass after Andersen's death before the public was made aware that the poet also produced visual art: His authorship was a public matter, but his visual arts was considered as more of a private affair.

Surprisingly little has been written on Andersen's visual art works although there are numerous papercuts, drawings and collages in existence. The latter art form can mainly be found in the picture books Andersen composed for the children of the families he felt most attached to. Kjeld Heltoft's two monographic studies from 1969 and 1972 remain the only full volumes dedicated to Andersen's visual art forms in Danish. In English, the single monographic study of the papercuts has been written by Beth Wagner Brust in 1994. Two of Andersen's picture books to Christine Stampe and her sister Astrid Stampe have been published in photographically reprinted editions with commentaries in 1984 and 2003.

Except from these studies Andersen's visual arts have only been studied sporadically in the scholarly tradition. In museum exhibitions on Andersen his visual arts also tend to be regarded as something eccentric and peripheral to his artistic achievement. Nevertheless, the rich material bears witness to the fact that Andersen was deeply engaged in visual arts throughout his life. A study of this material will hopefully not only offer a more nuanced and complex picture of Andersen to the reader, but also contribute to an appreciation of certain artistic techniques which can also be found in Andersen's written works.

Andersen's visual works can be divided into three groups: papercuts, drawings and collages. These three groups can be further specified in terms of chronology. The collages came into being between the 1850s and 1874. Andersen tended to work on drawings in certain periods of time, 1830–33, 1833–34, and 1840–41. In contrast, Andersen produced papercuts continuously during his whole life. The first preserved papercut is from 1822 while the last one was made in 1874, the year before Andersen died. As such, papercuts remained a constant preoccupation for Andersen in his life. One may therefore presume that the artistic techniques Andersen used in producing his papercuts remained stable. For this reason, the papercuts are remarkable. In the following sections, Andersen's papercuts will thus be discussed closely.

The Papercuts

When Andersen died on August 4, 1875, there were no papercuts in his estate since he did not collect them. They often came into being in social settings where he as a *maître de plaisir* entertained a group of people while producing them. At his death Andersen's papercuts were thus scattered in numerous homes in Denmark and the rest of Europe. For this reason, we cannot know exactly how many have been preserved. Presumably many of them can still be found in private ownership and some have most likely been destroyed.

With the inauguration of the Hans Christian Andersen Museum in Odense in 1905 an effort to collect the poet's visual work commenced. The museum now holds the largest collection of Andersen's art. 176 papercuts have been preserved in public Danish ownership, and if one includes the papercuts which were glued to the pages of the picture books for children, the estimate goes up to around 400. This is a sizeable amount, but still not equivalent to the mistaken numbers of a 1000 and even 1500 papercuts one may find in scholarly works on Andersen.[1]

The Social Space

As a writer Andersen normally wrote alone. A study of Andersen's papercuts therefore offers us knowledge of a different aspect of his artistic capabilities in that they were made in an intimate social setting. We know from reading Andersen's diaries and letters and other writers' memoirs of Andersen that he appreciated social gatherings. Evenings in Copenhagen were, for example, often fully reserved for dinners except Sundays which Andersen wanted to have at his free disposition. Being a bachelor, Andersen's intense writing sessions were performed solitarily, unless he was travelling. Andersen was perceived as a highly interesting guest who could entertain an entire company, relating anecdotes, reading manuscripts aloud and performing other artistic activities such as producing papercuts with his scissors. Andersen also enjoyed the companionship. He liked to converse and found it joyful to narrate his tales. It was also useful for Andersen to hear reactions from his audience so that he could improve his texts before publication. In fact, several of Andersen's fairy tales, including "The Emperor's New Clothes" ("Keiserens nye Klæder," 1837) and "Psyche" ("Psychen," 1862), received their final form only after he had read them aloud to friends and acquaintances.

Andersen's literary art form was of course intimately connected to the printing press. By means of the book Andersen attained a wide dissemination and high esteem, but his readership remained amorphous and anonymous. The published book as medium barred Andersen from dialogue and the human presence of the spoken word. It is worth remembering that Andersen's first series of published fairy tales are "told." All his fairy tale collections from 1835–42 were subtitled "told to children." Andersen's fairy tale narrators often address readers directly and his rhetorical art is particularly rich in onomatopoetic words and linguistic double meanings which are only accessible audibly. These writer's strategies can be seen as Andersen's poetic effort to establish a spoken presence with his unknown readers. Andersen was a child of folk culture and as such he grew up in a culture dominated by the oral tradition. It is this oral folk culture which Andersen in different ways tries to reestablish in his literary works.

Andersen papercuts are in this respect highly interesting. Whereas Andersen wrote in a solitary setting, his papercuts were formed and created through direct interaction with other people. They were produced in a social space. They can therefore be regarded as graphic reminiscences of a cultural tradition which is much closer related to folk oral culture than the written word and the book medium.

There are several memoirs which contain information on how Andersen's worked on his papercuts. Rigmor Stampe (1850–1923), the big sister to the aforementioned Astrid and Christine Stampe, recalls in her memoirs from 1918 how Andersen produced his papercuts:

> All Andersen's cuttings played a big role for our family's children. While Andersen was seated and talking, he folded a piece of paper and let his scissors run through it in winding movements. He then refolded the paper and there were the finished figures. They were so to speak little fairy tales, not in the sense that they were illustrations of his written fairy tales, but rather expressions of the same phantasy as you can find in these. One immediately recognises Andersen in them. They do not appear as other papercuts, but they do look alike. As in his poetry he kept reusing certain motives: castles, swans, pixies, angels, cupids, and other phantasy figures, many hearts, a dead man hanging in the gallows, a chamberlain with a key, a mill in the shape of a man – the wings being his arms and legs – and many others. He cut them for the children of the families he visited, but often the adults also received some. (133)[2]

Josefa Dürck-Kaulbach (1851-1936), daughter of the German history painter Wilhelm von Kaulbach, also offers a beautiful reminiscence of Andersen in the midst of a social gathering where where he makes his papercuts:

> After dinner the writer – who did not smoke – retired with us ladies to the salon and asked for a pair of scissors and a large sheet of paper. The latter he folded a number of times with great care with his soft and flexible fingers and then cut out with great skills the most charming things, which he distributed amongst us. While doing so, he told us about his life, then involuntarily (as it seemed) leaving the terra firma of existence and float-

ing off into the land of fairy tales, carrying all of us with him on his wings. Then he told us how he had often sat by the seashore and looked into the water. Once, he had walked far out along a jetty and seen a shipwreck deep down in the water where fishes swam in and out. Then he had noticed how a huge creature dragged something along with it in its mouth, unwilling to share the thing with others. When he looked more closely, he saw it was a small golden crown – and now his imagination took over and image upon image unfurled. We sat listening breathlessly. Some of us were in tears since our writer, sitting there in front of us directing the scissors with his restless fingers as he cut out ballet dancers, engaged us in so many sad experiences. When he had ended his story (or did it end because he had finished cutting the paper?), he spread out a whole series of cut-out ballet girls in front of us who were holding each other by the hand, their feet in the air. Andersen was delighted at the success of his venture. He took more pleasure in our amazement of his papercut than in the impression his story had made on us. (1921, 108)[3]

We are made aware in these interesting recollections that Andersen's papercuts were made in a short time since he narrated a tale while he let "his scissors run." The content of the tale – as it appears in Kaulbach's description – is to begin with presented realistically and then Andersen transforms it into the realm of the fantastic while producing a copious number of pictures – "Bild um Bild" – as the German original phrasing states. Andersen, then, elegantly stops the narrative at the same time as he is done with his papercut which he unfolds for everyone to see. This can be compared to how Andersen begins his narration of "The Snow Queen" ("Sneedronningen," 1845): "Now then! We will begin. When the story is done you shall know a great deal more than you do know." His audience may well see the pair of scissors in function, but they did not know what the outcome would look like before Andersen stops using the scissors and shows them what sort of figure he has brought to life. Stampe's and Kaulbach's way of characterising Andersen's papercutting technique can be compared to how princess Helene von Racowitza described Andersen's paper work in her memoir from 1909:

> He turned everything into a fairy tale. It was even more fascinating when he revealed himself as the "Student of little Ida's flowers"; that is to say, while he was telling stories, he cut out the most fascinating things with

scissors – castles, gardens, flowers and butterflies, elves and gnomes – in fact, all kinds of wonders. For many years I treasured a butterfly on whose outspread wings a fairy danced. (1910, 24 [1909, 16f.])

Thus, there seems to be a connection between language and image in Andersen's papercut art form. The papercuts were made at the same time as he was telling a story. The simplicity of the papercuts tells us that the relation between the papercuts and the story was of a more symbolic kind rather than purely illustrative and descriptive. Many of the papercuts appear bizarre because the original context in which they were produced remains unknown. When Andersen on August 18, 1850, was engaged in cutting paper models for the children of Georg Frederik Wilhelm Lund, the father made a notice of the names of the cuts. The strange looking woman is called "Female devil who eats little children," but although this is highly interesting information, we unfortunately do not know anything about the story told. In fact, the titles of Andersen's papercuts remain unknown more often than not. Therefore, the demonic figure who looks like a woman with four breasts (or maybe rather a jester dressed in his particular costume) also appears enigmatic to us today.

Andersen's papercuts should not be seen as mere decoration. The art works meant something, and they could also be of use. When his swan and ballerina papercuts were placed on a table, they could move across it when somebody blew on them. This is what the daughter of the author Carsten Hauch, Marie Rørdam (1834–1915), tells in her memoir. During his visit to B.S. Ingemann in Sorø, Andersen would also often visit the Hauchs: "For us it was a big event to see him [Andersen]. He would cut the loveliest things in paper: Churches with high towers, dancers who could stand up by themselves and when you blew on them it looked like they danced, also dervishes and other figures." (Rørdam 1911, 38). Also, baroness Bodild von Donner (1852–1927) wrote in 1926: "When I was a child I was delighted when he cut out chains of little dolls in white paper that I could put on the table and blow on so they would move forwards." (*Anderseniana* 1938, 312f.).

Andersen also cut so-called "Dolls" for the Christmas tree. These large human figures with colorful dresses made out of glazed paper were his original inventions. In the fairy tale "The Fir Tree" ("Grantræet," 1845) Andersen mentions them:

Female devil who eats little children. Papercut by Hans Christian Andersen from August 18, 1850. The Hans Christian Andersen Museum.

Figure with breasts or costume? Papercut by Hans Christian Andersen from Nørre Vosborg, 1859. The Hans Christian Andersen Museum.

Bootjack. Christmas tree decoration made by Hans Christian Andersen for the Ørsted family's Christmas tree, undated but before 1850. The Hans Christian Andersen Museum.

The first known papercut by Andersen. A soldier – perhaps for a doll theatre, made for the Hjort family in Sorø 1822. The Hans Christian Andersen Museum.

Then two servants came in fine livery and carried the fir tree into a big splendid drawing-room [...]. The servants and even the young ladies helped it on with its fine decorations [...]. Among its green branches swayed dolls that it took to be real living people, for the tree had never seen their like before. And up at its very top was set a large gold tinsel star. It was splendid, I tell you, splendid beyond all words!

Even though the dolls were cut for the Christmas tree, the children were of course free to play with them. The design of the dolls may very well be closely related to the dolls Andersen made as a child for his puppetry. In a letter from Christmas 1857 Andersen's friend Henriette Wulff, whom he had known since 1822, also mentions the dolls: "When you write that you have made doll papercuts for the Christmas tree, I find it difficult to express the strange feeling of longing for the time we spent together, *far far* back, when you cut for us *quasi* children at the academy." (Andersen 1959, 2:354).[4] It seems possible that Andersen was already engaged in papercutting as a child. His favourite childhood amusement was to play with his puppetry which his poor father had made for him. And the cobbler's son of course made the dolls himself. He had easy access to the tools needed in his father's workshop. The oldest preserved papercut by Andersen is from 1822 and represents a soldier who may have been part of a puppetry.

The Characteristics of the Papercuts

Andersen's papercuts have certain characteristics. Almost all of them are made out of one piece of folded paper and, likewise, most of them have only one symmetry axis. As a highly skilled improviser Andersen produced such papercuts in social gatherings where it was convenient for him to make them by use of only one symmetry axis. In this way he could do the whole work with half the effort and in half the time. There are also papercuts made by Andersen which have more than one symmetry axis. One symmetry axis produces two mirror images whereas more axes create a cross point at the intersection where they meet. The attention of the viewer is drawn to this point and the individual motives in the periphery appear to revolve around this alluring centre. It is as if the motives enclose themselves around something unknown similar to the coloured glass grains in a kaleidoscope. Some of these papercuts could be used as bouquet holders that is as an

Hans Christian Andersen's bouquet holder for Maria (von) Moltke (1809–95) made around 1849 at the manor house of Glorup. Notice that the countess' initials "M v M" have been cut out beneath the female figures.

exquisite napkin which could be folded around the bouquet so as to hide the flower stems. When used as a bouquet holder the cross point becomes the focal point which engulfs the lower parts of the bouquet.

In his 50s Andersen began creating large and complex papercuts full of motives represented in a kaleidoscopic fashion. Andersen entitled these large-scale arabesques "cut-out fairy tales." This was most likely not because the papercut depicted a specific fairy tale, but rather because the motives evoked a fairy tale-like atmosphere. The so-called Melchior papercut, which the sick Andersen made in 1874 for his close friend Dorothea Melchior, includes 17 mirrored motives. The papercut, which was Andersen's last big papercut, conjures a wistful mood. The central motive is a crucifix and the papercut's four corners are tragedy masks. The tragedy masks are also dominant in terms of numbers compared to the other figures, thereby strengthening the dark mood of the art work. The two skulls left of the crucifix at the center of the papercut make it clear that Andersen intended his last big papercut as a memento mori.

The Melchior papercut, 1874. Hans Christian Andersen's House.

The Traditions of the Papercut

Today we do not think much about how Andersen's papercuts were made. It seems natural to us that a papercut is made by cutting a folded piece of paper. However, Andersen's contemporaries considered his papercuts to be strange.[5] They did not resemble the typical and cherished papercut of his time, the silhouette, which can be defined as the non-mirrored shadow picture of a human, a face profile or a scenery. The tradition is named after Étienne de Silhouette who was in charge of tax collection in France during the reign of Louis XV of France. Mr. Silhouette had silhouettes of his friends hanging on the walls of his castle. This fact and the fact that much anger was directed at him due to his work as a tax collector caused people to link his surname with the shadow pictures as a sort of disdain for the art form which was at this time regarded as inferior.

The decision by the French Academy in 1835 to adopt his surname as the official designation for a shadow picture makes it clear that the silhouette was not despised in Andersen's time. The shadow picture excels in its objective and proportional accuracy in demarking contours. One may argue that there is a direct line from renaissance work on linear perspective around 1450 to camera obscura and the photo camera which Andersen was fascinated by. A constant is integral to shadow pictures in the sense that the contours are delineated by light. It is humans who mark and cut the silhouette, but the line which the light draws is objective, a word still used for the most important component of the photo camera: the lens.

Bonding Letters

Andersen's papercuts do not have anything in common with the art of the silhouette. It is, however, connected to a certain tradition which is almost forgotten today. The tradition of the so-called "bonding letter" ("bindebrev") dates back to the 16th century.[6] In Andersen's time the tradition was kept alive solely among common people.

The typical bonding letter was a cut-out arabesque with for example string ornaments, cut-out figures, animals and plants. Along the string labyrinth or at the centre of the bonding letter one would often find a "bonding verse" written – a descriptive or mysterious poem which would often refer to the visual appearance of the arabesque or bind the receiver of the bonding letter to the sender's wish or request. The string ornaments symbolise the inextricable knot and the bonding letter was normally provided with a silk thread full of knots which the receiver of the gift would barely be able to untie. The bond, which the bonding letter and the knot string expressed, was interpreted as a kind of magic link to which the receiver was bound. The notion of the magic knot is older than the bonding letter and can be found far back in Western culture. It forms a central part of the anecdote of Alexander and the Gordian knot which he solves in a dramatic - and at the same time simple – way.

When the Viking king Harald Bluetooth introduced Christianity in Denmark in 966 he let a rune stone be carved to commemorate the conversion of the Danes. The carvings on the large Jelling stone, as it is called, shows us the crucified Christ who is tied in a knot string arrangement which, similar to a rubber band, does not have a begin-

The Large Jelling Stone.
Photo: Roberto Fortuna.

ning or end. In this way it was made visually clear to everyone that the kingdom was "bound" to the new faith.

This knot string "mystique" – the idea that you can tie wishes and demands in a knot - was also frequent in the 18th century. The receiver of a bonding letter in this period was typically bound to hold a feast. The knot could also concern love demands. One was allowed to free oneself from the bond if the person in question could solve the knot or the riddle which was tied to the verse. In a Danish context the bonding letter magic has now become a harmless tradition. At Easter, people send anonymous and exquisite papercuts to each other that contain some kind of verse. If you do not guess the name of the sender implied in the verse you have to give the sender a chocolate egg. The bonding letter was not so toothless in Andersen's time. One tied one's wishes and hopes to the knot. In the fairy tale "The Snowdrop" ("Sommergjækken," 1863) the tragic narrative is based on the fact that the receiver of the love bonding letter is faithless: At the end the young man who was supposed to be bound as the boyfriend to a young girl

Bonding letter to Peder Hansen in Myllerup from Else Jørgensen in Hesle on the name day February 22 ("Peter's chair"), 1853. Odense City Museums.

is left shaken and hurt when she in spite of her letter chooses another lover. Andersen was familiar with the bonding letter and knot string tradition from his childhood in Odense where his father was known and respected for his bonding letters.[7] Unfortunately none of his letters have been preserved.

There is a striking similarity between Andersen's large arabesques and those bonding letters made by his contemporaries which have

Andersen arabesque from 1864, which was sold to the benefit of those families who lost relatives during the 1864 War against Prussia. The verse in the middle binds the buyer of the letter to be generous. Hans Christian Andersen's House.

been preserved. Both are characterised by unbroken and closed tracery. Andersen would also often write a verse at the centre. In the example above, the buyer of the papercut is bound by the verse to be generous towards those who have lost relatives in the war in 1864.

Playful Riddles and Intermediality

Many of Hans Christian Andersen's more simple papercuts also contain a playful riddle which is embedded in the imagery. This is why Andersen's papercuts in their simplicity assume the character of a symbol or a logogram or semiogram like the Egyptian hieroglyphs. Whereas the art of the silhouette has realistic proportions and naturalistic representations, no such thing is to be found in Andersen's papercuts. On the contrary. Andersen did not seek out realistic representations. His papercuts rather appear unrealistic: Neither a pierrot nor a dancer can stand on a swan or the wings of a butterfly. When interpreting the papercuts it is important to use another conceptual approach where the hierarchical dimensions between words, material, expression and appearance are taken into account.

Andersen's paper cutting can be regarded as an intermedial art form in the sense that it combines and is formed by other art forms. Intermediality has been known for quite some time.[8] Many linguistic descriptions and metaphors are, for example, characterised by synesthesia, that is their connection to different sensory modalities. The German romanticists Friedrich Schlegel and Novalis conceptualised the idea of a universal poetry which would be marked by a desire to transgress the boundaries of poetry and reach the realms of music and painting.[9] In our time, theories of intermediality have gained traction in the Humanities and new insights have thereby been formulated (Heitmann 2003; Sanders 1997; Müller-Wille 2017). In terms of Andersen's papercuts one can perceive their intermedial aspect in the way they address our perceptions of visual art and language, visual art and poetry. In other words, there is a crucial element of interplay between word and image in Andersen's papercuts.

Andersen's papercuts are not insignificant ornaments. They contain a message that can be decrypted in a similar way to hieroglyphs in which the motive can be decoded iconographically, phonetically and metaphorically. In the act of interpretation, the meaning of the papercuts comes alive. We may at the same time get an insight into the conceptual thought behind the work and how Andersen conceived and made use of language. In the following some examples will be discussed which encapsulate Andersen's use of signs and his knowledge of the different layers of consciousness.

The head of flower. Papercut to Mathilde Ørsted, year unknown. Hans Christian Andersen's House.

This papercut, which represents a face with petals, contains a little riddle. The papercut can be decoded as a simple rebus: the motive as a whole forms the word 'flower head.' It is the two motives' ideograms which in their composition produce the word.

The newspapercut, which depicts a man with a large broad-brimmed hat, is a Brazilian. In decoding the cut-out it is helpful, of course, that the word "Brazil" is printed in bold gothic on the hat. In interpreting the meaning of the papercut our attention should be drawn towards the motive (a man) in combination with the material dimension of the papercut (a newspaper). From a newspaper article on Brazil Andersen has cut the shape of a man so that we see him standing there in the middle of the events beneath the country's sun.

The papercut of a man who holds a board which is filled with things is a fine image of a so-called plaster maker who carries his goods on a board over his head. The plaster makers, who produced and sold artifacts made of plaster, were common in Andersen's time. In a letter novel by F.C. Sibbern from 1826 one of these are mentioned: "This morning [...] I saw down the road [...] a plaster maker with his long board on his head." ([1826] 1851, 240). Andersen's plaster maker seems, though, burdened by the weight of the board. One could therefore decode the motive as a version of Atlas who according to the Greek myth upholds the whole world. Another possible decoding would be to regard the papercut as the visual equivalent the idiomatic

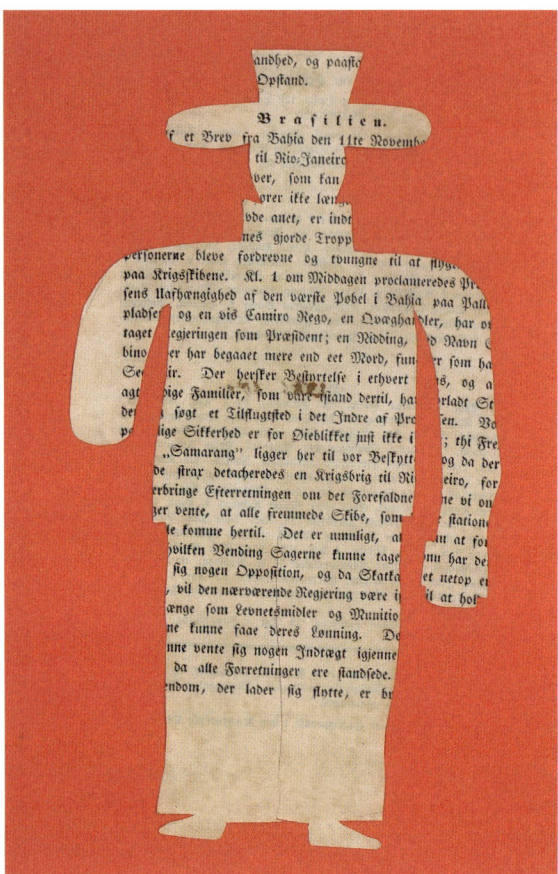

The Brazilian. Newspaper cut by Hans Christian Andersen for the editor Liunge's daughter Louise (born 1830), year unknown. Hans Christian Andersen's House.

expression: "The world turned on its head." Such visualisations of idioms were much appreciated in Copenhagen in the 1830s and were referred to by the German word "Krähwinkel" which has a slightly different meaning in German.

In another papercut two dancers or elf girls are balancing on the wings of a butterfly. This image can be decoded as Psyche who in Greek mythology is associated with womanhood and butterflies. Andersen liked to adorn his flower bouquets with this motive which allegorically represents the soul. In Christian symbolism the three stages of the butterfly (caterpillar, cocoon, butterfly) represent life, death and resurrection. This is the reason why the butterfly is often found as an ornament on tombstones where it symbolizes immortality. In his papercut Andersen combines the motive of the butterfly with female

Plaster maker. Papercut by Hans Christian Andersen for the Castenschiold family from the manor Borreby, year unknown. Hans Christian Andersen's House.

Psyche. Papercut by Hans Christian Andersen to Mathilde Ørsted. Hans Christian Andersen's House.

The Mill Man. Papercut by Hans Christian Andersen, year unknown. Hans Christian Andersen's House.

figures thereby relating it to the myth of Psyche and thus to the idea of the immortal soul. Andersen did not believe in the resurrection of the body, but he did have faith in the immortality of the soul. In the poem "The Old Man" ("Oldingen") belief this is clearly expressed:

> Each soul God has created in his image
> Is indestructible, cannot be lost,
> Our life on earth is the seed of eternity,
> Our body dies, but the soul cannot die!
> (1874, 7f.)

Andersen chose these verses for his tombstone in Assistens Churchyard.

The interplay between word and picture is clearly present in the papercut "The Mill Man" ("Møllemand"). This motive is frequent in Andersen's visual art. In this example the wind mill is cut out so it looks like a man. The man's arms are the wind mill's wings, but if you look carefully you will realise that there are no hands at the end of his arms. Rather Andersen has provided the man with pens instead of hands. In Danish a miller is also called a "maler" ("painter") in the sense that he grinds (maler) corn. This double meaning is evident in the papercut. The mill port can be opened so that everyone can see

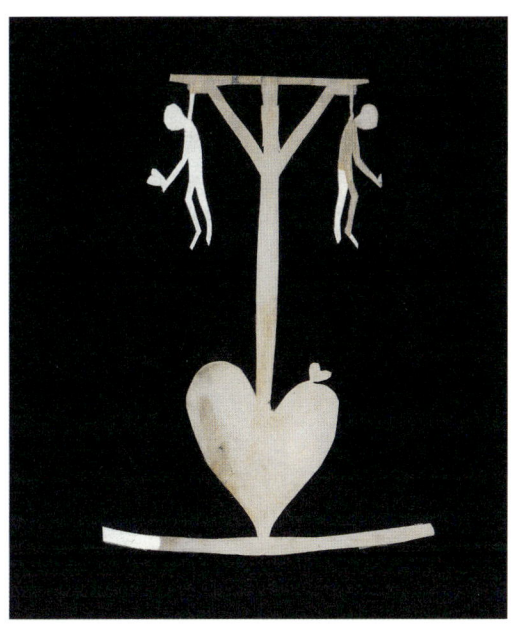

Thief of hearts. Papercut by Hans Christian Andersen to the Serre family at the manor house of Maxen, Dresden. Hans Christian Andersen's House.

what the mill man has been painting. A privately owned papercut has been preserved where Andersen's friend, the art painter Carl Bloch, has drawn a little face for everyone to see when the port is opened.

These examples show how it is possible to comprehend Andersen's mysterious choice of motives and style. As discussed, a fundamental aspect of Andersen's papercuts is the mirroring which he produces by cutting along a symmetry axis. Andersen's exploration of the possibilities of mirroring is an important part of his play with the relations between images and words. Some of his papercuts can be interpreted easily like a simple rebus, but others are far more demanding. In fact it is often crucial to focus on the mirroring when interpreting the semantic field between word and image.

The papercut "Thief of Hearts" ("Hjertetyven") is a beautiful example of this. At first sight the papercut appears symmetric, but the motive of the two hanged men contains a crucial asymmetric detail. Andersen has cut out the heart held by one of the men and while cutting the large heart on which the gallow is placed Andersen has cut another heart so it looks like the man has dropped the one he was holding. 'Thief of hearts' is Andersen's synonym for Amor, the god of love who steals somebody's heart and gives it to someone else. In his poem "Thief of Hearts" ("Hjertetyven") from 1831 Andersen ironically calls Amor "a thief who should be hanged." (Andersen 1831, 44) The man who still holds a heart in his hand can thus be interpreted as Amor. The other man, however, has, as the Danish idiom states, "lost his heart" and due to unrequited love has committed suicide. The exquisite asymmetry of this papercut incites the viewer to reflect on two different love narratives; one is about those who strikes with love, the other deals with people struck by love.

Ambivalence, Mirroring and Duality

Hans Christian Andersen's papercuts are expressions of an artistic sensibility which joyfully works in ambivalence. When one considers the fact that Andersen produced papercuts during all his writer's life it is reasonable to presume that one can find many similarities between Andersen's ambiguous papercut art and his literary art. That this is so has been demonstrated by Andersen studies (Kofoed 1967; Bøggild 2012). In this context it is important to point out that Andersen's papercuts really do contain this characteristic. In his article "From Word to Picture – and Back" ("Vom Wort zum Bild – und retour") Edgar Pankow writes:

> It is seldom that poets who dare to change media and move from word to picture decide to do so solely out of sense of productive abundance. Changes of media are always also a sign of an experience of deficiency: an interruption of communication, an aesthetic incompatibility, a psychological resistance. They do not just work additively by simply adding the image to the word or the word to the image. Changes in media establish relations and interspaces which did not exist before. They open up roads and detours and offer new artistic possibilities albeit at the price of new complications. (2013, 334)

In the transition from word to image one can find traces of words, Pankow argues, and adds: "Poets do not abandon words when they act as painters and designers. Rather the engagement with imagery reacts with the engagement with words." (334).

Andersen's use of rhetorical ambivalence in his fairy tales is capable of entertaining and rousing thoughts among both children and adults. Rereading the fairy tales, one discovers new depths which one was overlooked when reading them the first time. The humour of ambivalence - from simple jokes to complex and stark ironies – is an extraordinary aspect of them. The complex effects of this is the reason why they can be enjoyed by all ages. Even though translations cannot adequately cover the full range of Andersen's Danish semantics, his narrative art, which is so full of ambivalent images, do cause readers from different cultures to ponder the stories over and over again.

A Poet for All Ages

Shortly before his death, when he was lying sick in bed in Dorothea Melchior's country house "Solitude," Hans Christian Andersen reflected on his fairy tales in a letter to his young friend Johan Collin the younger:

> My goal has been to be a poet for all ages [...]. The naïve was only a part of the fairy tales. Humour, on the other hand, was the real salt in them, and the fact that my written language was built on the vernacular is related to my Danishness. (1875)

In order to be able to write "for all ages" an author must be able to write with two tongues, so to say. Andersen was constantly capable of exploring double meanings between language and image. In all of his fairy tales readers find dualities and mirror effects. This is also an omnipresent characteristic of his papercuts.

Note: All illustrations in this chapter have been published with permission from Odense City Museums.

References

Andersen, Hans Christian. 1831. *Phantasier og Skizzzeer*. København: Forfatterens Forlag.

Andersen, Hans Christian. 1874. "Oldingen" [The Old Man]. *Julebog 1874*. By Karl Schmidt. Odense.

Andersen, Hans Christian. 1875. Letter from Hans Christian Andersen to Jonas Collin, June 6, 1875. The Royal Library, Den collinske Brevsamling XV–XVI; Fasc. 4. Transcription by Ejnar Stig Askgaard. Unpublished.

Andersen, Hans Christian. 1959. Letter from Henriette Wulff, December 23, 1857. In *H.C. Andersen og Henriette Wulff. En Brevveksling*. 3 vols. Edited by H. Topsøe-Jensen. Odense: Flensted.

Andersen, Hans Christian. 1984. *Christine's Picture Book – Hans Christian Andersen and Grandfather Adolph Drewsen*. Introduction and notes by Erik Dal. Kingfisher Books Ltd.

Andersen, Hans Christian. 2003. *Hans Christian Andersen and Adolph Drewsen. Astrid Stampe's Picture Book*. Published by Odense City Museums, edited by Karsten Eskildsen. København: Gyldendal.

Andersen, Jens. 2008. "The Man who Wrote with Scissors." In *Cut-Outs and Cut-Ups: Hans Christian Andersen and William Seward Burroughs*, edited by Hendel Teicher. Dublin: Irish Museum of Modern Art.

Anderseniana. 1938. *H.C. Andersen paa Holsteinborg*. Vol. 5-6. Edited by Chr. M. K. Petersen. København: Levin & Munksgaard – Ejnar Munksgaard.

Bredsdorff, Elias. 1979. *H.C. Andersen. Mennesket og digteren*. København: Fremad.

Bruhn, Jørgen. 2008. "Intermidialitet. Framtidens humanistiska grunddisciplin?" *Tidsskrift för Litteraturvetenskab* 38(1): 21–38.

Bøggild, Jacob. 2012. *Svævende stasis. Arabesk og allegori i H.C. Andersens eventyr og historier*. Hellerup: Forlaget Spring.

Bøgh, Nicolaj. 1905. "Fra H.C. Andersens Barndoms- og Ungdomsliv." *Personalhistorisk Tidsskrift*, Vol. 5.2: 58–79.

Dürck-Kaulbach, Josefa. 1921. *Erinnerungen an Wilhelm von Kaulbach und sein Haus*. München: Delphin-Verlag.

Heitmann, Annegret. 2003. *Intermedialität im Durchbruch. Bildkunstreferenzen in der skandinavischen Literatur der frühen Moderne*. Freiburg im Breisgau: Rombach.

Heltoft, Kjeld. 1969. *H.C. Andersens Billedkunst*. København: Gyldendal.

Kofoed, Niels. 1967. *Studier i H.C. Andersens fortællekunst*. København: Munksgaard.

Müller-Wille, Klaus. 2017. *Sezierte Bücher. Hans Christian Andersens Materialästhetik*. Paderborn: Wilhelm Fink.

Pankow, Edgar. 2013. "Vom Wort zum Bild – und retour." In *WortBild Künstler. Von Goethe bis Ringelnatz. Und Herta Müller*. Pliezhausen: Karl Grammlich GmbH.

Rørdam, Marie. 1911. *Tilbageblik paa et langt Liv.* København: G. E. C. Gad.
Sanders, Karin. 1997. *Konturer. Skulptur- og dødsbilleder fra guldalderlitteraturen.* København: Museum Tusculanum.
Sibbern, F. C. (1826) 1851. *Udaf Gabrielis's Breve til og fra Hjemmet.* København: C. A. Reitzel.
Stampe, Rigmor. 1905. "H.C. Andersen som børneven." *Illustreret Tidende*, no. 27, 396.
Stampe, Rigmor. 1918. *H.C. Andersen og hans nærmeste Omgang.* København: H. Aschehoug & Co.
von Racowitza, Helene. (1909) 1910. *Princess Helene von Racowitza: An Autobiography [Von Anderen und mir. Erinnerungen aller Art]*. Authorized translation from the German by Cecil Mar. London: Constable.

Notes

1. See for example Bredsdorff 1979, 383; H C. Andersen 1984, 257; J. Andersen 2008, 142. The reason why these researchers have estimated the number of Andersen's papercuts to be so high is their systematic misreading of Kjeld Heltoft's *H.C. Andersens Billedkunst*, 1969, p. 9. Heltoft's number includes both papercuts, collages and inkblot drawings.
2. Unless otherwise indicated all translations are mine.
3. The episode from Kaulbach's home is quoted by Josefa Dürck-Kaulbach (1851-1936) after her sister-in-law Sophie Kaulbach, née Schroll (1850-1920).
4. Henriette Wulff was the daughter of captain commander P. F. Wulff (1774-1842) who directed the Sea Cadet Academy which until 1827 was housed in Amalienborg in Copenhagen.
5. The strange qualities of Andersen's papercuts are mentioned in the preserved memoirs about his art of cutting by sir Henry Dickens, princess Helene von Racowitza, Rigmor Stampe and Axelline Lund. In several memoirs, the style of the papercuts is compared to that spirit the autobiographers identified in Andersen's fairy tales. The simple fact that the mostly brief description of Andersen is connected with a description of his papercuts in the memoirs conveys the strong impression his art work must have made. Rigmor Stampe wrote it like this in Illustreret Tidende (no. 27, 1905): "The execution was not characterised by meticulousness, but by ease and swiftness, and the expression was steady and characteristic. Some of the spirit from the fairy tales were found in the figures, and this made them so attractive: One remembered them."
6. The tradition of the "bindebrev" is not known in the English-speaking world and therefore there is no term for this kind of letter in English. "Bonding letter" – which signifies obligation as well as emotional attachment – seems to be the best possible translation.
7. As an older man Hans Christian Andersen told his young friend Nicolaj Bøgh about his father. Bøgh mentions that Andersen told him that his father "could write verse, for example a verse on a virgin with one eye who gave birth to a child. He also made 'bonding letters' which the neighbours marveled at." (Bøgh 1905, 60).
8. See Jørgen Bruhn (2008, 24). In Bruhn's article one also finds a thoughtful historical overview of intermediality as a humanistic discipline.
9. E.T.A. Hoffmann's "Die Fermate" (1815), which takes its point of departure from J. E. Hummel's painting by the same name, and "Ritter Gluck" (1809), which point of departure is the overture to C. W. Gluck's opera Iphigénie en Aulide (1774), are good examples of this expansion of the field of poetry.

Hans Christian Andersen's Discovery of the Poet as National Icon
The Public Memorial as Urban Phantasmagoria

Jakob Stougaard-Nielsen
University College London

Taking my starting point in Hans Christian Andersen's travelogue A Visit to Portugal, 1866, *I consider his experiences as a literary tourist of the modernisation and restoration of urban, national spaces in Lisbon, embodied in his consideration of a monument to Camões, and in Paris, as reflected in his modern tale "The Dryad." I consider how these impressions impacted on the canonisation of Andersen, as he would later consider plans for his statue to be erected in Copenhagen. Andersen's understanding of the iconicity of authors in relation to urbanisation and nation-building is then placed in relation to a wider wave of commemorations that passed over Europe in the nineteenth century, where famous authors were used as guarantors of the nation's sense of achievement – as central to the formation of modern nations understood as imagined communities. It is argued that Andersen understood the veiling and forgetting of colonial subjugation and the past inherent to canonisation and nation building.*

In his biography of Hans Christian Andersen, Jens Andersen portrays the author as the nineteenth-century traveller *par excellence*: he discovered new travel destinations, was constantly restless in his pursuit of new sites and sights and in his quest for new experiences and inspiration. In his travel writings we often find what the biographer calls Andersen's constant "spiritual travel ideal": the "pure striving for development and maturity," which he thought could be acquired "only in the world, among people" (J. Andersen 2005, 481). Hans Christian Andersen was a cosmopolitan traveller for whom "it was strangely easy [...] to traverse borders and cultures, religious creeds and political systems without fear of the foreign" (482).

In Andersen's travelogue *A Visit to Portugal, 1866* (*Et Besøg i Portugal 1866*, 1868), based on his journey to the Iberian peninsula via Holland and France, however, Jens Andersen finds an aging author whose restlessness has been replaced by a more contemplative spirit, perhaps resulting from his romantic notion of Portugal as a rare and surprising oasis in the periphery of an unstable, deteriorating and conflict-ridden Europe, and, perhaps, his memories of formative reading such as Lord Byron, who visited Portugal in 1809 and described the picturesque town of Sintra as "the most beautiful, perhaps, in the world" (letter to Francis Hodgson, July 16, 1809).[1] Sintra is the town near Lisbon where Andersen was invited to stay with the O'Neill brothers, the sons of the Danish Consul in Lisbon, Jorge O'Neill, whom Andersen had met as a young man at the home of the Wulff family (J. Andersen 2005, 484-486).

While the already then world-famous Danish writer of fairy tales is inseparable from the cosmopolitan worldview and restless spirit of a constantly travelling author, whose literary endeavours developed and were shaped by a Europe in flux, "in the world, among people," Andersen's 1866 travels to Portugal and Paris were instrumental in shaping his view of the social role of literature and authors, and how his likeness and his authorship could be used and "commemorated" to serve the formation of a national community in the wake of the Prussian decimation of the Danish army, national pride and identity in 1864, only a few years prior to his journey.

Andersen the aging traveller, is one whose attention and imagination is constantly engaged with notions of nationhood, restoration, legacy and memory, where particularly his experiences as a "literary tourist" of the modernisation of urban and national spaces in Lisbon and Paris in 1866 are complemented with his simultaneous and ongoing attempts to authorise and authenticate his own literary persona, and ensure and monumentalise his literary legacy for future purposes. In this sense, Andersen's self-reflexive canonisation must be seen in relation to a wider "wave of commemorations that passed over Europe in the long 19th century," where cultural heroes such as famous authors were used as guarantors "of the nation's continuity and sense of achievement" – as central to the formation of modern nations understood as what Benedict Anderson has termed "imagined communities" (as quoted in Leerssen and Rigney 2014, 9).

In the following, I shall discuss a shorter passage from *A Visit to Portugal* wherein Andersen contemplates Lisbon as a restored, modernised urban space and records his impression, as a literary tourist, of the unfinished monument to Luís de Camões, the author of Portugal's national epic *Os Lusíadas* (1572). I shall follow Andersen as he makes his way back to Denmark, stopping in the middle of Paris, where, presumably, a seed is sown for his melancholic urban tale about the demise of a wood nymph, and by association old France, in the phantasmagoric spectacle of the Paris World Exposition, "The Dryad" ("Dryaden," 1868), published the same year as his travel accounts from Portugal were published together in a single volume. Here, I shall consider a seemingly sentimental scene where the narrator is found contemplating a modern and thoroughly urban tragedy: the beautification of Paris with fresh, young trees arriving from the countryside to replace the old and infirm. I shall, in short, employ these allegories of transformation, commemoration and urban renewal, found in texts deriving from Andersen's travels to Portugal and France, to consider how Andersen, in old age, moulded his own author image, not only by producing autobiographies and collected editions of his works, but literally by evaluating plans for the making of a monument to himself in the shape of a statue to ensure his long-lasting presence in the Danish public sphere. The well-known story about Andersen's dissatisfaction with a planned statue to be erected in his honour, featuring a group of children, including a boy leaning against the author's groin, is to my mind not merely an example of, as Jackie Wullschlager has it, how "small things upset him absurdly," but should instead be considered a conscious and inspired attempt on his part to canonise a particular cosmopolitan image of himself for a modern, urban, Danish imagined community (2001, 436).

In Lisbon: Restoration and Phantasmagoria

Hans Christian Andersen's visit to Lisbon, as recorded in the third chapter of *A Visit to Portugal*, gives us, I believe, interesting insights into how the restoration and modernisation of urban spaces, amounting to a veritable national restoration in the case of Portugal, was closely aligned with public canonisations and memorialisations of national authors in the late nineteenth century – at least so it might have appeared to the mind of a well-versed, experienced literary traveller and tourist such as Andersen. Andersen's reflection, as we shall see, can be considered an example of the intimate linkage between nineteenth-century nation-building and "the self-reflexive cultivation of the past as a resource for collective identity" (Leerssen and Rigney 2014, 4); a connection cultural historians such as Eric Hobsbawm (*The Invention of Tradition*, 1983) and Pierre Nora (*Les Lieux de mémoire*, 1984-92) have identified in different European contexts, revealing the processes through which "shared identity narratives" have been actively promoted "with the help of museums, monuments, archives, text editions, and narratives expressed in different media and genres" (Leerssen and Rigney 2014, 4). In addition, Andersen became the canonised object of, but also, in his own time, a participant in, what Joep Leerssen and Ann Rigney have defined as the central place afforded to the obsessive memorialisation practices and public celebrations of canonical writers. They argue that such canonisation and memorial practices peaked in the nineteenth century as:

> occasions for the extension of the private pleasure of reading into the public arena through its remediations in the form of visual displays, pageantry, and sculpture. In the process [public celebrations of canonical authors] provided the rapidly expanding literate classes with an opportunity to display their cultural 'pedigree' and cultural allegiances in an embodied manner and in the co-presence of like-minded citizens. (9)

It is my contention that Andersen's travelogue, and his travels in 1866 more generally, exemplify the author's own developing understanding of the importance of taking an active part in moulding and mediating his authorial legacy to take part in a much wider renewal of urban and national spaces and communities.

Andersen's first impression of Lisbon is one of defamiliarisation. Lisbon does not correspond to the descriptions he had previously seen or read: "I had," he writes,

> a picture in my mind's eye of what it would be like, but the light, fair city I now saw in reality was quite different. I could not but exclaim, Where are the filthy streets I have read about, filled with garbage, the wild dogs,

and the wretched figures from the African colonies, who are supposed to wander about with their white beards and black skins, suffering from horrible diseases? (Andersen 1972, 27)[2]

Andersen is told that the Lisbon he has in mind is the Lisbon of thirty years ago. Since then, he remarks, the country "which has undergone so many struggles [...] now seems to be developing in peace and harmony" (33).[3] It is not unlikely that Andersen is here projecting a similar hope for his native Denmark, which only a few years previously had suffered a deadly blow to its own sense of security and national identity on the battle fields of Southern Jutland.

The modernisation of Lisbon is partly expressed through one of Andersen's favourite symbols of the transformation of urban spaces and the arrival of modernity in his time, namely the introduction of gas lights. Gas street lighting was introduced in Lisbon in the 1850s and 60s, and we may recall that Andersen adopted the same figure in his tale "Godfather's Picture Book" ("Gudfaders Billedbog") published in 1868, the same year *A Visit to Portugal* was published in book form.

As a fantasy tale recounting a heroic Danish past from the odd perspective of a disappearing technology for the illumination of the streets of Copenhagen, this is essentially a tale which performs, as I have argued elsewhere, the function of an urban memorial to a national identity transformed by the advent of a type of modern technology (Stougaard-Nielsen 2013, 147). The impact of gas lighting, introduced in Copenhagen in 1857, is presented as the historical framework for "Godfather's Picture Book." The transition from an old to a new technology allows the frame-narrator, the Godfather, to retell and restore to the collective memory the history of Copenhagen in short descriptive vignettes, dwelling on discursive portraits of central characters, kings, heroes, scientists, and artists, and on the most significant historical events as witnessed by the old oil lamps over the centuries. In the logic of the tale, the old and soon-to-disappear oil lamps represent the storytelling Godfather. As the fragile picture book itself is prone to be torn by children and circulated as scraps, the collective memory in and of Copenhagen, the story suggests, will need to be continuously assembled and recollected in new material and oral enactments. It is clear that "Godfather's Picture Book," as well as Andersen's impressions from the streets of Lisbon, are not history lessons, but are instead modern explorations of the role of memory in the creation of collective identities and, not least, the significance of new technologies and mediation in a modern, urban memory culture.

In Lisbon, Andersen describes "the public promenade" of "the light, fair city" as "lit by gas in the evenings; there is a band, and from the flowering trees streams a perfume that is really almost too strong – it is just as if one were standing in a spice-shop or a confectioner's where they have just produced fresh-made vanilla ice-cream" (Andersen 1972, 27).[4] In Andersen's vision of an unrecognisable, almost unreal Lisbon, the bustling yet clean streets, doors and balconies freshly painted in the national colours of green and red, the large squares planted with trees and neat-patterned mosaics, the goldsmiths and the small, handsome theatre – in short, the modernised, restored urban, national stage on which he now finds himself – is intricately, yet simultaneously, almost ghostly, bound up with exotic sensations and with the political economy of empire and colonialism: the "wretched figures from the African colonies" of the past, whom he had expected to find in the streets, have been replaced by modern illumination, stagecraft and the *phantasmagoria* (in Walter Benjamin's sense of the term) of a confectioner's strong perfumes from exotic spices and vanilla.

We will see a similar ironic, perhaps even uncomfortable, celebration of urban and national restoration as Benjaminian *phantasmagoria* ("a consumer item in which there is no longer anything that is supposed to remind us how it came into being" and "an art of total illusion that also contained its own critique" [Gunning 2004, 11, 7]) in Andersen's conception of "Dryaden" – his seminal tale about the turbulent, modern experience of urbanity as display and stagecraft.

In Paris: Memory and Forgetting

On his way home from Portugal, Andersen stopped over in Paris where preparations for the following year's World Exposition were underway – an event that would result in his tale, "The Dryad: A tale from the Paris Exposition 1867," published in Denmark in December 1868. This was the tale that Andersen would later bemoan that Georg Brandes had overlooked in his critical assessment of Andersen's work. Brandes thought that one should not write fairy tales about something as modern and fleeting as a world exhibition. Andersen could, therefore, not be considered a great modern author – he should remain in the nursery as a great author of universal tales for children (Andersen 1963–90, 6:216; Brandes 1899, 126).

Based on Andersen's annotations to his Collected Works, we are led to believe that "Dryaden" was initially conceived as a response to a journalist who claimed that only Charles Dickens could write a tale about the Paris Exposition. Additionally, Andersen claims that the central motif, of what would become his response, was impressed on him when he visited Paris in April and May of 1867, shortly after the Exposition's opening on April 1, 1867 – during the first of his two visits to this wonder of the modern world.

However, according to his diary entry a year previously, in 1866, written down on his journey back to Denmark from Portugal, it appears that he had already witnessed the scene that would two years later grow into his bestselling tale "Dryaden." This is what Andersen writes about the view from his hotel room on April 13, 1866, with imagery closely resembling his impressions from the streets of Lisbon:

> Outside my windows was a small square with a fountain, which didn't spring, a patch of green grass with benches where people sat and stared at the greenery. There were seemingly withered trees who, like I, could not cope with the Parisian air, and as they hadn't left, they had languished. One day, to improve the view, two trees about to bloom arrived from the countryside, proclaiming spring had arrived. The two old trees were dug up and the new ones planted in their place. They reached up to my window and let themselves bathe in the gaslights, to be beheld by the modern Babylon below. A fairy tale could be written about the trees, their longing for the World City, and their imminent death therein. I think I shall write a fairy tale about them [...]. (1971–77, 7:74, my translation)[5]

In the tale itself, Andersen's narrator describes the same scene in which he, who has arrived in Paris by train with the swell of tourists, finds himself looking down from his hotel balcony contemplating a tableau which immediately impresses an allegorical meaning on his imagination. On the square below, workers are about to replace an old withered tree with a young chestnut tree. The dead tree lies on the square presumably withered from the polluted city air. Andersen reflects both in the tale and in his diary on the similarity between the longing of the tree for the great city and its inevitable demise and his own constant longing and troubles with the urban air. In one singular impression the tableau below enacts the conflict between the old world and the new, the loss of innocence and childhood, and the paradoxical notion he had recently trademarked, captured in the first programmatic lines of the story: "Our time is the time of fairy tales."

Andersen, as the editor and annotator of his own literary monument, his Collected Works, insists that the kernel of this tale is located in his own authentic experience of visiting the Exposition – "We saw it ourselves, during the Exposition in Paris in 1867, during our time, the great, wondrous time of fairy tales," as he ends the tale. As I have argued elsewhere, it appears that Andersen may have borrowed the scene from his fellow traveller, the editor of the paper *Figaro*, the writer and journalist Robert Watt, who not only accompanied Andersen on his visit to the Exposition in 1867, but also published, in December of that year, an extract from Andersen's travel accounts from Portugal in the paper *Dagens Nyheder*. Watt also wrote travel accounts himself, such as a series of vignettes from Paris for the illustrated newspaper, *Illustreret Tidende*, published in 1865, which Andersen must have read. One such account, entitled "On the Boulevards," offers excited eye-witness reports from the hustle and bustle and spectacle of Parisian street life and from the famous cafés where modern life could be observed in detail.

Apart from being similar in tone to Andersen's reports from a modernised Lisbon, Watt's reports from Paris also had direct influence on what would become Andersen's "Dryaden." In the same article in which Watt praises Paris as the delightful and magnetic centre of the world, we find a description of the artificial dressing that is also the history of the boulevards: a description of the shining front of the boulevards and the city at the cost of much suffering. Watt writes about the trees that line the boulevards:

> Daily you see workers preoccupied with uprooting the old and infirm trees to replace them with the young and healthy. You occasionally see small wagons on which the fertile and hopeful child of the forest struts as it is taken to its new home where its life force will soon be spent. It is as if Parisian life rapidly exhausted its vitality, and soon the wagon will make a stop by the now withered tree to take it away from the beautiful city that became its deathbed [...] to the passing observer the boulevard maintains its constant smiling, shiny facade. (Watt 1865, 363, my translation)[6]

Watt, like Andersen, is evidently inspired by the symbolism of the young trees meeting their demise in the city – consumed, so to speak, by the passing consumer-observer tourists for whom they are displayed, implicating also the young author-traveller. The trees and gas lights become, again, figures for the smiling front veiling the labour, death, and sacrifice behind the urban spectacle.

Both Lisbon and Paris please the aging author's touristic gaze; they are modern, efficient urban settings strangely uncanny and pleasing to the eye. At the same time, they necessarily evoke their opposites through a phantasmagorical veiling of suffering and the past: In Lisbon, exploitation, violence and decease lie in the shadows of the modern gas-lit city, suppressed by the exotic perfumes of spice shops, its colonial past veiled by the monumentalisation of the author as a national icon; in Paris, trees and humans deeply connected to the national past and the natural environment are up-rooted to serve, momentarily and fatally, as mere decorations in the de-humanised, urban spectacle. Andersen was never naïve about this paradox that the desire to renew and to modernise came at the cost of selective forgetting – his own biography and work can itself be seen as such a constant veiling and self-reflexive process of forgetting. These themes of rapid urban change, of individual and cultural loss and forgetting paired with the figure of the storyteller capable of reflecting this change and providing some sense of historical and collective cohesion and continuity are condensed in the short passage in *A Visit to Portugal* that follows Andersen's initial impressions of the urban phantasmagoria.

The Author and the National Memorial

Andersen's seemingly – but only seemingly – casual ramble through the streets of Lisbon takes him to "one of the high-lying and most frequented parts of the city," where, he writes, "they are going to put up a monument to Camões. The place is already planted with trees and flowers, and the plinth has been put up but not the statue – it was rejected and another is being cast" (Andersen 1972, 28).[7] On the square, which since 1860 had carried the name of the extensively mythologised and romanticised poet of the sixteenth-century national epic *Os Lusíadas*, Andersen strikes up a curious, perhaps imagined, conversation with a non-descript guide, perhaps one of the O'Neills, about the soon to be erected monument to Camões:

I asked if Camões' slave would be there with him – I was thinking of him sitting at the base, his hand outstretched, just as he had sat here in the streets during Camões' lifetime, begging for his poverty-stricken, abandoned master, who was likely to die of hunger. The answer to my question was that such a representation would be an enduring reproach to the nation which had paid no heed to its great poet while he lived. How the monument will turn out I do not know, but Camões' own work will always be his best memorial. By that work, more than by bloody wars and geographical discovery, is the name of Portugal rooted in the memory of all races in all lands. (Andersen 1972, 28)[8]

According to Paulo de Medeiros, the invention of Camões as a national icon began in the nineteenth century. By German Romantics, such as Friedrich Schlegel, the tragedy of the poet's life became representative of the demise of Portugal and its loss of independence (De Medeiros 2014, 283). As Schlegel considered both Germany and Portugal to be in decline in his own time and viewed the situation to be even harsher for Germany, as its national glory was "not preserved in poetry as in Portugal," the nineteenth-century invention of Camões as a national icon can be understood as "a direct result of Romantic concepts of literature and the national spirit" (283).

The invention of Camões culminated in the tercentenary celebration in 1880, centring on mass commemorations around the statue that would be erected on the empty plinth Andersen is contemplating, and Camões' figure was soon put into the service of nation and empire such as in campaigns of colonialisation in Africa (De Medeiros 2014, 290). Such political appropriations of the poet occurred well after Andersen's visit to Portugal; however, it is possible to see in Andersen's 'use' of Camões an intuitive understanding of the author's potential for political and national appropriation and the resistance to such uniform and simplistic canonisation latent in the legend and work of the author himself. It is indeed possible, according to de Medeiros, to see in Camões' work a writer who both celebrated and problematised "imperialism and its attendant forms of colonial subjugation, but he himself, though destitute, relied on the services of a slave in order to ease his old age and his blindness." (293). Andersen's imagination of Camões' future statue in the colonial phantasmagoria of Lisbon's sanitised streets looks awry to the forgotten "wretched figures from the African colonies," as the spectacle of modernity in "The Dryad's"

Parisian streets and the new urban consumer culture is dependent, in Andersen's tale, not only on the veiling of labour but also the forgetting of the natural environment and the past.

Andersen himself seems to be putting Camões in the service of a distinct anti-imperialism insisting that his poetic work alone is what places Portugal in relation to the rest of the world. Andersen stresses the epic itself as Camões' "best" memorial, and that by his poetic work "more than by bloody wars and geographical discovery, is the name of Portugal rooted in the memory of all races in all lands. His own life reads like a poem and has been so used," Andersen adds, perhaps with a slight nod to his own world-famous authorial self-fashioning in, for instance, his autobiography *The Fairy Tale of My Life* (1855).

In his travelogue, Andersen mentions Ludwig Tieck's artist-novel *Der Tod des Dichters* (*The Death of the Poet*) from 1833, as a "beautiful" example of such discursive memorials to and retellings of Camões' life, which should make us think that Andersen was at least as interested in the romantic myth of the poet's life as in his famous epic of discovery. Andersen had befriended Tieck since his first European travels in the early 1830s so he may have read Tieck's novel much earlier in his own career.

It might be Tieck's sentimental account of the poet's last tragic days in Lisbon – unrecognised by his compatriots, infirm, poor and only supported by his adoring slave – that Andersen has in mind when he imagines what would make a pertinent subject for the future monument – and, perhaps, what he could have feared as his own future destiny, since he never rid himself of the fear of poverty and misrecognition.

Andersen was perhaps more subtly attracted to the unfinished memorial to the poet as it lent itself to an ironic account of national and urban restoration that he offers in his travel account from Lisbon. Following Nora, we should understand public memorialisation as intimately connected to or a by-product of processes of modernisation and urbanisation, as public memorials and monuments were designed to "re-establish a meaningful relationship to an ever-receding past" (Leerssen and Rigney 2014, 6). However, Andersen's part sentimental, part critical suggestion that Camões should be immortalised with his slave at his feet unveils the extent to which "the processes of canonization and of public memorialization go hand in hand" (254), the extent to which the obsession with memorials to national poets in the nineteenth century had less to do with the celebration of poetic achievements and more to do with nation branding – a purpose for which the author figure needs some fitting.

The Sculpted Author as Testamentary Act

What Andersen finds in Lisbon is, then, not only a surprisingly civilised paradise, but also, more importantly, an introduction to the very public processes with which a nation, not dissimilar to his own, appropriates literary icons to serve different purposes than those perhaps intended by the poet or based on historical facts, which, with increasing speed, disappear into the past. Yet this malleability of authenticity, of the author's legacy through public memorials, would also become relevant to Andersen towards the end of his life when a competition was held to create a memorial sculpture of the author in Kongens Have (The King's Garden in Copenhagen). The anecdote of Andersen being infuriated by several of the shortlisted models for the sculpture, which in most cases included children sitting at the feet of Andersen, sitting on his lap or standing by his side captivated by the storyteller, suggests that Andersen had learned a thing or two about the significance of public memorials to the afterlife and legacy of his authorship. In his diary on June 4, 1875, he noted a visit from the sculptor Saabye who would eventually be selected for the work:

> At home a visit from the sculptor Saabye, to whom I said loudly and clearly that I was dissatisfied with his statue of me, that neither he nor any of the sculptors knew me, that they hadn't seen me read, that I didn't tolerate anyone standing behind me and never had children on my back, on my lap or between my legs, that my tales were just as much for older people as for children who only understood the outer trappings and did not comprehend the whole work until they were mature – that naiveté was only a part of my tales, that humour was really what gave them their flavour. (1971–77, 10:458-459, my translation)[9]

In a sense, there is not a major difference between editing out Camões' slave and editing out the listening child at the feet of the monumentalised poet. However, in Andersen's case, he had the opportunity to do the editing himself as, what Michael Millgate has termed, a "testamentary act." Such acts include "the ways in which writers famous in their own time have sought in old age to exert some degree of posthumous control over their personal and literary reputations – over the extent and nature of future biographical investigation and exposure, and over the interpretation and textual integrity of their published works" (Millgate 1992, 2). Wanting to be recognised as more than a storyteller for the nursery, Andersen's complaints about the plans for his statue show him actively engaged in self-canonisation, less preoccupied with how he was seen and more with how he *desired* to be seen – and, of course, his work to be read in the present and the future.

Andersen was at the time consciously and actively engaged in canonising his authorship as a modern, cosmopolitan and 'serious' one, even if, as Jens Andersen writes in his biography, Andersen did not write much during his 1866 travels. However, the active modernisation of his authorship, reflected in tales such as "Godfather's Picture Book" and "The Dryad" originated in his experiences of modernised urban spaces in Lisbon and Paris. Andersen's experiences as a literary tourist in 1866, too, suggest to me that he had by then developed a very modern understanding of nation branding and the centrality afforded literary icons therein. He had come to understand that authentic experiences and our ubiquitous desire for 'mythic' origins are necessarily the products of constant rewritings and interferences serving to re-fashion national and authorial identities for new, sometimes problematic, purposes. Andersen had realised that strategies for modernising and revising national narratives and iconic national poets are not substantially different from the strategies available to an author with a desire to modernise, revise, canonise and memorialise his own authorship.

References

Andersen, Hans Christian. 1971–77. *H.C. Andersens Dagbøger 1825-1875*. 12 vols. Compiled by Kåre Olsen and H. Topsøe-Jensen and edited by Helga Vang Lauridsen, Tue Gad, and Kirsten Weber. København: Det Danske Sprog- og Litteraturselskab/Gad.

Andersen, Hans Christian. 1972. *A Visit to Portugal 1866*. Translated by Grace Thornton. London: Peter Owen.

Andersen, Hans Christian, 1963–90. *H.C. Andersens Eventyr*. 7 vols. Edited by Erik Dal. København: Det Danske Sprog- og Litteraturselskab/Hans Reitzels Forlag.

Andersen, Hans Christian. (1868) 2006. *Et Besøg i Portugal 1866*. In vol. 15 of *Andersen. H.C. Andersens samlede værker*, edited by Klaus P. Mortensen, 419-479. København: Gyldendal, 2003–2007.

Andersen, Jens. 2005. *Hans Christian Andersen: A New Life*. Translated by Tiina Nunnally. New York: Overlook Duckworth.

Anderson, Benedict. 2006. *Imagined Communities: Reflections on the Origin and Spread of Nationalism*. London: Verso.

Brandes, Georg. 1899. "H.C. Andersen som Æventyrdigter." In vol. 2 of *Georg Brandes Samlede Skrifter*, 91-132. København: Gyldendal, 1899–1910.

De Medeiros, Paulo. 2014. "Whose Comões? Canons, Celebrations, Colonialisms." In *Commemorating Writers in Nineteenth-Century Europe: Nation-Building and Centenary Fever*, edited by Joep Leerssen and Ann Rigney, 283-294. Houndmills: Palgrave.

Gunning, Tom. 2004. "Illusions Past and Future: The Phantasmagoria and its Specters." MediaArtHistories Archive. http://www.mediaarthistory.org/refresh/Programmatic%20key%20texts/pdfs/Gunning.pdf.

Leerssen, Joep and Ann Rigney, eds. 2014. *Commemorating Writers in Nineteenth-Century Europe: Nation-Building and Centenary Fever*. Houndmills: Palgrave. Kindle.

Millgate, Michael. 1992. *Testamentary Acts: Browning, Tennyson, James, Hardy*. Oxford: Clarendon Press.

Stougaard-Nielsen, Jakob. 2013. "The Fairy Tale and the Periodical: Hans Christian Andersen's Scrapbooks." *Book History* 16 (1): 132-154.

Watt, Robert. 1865. "Billeder fra Paris II: Paa Boulevarderne." *Illustreret Tidende* 6 (306): 363-364. http://www.illustrerettidende.dk.

Wullschlager, Jackie. 2001. *Hans Christian Andersen: The Life of a Storyteller*. New York: Alfred A. Knopf.

Notes

1 Hans Christian Andersen's letters can be located on the Hans Christian Andersen Centre's homepage: http://andersen.sdu.dk/brevbase/

2 " [...] forud dannet mig et Billede af denne By, men hvor langt anderledes lys og smuk laae den nu for mig i Virkeligheden. Jeg maatte udbryde: hvor er her de smudsige

Gader, jeg har læst om, de udkastede Aadsler, de vilde Hunde og de ynkelige Skikkelser fra de afrikanske Besiddelser, der med hvidt Skæg i den sorte Hud og med væmmelige Sygdomme her skulle drive om." (H.C. Andersen [1868] 2006, 437).

3 "der har prøvet saa mange Kampe [...] nu synes at groe i Hvile og Velsignelse" (H.C. Andersen [1868] 2006, 442).

4 "om Aftenen oplyst ved Gas, her musiceredes, og fra blomstrende Træer strømmer en Duft, næsten altfor stærk, det er som stod man ved en Kryderbod eller et Conditori, hvor just Vanille-Iis blev lavet og frembaaren" (H.C. Andersen [1868] 2006, 437).

5 "Udenfor mine Vinduer var en lille Plads med et Springvand, som ikke sprang, lidt grønt Græs med Bænke foran, hvor Folk sad og stirrede paa det Grønne, der stode vistnok uddøde Træer, de havde som jeg ikke kunnet taale Pariser Luften og da de ikke kom afsted, vare de gaaet ud; for nu at hjelpe her paa kom en Dag to store halvudsprungne Træer ude fra Landet, de var en Forkyndelse af Foraaret, to gamle Træer bleve gravne op og de nye plantede istedet, de naaede op mod mit Vindue og lode sig bestraale af Gaslamper, beskues af hele Nutidens Babilon neden under. Der kunde skrives et Eventyr om de Træer, deres Længsel efter Verdens Byen, og deres snare Død derinde. Jeg skriver vist et Eventyr derom [...]." (H.C. Andersen 1971-77, 7:74).

6 "Dagligt seer man Arbeidere sysselsatte med at borttage de gamle, sygelige Træer, for at sætte unge og friske istedet. De små Vogne, hvori det frodige, haabefulde Skovens Barn kneiser, medens det føres til sit nye hjem, hvor dets Livskraft saa snart skal nedbrydes, møder man jævnligt. Der er, som om Pariserlivet hurtigt opbrugte dets Kraft, og snart holder atter Vognen ved det nu henvisnede Træ, for at føre det bort fra den Skjønne By, der har været dets Sotteseng [...] for den flygtige Iagttager har Boulevarden bestandigt det samme smilende og glimrende Ydre." (H.C. Andersen 1865, 363).

7 "Camoens' Monument reises; Pladsen er allerede beplantet med Træer og Blomster, Fodstykket stillet op, men endnu ikke Statuen, den blev forkastet; en ny er under Arbeide." (H.C. Andersen [1868] 2006, 438).

8 "Jeg spurgte: 'Kommer Camoens' Slave derpaa?' Jeg tænkte mig denne siddende paa Fodstykket, udstrækkende Haanden, som han i Camoens' Levetid sad her i Gaderne og tiggede til sin fattige, forladte Herre, der var nær ved at døe af Sult. 'Den Fremstilling,' svarede man mig, 'vilde jo være en vedvarende Bebreidelse mod Nationen, der ikke tænkte paa sin store Digter, da han levede.' Hvorledes Monumentet bliver, veed jeg ikke, hans eget Værk vil altid blive hans bedste Monument, ved det er Portugals Navn, mere end ved blodige Kampe og Landes Opdagelse, groet i Erindringen hos Slægter i alle Lande." (H.C. Andersen [1868] 2006, 438).

9 "Besøg hjemme af Billedhuggeren Saaby, som jeg denne Gang sagde klart og tydeligt at jeg var utilfreds med hans Statue af mig, at hverken han eller nogen [af] Billedhuggerne kjendte mig, havde ikke seet mig læse, at jeg ingen taalte da bag ved mig og ikke havde Børn paa Ryggen, paa Skjødet eller i Skrævet; at mine Eventyr vare ligesaa meget for de Ældre som for Børnene, disse forstode kun Stafagen og som modne Folk saae og fornam de først det Hele. At det Naïve var kun een Deel af mine Eventyr, at Humouret var egentligt Saltet i dem." (H.C. Andersen 1971-77, 10:458-459).

ETHICS AND VALUES

Ethics of the Discarded:
Empathy with the Inorganic
Hans Christian Andersen's use of waste, rubbish, and other stuff

Karin Sanders
UC Berkeley, San Francisco

This chapter argues that Hans Christian Andersen saw a potential in wasted objects or misplaced things that allowed him to craft a material poetics where the devalued gained or regained some form of agency. His imaginative fairy tales about broken and discarded things are not so much meant to trouble our conspicuous consumption of goods as they are intended to prod us to consider or reconsider the world we share with material stuff of all sorts. Often there is an ethos of inclusion in the tales where seemingly non-aesthetic rubbish is given free passage into cultured aesthetic forms. Andersen demonstrates how debris could be recuperated and parsed for critical insights into both social and aesthetic value systems in ways that not only opened for new understandings of enchantment, but also preceded early twentieth-century avantgardes' use of recyclable trash.

Hans Christian Andersen's many stories of misplaced coins, shattered piggy-banks, chipped teacups, broken bottles, wasted tops, trashed balls, and frayed collars speak volumes about his investment in the discarded. But is there a deeper correspondence hidden behind the mélange of broken objects in Andersen's oeuvre, one that points to a sense of obligation in the human world? Can Andersen's object tales, for example, be seen as a way to disrupt a given social order in the community of persons? Andersen's stories of decayed and aging objects often suggest that there is added value to the ostensibly valueless and his many transient things frequently claim poetic power to control social anxieties. Yet, to what degree is there an *ethics* attached to discarded or useless 'stuff' in his tales? How does Andersen weigh human values against material value and how can we ponder what kinds of environmental, philosophical and poetic economies emerge in his tales?

Let me start with three short quotes. The first comes from Gay Hawkins' *The Ethics of Waste* where she notes that: "Waste is reduced to a product of culturally and historically variable human practices; what we want to get rid of tells us who we are." (2005, 2). The second comes from Leah Price's *How to Do Things with Books* from a chapter on books as waste in which she adds a historical dimension, namely that "Modernity can be defined not just by what's produced, but by what's discarded, and when." (2012, 219). Finally, Zygmunt Bauman in *Wasted Lives: Modernity and its Outcasts* notes that: "Waste may be described as simultaneously a most harrowing problem and a most closely guarded secret of our times." (2003, 26).

All quotes suggest that there is a great deal of anxiety and emotion bound up in our relation to rubbish, junk, trash or garbage. Nothing it seems is more prosaic and less poetic than byproducts or useless stuff. This is particularly obvious at a moment in time, during the industrial revolution, where the production of goods exploded and commodification culture became a concern that resonated in fiction literature. A time where waste (as discharge of increased wealth) became a noticeable topic for a literature increasingly interested in sharpening the notion of prose in realistic terms, giving the mundane and ordinary place of pride.

The concept of waste is associated with sorting and categorising, but it is also about restrictions, about figuring out when something is, or is not, in its proper place. "Nothing is inherently trash," as Susan Strasser notes in her *Waste and Want: A Social History of Trash*, it is rather a matter of thresholds or "physical boundaries." (1999, 5). Dirt is not dirt, she suggests, if it is properly located on the *outside*; but if dragged *inside* (into the living room for example) its dirtiness becomes noticeable, even intolerable.

In the following I will argue that Andersen examined the threshold between what was considered to be appropriately *inside* or *outside* proper boundaries. He used the potential in wasted objects or misplaced things (and persons) to voice not only a social indignation but also to craft a *material poetics*. Devalued materials gain new value in his object tales and Andersen develops an ethos of inclusion where seemingly non-aesthetic stuff is given free passage into cultured aesthetic forms. It is often a restoration of agency to the discarded, and sometimes also of dignity.

The Stuffiness of Prose

Sorting through trash makes everyone a *bricoleur*. Or as Andersen's contemporary Charles Baudelaire notes, in modernity the poet becomes a "ragpicker" who recuperates scraps of rubbish from actuality. Certainly, as many have shown, latest Klaus Müller-Wille in his *Sezierte Bücher* from 2017, ragpicking, for Andersen as for Baudelaire, generates an inventory of images that offers new meanings to that which is otherwise deemed useless if not meaningless.

Although this essay is interested in Andersen's fairy tales and not his novels, to fully understand what is at stake in the fairy tales' use of waste and rubbish and broken things it is useful to take a short detour to the nineteenth century novel, since the novel as a genre brings not only realism and the prosaic to the fore, but often does so overstuffed, sometimes claustrophobically, with paraphernalia. Realism, as Sara Danius has emphasised in *Prose of the World*;

> was accompanied by a historically new emphasis on things: on inert matter, everyday objects, household goods, commodities, kitsch, curiosities, *bibélots*. And because realism wanted to incorporate the thingness of the world into its descriptive discourse, it developed a penchant for the detail – say, blue soap. (2006, 27).

Andersen's novels may well prove to bring some insights into this tendency as well. Think for example of the eccentric rooms of Mr. Svane in the novel *To Be, or Not to Be?* (*At være eller ikke være*, 1857), full of old and ragged cut-outs on the walls and an abundance of "Nipserier og Legetøj" ("trinkets and toys") on top of a painted and overornamented cabinet (Andersen 2003–07, 6:20). My point here is that Andersen's fairy tales, while seemingly far removed from the novel, often make ironic remarks and test our everyday anxieties about material things in ways that resonate with the novel. Said differently, his fairy tales echo in a more fantastic form many of the same everyday concerns that fill prose literature like novels in the nineteenth century.

The fondness for details and everyday objects can be found most crowdedly in the Victorian novel. In fact, as the American literary scholar Elaine Freedgood demonstrates in *The Ideas in Things*, also 2006, the Victorian novel in particular "showers us with things [in the form of] cavalcades of objects [that] threaten to crowd the narrative right off the page." (1). We can think here of how Marx's theory of exchange (commodification and fetishising) makes the overflow of things in novels into social hieroglyphs. She concludes that: "Fictional objects become exchangeable figures used in the novel's symbolic system to make a point about the mechanicalness, one-dimensionality, and deadness of industrialised people. Thus, fictional things are themselves commodified." (141). Like Hawkins, Price, Bauman and Freedgood, Francesco Orlando in his *Obsolete Objects in the Literary Imagination* argues that fiction literature is a privileged site that allows the reemergence and reconsideration of discarded things that are "diminished in their functionality" and therefore point to "the very relationship between human beings and the physical world subjugated by them." (2006, 2, 3). Prose fiction, to follow Orlando, opens up for the "accursed, abject, foul, squalid, shady, dreadful, pitiable, moving, extravagant, or ridiculous," in ways that resemble "the return of the repressed, which elsewhere," as he notes, "would not be of a material nature" (6). Even the most troubling object can be "reversed through verbal fantasy into their resplendent opposites." (306).

Yet, in a single and short reference in a footnote to Andersen's mermaid, Orlando does not find this kind of potential in Andersen's world (2006, note 519, 455). He refers briefly to the little mermaid's fraught visit to the witch's cave and rather too hastily concludes that the insistent darkness there is one-dimensional and therefore does not open up the potential of 'reversal' into opposites. Andersen's tales, Orlando suggests, seem unable to create a space for what he calls "the return of the *antifunctional* repressed." (7).

I disagree. For if we take a closer look at Andersen's tales, we see that the imaginary space in his works is particularly open to the anti-functional or nonfunctional. In fact, Andersen's works are full of "returns" of trashed or discarded or repressed things that trouble conventional social orders or mental geographies and clearly demonstrate ambivalence and a willingness to disrupt the proper order of things.

Andersen knew well that prose literature could function as a privileged site for the inconvenient or discarded and his works often recuperated and revaluated useless stuff in its many forms to challenge both social and mental orders.

Orlando's hasty claim may well be a result of a common misreading of the potential in Andersen's fairy tales, overlooking its engagement with a prosaic world. Yet, there is a particularly pervasive ethos in regard to useless objects in Andersen's work, acutely sensitive to anything disenfranchised, offering things-as-waste up as a rich opportunity to investigate not only the relationship and interaction between humans and the material world, but also to a broader understanding of what Walter Benjamin and other materialist historians would later see as "a phenomenological hermeneutic of cultural debris." (Hawkins 2005, 73). For Andersen cultural debris could be recuperated and parsed for critical insights into both social and aesthetic value systems in ways that not only opened for new understandings of enchantment, but also preceded the early twentieth-century avantgarde's use of recyclable trash.

The Currency of Abject Objects

Wasted objects, Andersen acknowledged, acquired a new kind of currency because they challenge our sense of ethics and make a claim on us as readers by forcing us to ponder *how* we see the world and how *we* are implicitly complicit in the broken and decaying objects' stories. His imaginative fairy tales about broken and discarded things are not so much meant to trouble our conspicuous consumption of goods as they are intended to prod us to consider or reconsider the world we share with material stuff of all sorts.

It is useful here, I think, to recall how radically different Andersen's understanding of the fairy tale genre was from that of the Brothers Grimms' understanding of the folk tale. Where the Grimms in their 1812 preface to the first collection of *Kinder- und Hausmärchen* argued that folk tales were gems that needed to be recovered from a storm of destruction, and that folktales testified to an authentic culture that could survive only "where there are imaginations not yet deformed by *the perversities of modern life*." (Grimm and Grimm 2004, 402, my emphasis). Andersen saw the "perversities of modern life" as a possibility and resource to allow fairy tales to respond to the reality of a contemporary world. What the Grimms' viewed as disenchantment and perversity, Andersen saw as the possibility for re-enchantment of things and persons that fell outside the categories of the proper. The worlds he conjures in his fairy tales are not just secondary worlds, but worlds that look or sound very familiar, even if strange, full of material metaphors that address real problems for real human beings.

It would be a mistake however to see Andersen's use of useless objects as a mere extension of his social indignation. Broken things in his stories are not just about being violated, misunderstood, or misread, or about being in need of finding one's proper place in the (human) world of things. They are far more complex. Broken things gain value in Andersen's tales precisely because of their lack of conventional worth; in fact, his failed objects are reassigned a positive value contingent precisely on their material predicament.[1] This point is also made by Brigid Gaffikin who sees what she calls "positive evaluations of the objects' brokenness, [or] 'failure'." (2004, 186). From a different perspective Anthony Curtis Adler has noted that Andersen's broken things "are never thrown out, but only away," and therefore "it is best to speak of them not as objects, standing in a simple relation to the consciousness of presence or absence, but as *abjects*, sent to the limit of the world without yet ever quite being eliminated." In fact, many of Andersen's things exist, he goes on, "at the frivolous margins of the world." (2012, 115). This means that they are outside normal circulation logic. They have no natural end. No finitude! Yet, worn out, they are often and paradoxically just as vibrant as any freshly formed object. Their uselessness and age *is* their currency. If Andersen's failed objects are abject objects, they are not worthless or without things to say.

One such abject object, denied a 'natural' demise, but given a rich story to tell, is found in "The Bottle Neck" ("Flaskehalsen," 1858). The prosaic bottle in this fairy tale is repeatedly turned upside-down, swirled into the air, thrown into depths, maltreated, misused, overlooked, and finally smashed to pieces. Throughout, Andersen bends the poetic cliché of empty vessels in need of substance, filled to suggest psychological, spiritual or emotional voids; he avoids sentimental predeterminations by emphasising the random materiality in each of the bottle's 'fillings.' Whether it is wine, medicine, boot polish, a handwritten paper note, a candle, or water, each substance comes with a story of being thrown up in the air or cast deep into the sea, of being hidden in dark cellars, or being blackened or illuminated; a continual topsy-turvy journey that turns into an allegory of life's unavoidable (uncontainable) serendipity. Not being filled feels to the bottle like an existential void: "empty and corkless, and [it] felt strangely dull as if it lacked something, though it didn't know what."[2] The turbulent and episodic life of the bottle is framed to follow the length of a human life, but the reader is constantly made aware of the impossibility of this anthropomorphic possibility and encouraged to be skeptical about the very nature of speaking objects.

Here, as elsewhere, Andersen regularly undercuts his own active use of anthropomorphism; he never avoids the obvious paradox of the artifice but relishes it. That is to say, when he allows his objects to reflect (within the pages of the very tales that tell them) on their own production, their own being, and their own possible misreading or even destruction, he brings a complex understanding of the creative process to the reader. When illusions are created and broken, sometimes within a single utterance, readers are forced to reflect: "I know that things cannot speak;" or "I know that fiction is just marks on a piece of paper," and so forth. The bottle's story, as it turns out, concerns not only the implausible life of a thing, but also a plausible although stilled life of a very ordinary human being, a young girl, whose sad and prosaic life is tied up in the adventurous story of the bottle; until, that is, they are reunited, each as broken debris. She, as a shriveled old maid, who has never lived, and "it" in a rather humiliating position as an upside-down birdbath with a cork in its bottom, inside the old maid's birdcage. Both are leftovers in a world where humans and things intersect and reflect each other in ways that unwrap feelings and emotions like longing, grief and nostalgia.

Like the bottle, the eponymous darning needle from the tale of 1847 (first published 1846), "The Darning Needle" ("Stoppenaalen") is possessed with human feelings such as pride. Like the bottleneck, the needle refuses to be what it has become. They are both anxious and vain beings that insist on their own importance even in changed circumstances and distorted forms. The darning needle imagines itself as a sentient and sensitive soul born of a sunbeam. It is in fact made of steel, or perhaps the more brittle iron, exhibiting a remarkable, almost irrational, resilience, so that, although we know that the needle was broken at the onset of the story, in the end, this tiny gadget survives its own story: "'I'm breaking! I'm breaking!' But she didn't break, though the wagon went over her; she lay at full length along the cobblestones, and there we'll leave her."[3] The final remark from the narrator makes clear that there is no transcendent afterlife for this material thing, except to be left in its own robust animation.

This is also the case in "The Sweethearts" ("Kjærestefolkene," 1844), where excessive bouncing leads to nowhere but eventually lands a Moroccan leather ball in the gutter where it is left for years to come. In the meantime, the top, repainted, gilded in fact, became so animated that it jumped straight "into the dustbin, where all sorts of rubbish was lying – old cabbage stalks, dust, dirt, and gravel that had fallen down through the gutter."[4] Here in the dustbin it recognised its old flame, the ball, now faded like a wrinkled old apple, which for years had been lying in the gutter in diminished circumstances unrecognisable as trash, rubbish.

Transient and Durable Things

According to Michael Thompson's *Rubbish Theory* from 1979 the value and "possession of objects" is contingent on our ability to "discard objects." ([1979] 2017, 1). This contingency is itself contingent on a paradigm that states that "there is a status difference between the condition of being rich and the condition of being poor, the former being higher that the latter. The condition of richness or poorness is determined by the quality of objects one possesses: a poor person possesses few objects, a rich person many objects." (1). A poor person cannot afford to throw away any objects; a rich person can waste things. But at the same time there has to be a consensus about what is valuable. It is this consensus that Andersen questions in many of his stories.

What has happened in the sweetheart story is that Andersen has placed the ball in the *transient* and the top in the *durable* category to use Thompson's categories. The ball will most likely remain trash, or might, if found, become a secondhand object, while the top may well end up as an heirloom and an antique. In this economic system, they clearly age differently. While one loses worth, the other gains worth. But the fate of each is arbitrary. That is Andersen's main point. Serendipity decides if you are lost or found, transient or durable. A toy is just a toy, but its value changes depending on circumstances.

The cracked bottle, the broken needle, the weather-beaten ball and the restored top along with a host of other things in Andersen's works, all have one thing in common: they are commonplace household items or simple toys. They belong to the intimate sphere of human life: the kitchen and dining room, the living room and the nursery. Neither of them is particularly valuable in a conventional sense; there are no precious diamonds or pearls here. Instead there is a constant flux between hubris (excess worth) and humiliation (worthlessness) in the objects' fates. The unremarkable darning needle and the other broken objects stubbornly see themselves as unique and exceptional, no matter how brutally they are humiliated or debased. They continue to put on airs even as they fall into the gutter. The harder an object falls into the rubbish category the more it gains in poetic value. Said differently, the displaced, disrupted, misunderstood or buried objects earn interest in a value scheme of fiction "matured in a greedy imagination, and not in a bank." (Orlando 2006, 9).

When Andersen makes use of ordinary objects as social metaphors, granting them value through the process of suffering, it is not only because literature tends to love misery, but also because he has a point to make. Things are often placed in miserable situations where they routinely misjudge their own predicament in ways that seems geared for the readers to grasp the predicament properly. That is to say, the frequent misreading of circumstance by the things themselves within the tale serve as a curative (or warning) for the reader to remain vigilant and skeptical about what is articulated by the things and by their proxy narrators.

Although Andersen's own lifetime was not yet marked by the massive amounts of disposables we now know, the mechanical production of more and more goods rubbed off on his imagination and allowed him to see that discarded things, like waste, "can generate powerful emotions" (Hawkins 2005, vii) and not least, to use Hawkins' phrase "becomes recognizable and representable as the dead matter that affirms our living subjectivity, or sense of self" (2). The inanimate, in other words, reaffirms the dynamic between material stuff and human lives. It becomes "a social text that discloses the logic or illogic of a culture." (2).

If we see waste as "discarded, expelled, or excess matter" (Hawkins 2005, vii), Andersen can be said to add a measure of "empathy with the inorganic" – the emotional appeal that Benjamin in 1938 noticed in Baudelaire's enthusiasm for animated toys. Andersen was interested in a kind of restitution of broken persons and things and expressed empathy with the inorganic not only to press his readers then and now, to pick up seemingly mute things and listen to their stories, but also to give unwanted stuff life stories to tell, worth listening to. Not least because rubbish, garbage and waste *tell on us*, as Andersen demonstrates, and disclose our practices, prejudices, values and secrets. His use of vibrant storied matter, to borrow Jane Bennett's term (2010, viii), makes for good stories indeed. Yet we should be careful to avoid seeing this as a simple mapping of human concerns onto inanimate matter even though precisely this meshing of the world of humans and things is suggestive, making things and humans both strangers and partners.

Andersen's use of rubbish and waste and broken things should not be seen as a curiosity about repulsive stuff *per se*. During his lifetime, human waste cramped the gutters, filled the air with noxious fumes, and created health hazards such as cholera epidemics. In general Andersen avoided the kind of dirt we associate with filth and slime and ooze, human by-products like faeces and the like; the kind of dirt that Mary Douglas writes about in *Purity and Danger* (1966, 36, 121). Instead Andersen had an eye for the fact that waste of no value or even negative value can be used in literary language as both an oxymoron and a paradox as I will illustrate in the next example.

Mud and the Power of Nonsense

So far Andersen's use of anthropomorphism in his fairy tales, his summoning of human agency to give life and voice to mute objects has centered our attention on *objects as subjects* in storytelling. But Andersen also makes use of discarded stuff as verbal action aids. The mud in "Clumsy Hans" ("Klods-Hans. En gammel Historie fortalt igjen," 1855) is used precisely as worthless stuff with linguistic, indeed ironic value. That is to say, there is a restructuring of value in the tale that feeds off of the paradoxical and challenges ordinary economies or social or aesthetic orders. Although this is not an original Andersen tale, but retold from a folk tale, Andersen knows how to mime the story's brilliant use of useless matter. It is precisely the mud's apparent lack of value that gives this slippery substance its currency as valuable material for Andersen. Along with the other valueless objects in "Clumsy Hans" (a dead crow and an old wooden shoe) the mud actually gains currency as the 'stuff' that ultimately earns our clumsy hero the most valuable price: the princess and half the kingdom.

Clumsy Hans, of course, is himself essentially valueless waste; at least in the established social order of the story. He is a marginal, almost residual character introduced into a story well under way and after his two more 'worthy' brothers. Andersen's shrewd use of the outcast and his understanding of the value of that which falls outside of a seemingly natural economic system allows him to pry open our collective blindness to all those things and persons we often do not notice even if we step on or over them. We habitually turn our eyes away from things or persons of no value.

But Andersen forces the reader to look again. He makes us reconsider, of all things, the potentials of mud. Children already know that mud matters (just as dead crows and old shoes can be inspiring, if morbid, playthings). Andersen makes use of this knowledge and promotes the slippery substance as a valuable currency. The mud (along with the other useless things) allows Hans to be "witty" in ways that wins the princesses' heart and drives the plot. Indeed, when he throws the mud in the face of the pedantic alderman (Oldermand) it underscores the sway of abject matter: it can make the powerful look ridiculous. To make this happen, Hans pronounces (against all reason) that the dead crow is food, that the old shoe is a pot to cook in, and that mud is gravy. Again, it is by wit that he persuades the readers and the princess and wins the competition. The wittiness in handling the crow, shoe, and mud skilfully echoes the wit of the story's plotline. Useless things can both earn a princess and a kingdom and provide material for brilliant storytelling.

There is nothing magical or extraordinary about mud. Mud is a poor substance. But if used, as in Andersen's tale, to call attention to the discarded and wasted, it promptly becomes rich with literary value. Perhaps Andersen can be seen as an early observer of what Bennett calls thing-power: "*Thing-power* ... has the rhetorical advantage of calling to mind a childhood sense of the world as filled with all sorts of animate beings." (2010, 20). Yet, the add-on value through speech acts, in this tale, has as a starting point useless junk and a hero who is seen as unable to master (proper) speech: "you don't know how to talk properly," as his father says.[5] This deficit makes a difference since the added value not only comes about by going against the grain of regular conventions of value (the dead crow, wooden shoe, and mud) but by making absurd claims. The father is seriously misreading the eloquence of his three sons and is unable to predict the persuasiveness of his youngest son's tongue. It is the verbal skills of Hans that has currency, not the book-learnedness of his brothers. But Hans' articulateness comes about by subverting normal or reasonable rhetoric. To those in power, he speaks nonsense.

Andersen's narrative technique is in other words repeatedly reliant on a world turned topsy-turvy. It is contingent on *nonsense*. The etymological meaning of the word in English, as Susan Stewart has pointed out, is that "which is not sense; spoken or written words which make no sense or convey absurd ideas; also absurd or senseless action," but it can also mean "unsubstantial or worthless stuff or things" or even a "want of feeling or physical sensation." (1978, 4). It can be something that belongs to marginal beings; those who have not yet gained the ability to resonate or those who have lost the ability to do so, like the child and the mad: stock characters for Andersen. Through the imaginative and eloquent nonsense of a marginal character Andersen allows otherwise useless stuff to be (preposterously) useful.

Picking up the Trash

When Andersen picks up the trash or 'pens' debris he implicitly points to an otherness in material residue that is not, to use Peter Schwenger's phrase from his book *The Tears of Things: Melancholy and Physical Objects*, "indifferent to human existence," but "a constant-and enduring parallel universe of matter." (2006, 81). "From the point of view of such objects," Schwenger goes on "the narratives and structures that give shape to our lives are nothing but sheds and patches, tacked together over the insubstantiality of the subject." (82). The troubled solidity of objects, their *trashability,* in turn troubles the same qualities in the subject, presses on or even dissolves our assumptions of solidity. Like things, *we* can be trashed.

Andersen is not interested in the forensics of discarded things or the gooeyness of dirt, but in their ethos, their aesthetic and social significance where the civilising process that pushes dirt to the side as shameful and abhorrent is analogous in some respects to a more general process of discarding, overlooking, alienating. In the nineteenth century, the culture of excess rears its head and the economy of the discarded took on a different valence that it had before. Andersen was more than willing to pick up the wasted objects from the trashcan, consider how their nature of brokenness could make them into material metaphors for human anxieties and show how the wasted can create something new in prose literature.

Andersen's broken things are in this sense recuperated as valued characters that are given voices to speak directly about the ambivalence and irony of our relationship to trash. At the same time, in Andersen's thinking, there is an implicit path of regeneration and reuse, not entirely different from his frequent use of the eternal return of the ephemeral (consider his bird phoenix principle). Andersen's use of regeneration as a model gives vitality to trash that also points to a dynamic act of restoration of human actors.

Picking up the trash then means restoring dignity to those (or that) who have lost theirs (or its). This, I would argue, is an aesthetic and ethical claim, as well as a social and historical argument. Not least because, for Andersen, as always, the disenchantment of an over-stuffed modernity contains a possibility for re-enchantment of the mundane and low forms of prosaic life, of rubbish, trash, waste.

References

Adler, Anthony Curtis. 2012. "The Abject Life of Things: H.C. Andersen's Sentimentality." *Angelaki: Journal of Theoretical Humanities* 17 (1): 115–130. doi:10.1080/0969725X.2012.671673.

Andersen, Hans Christian. 2003–07. *Andersen. H.C. Andersens samlede værker*. Edited by Klaus P. Mortensen. 18 vols. København: Det Danske Sprog- og Litteraturselskab/Gyldendal.

Bauman, Zygmunt. 2003. *Wasted Lives: Modernity and its Outcasts*. Cambridge: Polity.

Bennett, Jane. 2010. *Vibrant Matter: A Political Economy of Things*. Durham: Duke University Press.

Danius, Sara. 2006. *The Prose of the World*. Stockholm: Coronet Books.

Douglas, Mary. 1966. *Purity and Danger: An Analysis of Concepts of Pollution and Taboo*. London: Routledge.

Freedgood, Elaine. 2006. *The Ideas in Things*. Chicago: University of Chicago Press.

Gaffikin, Brigid. 2004. "Material Witnesses: Hans Christian Andersen's *Object tales* and the Memories of Things." *Edda: Scandinavian Journal of Literary Research* 2004 (3): 186–200.

Grimm, Jacob, and Wilhelm Grimm. 2004. *The Annotated Brothers Grimm*. Edited and translated by Maria Tatar. New York/London: W.W. Norton & Company.

Hawkins, Gay. 2005. *The Ethics of Waste*. Lanham, Maryland: Rowman & Littlefield Publishers.

Müller-Wille, Klaus. 2017. *Sezierte Bücher. Hans Christian Andersens Materialästhetik.* München: Fink-Verlag.

Orlando, Francesco. 2006. *Obsolete Objects in the Literary Imagination: Ruins, Relics, Rarities, Rubbish, Uninhabited Places, and Hidden Treasures.* New Haven: Yale University Press.

Price, Leah. 2012. *How to Do Things with Books.* Princeton: Princeton University Press.

Schwenger, Peter. 2006. *The Tears of Things: Melancholy and Physical Objects.* Minneapolis: University of Minnesota.

Stewart, Susan. 1978. *Nonsense: Aspects of Intertextuality in Folklore and Literature.* Baltimore: Johns Hopkins University Press.

Strasser, Susan. 1999. *Waste and Want: A Social History of Trash.* New York: Holt Paperbacks.

Thompson, Michael. (1979) 2017. *Rubbish Theory: The Creation and Destruction of Value.* London: Pluto Press.

Notes

1. For the purpose of simplicity and clarity, I use 'thing' and 'object' interchangeably here and do not adhere to the strict (albeit often useful) distinctions offered by Bill Brown and other thing theorists. Similarly, I do not distinguish here between the many inflections of waste, junk, rubbish and garbage, but see them all as part of Andersen's particular use of discarded stuff.
2. "tom og propløs, følte sig saa underlig flau, den savnede Noget, men vidste ikke selv, hvad den savnede" (Andersen 2003-07, 2:162).
3. "'jeg knækker! jeg knækker!'" men den knak ikke, skjøndt der gik et Vognmandslæs over, den laae paa langs -- og der kan den blive liggende!" (Andersen 2003-07, 1:405).
4. "i Skarnfjerdingen, hvor der laae alle Slags, Kaalstokke, Feieskarn og Gruus, der var faldet ned fra Tagrenden." (Andersen 2003-07, 1:282).
5. "Du kan jo ikke tale!" (Andersen 2003-07, 2:121).

Hans Christian Andersen between community and commons
"The Ugly Duckling" and "The Fir Tree" revisited

Anne Klara Bom
University of Southern Denmark, Odense

One of the criteria that must be met if newcomers want to become Danish citizens is that a citizenship and naturalisation test must be passed. The tests are based on a learning material that the newcomers must learn by heart. Hans Christian Andersen holds a prominent position in all versions of the learning material. Through the lens of sociologist Nikolas Rose's (1999) notion of ethico-politics, this chapter examines how Andersen is presented and "harnessed" in this material. With this use as a point of departure, "The Ugly Duckling" and "The Fir Tree" are presented as examples of fairy tales that can be reframed as cultural commons in future encounters with newcomers and thereby be of use in future integration practices in Denmark.

Hans Christian Andersen's fairy tales are both institutionalised on curricula in many countries and chosen as bedside stories in families across borders. When the fairy tales are found valuable enough to be passed on to the next generation (and the next), they are sustained as literary world heritage, and they can thus be considered cultural commons: elements that should be equally accessible to everyone. In debates on how to secure sustainability in the world, "the tragedy of the commons" has been a theme for decades. In these debates, 'commons' are defined as goods that are not privately owned; for example, air and water. The 'tragedy' is when different actors start depleting or spoiling the commons out of self-interest (Hardin 1968). Within the cultural sphere, commons and the tragedies of them are also widely discussed. Here, commons are for example literature, arts and other kinds of heritage. The tragedy of cultural commons occurs when various actors either try to benefit from the common without taking responsibility for its maintenance (so-called "free riders") and/or when scarce attention is paid to commons in processes where they are passed on to the next generation (Bertacchini et al. 2012).

According to sociologist Nikolas Rose, one of the most significant threats to the cultural common is communities, because governing through community can result in communities that "harness" the common (1999, 176; Parmett 2012, 174). In line with this, political economist David Harvie (2004) suggests that we need to explore the nature of the communities we are already part of and ask how they produce or prevent commons. With these statements as points of departure, the purpose of this chapter is twofold: First, I present one particular case where Hans Christian Andersen is harnessed by the Danish government when he is put to use in naturalisation and citizenship tests and the learning material for them. This case is chosen in continuation of cultural scholars Sara Ahmed and Anne-Marie Fortier's argument that communities can be thought of as "effects of how we meet on the ground, as a ground that is material, but also virtual, real and imaginary." (Ahmed and Fortier 2003, 257). Multiple choice tests and a learning material that must be learned by heart is an example of how people are met on the ground in Denmark. This very real and material ground is also imaginary, as it conveys a particular narrative about Denmark and Danish values. In the material, Hans Christian Andersen is placed as a representative for this specific version of a Danish community. The second purpose of this chapter is to pay a revisit Hans Christian Andersen's fairy tales "The Ugly Duckling" ("Den grimme Ælling," 1844) and "The Fir Tree" ("Grantræet," 1845) and ask the question: Can these fairy tales be reframed as cultural commons in future encounters with our newcomers? And if so, can communities be thought of as frameworks that hold potential to sustain the common rather than prevent it? Aside from the fairy tales, the material in the analysis consists of the learning material for the tests and relevant statements from Facebook.

Community and Commons as Ethico-political Questions

Ahmed and Fortier's definition of community as effects of how we meet on the ground requires that community is examined not as a solution, but as "a question mark and a mark of questioning" (2003, 251). We must ask questions and feel unsettled by the notion *community*, they argue, we must look at the work that the word community does because this will enable us to think about what it could do in the work that we do as scholars (252). Thus, it is a case for cultural studies to look at ways in which communities are shaped in order to ask the question: Could they be shaped differently? The analytical framework for Nikolas Rose's work on community is "the conduct of conduct," a term that seeks to cover the equivocal nature of government and governing as comprising "all endeavours to shape, guide, direct the conduct of others" *and* the ways people are urged and educated to govern themselves (1999, 3). Rose illustrates how community, since it was offered as a solution to the emerging problems of governing a diverse and dispersed citizenry in the 1960s and 1970s, has been framed as both the diagnosis and cure of economic and social ills in the Western welfare societies (Parmett 2012, 173). This makes him ask: "if community, in so many guises and forms, is proposed as a solution, what is it in our welfare democracies that it is seen as a solution *to*? If there is an answer, there must be a question." (Rose 1999, 173). This question, according to Rose, is how governing can be relocated from state to citizenry through what he terms *ethico-politics*, defined as "self-techniques necessary for responsible self-government and the relations between one's obligation to oneself and one's obligation to others." (188). Communities can be framed as the platforms responsible for carrying out governmental politics, he argues, but it requires that they are ethically governed and that they govern themselves in correspondence with present ethical guidelines.

Rose distinguishes between two kinds of ethico-politics: The kinds that operate at the "pole of morality" and the kinds that operate at the "pole of ethics." Ethico-politics at the pole of morality has an uncontestable code of conduct that is put to use with the aim of managing people's self-conduct in ways that produce politically desired ends (1999, 193). They refer to community as essence, origin and fixity, and thus, Rose suggests that potential new forms of community can only emerge from ethico-politics that operate at the pole of ethics. Such politics are characterised by a reluctance to govern too much, and they refer to community not as fixed but as locally and situationally constructed, and thereby as indeterminate spaces of becoming where the "collective unworking of identities and moralities" can take place. In communities where such agonistic ethico-politics are explicated, Rose states, "the values of different forms of life would be directly at stake" (195) as practices of inclusion and exclusion and other non-individuated subjectivity formations are replaced with "opening up the evaluation of forms of life and self-conduct to the difficult and interminable business of debate and contestation." (192). The difficulties of realising these communities of becoming appear to centre on the question: How is it possible to leave thoughts about community as a synonym for commonality (and thereby thoughts about inclusion and exclusion) behind and replace it with debate? It is obvious that the conduct of such ethico-politics would require both physical and emotional labour, as Ahmed and Fortier put it (2003, 257). In a recent essay, Ahmed reflects on the kind of emotional labour that is at stake when national governments govern through communities with specific regard to newcomers. She sees it as matters of *attunement*:

> The problem with attunement is [...] that it can easily become not just a description of an experience but also an ideal, as if the aim is to be in harmony, to be in tune with others. When attunement becomes an aim, those who are not in tune or who are out of tune become the obstacles. (2014, 20).

The figures that find themselves or are found to be out of tune are also responsible for the affective labour it requires to get attuned: "Some bodies have to become attuned to others, those who are already, as it were, 'in the room'," as Ahmed phrases it (22). She points to what she terms *diversity work* as a possibly more balanced way to work on attunement. Diversity work seeks to "minimise differences" so that newcomers can appear more in tune with the community they arrive in (22), and the minimising is the responsibility of those who are already "in the room." The way I read it, Rose would think that such diversity work can only be carried out as radical ethico-politics that operate at the pole of ethics.

But how would such politics affect handlings of the commons? In a revisit to Hardin's thesis on the tragedy of the commons, Marxist theorists Michael Hardt and Antonio Negri argue that the original focus on the potential tragedies that occur as results of scarcity of material goods was developed within a framework where "the public" was considered a patrimony of the state and "general interest" an attribute of sovereignty (2005, 206) and therefore, it does not offer a fruitful platform for analyses of today's societies where immaterial logics of capitalism such as affect, information, knowledge, experience and relationships, dominate (Hardt and Negri 2009). Instead, Hardt and Negri suggest that the idea of "the public" must be replaced with the premodern idea of *the multitude*: a gathering of individual people where individuals control those goods and services that allow for the reproduction of the multitude itself (Hardt and Negri 2005, 206). Or put in another way: "every social function regulated by the state that could be equally well managed in common should be transferred to common hands." (Hardt and Negri 2012, 79). In a recent article, heritage scholar Helen Graham points to "productive connections" between the multitude and the commons in a museum context. She states: "As such, when brought into a museological context, Hardt and Negri make room for an argument that we need not focus so much on the scarcity of materiality culture but focus on the common ideas, knowledge and social relations that can be generated from use-as-access." (Graham 2017, 156). This, Graham argues, requires that heritage is perceived as a process; a perception that categorises all heritage as intangible because heritage is primarily about what is valued (Harvey 2001; Smith 2006; Graham 2017). This goes for Hans Christian Andersen's fairy tales as well, and if we follow Ahmed and Rose, the fairy tales could be obvious objects of diversity work if they were detached from a national context and posed as ethical questions in debates on what we find valuable and why. Thereby, they would work as ethical frames through which newcomers could be met on the ground.

Ethico-politics at the Pole of Morality: Hans Christian Andersen in the Tests

The naturalisation and citizenship tests exist as a result of a shift in migration and integration policies that was initiated in Denmark in 1998 with an Integration Act that had as its aim to "make it possible, through an integration effort, for newly-arrived refugees and immigrants to become *active participants* in society as a whole, *self-supporting* and with an *understanding* of Danish fundamental values and norms." (Ersbøll 2010, 112). In this act, integration was presented as a two-way process with the host municipality and the immigrant/refugee as central actors. Over the years, however, the rules and requirements for immigrants and refugees have been restricted several times, and this has affected both the migrants who wish to obtain permanent residence in Denmark and those who wish to apply for naturalisation. A noteworthy restriction came in 2005 when the government presented a new plan for integration called *A New Chance for Everybody* (*En ny chance til alle*). In this plan, a revised conduct of conduct emerged as it was explicated that an *understanding* of Danish values and norms was not enough anymore. Instead, the criteria were formulated like this:

> A diverse society can be an enrichment [...]. But, simultaneously, it places demands of openmindedness, openness, equivalence, accept, respect and trust. And it presupposes that there is approval and acceptance of fundamental values. Respect for the freedom of speech and the individual's freedom of rights and personal integrity must be values that everybody – regardless of cultural background – upholds. (Regeringen 2005, 32, my translation)

Human Rights scholar Eva Ersbøll has argued that this restriction reflects a shift in balance because the immigrants are not only expected to *understand*, but now to *accept* and *uphold* Danish fundamental values (Ersbøll 2010, 115, 149). In line with Ahmed it can be argued that the revised text frames the immigrant as even more "out of tune" than before, and as the only one responsible for getting attuned with the community he or she wants to be a part of. The tests were introduced as a result of this restriction. Today, the active citizenship test is a multiple-choice test with 25 questions about "the Danish democracy and everyday life, and about Danish culture and history" that must be passed by applicants for permanent residence in Denmark. The naturalisation test is also a multiple-choice test, but with 40 questions about "Danish society, Danish culture and history." Both tests are supplied with learning material published by the responsible ministry.

It has been argued that with the test systems, the Danish integration policies have developed from reflecting a liberal-republican model of citizenship towards a more communitarian one. Within the communitarian framework, "citizenship requires assimilation since it places the emphasis on the maintenance of a community's distinctive identity, as articulated by the majority community." (Kostakopoulou 2010, 5). Rose argues that for communitarian scholars (and for communitarians in general) a *remoralisation* of communities is the goal: The only way to "moral order" in multi-cultural societies is if all citizens refer to a "core of values shared by the members of all communities," and if this core is embodied in the rituals of everyday life (1999, 183). In *A New Chance for Everybody*, the accentuated moral values are freedom of speech, freedom of rights and personal integrity. In the learning material for the tests, however, it becomes clear that in order to be able to uphold and recognise these values in the Danish community, Danish history and culture must be learned by rote. In the naturalisation test, thus, half the questions can be considered communitarian (concerned with names, events, historical and geographical issues), and the other half as republican: questions that deal with useful and usable everyday knowledge for the participants (Ersbøll 2010, 144).

In all versions of learning material for both tests, Hans Christian Andersen's sections represent the communitarian questions. The material for the naturalisation test was first published in 2007 with the title *Denmark Before and Now* (*Danmark før og nu*), and again in 2015. In the version from 2007, Hans Christian Andersen appears in the section on Danish literature:

> Danish literature from 1800 till today comprises several great authors and storytellers. One of the most famous is Hans Christian Andersen (1805–1875), who was born in Odense. He wrote fairy tales that have pleased both children and adults in Denmark and in the rest of the world for two centuries. Hans Christian Andersen's fairy tales are translated into more than 125 languages. His tales about The Little Mermaid, The Ugly Duckling and The Fir Tree are among the most read. Even though Hans Christian Andersen is most famous for his fairy tales, he wrote novels and poems as well. (Ministeriet for Flygtninge, Indvandrere og Integration 2007, 90–91, my translation)

This small portion of words in the 2007 publication is accompanied by a picture of a statue of Andersen, and in 2015 by a photograph taken of him (Udlændinge-, Integrations- og Boligministeriet 2015, 76). In the textbook for the citizenship test, another picture of a statue of Hans Christian Andersen is chosen for the front page of the chapter called "Danish Culture," and the text about him goes as follows:

> Hans Christian Andersen (1805–1875) was a Danish author who became world famous for his fairy tales. Hans Christian Andersen was born in Odense as the son of a poor cobbler. He moved to Copenhagen when he was 14 years old. Among others, he wrote novels, poems and fairy tales. Hans Christian Andersen's fairy tales have been translated into approximately 125 languages. Among his most famous fairy tales are The Fir Tree and The Ugly Duckling. These fairy tales show Andersen's unique ability to equip animals and plants with human voices and – with animals and plants – to tell stories about human mistakes and dreams. (Udlændinge-, Integrations- og Boligministeriet 2016, 111, my translation).

As these examples illustrate, the text books present Hans Christian Andersen as a key figure in the majority culture (for those who are already "in the room") that all potential new citizens must be familiar with if they want to attune to the Danish community. The knowledge that can be required of newcomers, however, is reduced to the facts presented in the above quotes. In different tests over the years, applicants have for example been asked questions like: In what city was Hans Christian Andersen born? Which author wrote "The Little Mermaid"? In what period of time did Hans Christian Andersen live? Hans Christian Andersen is one of the most famous authors in Denmark. Which of these fairy tales did he write?

Following Ahmed, we need to ask what the word community does – or what kind of Danish community that is presented – in these examples. Law scholar Robert Kahn uses the restrictive initiatives in Danish integration politics as an example of what he terms the "exclusivist turn in European civic nationalism" that reflects a "love it or leave it position:" The newcomer is free to join the political community but *only if* he or she accepts the national values (2008, 529). Ersbøll argues that permanent residence and citizenship in Denmark is presented as something that must be "strived for" (2010, 133) and "earned" (139, 149). A part of this striving is learning by rote: Both tests can be passed if the applicants know the learning material by heart. In line with Rose it can be argued that community here is presented as a communitarian solution to the problems of governing a diverse and dispersed citizenry. Quoting communitarian scholar Amitai Etzioni, Rose defines the goal with such governing like this: "the moral voice of the community 'is the main way that individuals and groups in a good society encourage one another to adhere to behaviour that reflects shared values and to avoid behaviour that offends or violates them.'" (Etzioni 1997, 124, as quoted in Rose 1999, 184). Thus, the conduct of conduct that is reflected in the tests can be perceived as ethico-politics that operate at the pole of morality, and the Danish community is presented as essence, origin and fixity (Rose 1999, 195).

In a similar vein, rhetoric scholar Louise Schou Therkildsen argues that the learning material from 2007 comprises three narratives about a Danish community with essentialistic traits, norms and values (2013, 151). First, the contemporary Danish community is described as an organic, homogenous unit founded in a substantial, historical community (154–156). Second, the population is described as fairly homogenous and thus, the diachronic parallel in the first narrative is here supplied with a description of synchronic similarities (157). Third, it is accentuated that Danes are democratic people, and the norms for democratic execution are described as an internalised practice in all Danes: By participating in "everyday democracy" via for example associational life, Danes are trained to "discuss cases, try their arguments and compromise, in order to find reasonable solutions." In this sense, democracy is about more than voting: A democratic citizen is an individual who has argumentative skills that can be used in debates (158). The content of these three narratives, Therkildsen states, creates a static image of an already completed nation, a closed, excluding community, with a population that has an unchangeable core (161). This results in a positioning of the applicants as excluded and as the only ones who must be willing to change in order to be integrated in the community (162). In such a community, every citizen would of course know the answers to *all* the republican and communitarian questions. This, however, is not exactly the case. In the aforementioned integration plan *A New Chance for Everybody*, the Danish community is supplied with characteristics like openmindedness, openness, equality, accept, respect and trust, all founded in the fundamental values freedom of speech, freedom of rights and the right to personal integrity. But with the test systems, these stated values of community are surrounded by what must appear as an almost insurmountable fence for potential new citizens. This makes Ersbøll conclude that "future citizens have to do better than the average Danish citizen in order to become member of the Danish citizenry." (2010, 150).

Every year, the naturalisation test is published in the media after the test day. Danish newspapers use their online platforms to entice their readers to take the test. "Test yourself," the headlines say, frequently accompanied by "Can you become Danish?" (*Jyllands-Posten* 2017; *Berlingske* 2017) or even "Are you smart enough to become a Danish citizen?" (*Berlingske* 2012; *B.T.* 2016, 2017). And every year, many Danes take the test online in order to see whether or not they can be a part of the club. Quite a lot of them post their failed results as comments on the different newspapers' social media sites. It is beyond the scope of this chapter to conduct a thorough analysis of these comments, but it is safe to say that every year, the publication of the tests activates online debates on the existence and content of them, and the debates always evolve around the question: When are you Danish? Despite differences of opinion, online debaters seem to agree that the tests are a bad political decision. But even though the debaters oppose the conduct, their opinions differ when it comes to the conduct of conduct, namely the idea of the Danish community as an essence with an unchangeable core. Articulations that affirm the conduct of conduct are for example: "A test should not decide whether or not you are Danish, it should be decided by where you are born, if you speak Danish and if you have Danish values," (Huus 2017, n.p.)[1] or:

> You are Danish if you cheer for Denmark in a football match against for example Turkey, or when you wave the flag if the royal family has something to celebrate with the population, or if you participate, help and contribute to the local sports club and if you are a part of a community. If none of the above is spot on, you are probably not in the right spot on Planet Earth. (Hansen 2017, n.p.)

On the other side, expressions that appear to oppose the conduct of conduct tend to mock the tests: "Another ridiculous retrospective test that at best can give you a hint as to whether you are qualified to study history at the university college" and "Yes I passed, and so what? Does that make me more Danish? Hardly! Am I good at rote learning? Yes, probably. What is left is the question; how to become a modern Dane who can juggle with multi-cultural values and a Danishness that has room for us all?" (Mammen 2016, n.p.) It can be argued that in this latter category there could be potential for ethico-politics that operate at the pole of ethics: politics that do not refer to any "true discourse" about what it takes to be a part of the Danish community, but instead recognise diversity by arguing for "the powers of 'other communities' and 'other subjectivities', for an experimental ethical politics of life itself," as Rose puts it (1999, 194).

To sum up: The community presented in the learning material for the tests is dominated with essentialistic elements. Danish identity is something you are born with, and, as a newcomer, you will always already be positioned as "out of tune." Following Ahmed, community is here presented as a solution, and the governing through community, to use Rose's term, can be characterised as ethico-politics at the pole of morality. And Hans Christian Andersen? He adorns the learning material in static versions: As an object for rote learning, visualised as a statue. In this version, he is a representative for the majority culture, a gatekeeper. A common good, but only for the Danes.

Another Community? Ethico-politics at the Pole of Ethics

As mentioned in the beginning of this chapter, Ahmed places it as an obligation for cultural studies scholars to ask whether communities can be done differently, and Rose emphasises that the aim of governing through community can be counterposed by communities themselves: While governments and communitarian scholars wish to *reinvent* community in order to relocate power and thereby govern better (1999, 194), this "new game of power" (188) holds potential for re-thinking or re-imagining community as a "name for the forms of collectivization that create [...] new types of non-individuated subjectivity." (196) Such mobilisations require dialogue and debate. In her essay, Therkildsen suggests that a narrative about the Danish *citizen* as a common identity based on actions rather than on similarity and up-bringing would be more constructive in the meeting with applicants for Danish naturalisation or citizenship:

[...] argumentation and debate are competences that are appraised as valuable in the book. And at the same time, they are practices that inevitably involve disagreements, dynamics and development; we argue and debate with the intent to reach a common goal or a common attitude. Frequently these goals are not achieved, and we must agree to disagree – until the next option comes up, and it may be possible to reach a compromise. (2013, 162, my translation)

If Therkildsen's suggestion was put to use, becoming Danish would demand skills that could actually be achieved.

Hans Christian Andersen's fairy tales seem to be a rather obvious case for practicing debate skills and argumentation, because they present more nuanced descriptions of the values of community. The nuances are a consequence of the fact that Andersen's fairy tales are never moralising (Thomsen 2017a). Instead, questions about good and evil, right and wrong, remain open in the fairy tales. As Andersen scholar Torsten Bøgh Thomsen puts it: "Andersen's texts give room for statements and convictions to stay in a tension, an undecidedness, instead of settling in an unequivocal view of the world or art." (Thomsen 2017b, 63, my translation). Because Andersen avoids answers and static morals when he deals with the conditions of human life, the texts are still open for ethical debates today: They incite their readers to be curious and to never stop asking questions, and this is probably one of the reasons why Andersen is sustainable across borders and generations.

For reasons unknown, "The Fir Tree" and "The Ugly Duckling" are the two fairy tales continuously mentioned in every version of learning material for the tests. For the purpose of the essentialistic discourse, the selection of these fairy tales can be seen as an obvious choice, as they have both been objects to hegemonic readings that are concerned with the *essence* of their content, and such closed readings can easily work as platforms for essentialistic readings. The literary research on Hans Christian Andersen has existed for decades, and when it comes to "The Fir Tree" and "The Ugly Duckling," a common sense has manifested itself in the scholarly community. The dominating discourse on "The Fir Tree" is that it is a story to remind us that life is now. No matter where the tree is, it always longs for something else, something different: the joy, happiness and success that must be in store for it. Andersen scholar Johan de Mylius, for example, contributes significantly to this hegemonic reading. By use of phrasings like "it is a story about" (2005, 111) and "the actual story" (108), de Mylius emphasises the admonitions from the tree's surroundings to live in the moment, when he states: "'Carpe diem!' seize the day, echoes here, and that is, to put it shortly, the theme in the narrative about the fir tree." (109). Here, de Mylius points out and isolates one possible interpretation as the true meaning of the fairy tale. A significant trait in this way of reading Andersen is the idea that there is an unavoidable relation between Andersen as a person and the plot in the tale (110). Similar biographic readings have been applied to "The Ugly Duckling" since the fairy tale was published in 1843. Almost all readings, analyses and comments place themselves in continuation of Georg Brandes' statement that the fairy tale is the "quintessence of its author's entire being" (Bredsdorff 1975, 113-114) de Mylius, for example, accentuates this fairy tale as the one in which Andersen's private mythology was given "eternal expression." (de Mylius 2016, 12). He points to one exception from this discourse when he mentions an interpretation presented by the poet Carsten Hauch in a letter written to Andersen shortly after the publication. Hauch frames the tale as a "universal statement about one of the basic terms of life" when he writes: "The story about the cat and the chicken who consider themselves as belonging to the best part of the world and who despise everything that cannot purr or lay eggs repeats itself every day on earth." (Hauch, as quoted in de Mylius 2005, 63-64). As this reading of the fairy tale stands alone, however, it can be argued that the dominant biographic readings of both fairy tales have an excluding effect on other possible uses of the texts. They convey the idea that we all know what the stories are about, and thus, they can easily be adapted in an essentialistic discourse without further reflection. For example, it could seem fair to ask if the duckling would have had a happier life if it had just been born among swans in the community it was meant for. And wouldn't it have been easier for the fir tree if its roots had not been cut and if it had just stayed in its natural surroundings? But if we keep asking questions, there is more to both fairy tales than what meets the essentialistic eye, and both fairy tales can be of use if community is posed as a question rather than a solution. In the closing remarks of her extensive critique of the naturalisation tests, Ersbøll uses Hans Christian Andersen when she appeals to another Danish community with other values. Her reference point is The Ugly Duckling's stay with the old woman in the farm house. She lives with the chicken and the cat who both prefer the closed, excluding community. Ersbøll argues:

> We know about the consequences of being on trial and demanded the impossible from the famous Danish author H.C. Andersen's fairy tale The Ugly Duckling – which foreigners also have to be familiar with, since it is mentioned in the textbook "Denmark past and present" that has to be read and remembered in order to pass the naturalisation test. The 'ugly duckling' is a young swan born in a duck-yard and an outsider from the very beginning. It flies over the fence and lands near a hut where an old woman lives with her cat and hen. The woman takes the duckling for a duck and it is 'admitted on trial' in order to see whether it can lay eggs. 'Lay eggs, or purr', is the message from the hen to the duckling, which can do neither of these things. When we read the fairy tale about the ugly duckling that becomes the most beautiful swan, we normally take the side of the duckling. (2010, 151)

In this quote, Hans Christian Andersen is put to use not as a static image that conveys equally static morals, but as a medium that can be used to question the values of community in alternative ways. This is clear when Ersbøll explicitly appeals to a community by use of the word *we* – a *we* that normally take the side of the duckling.

"The Ugly Duckling" and "The Fir Tree" Revisited

Before I return to "The Ugly Duckling," let's take another look at "The Fir Tree." Almost throughout the entire fairy tale, the tree is overloaded with excitement for the future and it is completely occupied with the thought: Who am I and what will become of me? The tree passively awaits that somebody will arrive and act for it so it can be clear who it is. When this happens and the tree's destiny as a Christmas tree is revealed, it is cut by its roots and its agency is irrevocably lost for good.[2] For the rest of the tale, the tree is moved from community to community: From the forest to the living room to the attic to the courtyard and finally, into the fire. Every move is seen from the tree's point of view, and it keeps up the excitement for far too long, because it doesn't know what the author and the readers know: That its destiny was sealed the moment it was spotted as "the splendid one."

If this fairy tale is to be used to pose community as a question, it can be constructive to follow the *moving* of the tree with the knowledge we have as readers. When the tree is removed from its natural surroundings, it is bestowed with its central role in one of the most important traditions in Denmark: Christmas. And its function for the rest of the tale is the primary function of the Christmas tree: it is a gathering point. On Christmas Eve, it is both danced around and used as a gathering point when the little fat man tells stories to the children. When its function as a Christmas tree comes to an end and it is moved to the dark attic, it is still a gathering point: The mice gather around it and listen to its story. This community, however, turns out to be a narrow one as the rats let the tree know that they only want to listen to stories about things they themselves desire. Still not knowing who or what it is, the tree is once again moved to the courtyard. But the world has changed, and the tree realises that its significance and function has changed with it when one boy who danced around it and was astonished by it on Christmas Eve calls it "that ugly old Christmas tree" and treads on its branches "until they cracked beneath his shoes." For the last time, the tree is moved when it is chopped to pieces and placed in the fire. And for one last time, the children gather around it and enjoy watching it burn. The last lines in the fairy tale go as follows: "The children played on in the courtyard. The youngest child wore on his breast the gold star that had topped the tree on its happiest night of all. But that was no more, and the tree was no more, and there's no more to my story. No more, nothing more. All stories come to an end."

From these lines it is clear that even though both the story and the tree's life have come to an end, life goes on: The boys still play in the courtyard and the gold star did not burn with the tree. And year after year, children will again be astonished by trees in living rooms on Christmas Eve and each particular tree will lose its meaning and function when Christmas is over. If this cycle ever stops, it will be because Christmas trees have lost their function as unifying symbols. Social anthropologist Thomas Hylland Eriksen (2010) argues that unifying symbols are the "invisible glue" that creates social cohesion in every society. Following a similar argument, scholar Michael Böss states: "No common symbols, no community," and he continues his argument by accentuating that it is pivotal for citizens as well as for humans in general to "express ourselves in symbols about the aspects of life and society that cannot be measured and weighed and expressed in a rational language." (2012). In this context, the fairy tale about the fir tree can be used to question community in debates with newcomers. The dialogues could evolve around unifying symbols and we could ask each other questions like: How are unifying symbols put to use in ethical and unethical ways? What is the use and status of unifying symbols in Denmark? If such debates took place, it would be possible to direct new analytical attention to the work that the word community does when unifying symbols are supplied with affective meanings in everyday life in Denmark.

Unlike the fir tree, the ugly duckling does not find itself in its natural surroundings when its story begins – quite the contrary. But like the tree, the duckling doesn't know who it is. The only thing it *does* know is that it is not at all like the others, and therefore, it is ugly and unwelcome in the community, even though it learns all the facts about the community in the duck yard by rote: A good duckling must bow to the old duck, it must spread its feet wide apart, bend its neck and say quack. Even though de Mylius supports and contributes to the hegemonic interpretation of the fairy tale as a reflection of Andersen's biography when he refers to the connection between life and story as "obvious" (2005, 67-68) and when he states that the fairy tale is "rightly perceived as an interpretation of his life" (2016, 417), he simultaneously argues that this excluding interpretation of the tale can have as a result that other possibly significant themes in the text are missed. He points specifically to the question about what it is that makes the duckling move from one environment to another and argues that the move is "a move away from a given point of origin. Escape is the actual motif" but differentiates the motif from the duckling's goal with the move: To find its identity (2005, 69). If this statement is taken as a point of departure, the fairy tale can be re-opened in another context: Unlike the fir-tree, the duckling has the ability to move at its own will, and so it moves and moves from community to community. One of them is the house with the cat and the chicken mentioned earlier, where the two animals brag about their primary functions: They can lay eggs and purr. When they do so, the instinct to float on water is awakened in the duckling. The animals mock him for having this instinct: "If we don't understand you, who would?" they ask. The implicit message to the duckling here appears to be "You are not a part of our *we*, and therefore, you don't have a place in the world." The duckling, however, does not give up in its search for identity. It leaves the narrow-minded community in the farmhouse, and after a small unfortunate detour to hostile humans, it suddenly finds itself in a garden where it sees the swans. Based on all the experiences it has gathered in its lifetime, it prepares to die: "I shall fly near these royal birds, and they will peck me to bits because I, who am so very ugly, dare to go near them," it thinks. Thus, the duckling acknowledges that life as it knows it has come to an end. But it turns out that this is not a moment of death but a moment of transformation: The duckling is a swan and has finally found a *we* to be a part of. Unlike the fir tree, the duckling is not filled with longing for all the things in life it didn't appreciate because there has not been much of it. Instead it sends a tribute to all the horrors: "He felt quite glad that he had come through so much trouble and misfortune, for now he had a fuller understanding of his own good fortune, and of beauty when he met with it." So, to answer the question posed earlier: No, the duckling wouldn't have been happier if it had just been born among swans from the beginning. It is the horrifying search for identity that enables it to feel happy and appreciate a community where it is welcomed.

With this approach it can be argued that Hauch's interpretation of the fairy tale as a reflection of one of the basic terms of life and de Mylius' argument about the significance of social identity appear as more proper frames for ethical dialogues with newcomers: The duckling doesn't realise who it is until it becomes a part of a *we* among the swans. As a debating point, this fairy tale could be put to use in general ethical dialogues about the content and function of communities *and* about the consequences of moving oneself from one community to another. Relevant questions in such debates could be: What characterises the narrow communities the duckling meets in its search for identity? How is *we* articulated and used in Denmark in different discourses? Such debates would have an illuminating potential in cultural research on what the word community does for individuals when they are positioned as newcomers.

Concluding Remarks

Community, Ahmed and Fortier argue, is an unsettling concept that requires physical and emotional labour. Communities are "never fully arrived at" even when *we* already inhabit them" (Ahmed and Fortier 2003, 257), and therefore, community must always be posed as a question rather than as a solution.

Hans Christian Andersen can be perceived as a common good across borders but using him in naturalisation and citizenship tests reflects a perception of Andersen as privately owned by the Danes. In this version, a community harnesses the common, as Rose would argue. The fairy tales, however, present communities in ways that avoid moralistic solutions and absolutisms and incite us as readers to keep asking questions. If dominant values in Denmark, as it is suggested in *A New Chance for Everybody*, are freedom of speech, freedom of rights and the right to personal integrity, it would seem fair if they were reflected in the ways newcomers are met on the ground. As I have argued in my discussion of "The Fir Tree" and "The Ugly Duckling," these fairy tales hold the potential to function as commons if they are put to use as mediums through which the values of community can be can be debated and re-imagined in ethical dialogues about the contents, effects and functions of the word community in Denmark. From such use, another sense of community would emerge: Community as a framework through which commons are to be dynamically sustained. Here, community is something that does rather than is, as philosopher Jean-Luc Nancy puts it. And – still following the thoughts of Nancy – community here is an alterity always already in common and thereby something that can only be born through communication where we expose ourselves to alterity (Nancy 1990, 29; Parmett 2012, 185). In such dialogical processes where we use our differences to ask questions, maybe community as essence could be re-imagined as community as being-in-common. And in such communities, the fairy tales are a cultural common that belongs to the world.

References

Ahmed, Sara 2014. "Not in the Mood." *New Formations* 82: 13–28.
Ahmed, Sara, and Anne-Marie Fortier. 2003. "Re-imagining Communities." *International Journal of Cultural Studies* 6 (3): 251–259.
Berlingske. 2012. "Test dig selv: Er du klog nok til at blive dansker?" June 1. https://www.b.dk/nationalt/test-dig-selv-er-du-klog-nok-til-at-blive-dansker.
Berlingske. 2017. "Test dig selv: Kan du blive dansker?" November 30. https://www.b.dk/nationalt/test-dig-selv-kan-du-blive-dansker-1.
Bertacchini, Enrico, Giangiacomo Bravo, Massimo Marrelli, and Walter Santagata. 2012. *Cultural Commons: A New Perspective on the Production and Evolution of Cultures.* Cheltenham, UK/Northhampton, MA: Edward Elgar Publishing.

Bredsdorff, Elias. 1975. *Hans Christian Andersen: A biography*. London: Phaidon Press.

B.T. 2016. "Test dig selv: Er du klog nok til at blive dansk statsborger?" December 1. https://www.bt.dk/danmark/test-dig-selv-er-du-klog-nok-til-at-blive-dansk-statsborger-0.

B.T. 2017. "Test dig selv: Kan du blive dansker?" November 30. https://www.b.dk/nationalt/test-dig-selv-kan-du-blive-dansker-1.

Böss, Michael 2012. "Grantræer og andre vigtige symboler." *Berlingske*, December 26. https://www.b.dk/kommentarer/grantraeer-og-andre-vigtige-symboler.

Eriksen, Thomas Hylland. 2010. *Samfunn*. Oslo: Universitetsforlaget.

Ersbøll, Eva 2010. "On Trial in Denmark." In *A Re-definition of Belonging? Language and Integration Tests in Europe*, edited by Ricky Van Oers, Eva Ersbøll, and Dora Kostakopoulou, 107–152. Leiden/Boston: Martinus Nifhoff Publishers.

Etzioni, Amitai. 1997. *The New Golden Rule: Community and Morality in a Democratic Society*. London: Profile.

Graham, Helen. 2017. "Publics and Commons: The Problem of Inclusion for Participation." *Arken Bulletin*, no. 7: 150–168.

Hansen, T. 2017. Commentary to the post "Test dig selv: Kan du blive dansker?" *Jyllands-Posten*, June 7 [Facebook site].

Hardin, Garrett 1968. "The Tragedy of the Commons." *Science* 162 (3859): 1243–1248.

Hardt, Michael, and Antonio Negri. 2005: *Multitude: War and Democracy in the Age of Empire*. London: Penguin.

Hardt, Michael, and Antonio Negri. 2009. *Commonwealth*. Cambridge, MA: Harvard University Press.

Hardt, Michael, and Antonio Negri. 2012. *Declaration*. New York, NY: ArgoNavis.

Harvie, David. 2004. "Commons and Communities in the University: Some Notes and Some Examples." *The Commoner*, no. 8. http://www.commoner.org.uk/index.php?p=15.

Harvey, David 2001. "Heritage Pasts and Heritage Present: Temporality, Meaning and the Scope of Heritage Studies." *International Journal of Heritage Studies* 7 (4): 319–338.

Huus, K. 2017. Commentary to the post "Nu er testen her: Er du klog nok til at blive dansker?" *B.T.* November 30 [Facebook site].

Jyllands-Posten. 2017. Test dig selv: Kan du bestå den nyeste indfødsretsprøve? November 30. https://jyllands-posten.dk/indland/ECE10071981/test-dig-selv-kan-du-bestaa-den-nyeste-indfoedsretsproeve.

Kahn, Robert. 2008. "The Danish Cartoon Controversy and the Exclusivist Turn in European Civic Nationalism." *Studies in Ethnicity and Nationalism* 8 (3): 524–542.

Kostakopoulou, Dora. 2010. "Introduction." *A Re-Definition of Belonging? Language and Integration Tests in Europe*, edited by Ricky Van Oers, Eva

Ersbøll, and Dora Kostakopoulou, 1–23. Leiden/Boston: Martinus Nifhoff Publishers.

Mammen, C. A. 2016. Commentary to the post "Test dig selv: Kan du bestå indfødsretsprøven 2016?" *Kristeligt Dagblad*, June 14 [Facebook site].

Ministeriet for Flygtninge, Indvandrere og Integration. 2007. *Danmark før og nu – læremateriale om historie, kultur og samfundsforhold til indfødsretsprøve*. København: Ministeriet for Flygtninge, Indvandrere og Integration.

Mylius, Johan de. 2005. *Forvandlingens Pris. H.C. Andersen og hans eventyr*. København: Høst & Søn.

Mylius, Johan de. 2016. *Livet og skriften. En bog om H.C. Andersen*. København: Gads Forlag.

Nancy, Jean-Luc. 1990. *The Inoperative Community*. Minneapolis: University of Minnesota Press.

Parmett, Helen Morgan. 2012. "Community/Common: Jean-Luc Nancy and Antonio Negri on Collective Potentialities." *Communication, Culture & Critique* 5 (2): 171–190.

Regeringen. 2005. *En ny chance til alle – regeringens integrationsplan*. København: Ministeriet for Flygtninge, Indvandrere og Integration. http://www.stm.dk/multimedia/En_ny_chance_til_alle.pdf

Rose, Nikolas. 1999. *Powers of Freedom: Re-framing Political Thought*. Cambridge: Cambridge University Press.

Smith, Laurajane. 2006. *The Uses of Heritage*. London: Routledge.

Therkildsen, Louise Therese Schou. 2013. "Du fødes som dansker. Essentialistiske fortællinger i læremateriellet til den danske indfødsretsprøve." *Tidsskrift for medier, erkendelse og formidling* 1 (1): 149–165.

Thomsen, Torsten Bøgh. 2017a. "Skyggepunkter, mudder og menneske-atomer – natur og materialitet i H.C. Andersens forfatterskab." PhD diss., University of Southern Denmark.

Thomsen, Torsten Bøgh. 2017b. "Vi have intet at hovmode os over. Den antiantropocentriske Andersen." *Passage* 77 (summer): 49–64.

Udlændinge, Integrations- og Boligministeriet. 2015. *Læremateriale til indfødsretsprøven af 2015 – danske samfundsforhold, dansk kultur og historie*. København: Udlændinge, Integrations- og Boligministeriet.

Udlændinge, Integrations- og Boligministeriet. 2016. *Læremateriale til medborgerskabsprøven – demokrati og hverdagsliv i Danmark*. København: Udlændinge, Integrations- og Boligministeriet.

Notes

1 All commentaries from social media sites are translated by the author
2 In his interpretation of "The Fir Tree" as a carpe diem-fairy tale, de Mylius also emphasises the tree's passivity when he states: "Everything that happens to the tree is expressed in the passive." (2005, 108).

Funen Means Fine
Andersen the Anti-nationalist

Torsten Bøgh Thomsen
University of Southern Denmark, Odense

In this chapter, I present the argument that the Danish writer Hans Christian Andersen, who is often perceived as a proponent of sentimental and national Romanticism, can be said to perform an ironic critique of universalist Romanticism in his writings – primarily his novels O.T. and Only a Fiddler. This is done by turning the Danish landscape into a travesty of an idyll through the employment of romantic irony. Romantic irony is not what one would typically associate with questions of community, nationalism or politics. But I argue that in Andersen's specific use of irony, it develops into a critique that can be called political in the way that it challenges the nationalist agendas of the Danish Golden Age by questioning its legitimacy. It does so through a debunking of idealism that emphasises its artificiality, and it often appears through the lens of a social indignation that contrasts with the Golden Age's cultivation of the national, the idyllic and the harmonious. This is a social indignation that emphasises the fates of those phenomena and groups of people left out of the worldview created by romantic idealism. Seen like this, Andersen's work can be said to carry a political undertone that comes across as a discrete critique of the propagandistic uses of art and literature.

Hans Christian Andersen was a writer that was heavily influenced by the tenets of German Romanticism. So much so that when his writings are taught in Danish schools and high schools, he is often presented as the poster boy for Romanticism in a universalist and nationalist sense.[1] Mostly it is fairy tales like "The Bell" ("Klokken," 1845) and poems like "Danmark, mit Fædreland" (1850, Denmark, my Native Land) that are foregrounded to support this view on the Danish poet. This was also the case in 2011, where the nationalist Danish People's Party used a line from this poem, "from here, my world extends," as its campaign slogan (Dansk Folkeparti 2010).[2] Andersen's authorship is thus staged as representative of a certain kind of community. Its texts are used to construct and maintain a concept of Danish society as a harmonious and completed phenomenon that represents some fixed values, and which is clearly demarcated in relation to other communities.

However, rather than being exemplary of Andersen's overall oeuvre, it would be more accurate to consider these seemingly harmonious texts as outliers in a body of work that for the most part is inquisitive, critical even, of the tendency of romantic aesthetics to turn into universalistic clichés and produce fantasies of national hegemony. This critique can be traced even in those works of Andersen that seem to adhere to the ideals of universal Romanticism. Among these, we find the passages in the authorship that deal with Funen and which will serve as my point of departure in this chapter. I am presenting the argument that Andersen can be said to perform an ironic critique of universalist Romanticism, a mockery even, by turning the Danish landscape into a travesty of a literary idyll in his writings. Furthermore, I argue that this can be seen as a critique of the nationalism that was an integral part of the nation-building project, the self-branding you could call it, of the so-called Golden Age in Denmark (1800–1850, approx.).

Romantic irony is not what one would typically associate with questions of community, nationalism or politics. But I argue that in Andersen's specific employment of irony, it develops a critique that can be called political, without being linked to party politics, however. It becomes a way to challenge the overtly nationalist agenda of the Danish Golden Age by questioning its legitimacy. It does so through a debunking of idealism that emphasises its artificiality, and it often appears through the lens of a social indignation that contrasts with the Golden Age's construction of the national, the idyllic and the harmonious. This is a social indignation that emphasises the fates of those groups of people left out of the worldview created by romantic idealism. Behind the beautiful landscapes of the oil paintings of the Golden Age lies a darker social reality that peeps through the cracks in the surfaces instigated by romantic irony.

Andersen's Take on Sentimental Romanticism

Andersen's novel *O.T.* (*O.T.*, 1836) presents to the reader the two friends, Otto and Vilhelm, who are both students in Copenhagen. At some point they have to travel across Denmark to get from Copenhagen to Otto's birthplace in Jutland. Consequently, they pass Funen, the island in the middle of Denmark, famed for its lushness and fertile soil. This is also the birthplace of the author of the novel and historically known to be one of the richest and thus most powerful and influential provinces in Denmark. Up until the beginning of the 20th century, the island's main city, Odense, was the second-largest city in Denmark next to the capital, Copenhagen, and had been so for centuries. The chapter describing the two friends' journey through Funen begins with a little poem:

> The name of *Funen* means fine
> And that is to say:
> That Funen is a garden fine
> For the entire realm of Denmark!
> (Andersen 2003–07, 4:409, my translation)[3]

This charming little poem is allegedly the origins of the saying that is well known in Denmark today and simply goes: "Funen is fine." In the novel, Funen is presented as a fairytale realm, the gem of Denmark, the place where everything is cuter and neater than anywhere else. As the two friends are ferried away from Zealand over Storebælt, the narrator comments:

> The barrenness that the last view of Zealand presents means that you are doubly moved by the fullness and fecundity with which Funen appears. Green forests, rich fields and manor houses and churches strewn around. [...] Villages and peasant huts have a more prosperous appearance here than in Zealand where you would often mistake a family residence for a pile of manure raised on four poles. From the road you only see clean houses, the windowpanes painted, flowerbeds by the entrance door, and where flowers are cultivated there is always [...] a greater culture at the peasant's – he also thinks about the nicer things in life. (Andersen 2003–07, 4:409, my translation)

This idealisation of the landscape and rural community of Funen is in accordance with the ideals of sentimental Romanticism that were in vogue at this time in Denmark. According to this artistic movement, the world was to be presented in its most harmonious, pleasant and beautiful state, and the narrator or painter had to elevate the surroundings to this ideal state by use of his or her sensibility. Thus, art happens in a meeting between the empirical world and the artist's senses – or, one could say; in a meeting between nature and culture.

In 1795 the German poet Friedrich Schiller published the dissertation *Über naive und sentimentalische Dichtung*, in which he discussed the change in literary representations of nature that he located in the shift from classical to romantic art. Previously, he argued, it was assumed that there was an immediate relationship between the human and its environment, which allowed the artist to depict reality directly. This is an understanding of the immediacy of nature, which is also contained in the classicist artistic dogma "Ars imitatur naturam" ("art imitates nature"). Contrary to this, the romantic artist stood in a displaced and alienated relationship with these surroundings. Schiller can be said to write on the basis of an Enlightenment-based, Rousseauian idea that the human being loses his connection to his natural surroundings in society (Rousseau 1998, 5–21), and the Kantian point that human beings always only have access to their own translations of the world as it is *für uns*, and in principle are cut off from acknowledging it as it is on its own, *an sich* (Kant 2007). The original naïve approach to nature was thus lost, and the romantic artist's approach to the world was therefore in principle sentimental. In this regard, sentimental should not be understood as one particular emotional attitude to the world, but more in the sense that the world is always perceived by us through our consciousness and senses that will colour it in one direction or another. Conversely, this also meant that by uniting human sensibility and empirical reality in art, the possibility arises to reconstruct a harmonious relationship between the human and non-human (Schiller 1962, 707–708).

Andersen might have been acutely aware of this view on art. In some of his texts he lets his narrator express an understanding of landscape depiction that is very close to Schiller's. I am specifically referring to his first travelogue *Shadow Pictures* from 1831, in which the narrator states:

> It is not only the proud mountainsides with their immense forests and tall bushes which swell over the rushing river or the dead masses of stones from a half-collapsed building that make a region romantic. It is not until this region because of its very nature is imbued with some sort of legend that it achieves the perfectly magical illumination that raises it in the eye of the soul. Then the dead masses come alive, they are no longer empty decoration, action takes place, every leaf and every flower suddenly stand as a talking bird, the wellspring becomes a singing fountain striking its eternal trickling chords to this melodrama of the Spirit. (Andersen 2003–07, 14:124, my translation)

Only when the dramatic nature has occasioned some sort of cultural augmentation, which, like an Instagram filter, is layered upon the surroundings, can we talk about truly sentimental romantic scenery.

Accordingly, the landscape of Funen described in *O.T.* is brimming with legends. After having appreciated the horticultural skills of the Funic peasantry, Otto and Vilhelm admire the vast amount of wild red poppies that grace the roadside. Their coachman explains that they are reminiscent of the Spanish soldiers that were deployed in Funen in 1808 by Napoleon Bonaparte. At some point these soldiers were attacked by British soldiers but managed to escape onto their ships. However, they did not have time to bring their horses with them to safety and these were killed on the open field dyeing it red with the blood of Andalusian stallions. And that is why, the legend concludes, the Funic countryside is so rich in blood-red poppies. This seems unmistakably romantic. It expresses a view of the Danish nation and community in which the very landscape has managed to absorb and domesticate an external influence and turn something foreign and warlike into something neat and pacifist. But the passage does not end here. The coachman continues to spin his yarns, however in a somewhat coarser manner, telling the tale of a young woman who was expecting a child by one of the soldiers who fled:

> It is from this place too that we have the tale of the priest's daughter, who was crying and was ever so inconsolable, when the Spaniards were gone. But she wasn't exactly weeping for the loss of her boyfriend [...] she was crying because if the innocent child took after his father, it would be speaking Spanish and not a soul would understand it. (Andersen 2003–07, 4:410, my translation)

This legend seems somewhat less romantic. In fact, it is quite frivolous, and not exactly something that would fit smoothly into the literary preferences of the delicate bourgeoisie in Denmark in the early 1800's. No matter how good-natured and innocent this little joke about the naïve priest's daughter is, I cannot help but reading it as a little crack in the varnish, a little shade of irony in the otherwise brightly glorifying text about Denmark. Whereas the legend of the Andalusian stallions showed the Danish landscape as capable of completely absorbing and neutralising a foreign influence, this little anecdote focuses on the meeting of cultures, and seems to suggest that the idea that cultures should be radically incompatible is immature and ill informed. But at the same time, this second story allows both cultures, the Spanish and the Danish, to exist in their own right, which makes it more complex and ambivalent. Neither one is absorbed into the other. The image of complete assimilation (blood to flowers) is contrasted with recognition of cultural differences (in this case lingual) combined with a satirical mockery of the idea that this automatically entails cultural incompatibility. We move from an antagonistic view on different cultural communities, in which one must surrender completely to the other, to a more dialectic understanding in which one can literally exist within the other like an unborn baby in the woman's womb.

If we return to the previous passages with this little disturbance in mind, they may also not be as unequivocally adorable as they seemed at first glance, or rather; they are probably too adorable, too sugary, too unambiguous, which somehow makes them deeply ambiguous. Take for instance the poem "Funen is fine." Not only does it present a sublimation of Funen into a cute little garden that seems somewhat overdone, but if we look at the rhyme on the second and fourth line we find that it is an identical rhyme – a word that rhymes with itself. This construction of rhyme is somehow banal and pompous at the same time – simple and self-absorbed. It mirrors itself like Narcissus falling in love with his own reflection on the water surface. There is a self-importance to it that may seem childish, ridiculous even. And as such, the poem can be read as a critical analogy on sentimental Romanticism in general and its tendency towards self-mirroring, complacency and self-infatuation.

I believe that Andersen, in these passages, is piling romantic aesthetics on top of itself in order for it to implode. He accelerates romantic aesthetics causing it to go into a loop and become self-referential – a romantic self-awareness of writing as a romantic. This stylistic self-awareness I see as an ironic gesture that is reminiscent of the dark romantic irony that Friedrich Schlegel conceptualised. Schlegel championed an ironic style that, contrary to the idealism of Friedrich Schiller and Friedrich Schelling, cultivated the fragmentary. It was a version of Romanticism in which the artist was aware that in its effort to transcend its own limitations and connect with the ideality of nature, human consciousness would continuously be confronted by these same limitations and constantly be reminded that it cannot escape its own conditioned sensation and cognition. Romantic irony blends, as Schlegel expressed it, enthusiasm with irony (1967, 319). It is therefore a self-reflexive form of Romanticism that does not necessarily believe that the absolute can be realised in the work of art, but rather that the work of art can make human literary and artistic forms collide, allowing mutually exclusive statements, opinions and aesthetics to chase against each other and thereby create glimpses into the underlying cohesiveness of things. Thus, romantic irony is not to be understood in the contemporary sense of the word irony, in which it means saying something and meaning the opposite. It is rather an understanding of art in which no statement in a text is left uncontradicted.

The passage about Funen in *O.T.* can be seen as a late romantic version of this kind of irony – an awareness that the romantic love of nature and folk life, which had once invigorated art and literature, was slowly turning into predictable clichés that could be exploited for nationalist purposes.

I find this ironic self-awareness even more pointed in the passage that contrasts Funen and Zealand. If the intention was exclusively to enhance the Funic landscape, then the image of the pile of manure interferes. I believe that it is here to suggest that the language of sentimental Romanticism is turning into a big pile of manure itself. The laughable image of a pile of manure competes with the beautiful Funic scenery for the reader's attention, turning the idyll into a travesty by breaking the idealisation with grotesque imagery and a coarse metaphor. A travesty is, according to the Cambridge Dictionary, defined as: "something that fails to represent the values and qualities that it is intended to represent, in a way that is shocking or offensive." Usually, this happens unintentionally, but in the case of Andersen, I argue that this travesty of the idyll, and in a broader perspective romantic idealism, occurs deliberately due to an employment of romantic irony.[4]

I read these passages as examples of Andersen's double communication, which describes a stylistic trait with which the narrator manages to get several points that might be contradictory across in the same text. It also applies to the way that particularly Andersen's fairy tales contain an overt plot that can be easily decoded by children, and a more complex meaning intended for adult readers. This is a point that has often been emphasised in Andersen research. Recently, Jacob Bøggild (2012) has analysed this double communication in connection to the concept of romantic irony in his dissertation *Svævende stasis*, and I believe that his interpretation is also applicable to this context. For those who want sentimental, patriotic landscaping and glorification of Denmark, there is surely plenty of that in *O.T.* The narrator delivers perfect branding of Funen as a fairy tale realm of castles and peasants, soldiers and horses and exotic Spanish blood. But for those who want to look past this façade, this mocking pastiche, it is dark romantic irony and tongue-in-cheek cynicism all the way through.

Romantic Irony as Anti-nationalism

The question will then be: Why would Andersen do this? Is this just a stylistic play or some sort of art for art's own sake – an investigation of romantic aesthetics? I believe so, but I also think that on a higher level, Andersen might have political reasons for delivering this kind of debunking of Romanticism. In Denmark, Romanticism was closely connected to nation-building, and especially from the 1840's and onwards national Romanticism was arguably the most dominant artistic paradigm in Denmark. And contrary to what people might believe, Andersen was no nationalist. Andersen was and throughout his life remained cosmopolitan. And he was particularly critical towards what he saw as a specifically Danish tendency to self-complacency, to wall oneself in, cut oneself from the world and think too highly of oneself. Sometimes this resulted in decidedly anti-nationalist texts from the hand of Andersen.

Of particular interest in this regard is his use of female Jewish characters in the novels *To Be, Or Not to Be* (*At være eller ikke være*, 1857) and *Only a Fiddler* (*Kun en Spillemand*, 1837). In these two novels, Esther and Naomi, respectively, offer cultural side-glances on Denmark and often have some very critical remarks when it comes to the

Danish community and national identity. Here is a passage from *Only a Fiddler,* where Naomi speaks particularly bluntly:

> Yes, the climate was the aiding topic in the recurring conversational quarrels in the Count's home. Let poets and patriots sing and say as much as they like about the loveliness of Denmark, Naomi however declared that we live in a miserable climate. "If the Heavens had considered," she said, "that our admiration of nature should've risen to this degree, we would surely, like the snail, have been created with houses on our backs. Then we would have been relieved of this constant looking out for capes, cloaks and umbrellas that form such an integral part of our person as it is now. [...] I'm no poet who sings in order to become knighted!" Naomi said, "I'm no patriotic speaker, who wants to be accepted in the great grade-book of the Danes, the 'Statskalender': I appreciate what is beautiful, and if other people didn't do that to such an excessive extent, perhaps I would be excited too!" It was true. Perhaps she admired more than others the green, fragrant forest, the boldly shaped clouds, the sea and the burial mounds with the blooming blackberry vines. But she also knew that there are greater wonders in God's great creation and that our climate is terrible. (Andersen 2003-07, 5:194, my translation)

From a narratological perspective, the choice of words in the little sentence "It was true" stands out. The narrator pops up out of nowhere to sympathise with these anti-nationalist sentiments, and even though it would be a stretch to make *O.T.* and *Only a Fiddler* comment directly on each other, I think that it is interesting to contrast Naomi's thoughts on nationalistic appreciation of nature with the appreciation that appears in *O.T.* Also, I would like to stress the fact that *Only a Fiddler* was published only a year after *O.T.* making the two novels virtually contemporaneous.

So, when Andersen is pigeon-holed as a sentimental romanticist and his works used in nationalistic propagandistic ways, I would like to counter this narrative by pointing out that focusing solely on the idealising texts in his oeuvre involves ignoring the significant part of his texts that are skeptical towards this idealisation.

Social Indignation as a Vehicle for the Politics of Romantic Irony

It might seem counter-intuitive to read political messages out of works such as Andersen's, which in general appear distinctly apolitical. Indeed, the writer himself stated that he wanted nothing to do with politics. He "felt no skills or necessity to meddle with things like that" (Andersen [1855] 1975, 1:255, my translation). Thus, he is definitely not a partisan or associated with any kind of political party. But his texts are political in the sense that they are critical towards universalism, which we also know from fairy tales like "The Emperor's New Clothes" ("Keiserens nye Klæder," 1837). However, this anti-universalism is often launched discretely as attacks against the universalist tendencies in Romanticism. And – especially in the novels and the travelogues that allow themselves to be more explicitly critical than the fairy tales – it is done by the use of nature as a theme – particularly ugly or dirty nature. It is an aesthetic vocabulary of Andersen's, one could say.

Returning to the joke about the priest's daughter that interfered with the romantic description of the Funic countryside, I think we might add another layer to this critique that tinges the writings of Andersen in an even more political way. I am arguing that the beautiful romantic imagery of nature is often nuanced through the introduction of social affairs and particularly through the display of social indignation. Amidst the sentimental construction of an idyllic countryside, the reader is suddenly made aware of social factors, here the precarious lives of young women in the 19th century in a way that conflicts with the harmonious idealisations. And if we pan out to other texts in the authorship, we find that this is a recurring trope.

In her article "Denne Deilighed og dette Griseri," literary researcher Camilla Storskog discusses Andersen's travelogue *A Poet's Bazaar* (*En Digters Bazar*, 1842) as a representative of the romantic travelogue. Storskog states that the romantic travelogue distinguishes itself from the traditional travelogue by having a clear focus on the narrating subject and its emotional experience of the outside world – in other words: by being sentimental in the sense that Schiller understood the term. Storskog writes:

The most prominent task of the travelogue is therefore to provide a forum for the traveller's personal needs to express him or herself, a development that it of course shared with most other of the contemporary art forms at that time. In terms of content the romantic travelogue is distinguished by renewing the ways of describing nature and by placing the experiencing subject in a central role in the narrative [...]. The composition is characterised by a large variation in form and by the romantic fondness of 'creating' rather than 'depicting', which in H.C. Andersen's *A Poet's Bazaar* (1842) may also involve transforming reality into fiction. (Storskog 2008, 19, my translation)

Storskog ends up placing *A Poet's Bazaar* as more or less exemplary of this genre, the romantic travelogue, not least because of beautiful renderings of the Italian landscape and folk life such as these:

It was grey weather but the mountains were beautiful, many trees were quite green. One small town after another rose in front of us, each was lying like a sphinx on the top of a hill and seemed to ask: 'Do you know what lives and goes on here?' – 'We hurried past' A begging woman was kneeling on the road and kissing the ground. 'We hurried past!' we met armed soldiers who encircled a cart on which four robbers were laying in chains, large black-bearded fellows. An old hag was sitting by them, backwards in the direction of travel, nodding at us and seeming as jolly as ever. 'We hurried past!' (Andersen 2003–07, 14:289, my translation)

Storskog uses this quote to make the point that Andersen, despite also renewing the romantic travelogue in many ways – for instance through his depictions of the steam engine and other technological advances – also remains traditionally romantic when it comes to describing nature and folk life. According to her, when he does so he is the very emblem of the blasé 19th century poet who exoticises and dramatises social misery and crime at his convenience. And while this might bring an air of authenticity to the literary production it also reproduces classic Northern European stereotypes about the passion, frivolity and lawlessness of the South. It is, you could say, all appropriated into a romantic imagery that, as Storskog writes: "makes the heart of the poet cheer as he describes them [the people] from the lofty window seat of the carriage." (Storskog 2008, 26, my translation). To some extent, I can agree with Storskog that the passage shows a traditionally romantic blasé poet who does not invest much attention in the country visited but is more interested in himself and his own experience. But I believe Storskog overlooks the fact that the text itself seems aware of this. I read the repetition of "We hurried past" as a discreetly ironic pastiche of the travelogue as a genre. The quote signals an awareness that the travelling poet can at best reproduce a fleeting and deeply personal account of his journey. There is a meta-consciousness present, which creates an ironic distance between the narrator and the narrated. And this is done by the introduction of social misery, which, rather than supporting it, exposes the cliché descriptions of Italian nature and folk life.

An even more poignant example of this is found in the latter part of *Only a Fiddler*. In the third part of the novel, the reader is introduced to a short side story about the Romani people living on the heath of Jutland, which was back then perceived to be the wild west of Denmark. The narrator begins by describing India, where the Romani people were thought to stem from, in terms that showcase the orientalism of the 19th century. India is believed to be like the Garden of Eden and the narrator reminds us that ever since Adam and Eve were expulsed from this place, all human beings might in some sense be considered migrants living in some kind of diaspora. The narrator goes on to describe the Jutland heath as a rough and unforgiving environment in ways that correspond with a romantic fascination of wilderness. Then the social indignation takes over:

> Even to the north, to the barren heaths of Jutland, the youngest generation of the Pariahs migrates. We call them gypsies, scoundrels. The field of grain is their summer tent, the deep ditch their winter chamber. The children of the Pariahs don't have like the fox its cave, like the bird its nest. They walk in sludge and storm over the rough heath. There, like beasts, they give birth to their kin. The place of birth is the place of custody, so the farmer always seeks to move the pregnant women over to the neighbour's district. Thus, she is often taken from place to place on the miserable, uncomfortable wagon, without straws to lie upon, and gives birth there to her child, which is doomed to wretchedness. (Andersen 2003–07, 5:218–219, my translation)

In compassionate terms, the narrator describes the fate of the Romanis. He is not content to present the landscape as magnificent and harsh.

The reader is also reminded that this harshness has real consequences for real people. The social indignation is clear, as is the criticism of the asocial farmer who chases the pregnant woman away from his premises. Furthermore, the wretched conditions of these people are described in detail in ways that make them tangible to the reader. Last but not least, Andersen focuses specifically on the pregnant woman and the child, which is not coincidental. It is the fate of the most vulnerable we are told about and thus encouraged to have compassion with.

Conclusion: Climate and Critique

When it comes to the tradition of research on Andersen, this argument is thus in continuation of an ongoing tendency to detach Andersen's writings from the frameworks set up by the established reception of it, primarily the dominant trends to read him as a sentimental romantic or to stage him as a national romantic. This ongoing tendency is reflected in Karin Sanders' (1997) focus on the ironic aspects of the writing and Jacob Bøggild's (2012) readings of his arabesque aesthetics, which, alongside the arguments offered in my own PhD thesis (Thomsen 2019), emphasises Andersen's inspiration from radical aspects of Romanticism. In addition, this study is drawing on the by now well-established tradition to consider Andersen a border figure whose writing is rooted in Romanticism but points to modern and modernist methods of writing (de Mylius, Jørgensen, and Pedersen 1993). However, scholarly considerations of the distinctly anti-nationalist perspectives in Andersen's authorship are unknown to me, and this theme would therefore be a fruitful ground for future studies. In addition to being able to enlighten the understanding of Andersen in particular, such studies would also supplement studies in the Danish Golden Age with critical analyses of nationalism in this period. As far as I know, these studies limit themselves to pointing out the nation-building and community-creating tendencies. There is a great job to be done in nuancing this image.

Much can be said against biographical readings or in general of resorting to biography to substantiate a point. And I also believe that the point about Andersen's reservations when it comes to nationalism and sentimental Romanticism can be brought to the fore just by analysing the aesthetic works of art. But in conclusion I do want to share a biographical detail to further underline the argument that Andersen was a globalist who loved Denmark but disliked the Danish tendency to nationalism and small-mindedness. In 1843 Andersen was in Paris, and whilst there he received news that when his play *Agnete and the Merman* (*Agnete og Havmanden,* 1833) had been shown at a theatre back in Copenhagen, some people among the audience had had the audacity to hiss at it. In a letter to his friend Henriette Wulff he wrote as a reaction to this:

> Here, in the foreign metropolis, Europe's most noble and renowned souls lovingly encircle me, meet me as kindred spirits whilst in my home the boys are spitting at my heart's best creation! If after I die I must be judged as I have been in life, I will declare: The Danes could be evil, cold, and satanic! – it is a people that fits the moist, mildew-green islands from which Tycho Brahe was banished, where Eleonore Uhlfeldt was imprisoned, Ambrosius Stub was the jest of lords. Many people will continue to be treated badly until the name of this people will be a legend only. [...] I am sick this evening – sick! My home has sent me a fever from its wet, cold woods, which the Danes glare at and imagine to love – but I don't believe in love in the North: I believe in evil, falseness – I feel this in my own blood and only by this feeling do I know where I come from! (Andersen 1843, April 29, my translation)

So, in conclusion: I argue that Andersen makes a travesty of the romantic idyll. He accelerates romantic aesthetics in order for it to implode and shows that it is quickly becoming – not just a cliché, but a potentially dangerous cliché. The originally beautiful and revolutionary romantic ideology had become exploitable by nationalistic interests. Andersen saw that and went against it. By use of social indignation and by inserting descriptions of vulnerable and precarious lives that sometimes verge on social realism, he nuanced the aesthetic ideals of sentimental and nationalist Romanticism thus reinvigorating an earlier form of Romanticism – the ironic one – through his compositions in which contrasts flicker and tremble in the internal tension of the artwork. Andersen had a profound appreciation of nature and Denmark but detested narrow-mindedness and self-righteousness. Looking back at Denmark from a cosmopolitan point of view, he never got tired of showing his readers that there were larger wonders in God's great creation and it was his firm conviction throughout his life that our Nordic climate is truly terrible.

References

Andersen, Hans Christian. 1843. Letter to Henriette Wulff from Paris, April 27-29. http://andersen.sdu.dk/brevbase/brev.html?bid=2818 (the letter is kept at the museum H.C. Andersens Hus).

Andersen, Hans Christian. (1855) 1975. *Mit Livs Eventyr*. 2 vols. Published by H. Topsøe-Jensen. København: Gyldendal.

Andersen, Hans Christian. 2003-07. *Andersen. H.C. Andersens samlede værker*. Edited by Klaus P. Mortensen. 18 vols. København: Det Danske Sprog- og Litteraturselskab/Gyldendal.

Binding, Paul. 2014. *Hans Christian Andersen: European Witness*. New Haven/London: Yale University Press.

Bom, Anne Klara, Jacob Bøggild, and Johs. Nørregaard Frandsen, eds. 2014. *H.C. Andersen i det moderne samfund*. Odense: Syddansk Universitetsforlag.

Bøggild, Jacob. 2012. *Svævende stasis. Arabesk og allegori i H.C. Andersens eventyr og historier*. Hellerup: Forlaget Spring.

The Cambridge Dictionary. 1999-. https://dictionary.cambridge.org/dictionary/english/.

Dansk Folkeparti. 2010. https://danskfolkeparti.dk/wpcontent/uploads/2017/06/Pia_Kjærsgaards_årsmodetale_20101.pdf.

Dansk Folkeparti. 2011. http://lokal.danskfolkeparti.dk/herfra_min_verden_gaar_sang. Accessed December 11, 2018.

Kant, Immanuel. (1781) 2007. *Critique of Pure Reason* [*Kritik der reinen Vernunft*]. Translated by Marcus Weigelt. London: Penguin Modern Classics.

Kofoed, Niels. 1996. "Hans Christian Andersen and the European Literary Tradition." In *Hans Christian Andersen: Danish Writer and Citizen of the World*, edited by Sven Hakon Rossel, 209-256. Amsterdam/Atlanta, GA: Rodopi.

Mylius, Johan de, Aage Jørgensen, Viggo Hjørnager Pedersen, eds. 1993. *Andersen og Verden*. Odense: Syddansk Universitetsforlag.

Rousseau, Jean-Jacques. (1762) 1998. *The Social Contract* [*Du Contrat Social*]. London: Wordsworth Editions Limited.

Sanders, Karin. 1997. *Konturer. Skulptur- og dødsbilleder fra guldalderlitteraturen*. København: Museum Tusculanums Forlag.

Schiller, J. C. Friedrich. (1795-96) 1962. "Über naive und sentimentalische Dichtung." In *Friedrich Schiller: Sämtliche Werke,* 5 volumes, Vol. 5, edited by Gerhard Fricke et al., 693-779. München: Carl Hanser Verlag.

Schlegel, K. W. Friedrich von. (1799) 1967. "Gespräch über die Poesie." In *Kritische Friedrich Schlegel-Ausgabe,* 23 volumes, Vol. 2: *Charakteristiken und Kritiken I (1796-1801)*, edited by Hans Eichner, 284-290. München/Paderborn/Wien: Ferdinand Schönling.

Segala, Anna Maria, ed. 2010. *Fiaba e modernità in Hans Christian Andersen*. Rome: Bulzoni.

Storskog, Camilla. 2008. "Denne deilighed og dette Griseri –! : om H.C. Andersens italienska resa i *En Digters Bazar* (1842) och den romantiska reseskildringen." In *Studi Nordici*, edited by Jørgen Stender Clausen, 19-35. Rom/Pisa: Fabrizio Serra Editore.

Thomsen, T.B. 2019 (forthcoming). *Skyggepunkter - menneske, natur og materialitet i H.C. Andersens forfatterskab*. København: Forlaget Spring.

Notes

1 A simple Danish Google search on "H.C. Andersen + Romantik" will show that as diverse websites as Wikipedia, studienet.dk and the Hans Christian Andersen Centre's website at the University of Southern Denmark list Andersen as romantic without reservations. The same goes for an English search for "Hans Christian Andersen + Romanticism." Furthermore, Niels Kofoed's characterisation of Andersen as "whole heartedly romantic and anti-academic eagerly concerned with folklore and the popular cause" (1996, 215) supports this view on his authorship. However, it should be mentioned that the understanding of Andersen as something other than a typical romantic writer has gradually become widespread in research on Andersen. Thus, arguments have been made to perceive Andersen as a cosmopolitan and internationally oriented writer rather than a Biedermeier author (de Mylius, Jørgensen, and Pedersen 1993; Binding 2014). Similarly, several efforts have been made to consider Andersen as a modern author, both in Danish and international contexts (Bom, Bøggild, and Frandsen 2014; Segala 2010).

2 A campaign song was also made to accompany the slogan (http://lokal.danskfolkeparti.dk/herfra_min_verden_gaar_sang) and the leader of the party back then, Pia Kjærsgaard, held a speech at the annual party meeting entitled "From here, my world extends" (https://danskfolkeparti.dk/wpcontent/uploads/2017/06/Pia_Kjærsgaards_årsmodetale_20101.pdf).

3 Since no officially recognised, standardised translations of the novels or travelogues exist, I have taken the liberty of translating my examples in this chapter myself. The existing translations are highly uneven in quality, exist in a lot of versions and are often re-written versions that have been stylistically embellished or otherwise altered.

4 The concept "travesty of the idyll" derives from a keynote delivered by Klaus Müller-Wille at the conference "Hans Christian Andersen and Community" held by the University of Southern Denmark, December 2017. For an elaboration of this argument as well as an in-depth discussion of Andersen and Romanticism (in Danish), see Thomsen 2019.

Underground Andersen
Political Allegory and the Fairy Tale

Marianne T. Stecher
University of Washington, Seattle

This chapter seeks to demonstrate how texts move from the 'passive' literary archive into 'active' cultural memory when activated by a collective political sentiment. The chapter also develops the idea that the term "underground" might suggest clandestine or subversive activities in modern, urban environments. Further, the term "underground" alludes to the new museum design by Kengo Kuma that creates underground spaces which simulate the imaginative universe of Andersen's fairy tales. The core analysis in the chapter rests on the potential for political allegory in the Andersen fairy tale, demonstrated by readings of two tales: "The Wicked Prince" ("Den onde Fyrste," 1840) and "The Little Green Ones" ("De smaa Grønne," 1868). These readings emphasise the historical and political contexts in which such tales might be circulated and interpreted. In a broader sense, this reading also illustrates how Andersen's tales continue to resonate with readers in a globalised, modern world.

Underground Andersen

Where does the Andersen fairy tale come alive? Does it thrive in illustrated publications, animated on-screen adaptations, and public commemorations, or reside in museums, library archives, and scholarly editions? Might the Andersen fairy tale also dwell 'underground'? How are Andersen's fairy tales embedded in cultural memory, and what determines which fairy tales a community of readers remember, appreciate, and celebrate? Aleida Assmann proposes that "The canon stands for the active working memory of a society that defines and supports the cultural identity of a group. It is highly selective and, as Harold Bloom has put it, built on the principle of exclusion" (2010, 106). There is a distinction between *active* and *passive* cultural memory, argues Assmann; between a society's working memory and its reference memory, between the *canon* and the *archive* (99). About the archive (i.e. libraries, museums), she writes insightfully: "The institutions of passive cultural memory are situated halfway between the canon and forgetting." (102). This chapter illustrates how certain texts (two halfway forgotten fairy tales by Hans Christian Andersen) might move from 'passive' cultural memory (the archive, the library, the scholarly edition) into the active, circulating sphere of cultural memory at a particular historical moment of collective political sentiment. Rather than consider Andersen's fairy tales that are widely perceived as "canon," or as belonging to our active cultural memory, this chapter digs into a passive cultural repository, into a figurative 'underground,' in order to illuminate the potential of the fairy tale, particularly its potential as political allegory.

Thus, it is the darkly ironic, modern, somewhat urban, and 'underground' aspect of Andersen's tales that is the focus of the present analysis. My term 'Underground Andersen' evokes several connotations that I will explore briefly here by way of further introduction. There are numerous associations with the term 'underground:' subterranean (underjordisk*)* or the underground (undergrunden). In a way, these terms relate to one another in their earthliness or worldliness in some regards. 'Underground' associations are largely secular, if you will, and may also tie into the biological or botanical metaphors which Andersen tales and stories often employ. In a metaphorical sense, they are the 'roots' of the plants and great oak trees reaching underground and bringing life to the fairy tales.

As demonstrated by much previous scholarship, Andersen's tales at times reflect the early tendencies of literary modernism; the term 'modernity' suggests fragmentation, disintegration, and the loss of traditional community. Further, an overarching characteristic of Andersen's work seems to be the co-existence of the traditional with the modern and an ambiguity created by that very tension between the traditional and the modern. Andersen is both the fairy tale writer and the dark visionary. Particularly in certain tales and stories published after 1850, Andersen is at times darkly prophetic and prescient with regard to the social, political, and technological developments that the future century (and millennium) would bring. Andersen's visionary statements about modernity's impact on the future of poetry – and the forms of poetry itself – are unforgettable and seem eerily realised today. I am thinking here of his late aesthetic manifesto, "The New Century's Goddess" ("Det nye Aarhundredes Musa," 1861) in which the narrator remarks, "the many 'immortal' productions of today's poets will, in the future, perhaps exist only in the form of charcoal tracings on a prison wall, seen and read only by a few curiosity seekers?"[1] In other words, Andersen's vision of future poetry might suggest the ubiquitous graffiti that exists today in urban and 'underground' environments, in prisons, in railway stations, under bridges, and in public washrooms. Modernity and the future of poetry are the topics in two later texts by Andersen that might be considered his artistic manifestos: "The New Century's Goddess" and the chapter "Poetry's California" ("Poesiens Californien"), published in 1851 as the last chapter in the poetic travelogue, *In Sweden* (*I Sverrig*). In these texts, Andersen ponders with both enthusiasm and trepidation the new world of poetry that the social, political and technological changes will bring. The significant changes brought by the Democratic Constitution of 1849, the removal of the city walls and ramparts of Copenhagen, industrialisation, the introduction of gas lighting of the city streets, and so forth, as Johan de Mylius points out:

> Relative to the scene-setting that it was given in the fairy tale texts from the 1840s, the theme here after 1850 has been supplied with new fuel, so to speak. It is the age after the great break in social and cultural circumstances: The introduction of the bourgeois democracy, the gradual and more and more visible urbanisation, the small beginnings of industrialisation [...]. (de Mylius 2004, 242–243, my translation)[2]

Andersen's so-called "manifestos" of 1851 and 1861 are superficially light-hearted and fanciful, but ultimately informed by a vision of a 'godless' world ruled by the machine, called Master Bloodless (Mester Blodløs), an agent who lacks both blood and soul. The voice of the narrator in Andersen's 'science fiction' texts welcomes the innovations of the future and, at the same time, expresses skepticism and dark premonition as argued in "Modernity, Technology, and Tourism: Hans Christian Andersen's Futuristic Tales." (Stecher 2014). Andersen suggests that the machine, which should be our servant, may in future become our lord and master.

Thus, Hans Christian Andersen's vision could often be dark and ironic. Although he became famous for texts that are written in a naïve genre – that is, the fairy tale – Andersen is hardly a naïve writer. Even well before the midpoint of the nineteenth century, Andersen articulated intellectual acuity and dark promotions regarding the future urban age. His vision of human society with all its flaws is expressed already in tales such as "The Drop of Water" ("Vanddraaben," 1847), after a visit to England. "The Drop of Water" depicts a microcosm of modern urban life and serves as a commentary on the overcrowded London metropolis with its contaminated waterways, which Andersen had just experienced. The modern philosopher and writer Villy Sørensen, who cultivated the darker or 'shadow' side of Andersen's work, composed modernist inversions of some of Andersen's canonical tales, such as "A Tale of Glass" ("En glashistorie," 1964), an ideologically provocative retelling of "The Snow Queen" ("Sneedronningen," 1845).[3] In an essay entitled "The Shadow of Hans Christian Andersen" ("H.C. Andersens skygge"), Sørensen offers the following observation about Andersen's legacy as a writer:

> Here in Denmark we have accepted that Andersen is a harmless children's writer, who not only wrote naively, but who also was himself naïve, and we have overlooked far too easily that from his very first debut – with the still undervalued *Foot Journey* – he was in possession of an unusual intellectual power and an irony that had not least an eye for "what was wrong with things." (2004, 57–58, my translation)[4]

Let us return to the earthly, or earthy, underground associations with Andersen's tales. Most obviously, there exists in the field of folklore, typologies of folk and fairy tales, such as the Aarne-Thompson Tale Type index and classification system, which feature subterranean, supernatural creatures, including *de underjordiske* (*the subterranean ones*). In folklore, the particular use of 'underground' relates to a widely accepted understanding of the world of the folk fairy tale. Just to take one example, folklorist Reidar Christiansen observes in his study *Norwegian folk tales* that the "huldre-folk," also referred to as *de underjordiske* are creatures of legend more closely related to humans than are the trolls or the giants (the so-called 'jotuns'). These creatures are referred to by "the whereabouts of their domain, which also include the ground under the houses. [...] But they often lived literally under a building, e.g., in a stable or a cowshed" (Christiansen 1964, xxxv). Christiansen suggests that we compare the term 'underjordiske' to the term 'kjellerman' ('cellar man'), which has also been used. Those living under the house (de underjordiske) are not to be confused with the guardian of the home, the *nisser* (or elves), who are actively interested in the prosperity of the people living there. However, these are typologies of folklore, and not the focus of this particular chapter. The point which I wish to emphasise is that the action of a *folk* fairy tale takes place in a parallel universe or domain (whether underground or underwater) to that of the earthy or human existence. In the 'underground' the magical and the supernatural has its origins and flourishes.

On the other hand, the world of the afterlife in Andersen's tales, as represented in the grave sites, tombstones, ghosts, and the angels of dead children, an entire spiritual 'underworld' that is a fascinating gothic (or late romantic) dimension of Andersen's work, is a deep site of textual exploration, which I have omitted deliberately from this investigation. Andersen's spiritual underworld with its relation to the afterlife is simply beyond the scope of this particular chapter in the context of the secular and political allegory.[5]

Beyond the field of folklore, one might also consider the representation of the underground dimension of Andersen's fairy tales in the architectural realm. The design for the new Hans Christian Andersen museum in Odense by Kengo Kuma creates underground spaces that simulate the universe of the Andersen's fairy tale and allows the visitor to experience the underground or 'underjordiske' world that holds great significance for the fairy tale genre in general. Kuma's design is constructed around this underground metaphor with two thirds of the museum's buildings constructed below ground level in order to create spaces for the otherworldliness of Andersen's fairy tales. This design will also create ground level space for enchanted gardens of large trees, lawns, box hedges, and large shrubs. The design thus evokes naturalistic and botanical metaphors and suggests that the origins of stories lie 'underground.' In the architectural context, one might also consider the new Frihedsmuseet (Museum of Danish Resistance) designed by Lundgaard and Tranberg, which is scheduled to open in 2019. This new museum will be entirely 'underground', a design which will evoke the idea of an underground movement or undergrundshæren (underground army), a deliberately metaphorical design (which may also help prevent arson attacks in the future). In this case, the notion of 'underground' suggests clandestine or subversive activities in modern, urban environments. Finally, what about the term underground in modern, urban environments? I come from Seattle where *Grunge* music emerged from the region's 'underground music' scene in the 1980s. This is a kind of musical or artistic subculture, like the popular or peasant folk tale, with its potential for counter-culture or subversive messages.

Allegory and the Fairy Tale

In the literary arts, subversive messages may be articulated via the allegory (whether intentional or simply unintentionally topical). This is particularly true of literature and pictorial arts produced by artists under religious or political censorship by oppressive regimes. I am thinking here the original fairytales or 'Contes de fées' of Madame D'Aulnoy and Charles Perrault and the implicitly subversive tales composed by aristocratic women of the French Salon, which existed in the periphery of the court of the extravagant monarch Louis XIV, 'Le Roi Soleil', the 'Sun King.' In particular, the early French versions of "La belle au bois dormant" ("Sleeping Beauty") in which Sleeping Beauty is awakened from her slumber by the prince and then marries him and bears their children. In this variant of the ancient tale, the concluding episode is remarkable (and unlike the later German versions): the queen, the prince's jealous mother, is depicted as a cannibalistic ogre who intends to devour her own grandchildren (she instructs her chef to prepare the tasty meal of grilled grandchildren with a sauce Robert). My point is this: one might easily in the context of the reign of the lavish French monarch read this tale allegorically; it has suggested to readers that the voracious ruler (Louis XIV) would 'consume' the French peasantry, his own people.

What then is an allegory, a 'political allegory'? How do I suggest that we understand the term in the context of 'underground Andersen'? By definition, the allegory is a symbolic fictional narrative that conveys a meaning that is not explicitly set forth in the narrative. The allegory is an extended metaphor that functions on multiple levels in the narrative. Several of Andersen's most famous texts can be read as literary allegories. These allegorical tales range from "The Ugly Duckling" ("Den grimme Ælling," 1844), which can be read as an autobiographical fable, to "The Gardener and the Noble Family" ("Gartneren og Herskabet," 1872), an allegory about literary criticism and Andersen's reception, to richly symbolic tales such as "The Story of a Mother" ("Historien om en Moder," 1847). In an earlier article, "H.C. Andersen's 'Historien om en Moder' – Allegory and Symbol in the Danish Golden Age," I argue that this tale is a highly symbolic allegory depicting the stages of grieving of the mother who, having lost her child, must come to terms with the death of the child (Stecher-Hansen 2004).

Obviously, writers often make use of the allegory to express sentiments or opinion in politicised contexts and, as such, the allegory has for centuries been popular as a vehicle for satire. A well-known twentieth-century literary classic exemplifying the 'political allegory' is George Orwell's *Animal Farm* (1945), which under the guise of a fable about domestic animals expresses disillusionment with the Bolshevik Revolution and illustrates how one tyrannical system of government is replaced by another. Such political allegory as a directed satire (targeting particular circumstances or people) implies that the author intends to convey an implicit meaning to the reader of the text. Nonetheless, political allegory as 'intentional satire' is generally *not* what one finds in Andersen's work – although, certainly, one can find examples of particular persons and circumstances that have been directly satirised by Andersen: the literary critic Johan Ludvig Heiberg as the 'music master' in "The Nightingale" ("Nattergalen," 1845), just to mention one example.

I would like to illuminate this particular poetic idiom, the allegory, in the context of the Danish Golden Age, the era during which Andersen's aesthetic sensibilities were formed. The allegory and the symbol are among the most important poetic idioms of vast generation of romantic writers and, therefore, I turn to an essay by Adam Oehlenschläger, entitled "About the Allegory in General" ("Over Allegorien i Almindelighed"), first published in his collected *Aesthetic Writings* (*Æstetiske Skrifter*) in 1854.[6] Oehlenschläger originally presented these reflections on poetic theory as a lecture at the University of Copenhagen in 1810. In the essay, the respected Professor of Aesthetics and one of Andersen's foremost literary mentors delineates a hierarchy of figurative language or poetic idioms. Oehlenschläger's remarks seem relevant to Andersen's own poetic manifestos (such as "The New Century's Goddess," mentioned earlier) and as reflections on the importance of the allegory in nineteenth-century literature, generally speaking. Specifically, Oehlenschläger argues that the most important element of poetry is the image (*billedet*) and he presents a hierarchy of poetic idioms that distinguish between the simile (*lignelsen*), the allegory (*allegorien*), and the symbol (*symbolet*). He claims that, whereas the first two idioms (simile and allegory) require of the reader only reason (*forstand*) or sense (*fornuft*), the symbol functions in a higher sphere of human cognition. Oehlenschläger, the quintessential romantic poet, states that in order to understand or grasp the symbol fully requires imagination (*fantasi*) and an intuitive spiritual or religious sensibility.[7] Although Oehlenschläger values the allegory as a poetic idiom, he relegates it to a category of rhetorical tools that belong to the earthly (*jordisk*) or secular realm:

> The allegory belongs to the realm of arts in so far as it encompasses a beautiful idea in a beautiful form. It is grasped by reason in so far as its meaning is clear, if not finite, then infinitely *earthly*. (Oehlenschläger 1980, 113, emphasis added, my translation)[8]

According to Oehlenschläger, the allegory is thus something less profound, whereas the symbol is something more. The symbol may not be grasped by mere reason or understanding for the full meaning of a symbol may only be sensed intuitively. Precisely because the symbol is a reflection of a divine (*guddommelig*) presence, it cannot be grasped by intellect alone and therefore Oehlenschläger situates the symbol in the context of religious faith and imagery. But this is not the case with the 'earthly' allegory! Although Hans Christian Andersen himself did not directly explore poetic theory in his writings, he certainly makes use of both allegory and symbol, also when laying out his aesthetic program in "Poetry's California" (*I Sverrig*, 1851) and in "The New Century's Goddess" (about the future of poetry to be written "in blood and ink").

Politics and Reading Fairy Tales

What then is the potential for Andersen's fairy tales to function as 'political allegories' (whether 'intended' or 'unintended'), and as a genre of underground literature or subculture literature? The allegory, as defined here with some help from Oehlenschläger, relates to the 'earthly' or secular world, not to the spiritual or religious realm; the allegory is simply an extended metaphor that conveys meaning, as determined by a readership at a particular point in history. One provocative example of fairy tales as political allegories that functioned subversively in an 'underground,' are the tales by Hans Christian Andersen that were published and distributed illegally during the German occupation of Denmark. In using the term "illegally published," I am referring to the long list of books and publications which were blacklisted by the German authorities in Denmark during this period and included "the works of numerous English and American writers, virtually all Jewish writers, and writers of all nationalities in any way critical of the ways of the Nazis or in any way sympathetic to the objectives of Marxism," as discussed by Jens Nyholm (1947, 264). Danish underground publishing included not only newspapers and periodicals (which circulated vital Allied news and information to the occupied population), but also included literary texts, "the production and distribution of some two hundred books and pamphlets, represented by approximately 275 editions" (264). Among these banned literary publications were certain texts by Hans Christian Andersen, along with new Danish literature and numerous translations of European and American literature. According to Nyholm, "the German pressure even in Denmark was strong enough to make the creation of a free Danish underground literature a necessity for the continuance of the country's intellectual life." (265).

Over twenty years ago, in 1996, Elias Bredsdorff presented his archival research from the Royal Danish Library on these underground publications of Andersen's tales in a keynote lecture at the Hans Christian Andersen conference in Odense, later published as "Intentional and Non-Intentional Topicalities in Andersen's Tales." (1999, 11–37). Although I wish to acknowledge my scholarly debt to Bredsdorff, I do not wish to repeat his findings here. Bredsdorff's study includes thirteen tales by Andersen, which were published illegally in Denmark during the occupation. Here I focus on only two of these tales, "The Wicked Prince" ("Den onde Fyrste," 1840) and "The Little Green Ones" ("De smaa Grønne," 1868), which Bredsdorff describes as follows: "two of the less known tales in particular which acquired an unexpected popularity and were read in many homes, in which they had previously been either completely unknown or forgotten." (1999, 16). My interest in the present context is not limited to Danish underground or resistance literature. The broader point of my reading – which Bredsdorff implies but does not pursue in his article – is that it is a readership, as much as an author, that produces the meaning of a text. This fact holds particularly true in the case of literatures of wartime published under conditions of censorship. It is a given readership that produces meaning – although scholars will still continue to investigate the circumstances of the origins of production of a text.

Now, let us turn to the earliest of the two tales: "The Wicked Prince: A Fairy Tale," published one hundred years before Denmark was occupied during the Second World War. Andersen's tale is a story about a megalomaniac tyrant who conquers one country after another, striking terror in the population: "Once upon a time there was a proud and wicked prince who thought only about how he might conquer all the nations of the earth and make his name a terror to all mankind."[9] Andersen's characterisation of the barbarous soldiers and the war-ravaged countryside evokes a horrific, painterly vision of military brutality: "his soldiers trampled down the grain in the fields, and put the torch to the peasant's cottage so that the red flames licked the very leaves from the trees, and the fruit hung roasted from black and limbs."[10] Andersen does not spare details regarding the destruction and cruelty of the tyrant's soldiers, who rape and terrorise women and children, demonstrating a demonic agency:

> Many a poor mother caught up her naked baby and tried to hide behind the smoking walls, but the soldiers followed her, and if they found her and the child, then began their devilish pleasure. Evil spirits could do no worse, but the Prince rejoiced in it all.[11]

In a literary analysis focusing on the origins of the text, readers might speculate that Andersen's tale alludes to Napoleonic forces ravaging the European countryside in the early 1800s. On the other hand, for the twentieth- or twenty-first-century reader, including those of occupied Denmark of the early 1940s, it is more immediate to envision the figures of Hitler (or Stalin) and their troops, who used scorch and burn tactics at the Eastern front (in the Ukraine and Belarus).[12] Other manic tyrants of the twentieth century and today's world emerge in the mind's eye.

In the tale, Andersen's princely tyrant suffers from fatal Hubris, when he wishes statues (*billedstøtter*) of himself placed, not only in the town squares and in the royal places, but also before the altars in the churches. The pastors warn him cautiously that he is great, but that God is greater! The evil prince defies them and declares that he will conquer God as well. And so, the plot of the tale evolves along the lines of the ancient Greek legend of Daedalus and his son Icarus, who flies too close to the sun with the waxed wings (fashioned by his father), and falls to his death in the sea below. Andersen's fairy tale ("more Christian than Greek," remarked one of my undergraduate students at the University of Washington) makes use of futuristic imagery in the depiction of a fantastical, flying military craft, complete with reloading canons:

> he had built a splendidly constructed ship in which he could sail through the air. It was as colorful as a peacock's tail, and seemed decorated with a thousand eyes, but each eye was the barrel of a cannon. The Prince could sit in the center of the ship and, upon his touching a certain button, a thousand bullets would stream forth, and the guns would at once be reloaded.[13]

Although the prince is defeated for a time (blasted from the heavens and lies in his ship, half-dead, caught in a tree), he is determined to force his will. He spends "seven years" building more aircraft, of the hardest steel ("af det haardeste Staal"), a kind of nineteenth-century Luftwaffe and gathers huge armies ("store Krigshære") that cover a radius of many miles, when the troops stand man to man. One could say that Andersen's vision of a massive, modern military force is shockingly prophetic, and, in this sense, the tale constitutes futuristic 'science fiction' as well as political allegory.

The Lord God sends out a biological army (a kind of germ warfare), a swarm of mosquitos. Special blankets swaddled around the prince's body fail to protect the tyrant. A single mosquito penetrates and bites his inner ear, and the poison infects his brain; "the poison rushed into his brain,"[14] a passage which reflects the author's fear of insect-borne fatal illnesses that plagued the contaminated urban waterways of nineteenth-century urban Europe. Finally, the prince is publicly humiliated in his madness, as he throws off the blanket and dances naked in front of the crude soldiers who now mock him: "[He] danced naked before the rugged and savage soldiers. Now they could only mock at the Mad Prince who had started out to conquer God and had been himself conquered by a single little gnat!"[15] The tale suggests that power corrupts – and arrogance, too – and like the emperor in "The Emperor's New Clothes" ("Kejserens nye Klæder," 1837), the evil prince suffers the ultimate humiliation: to parade or dance naked before his own people.

In the historical context of an occupation by a foreign military power, it perhaps comes as no surprise that this tale came to be celebrated (and banned) as a piece of resistance literature, an underground publication that gave moral courage to an occupied people. "The Wicked Prince" seems easily appreciated as an empowering allegory, because it may be read metaphorically as a story about how the small swarm (those who inhabit the natural order) is ultimately more powerful than the self-appointed tyrant or megalomaniac dictator. Furthermore, the prince's demise shows that it only takes one – a single, tiny organism – in the crowd of individuals (a swarm of attacking insects) to destroy (or assassinate) a tyrant. Obviously, Andersen could not have foreseen that this tale would be read and appreciated a century later in Nazi German occupied Denmark. Yet, that is the point: an allegory ought to resonate with various publics and in diverse political contexts. That is world literature and 'universalism.'

The second example of the fairy tale as political allegory is "The Little Green Ones," published later in Andersen's career, in 1868. Similar to the conclusion of "The Wicked Prince," this short tale is informed by a biological metaphor, or rather a botanical metaphor.[16] The story opens with a description of a rose bush (or rose tree) that not long ago had been green and blooming, but now appears sickly. The language of the text directly suggests the analogy of a military invasion: "A *regiment of invaders* were eating it up; and, by the way, it was a very decent and respectable regiment, dressed in *green uniforms*" (emphasis added).[17] The previously blooming rose bush perhaps alludes to mother Denmark (garden metaphors often seem to represent Denmark in Andersen's tales), invaded by a regiment in "green uniforms." By actual coincidence, the ordinary German soldiers stationed during World War II in occupied Denmark, called *flødeskumsfronten* (*the whipped cream front*) in reference to this light-duty occupied territory, indeed wore green uniforms. Much of this tale is narrated in the speaking voice of a "little green one," who openly protests his treatment by humans: "Humans detest us! They come and kill us with soapsuds – that's a horrible drink."[18] The play with words in the tale concerns not naming the green ones by their most "despicable and ugly" ("væmmeligt og stygt") name, a name that cannot be spoken out loud. So what is it?

The real allegory ('political', if you will) of the tale concerns censorship. No voice in the tale is allowed to name the invading green-uniformed pests for what they really are in order to avoid causing offence. I would emphasise here that Andersen's choice of words in the tale indeed suggests an invading military force, an army, (i.e. "quarters," "uniforms") and does not seem to suggest migrants or refugees fleeing into the country. The reader (or "human") perspective on the rosebush is that of a person whose words are censored: "And I, the man, stood looking at the tree and at the little green ones – whose name I'll not mention, for I shouldn't like to hurt the feelings of a citizen of the rose tree, a large family with eggs and youngsters."[19] Again, it seems clear to see how this tale, published with several other Andersen tales in an underground collection, was readily interpreted as an (unintentional) political allegory and appreciated by wartime Danes, who were weary of (or infuriated by) the Danish coalition government's collaborationist policies with Germany (called *forhandlingspolitik* or *the policy of negotiation*) and were legally forbidden from protesting or resisting them. The presence of uniformed German soldiers on the streets was in fact accepted by the vast majority. In *Occupied: Denmark's Adaptation and Resistance to German Occupation 1940–1945*, Nathaniel Hong describes the paradoxical situation in the first years of the occupation as follows:

> The German occupying power and the Danish coalition government shared a common interest in keeping the hearts and minds of the Danish people solidly behind the policy of cooperation and appeasement. [...] Denmark's national security, in this recipe, depended on suppressing discontent and visible opposition to occupation. [...] the Danish state had to police and suppress its citizens' freedom and democratic rights to save democracy. (2012, 48)

The allusion to censorship in "The Little Green Ones" indeed seems to suggest a government-imposed policy on citizens (rather than an ideology of the people) and thus it is not difficult to appreciate how the tale must have resonated with many Danes who – especially during the first three and half years of the occupation (up until the point when the coalition government resigned in late August 1943) – felt the sting of the government censorship.

In the very conclusion, Mother Fairy Tale (Eventyrmo'er), intervenes in this botanical drama to identify the green invader as "Bladeluus!" ("Tree lice!" [aphids]), which is the "invading regiment" that is eating up the rose tree (Dannevang). In the final line of the tale, Mother Fairy Tale makes a bold announcement, a sort of a meta-allegorical commentary, which surely also must have been celebrated by the occupation-era Danish readership and which might just as easily be (mis)interpreted as an invitation to politically offensive speech today: "You should call things by their right names; if you do not always dare to do so, you should at least be able to do it in a fairy tale!"[20] Indeed, these words by Hans Christian Andersen might be the most fitting conclusion to my remarks on relevancy of the political allegory in the fairy tale.

One final note on "The Little Green Ones" ought to mention the historical poignancy of this little tale, which was first published in 1868, just four years after the massive Danish defeat in the Dano-Prussian or Second Schleswig war of 1864 and the consequent loss of Schleswig-Holstein-Lauenburg (two-fifths of the territory of the Danish kingdom). It appears that the Prussian uniforms were blue, not green – nevertheless, we know from many references in his diaries and from his poetry of the period (including "At the Homecoming of the Soldier in 1864" ("Ved Soldatens Hjemkomst i 1864"), that Andersen was devastated by the Danish defeat in the war, a point which historian Tom Buk-Swienty has popularised in his documentary novels: "Hans Christian Andersen [...] was devastated by the war [...]. Though he was more than 300 kilometres from Dybbøl, he was plagued by ominous premonitions" (2015, 99). Apparently Andersen felt, similar to other Copenhageners, that the nation had been betrayed by Danish political leaders. Yes, we ought to call things by their real names and if we cannot do it openly, then we ought to be able to do so in a fairy tale! Apparently, Andersen really did so in "The Little Green Ones."

Naturally, a further exploration and expansion of my argument could investigate whether and how these Andersen fairy tales were read in other occupied European countries during the war. It is quite likely that a fairy tale such as "The Wicked Prince" had a wide circulation in clandestine, underground presses in other Axis-occupied nations. Generally speaking, it holds true that literary works which had been blacklisted and banned by Nazi Germany, such as John Steinbeck's allegorical novella *The Moon is Down* (1942), flourished in underground presses and translations and were circulated in hundreds of editions in occupied territories during the Second World War.

In conclusion, situating Andersen's tales in the context of political allegory is intended to stimulate a conversation about how Andersen's tales figure in the cultural memory of the Danes and citizens around the world. In other words, I have attempted to demonstrate how 'halfway forgotten' fairy tales by Andersen might migrate from the passive archives of cultural memory to become agents in active cultural memory, when these texts are galvanised by a collective political sentiment at a particular point in historical time. Andersen might be the fairy tale writer who 'conquered the world' – but Andersen is also the dark and ironic visionary who regarded developments in a modern and militarised global world with foreboding. In investigations of Andersen's tales in underground contexts and contemporary cyberspace, we may continue to discover references to world leaders and presidents who bring to mind Walter Benjamin's thoughts on "Der destructive Charakter" and whose names one would rather not mention.[21]

References

Andersen, Hans Christian. 2003–07. *Andersen. H.C. Andersens samlede værker*. Edited by Klaus P. Mortensen. 18 vols. København: Det Danske Sprog- og Litteraturselskab/Gyldendal.

Assmann, Aleida. 2010. "Canon and Archive." In *A Companion to Cultural Memory Studies*, edited by Astrid Erill and Ansgar Nünning, 97–107. Berlin/New York: De Gruyter.

Benjamin, Walter. 1972. "Denkbilder: Der destruktive Charakter" in *Walter Benjamin. Gesammelte Schriften* IV: 1, 396 - 398. Frankfurt am Main: Suhrkamp Verlag.

Bredsdorff, Elias. 1999. "Intentional and Non-Intentional Topicalities in Andersen's Tales." In *Hans Christian Andersen: A Poet in Time,* edited by Johan de Mylius, Aage Jørgensen, and Viggo Hjørnager Pedersen, 11–37. Odense: H.C. Andersen Center and Odense University Press.

Buk-Swienty, Tom. 2015. *1864: The Forgotten War that shaped Modern Europe*. Translated by Annette Buk-Swienty. London: Profile Books.

Christiansen, Reidar Th. 1964. "Introduction." In *Folktales of Norway,* translated by Pat Shaw Iversen and edited by Reidar Th. Christiansen, xix-xlv. Chicago: University of Chicago Press.

Hong, Nathaniel. 2012. *Occupied: Denmark's Adaptation and Resistance to*

German Occupation 1940-1945. Copenhagen: Frihedsmuseets Venners Forlag.

Kastbjerg, Kirstine. 2013. "Reading the Surface: The Danish Gothic of B. S. Ingemann, H.C. Andersen, Karen Blixen and Beyond." PhD diss., University of Washington.

Mylius, Johan de. 2004. *Forvandlingens pris: H.C. Andersen og hans eventyr.* København: Høst.

Nyholm, Jens. 1947. "Danish Underground Publications." *Scandinavian Studies* 19 (7): 261-269.

Oehlenschläger, Adam. (1854) 1980. "Over Allegorien i Almindelighed." In Æstetiske Skrifter 1800-1812, edited by F. J. Billeskov Jansen, 110-119. København: Oehlenschläger Selskabet.

Snyder, Timothy. 2010. *Bloodlands - Europe between Hitler and Stalin*. New York: Basic Books.

Stecher, Marianne. 2014. "Modernity, Technology, and Tourism: Hans Christian Andersen's Futuristic Tales." In *More Than Just Fairy Tales: New Approaches to the Stories of Hans Christian Andersen*, edited by Julie K. Allen, 95-104. San Diego, CA: Cognella Academic Publishing.

Stecher-Hansen, Marianne. 2004. "H.C. Andersen's 'Historien om en Moder' - Allegory and Symbol in the Danish Golden Age." In *H.C. Andersen: Old Problems and New Readings,* edited by Steven P. Sondrup, 97-116. Odense: Hans Christian Andersen Center/University of Southern Denmark Press.

Sørensen, Villy. 2004. "H.C. Andersens skygge." In *Sørensen om Andersen: Villy Sørensens udvalgte artikler om H.C. Andersen,* edited by Torben Brostrøm, 51-60. Copenhagen: Gyldendal.

Sørensen, Villy. (1964) 1988. "A Tale of Glass." In *Tutelary Tales* ["En glas historie." In *Formynderfortællinger*], 1-24. Lincoln: University of Nebraska Press.

Notes

1   "at det meget 'Udødelige,' Nutids-Poeter skrive, i Fremtiden maaskee kun existerer som Kul-Indskrifterne paa Fængsels-Murene, seet og læst af enkelte Nysgjerrige" (Andersen 2003-07, 2:382).

2   "I forhold til den iscenesættelse, det fik i eventyrteksterne fra 1840'erne, har temaet her efter 1850 fået tilført nyt brændstof, så at sige. Det er tiden efter det store brud i samfunds- og kulturtilstanden: Indførelsen af det borgerlige demokrati, den gradvise og mere og mere synlige urbanisering, den så småt begyndende industrialisering [...]."

3   See Villy Sørensen ([1964] 1988).

4   "Man har [her i Danmark] vænnet sig til at Andersen er en harmløs Børnebogsforfatter, som ikke blot fortalte naivt, men som selv var naiv, og man overseer alt for let at han fra sin første fremtræden - med den stadig undervurderede Fodreise - var i besiddelse af en ualmindelig intellektuel slagkraft og af en ironi som ikke mindst havde blik for 'hvad der var galt ved en Ting'."

5   Note the extensive analysis of the Gothic mode in Hans Christian Andersen's work in Kirstine Kastbjerg (2013).

6   As mentioned earlier, I have previously made use of "Over Allegorien i Almindelighed"

7   in the article, "H.C. Andersen's 'Historien om en Moder' – Allegory and Symbol in the Danish Golden Age" (Stecher-Hansen 2004).
7   Notably, Adam Oehlenschläger's poetic hierarchy is recognizable in Hans Christian Ørsted's dedication of 1833 in Andersen's poetry book, i.e. Ørsted's phrase about: "the true, the good and the beautiful" ("det sande, det gode og det skønne"), words which are echoed in Andersen's depiction of the learned man in "The Shadow" ("Skyggen," 1847).
8   "Allegorien hører hen i Kunstens Rige, forsaavidt den indslutter en skiøn Idee i en skiøn Form; den begribes allerede af Forstanden, forsaavidt dens Betydning er klar, og om ikke endelig, saa dog uendelig jordisk."
9   "Der var engang en ond og overmodig Fyrste, hvis hele Tanke gik ud paa at vinde alle Verdens Lande og indjage Skræk ved sit Navn" (Andersen 2003-07, 1: 238).
10 "Hans Soldater nedtraadte Kornet paa Marken, de antændte Bondens Huus, saa den røde Lue slikkede Bladene af Træerne, og Frugten hang stegt paa de sorte sviede Grene" (Andersen 2003-07, 1: 238).
11 "Mangen stakkels Moder skjulte sig med sit nøgne diende Barn, bag ved den rygende Muur, og Soldaterne søgte hende, og fandt de hende og Barnet, da begyndte deres djævelske Glæde; onde Aander kunde ikke handle værre; men Fyrsten syntes just det gik som det skulde." (Andersen 2003-07, 1: 238).
12 See for example Timothy Snyder, Bloodlands – Europe between Hitler and Stalin (2010).
13 "[han lod bygge] et kunstigt Skib hvormed man kunde gjennemfare Luften; det var broget som Paafuglens Hale og syntes besat med tusind Øine, men hvert Øie var en Bøssepibe; Fyrsten sad midt i Skibet, han behøvede kun at trykke på en Fjer da fløi tusind Kugler ud og Bøsserne vare igen ladede som før." (Andersen 2003-07, 1: 238-239, emphasis added). A note on translation. Andersen writes that the prince need only to press a "trigger" or pull a "spring" (*en fjer* may be a Fuen dialectic spelling of *en fjeder*) to shoot the cannons from the airship; Hersholt translates fjer as a "botton."
14 "Giften slog op i hans Hjerne" (Andersen 2003-07, 1: 239).
15 "[Han] dansede nøgen for de raae, vilde Soldater, som nu spottede den gale Fyrste, der vilde bestorme Gud og strax var overvundet af een eneste lille Myg" (Andersen 2003-07, 1: 239).
16 It is well known that H.C. Andersen was a disciple of the natural scientist H. C. Ørsted and was influenced by his cultural essays, published as Aanden i Naturen (1850-51). It is quite evident that Andersen's 'futuristic tales' were inspired by H. C. Ørsted's appeal to writers for a modern literature which would bridge the arts and sciences. Is it also possible also to discern Darwinian theory in Andersen's imagery in his later tales? The botanical metaphor in "The Little Green Ones" is quite striking. Note that Andersen's tale "The Most Incredible Thing" ("Det Utroligste," 1872), was published together with the first (Danish) introductory essay on Darwin by the botanist and writer Jens Peter Jacobsen, who sought to educate the Danish public regarding Darwinian theory; both texts were published in 1872 in Nyt Dansk Månedsskrift.
17 "Det [Rosentræet] havde faaet Indqvartering, der aad det op; foresten meget honnet Indqvartering i grøn Uniform" (Andersen 2003-07, 3:150).
18 "Menneskene taale os ikke; de komme og dræbe os med Sæbevand; det er en fæl Drik!" (Andersen 2003-07, 3:150).
19 "Og jeg, Mennesket, stod og saae paa Træet og paa de smaa Grønne, hvis Navn jeg ikke skal nævne, ikke krænke en Rosenborger, en stor Familie med Æg og levende Unger" (Andersen 2003-07, 3:151).
20 "Man skal nævne enhver Ting ved sit rette Navn, og tør man det ikke i Almindelighed, saa skal man kunne det i Eventyret" (Andersen 2003-07, 3:151).
21 With thanks to Finn Barlby for drawing my attention to his discussion of "Den onde Fyrste" ("The Wicked Prince"), its current relevance in today's world, as well as the ways in which it resonates with Walter Benjamin's essay, "The Destructive Character."

Communal Uses

(De-)Constructing Community in Twenty-First Century Literary Transformations of Andersen's "The Little Mermaid" and "The Snow Queen"

Julie K. Allen
Brigham Young University, Provo

The sensitivity to community dynamics that permeates the fairy tales of Hans Christian Andersen helps to explain their continuing relevance to contemporary social problems and their attractiveness to reader-rewriters. The global resonance of Andersen's tales has created an international community of readers whose creative responses to Andersen's works have resulted in a web of adaptations, across cultural, linguistic, and generic lines. This chapter explores how several recent literary adaptations of Andersen's tales "The Little Mermaid" and "The Snow Queen" – two of his best-known and most didactic tales which are fundamentally concerned with the issue of community-building and social fragmentation – function as a community of their own within which they transform Andersen's tales in various ways in order to expand and contribute to an ongoing discussion about the threats communities face and how, if at all, they can be restored.

"The Little Mermaid" ("Den lille Havfrue," 1837) and "The Snow Queen" ("Sneedronningen," 1845) are not only two of Hans Christian Andersen's most widely circulated tales, but also among his most didactic, particularly with regard to the topic of community. The narrator of "The Snow Queen" announces the story's educational intent from the outset: "When the story is done you shall know a great deal more than you do now,"[1] while the moral of "The Little Mermaid" emerges at the end of the tale, in the hope expressed by the daughters of the air that they will encounter good children, of the sort "who pleases his parents and deserves their love,"[2] so that their own probationary period before entering Heaven will be reduced. Both stories prove to be deeply concerned with the ways in which communities are constituted and compromised; each describes a process of fragmentation and alienation that the protagonists must remedy in order to achieve narrative resolution.

This focus on community dynamics may well be one of the contributing factors in both stories' appeal to reader-rewriters who have repeatedly adapted, reimagined, and transformed these tales into new texts which derive much of their meaning from their implicit dialogue with Andersen's originals. These transformed texts engage with the same questions of community destruction and reconstruction as Andersen's tales do, within recognisably derivative frames, but they often suggest radically different solutions than Andersen's, reflecting the distinct socio-cultural contexts in which each text was created. In a certain sense, these transformations and adaptations of Andersen's stories create a community of their own, a sort of proto-fandom, within which the idea of community can be explored, in particular the implicit suggestion made in both stories that communities are endangered by fear and pride but can be restored and rebuilt by acts of selfless love and courage.

Community (De-)Construction in "The Little Mermaid" and "The Snow Queen"

Community cohesion is a central theme in both "The Little Mermaid" and "The Snow Queen." "The Little Mermaid" begins with the narrator locating the community geographically, albeit somewhat vaguely, "far out in the ocean," deeper than "many steeples, [...] stacked one on top of another."[3] Down there in this remote, inaccessible location, is where the sea people live – in isolation from other people. The narrator's subsequent description of the undersea world is vivid and bright, but it serves primarily as a backdrop for a portrait of the widowed sea king's family – his clever, proud mother with twelve oysters on her tail and his six radiant daughters, whose beauty is circumscribed by their fish-tails. It is evident that they enjoy each other's company, playing together, tending their gardens, and listening to stories about the human world above. Similarly, the narrator of "The Snow Queen" offers a precise but generic geographic designator at the beginning of the second story; the community at the heart of this story lies "in the big city [where] it was so crowded with houses and people that few found room for even a small garden and most people had to be content with a flowerpot."[4] The reader quickly learns that this story concerns itself with people from the latter group, those whose share of the big city's resources is miniscule, but who are bound together by nature and affection into communities as close as families.

Yet at the same time both stories are haunted by the fragility of their communities. In "The Little Mermaid," the young mer-princesses' fascination with the human world is a dangerous one, forbidden until each girl's fifteenth birthday, that seems to call the value of their own society into question. The sisters' forays into the human world take up several pages, as each one reports on the alluring things she saw and heard, from church towers to the sunset, but in the end, these brief glimpses serve to inoculate the princesses against the desire to abandon their own home. Most of them soon tire of the novelty and declare "there was no place like the bottom of the sea, where they felt so completely at home."[5] It is only the youngest sister who finds herself incurably infected, an outsider within her own community, someone who no longer shares the same values and interests as the society that produced her, but who is willing to sacrifice her bodily integrity and her ability to communicate for the chance to live among humans and strive to obtain the soul that will qualify her to live eternally with the Christian God. On land, she is mute and misunderstood, petted and pampered, but ultimately unable to achieve her goal of integration, through marriage to the prince, into human society. Her sisters' sacrifice of their hair to provide her with the means of returning to her native land (or sea, if you will) represents the failure of her attempts to join a community that cannot see and appreciate her for what she is.

"The Little Mermaid" raises more questions about community than it answers. Does the mermaid's failure to win the prince represent a tragic failure of integration or is it instead a *felix culpa,* a fortunate fall that enables her to achieve her ultimate salvific goal – reunification with God – without relying on anyone else? Did her longing for the world above poison her chance of belonging completely to her community beneath the sea? Did she ever have a chance of acceptance on land or did her difference inevitably relegate her to the position of outsider? Is her reward simply a form of eternal enslavement or social acceptance at last? Can those who are othered by society ever find a place where they fully belong?

While the threat of community destabilization unfolds gradually in "The Little Mermaid," it frames the entire narrative of "The Snow Queen," the first story of which describes a dystopia of social alienation and community fragmentation through the depiction of the devil's magic mirror, "which had this peculiar power: everything good and beautiful that was reflected in it seemed to dwindle to almost nothing at all, while everything that was worthless and ugly became most conspicuous and even uglier than ever."[6] The mirror warps viewers' perceptions of the world and the people around them, turning "the loveliest landscapes" into "boiled spinach," and deforming the faces of "the very best people" into unrecognisability. The mirror mocks every "kind, pious thought," claiming exclusive truth value for its own twisted perspective. The devil's students run around claiming that now, through the mirror, "for the very first time you could see how the world and its people really looked."[7] The mirror's deliberate misrepresentation of reality is intended to corrode the bonds between individuals and divide communities, from private friendships and families to church congregations and neighbourhoods.

This first story of "The Snow Queen" describes in the abstract what the next story makes concrete – the dissolution of Kay and Gerda's safe, harmonious community and its replacement by a lonely struggle for survival. The devil's students are avid purveyors of this destructive force, shuttling the mirror around the world "until there was not a person alive nor a land on earth that had not been distorted."[8] When the mirror finally shatters into "hundreds of millions of billions of bits, or perhaps even more," it causes "more trouble than it did before it was broken" by invisibly permeating the entire world. Since "every little bit of glass kept the same power that the whole mirror had possessed," each particle has the power to make people focus on the negative: "These bits of glass distorted everything the people saw and made them see only the bad side of things."[9]

In the second story, this general phenomenon of community deconstruction becomes particular. After being contaminated by the mirror particles, Kay comes to regard his community with contempt. Psychologist John Gottman argues that "contempt is the most poisonous of all relationship killers – destroying psychological, emotional, and physical health." (Lisitsa 2013). Once Kay's opinion of his community has been poisoned by the mirror's shards, he is anxious to denigrate it and leave it behind. He can see only the imperfections in Gerda, their roses, even their beloved grandmother. He makes an art of mocking his neighbours: "before long he could mimic the walk and the talk of everyone who lived on that street. Everything that was odd or ugly about them, Kay could mimic."[10] Like the little mermaid, he longs to be part of a community he idealises, not the bright, colourful human world he already inhabits, but the perfect, orderly, supernatural sphere of the Snow Queen. That her palace offers Kay as little true friendship and comfort as the prince's palace does the mermaid reinforces the parallels between the two stories.

Both tales offer the hope of redemption, however, and the restoration of community cohesion, though in contrasting ways. Rather than replicating Kay's behaviour, Gerda holds on to the notion of their community and sets out on her quest to find him and bring him home. On the way she has the chance to join several new communities – to let the spring witch adopt her as a daughter, to become the pampered darling of the prince and princess, or the robber girl's tame plaything – but she resists every temptation in order to release Kay from his icy prison and bring him home. Her purity of heart is, as the Lapp woman informs the reindeer, what enables her to save him from the cold embrace of pure reason and social isolation. By the end of the tale, the two friends are reinstalled in the bourgeois Christian domesticity of their childhood home, having "forgotten the icy, empty splendor of the Snow Queen's palace as completely as if it were some bad dream,"[11] though Andersen offers no insight into whether Kay has developed enough emotional and social maturity to enable this harmony to endure. By contrast, the little mermaid rejects the chance – purchased with her sisters' hair – to rejoin her family and people by killing the prince, choosing non-existence instead, but that choice is denied her. By the power of an unseen agent, she is lifted up to join the daughters of the air in their fatiguing quest to earn themselves an immortal soul. She is welcomed into this new community on the strength of her own desire to a "share in mankind's eternal bliss,"[12] but it still requires three hundred years of good deeds, alongside her new sisters. Despite their disparate outcomes, both tales depict a process of recovering community by strengthening the bonds of love, trust, affection, and service that bind people together in families, churches, communities, countries, and across the globe.

Creative Engagement with Andersen's Texts

These two stories' depictions of the fragmentation of community and the solutions they seem to propose – primarily selflessness and sacrifice – have inspired and provoked dozens of artistic, literary, musical, and cinematic responses. Through these adaptations, a term that encompasses literary and cinematic texts that consciously echo distinctive elements of plot and character, the figures and motifs in the tales take on a life of their own, enter new cultural contexts, and become part of autonomous creative works that are in explicit or implicit dialogue with the works from which they derive. It is both the familiar elements of the originals that recur in adaptations and the unfamiliar, unexpected elements with which they are combined that give adaptations, as Linda Hutcheon puts it, "the comfort of ritual combined with the piquancy of surprise." (Hutcheon 2013, 4). Echoing Christina Bacchilega's observation that fairy tales undergo the same shape-shifting as many of their protagonists, Lucy Fraser describes such adaptations as transformations "in which the fairy tale morphs constantly into new shapes but remains somehow recognizable. (Fraser 2017, 7). Both terms – adaptation and transformation – offer useful insights into the nature of the process underlying the retelling and reimagining of familiar stories and the way in which readers respond to the multiplication of narrative levels, so I use them interchangeably in this chapter.

Successful transformations of Andersen's stories within a variety of different cultural traditions have produced new, artistically autonomous but inherently palimpsestuous works that are always already informed by their relationship to the works from which they are adapted. Gérard Genette describes adaptations as texts "in the second degree," created and received in relation to a prior text. This description echoes Roland Barthes' description of adaptations as "a plural stereophony of echoes, citations, and references." (as quoted in Hutcheon 2013, 6). While many adaptations can stand alone and be appreciated on their own merits, the implicit and explicit dialogue they engage in with the adapted work lends adaptations, by virtue of their intertextuality, a sort of double vision. However, this dimension only becomes apparent when the viewer/reader is familiar with the text being adapted. In such a case, our appreciation of a transformed text is inflected, positively or negatively, by our awareness of the original, and we continually compare the work we already know with the one we are experiencing. If a person encounters an adaptation first, they may not be initially aware of this duality, but it will colour their experience of the transformed text when (and if) they discover it, although the text they encountered first will now function as the original, to which the adapted work is then compared.

While the term "adaptation" encompasses both process and product, Russian philosopher Mikhail Bakhtin's notion of dialogism as it applies to the relationship not just between an original text and its retellings, but also between the adaptations themselves, offers a useful vantage point for discussing the discursive relationship between adaptations of Andersen's stories over the past nearly two centuries. Bakhtin argues:

> Utterances are not indifferent to one another, and are not self-sufficient; they are aware of and mutually reflect one another. [...] Every utterance must be regarded primarily as a *response* to preceding utterances of the given sphere (we understand the word 'response' here in the broadest sense). Each utterance refutes, affirms, supplements, and relies on the others, presupposes them to be known, and somehow takes them into account. (Bakhtin 1986, 91)

Extrapolating from Bakhtin's concept of the utterance, each textual expression in a living context of exchange is formed in relation to its context such that every adaptation is always already embedded in a history of expressions by others in a chain of cultural and political moments. Particularly when judged by their fidelity to the original, adaptations are often dismissed by critics and purists as "secondary, derivative, [...] and culturally inferior" (Hutcheon 2013, 3–4), but such an approach disregards how adaptations, rather than existing in individual one-to-one relationships with the original text, were formed in relation to their textual context and thereby make up a network that transcends the text itself. As Jørgen Bruhn, Anne Gjelsvik, and Eirik Frisvold Hansen note in the introduction to their volume on adaptation studies, "Adaptation must necessarily incorporate some kind of comparative element – seeing one text in relation to another" (Bruhn, Gjelsvik, and Hansen 2013, 5), which facilitates dialogue between different incarnations of a particular text that can become a source of pleasure and insight for readers and audiences. Since the scholarship about adaptations of Andersen has tended to focus on intermedial adaptations from text to film, notably Elisabeth Oxfeldt's 2009 study *H.C. Andersen på film,* this chapter occupies itself with the intertextual connections between Andersen's tales and certain literary adaptations of them that are recognisably indebted to Andersen's originals but diverge in significant thematic and generic ways. In the remainder of this chapter, I investigate how several literary transformations of "The Little Mermaid" and "The Snow Queen" participate creatively in a community of meaning-making in conversation with Andersen's originals and each other.

Re-envisioning "The Little Mermaid"

Adaptations of "The Little Mermaid," in media as diverse as opera, manga, orchestral music, theatre, film, and a range of literary genres, often depart radically from Andersen's text in their details, but many of them remain in dialogue with his story with regard to the fundamental question of community endangerment and redemption. While there are of course adaptations that downplay or omit community as a theme, each of the literary re-imaginings of "The Little Mermaid" discussed in this section – which include Scottish writer Naomi Mitchison's short story "The Little Mermaiden," originally written in 1936 but republished in 2014, Irish author Louise O'Neill's 2018 novel *The Surface Breaks,* American author Timothy Schaffert's dystopian story "The Mermaid in the Tree" from 2010, and the American novelist Marissa Meyer's short story "The Little Android" from 2016 – addresses the topic of community, questioning Andersen's apparent conclusions about how communities can be salvaged, and reframing specific aspects of the characters' choices to reveal differing sets of priorities. Moreover, while all of these texts can be read productively and enjoyably on their own, they gain nuance and depth when read in dialogue with each other.

Many adaptations of Andersen's story challenge the apparently happy ending of "The Little Mermaid," probing whether the destruction of community can ever be rectified and delving into the underlying causes of community fragmentation. Dafnia, the protagonist of Mitchison's melancholic short story "The Little Mermaiden," chooses, like Andersen's heroine, to abandon the fellowship of her own kind because of her desire to join the human world, but, unlike her predecessor, she ends up existentially homeless, adrift from all community bonds. Mitchison skips the description and backstory that Andersen provides, focusing instead on the mermaid's fate, but she offers glimpses of the development of the tragedy. Dafnia's sister, who narrates the story in retrospective, recalls how Dafnia chafed at their sheltered childhood and sought out the dangerous pleasures of the shore. She blames Dafnia's nature for her misalignment with the community of her birth: "It was as though something was wrong deep inside her, something that made her different from the rest of us mermaids." (Mitchison [1936] 2014, 202). In the sister's telling, the blame for the tragedy lies with Dafnia herself, who chose solitude over society and her own judgment over the community's priorities. This framing of the mermaid's desires as selfishness allows much less room for existential redemption than Andersen's mermaid's desire for a soul and Christian salvation.

In flouting her community's mores, Dafnia places herself outside her community of birth, tainted by her contact with the human world, but she remains unable to fully join the human community either. When she rescued the prince, still breathing, she violated her people's prohibition on touching live human flesh, preparing the breach with her sisters that came about when she went to the witch to acquire legs. The witch shaved her head and mutilated her body, "slit and carved and divided her, making her human-shaped," but, her sister recalls, "even so, she could not become wholly human, she could not have whatever this thing is which they claim is better for them than our calm sea-living for all time, [...] this troubled thing which humans call the soul." (Mitchison [1936] 2014, 206). She becomes something in-between, neither mermaid nor human, which the narrator describes in terms of miscegenation. For Mitchison's mermaid, the price of a soul is becoming "mixed with the human, the prince, as before she had been mixed with us and the sea." Having chosen exile and racial impurity, Dafnia is rejected by her family, ostracised and forgotten. As her sister recounts, "she was lost to us; it was no use remembering her." (208). Having failed to follow the community's rules, she is erased from her family's lives and their memories, a pariah.

Ultimately, Mitchison's story is less about Dafnia's failings than her sisters' inability to empathise with either her longing or her pain. One day her sisters come across Dafnia bathing, her hair going grey, her body "soft and blemished as land women's bodies are," and remember her after all. They ask whether she had found her human soul, and she confesses her failure, crying out, "it is all over. The land does not want me." When Dafnia begins to cry in despair, it is such a human thing to do that her sisters laugh, even as Dafnia walks into the sea. However, rather than drowning "as humans do [...], the waves washing against her were wearing her away as though she had been made of sand, a sand pillar." (Mitchison [1936] 2014, 208). Bereft of any emotional support, Dafnia simply dissolves into nothingness: "where Dafnia had been, there was nothing now but dancing waves and foam, and perhaps a mixing again with us mermaids and the sea world which is ours." No possibility of transcendence exists here, no *Deus ex machina* intervenes to validate her sacrifice and turn it into a reward. This ending reinforces the folly of the mermaid's choice to turn her back on her own kind while still reserving the possibility that she has been restored, in death, to the community to which by birthright she belongs.

While in Mitchison's story Dafnia's sisters censure their wayward sister, Louise O'Neill's novel *The Surface Breaks* defiantly valourizes the mermaid's rebellion against oppressive social norms, suggesting that unjust communities must be destroyed in order to be redeemed. O'Neill's protagonist, whose name Gaia evokes the primordial earth goddess, is born into a highly patriarchal and militaristic society. Her father ranks his daughters in order of beauty, mocks or beats them for gaining weight or losing suitors, and tries to marry her off at sixteen to Zale, a middle-aged general who covets her as a trophy and the key to her father's power. The kingdom, as the narrator refers to her home, is no peaceful utopia, but is fractured by social divisions. It is surrounded by the Outerlands, a liminal zone where those who don't conform to the Sea King's expectations – "the ones who pray to the forbidden gods, those whose bodies were hatched misshaped, maids who did not adhere to the standards of beauty my father prefers, those who are sterile or barren" (O'Neill 2018, 102) – are confined to a miserable, marginal existence on the fringes of society. Beyond the Outerlands lie the Shadowlands, home to the Sea Witch and her Slavic-mythology-derived Rusalkas, a race of drowned women who were once human – "the jilted, the victims, the orphans, and the abused" (291) – but now hunger for the flesh of human men. In O'Neill's transformation of this tale, the fundamental conflict is not between land and sea or Christian and pagan, but about how women are controlled by social indoctrination and male violence.

Gaia faces the choice of acquiescing to her father's demands in order to belong to this restrictive community or following her own will by striking out alone. Either way, she would seem to be following the example of her mother, Muireann, who first sold herself to the Sea King in order to broker an armistice between the Salkas and the Sea King, establishing a clear distinction between "good" mermaids who submit to authority and "bad" ones who follow their own desires, but then disappeared on Gaia's first birthday in an apparently selfish decision to pursue a human lover. Despite earnest attempts to conform to her community's misogynistic views, Gaia ultimately chooses to flee Zale's sexual assaults and seek refuge with a human man named Oliver, whom she, like Andersen's mermaid, saved from a shipwreck (though the danger he faced was from the Salkas, not the waves). She soon discovers that human society is not far removed from the misogynistic community she had fled. She comes to despise Oliver as weak and shallow, surrounded by men who view women as objects to be used and discarded. During an all-night party aboard Oliver's ship, which parallels the wedding feast in Andersen's tale, Gaia finally learns the full extent of her father's misogyny and cruelty from his sister Ceto, the Sea Witch, who had seduced Oliver in order to win Gaia's attention.

At this point, the novel takes a decisively feminist turn, challenging the reliance on faithful self-sacrifice that Andersen's tale seems to endorse as the means of healing breaches within a community. Gaia learns that the Salkas had surrendered the powers they were born with to please the mer-men but had only been exploited and abused as a result, just as her own mother had been murdered by her husband. Ceto explains: "We were told such powers weren't *mermaid-like*. We were told that no mer-man would want to be bonded with us if we were more powerful than they were. They warned us that our powers made us too loud. Too shrill. And so women became quiet because we were promised that we would be happier that way." (O'Neill 2018, 288). Emboldened by this knowledge and armed with the knife her sisters purchased for her with their hair to kill Oliver, Gaia throws off her self-hatred, regains her voice, confronts her father, rejects his authority, and embraces her own power. She uses this newfound strength to help reconstruct a community of strong mermaids, as she believes her mother would have wanted her daughters to be. Just before she transforms into a vengeful Rusalka, Gaia admonishes her sisters to "remember always how powerful you are. Never allow anyone to take that away from you, or try and make you feel small. [...] The kingdom needs you to be your true selves. [...] Living true is the most important thing any woman can do." (308–309). Rather than accepting the mermaid's alienation, as Mitchison seems to, O'Neill's radical feminist vision aims for a restoration of a lost community of self-assured women who know their own worth, ending with Gaia's plea, "Mother, can you hear me?" (309).

By contrast, in his story "The Mermaid in the Tree," Timothy Schaffert pays no attention to the mermaid's community of origin and its failings but concentrates on interactions between the mermaid and the human world, which fails her completely. Rather than camouflaging her physical difference behind the appearance, however excruciating, of legs, Schaffert's mermaid retains her inhuman shape. In the dystopian world of Schaffert's story, set in what seems to be a steampunk version of New Jersey, mermaids are objectified, exploited exoticisms who are both desired and despised by humans. They arrive most often as suffocated corpses, "washed up each year on the shore of Mud-puddle Beach" (Schaffert 2010, 174) to be cleaned up and displayed at the annual Mermaid Parade, while those who survive the transition to land find employment as entertainers, nuns, or prostitutes, all of whom are segregated from human society in different ways. Contrary to expectations of romantic literature, Schaffert's protagonist, nicknamed Rapunzel (shortened to Zel) because of her long hair, is not a seductress, but rather the victim of a fragmented, profit-driven human society that values her only as a commodity, quite literally. When Zel washes ashore, poisoned by botulism-tainted peaches, her tongue has been cut out by pirates to sell on the black market, as licking a freshly-cut mermaid tongue is supposed to strengthen the voice and perfect the pitch.

Unlike Andersen, Mitchison, and O'Neill, Schaffert allows his mermaid to experience reciprocated love, but emotion cannot triumph over systemic obstacles to her union with her lover that exclude them from the human community they exist alongside. Zel's romance with Axel, a human man, violates the societal prohibition on miscegenation between humans and merpeople. Their relationship is hollowed out by the desperate poverty that induces Zel to sell parts of her own body to black market vendors. After they consummate their illegal flophouse wedding and conceive a child, they plot to hang themselves in a suicide pact in order to protect their unborn child from similar exploitation, but Axel's attempt fails, condemning him to life and self-loathing. The story ends with Axel's wedding to a former girlfriend, Desiree, to which she comes armed with a bone of Zel's "little part-boy part-fish" child as insurance against her inevitable abandonment. Like Mitchison, Schaffert offers no happy ending for anyone, no redemption, reintegration, or transformation, but unlike O'Neill, his critique is focused on the human society that treated her like a commodity. No community is possible, he seems to suggest, in a world where everyone is only looking out for him- or herself.

Not all adaptations of "The Little Mermaid" double down on nihilistic despair, however, even when criticising social norms. Marissa Meyer's story "The Little Android," set in a futuristic cybernetic world, offers a more determinedly hopeful vision of transspecies' coexistence though one still rooted in self-sacrifice required by a world intolerant of difference. Meyer's 'mermaid' is not a fish out of water, but Mech6.0, an android who dreams of travelling the stars. Unlike mermaids in the sea, she has never had the experience of being part of an autonomous society, but has always been subordinated to her human owners, part of a community of slaves. Her unexpected affection for her supervisor Dataran, whom she rescues from a vat of oil, is an aberration that must be, as the mechanic working on her speculates, the result of a defective personality chip. Like Mitchinson's Dafnia, Mech6.0's failure to conform is ascribed to a fundamental flaw in herself. Androids are supposed to "keep working, not get involved with drama and upset," the mechanic tells her owner. "What this one did [...] it isn't normal. Something's wrong with it. The fact is an unpredictable android is a dangerous one." (Meyer 2016, 259). As with Schaffert's Zel, Mech6.0's divergence from social norms puts her in danger, but like O'Neill, Meyer suggests a way in which she can subvert the system that controls her and limits her choices.

Like Andersen, Meyer gives Mech6.0 a chance to control her own fate and determine her own identity, but that agency marks her as an outsider from both her community of origin and that of the man she loves. Unlike Andersen's mermaid, Gaia, and Zel, whose survival depends on the love of a man, Mech6.0 needs nothing from Dataran to ensure her own survival, thus removing the existential anxiety usually attached to the mermaid's marriage quest. To avoid being scrapped after the rescue, Mech6.0 swaps out her body for an ill-fitting humanoid escort-droid body missing its voice box and assumes a human name,

Star. Once she gets to know Miko, the girl Dataran loves, she experiences strange power surges that make her want to hurt Miko, causing her to feel like she was "disintegrating inside." (Meyer 2016, 272). Like Gaia, she is racked by self-doubt, wondering if the mechanic was right – "was she unpredictable? Was she dangerous?" But when Miko reveals her own secret, that she is a cyborg in a world where even part-human robots have no rights, Star has the opportunity to prove her humanity to herself. She sacrifices her own hopes for Miko's, trading places with her on a departing starship, facilitating Miko's elopement with Dataran. Rather than simply accepting her otherness and resigning herself to a life without the man she loves, Star takes on an agentive role, working proactively to ensure someone else's happiness. She proves her humanity just moments before her borrowed body shorts out, an experience that allows Star to imagine herself as simply one more star in the sea of millions [...] vast and bright and endless." (289). Like Mitchison, Meyer does not offer her mermaid a prolonged afterlife, but she gives her death – and thus her life – meaning, by allowing her to demonstrate her fundamental humanity. Like her aquatic predecessor in Andersen's tale, Star is able to conquer the world by self-mastery and selflessness, but without the prospect of a heavenly afterlife among her like-minded peers.

While these four texts represent just a fraction of the many literary adaptations of Andersen's tale, they illustrate a fairly diverse array of re-imaginings of the story's setting, character development, power dynamics, and didactic message. Each of them retains enough of the original's plot and narrative details to make the link to Andersen's original difficult to miss for people who have read it, but they also transform the story in ways that contribute to an ongoing conversation about the questions Andersen raised about the nature of community: what does it mean to belong to a community? What are the costs of choosing a different path than that sanctioned by your community? What benefits might the exercise of free will bring with it? How, if at all, can or should a fractured community be restored?

Reframing "The Snow Queen"

The scope and complexity of "The Snow Queen" have made it a popular subject for adaptations, many of which retain Andersen's depiction of community as integral to happiness, but they arrive there via different paths and describe very distinct communities. Some adaptations reproduce pivotal plot points of Andersen's story but flesh out the bare bones of it with specific historical and cultural context, from the clothes Gerda wears to period-appropriate conveyance, while others seek "equivalences in different sign systems for the various elements of the story: its themes, events, world, characters, motivations, points of view, consequences, contexts, symbols, imagery, and so on." (Hutcheon 2013, 10). Still other, looser adaptations, such as Disney's 2013 animated film *Frozen,* transform the plot and characters almost beyond recognition, while retaining the central quest narrative and the story's underlying focus on loyalty, bravery, and community. Most retellings, cinematic as well as literary, opt to omit the first story with its mythological qualities and focus on Gerda's quest, but the theme of the insidious mirror and its turbulent effect on communities often recurs in subtle ways. Like the preceding section on "The Little Mermaid," this section will examine recent literary adaptions of "The Snow Queen" – including Canadian author Eileen Kernaghan's YA novel *The Snow Queen* from 2000, American writer Francesca Lia Block's short story "Ice" also from 2000, and Australian author Karen Foxlee's YA fantasy novel *Ophelia and the Marvelous Boy* from 2014 – in order to demonstrate both how they relate to Andersen's original tale and how they engage in implicit dialogue with each other about the benefits and costs of community bonds.

Where Andersen assumes Gerda's contentment with the Christian norms of her community, Kernaghan's *The Snow Queen* explores Gerda's relationship to an imagined mid-nineteenth-century Copenhagen, Andersen's own time, and reveals how Gerda's journey changes her relationship to the dream of a picture-perfect bourgeois life that her community has taught her to value. The first lines of the prologue can be read as foreshadowing either the coming crisis in Kay and Gerda's relationship or Gerda's belief in the promises of middle-class morality: "Looking back, years afterwards, she thought she could name the day, the hour – almost the exact moment – when things began to go wrong." (Kernaghan 2000, 9). No shards of a magic mirror shatter the harmony of their community, but rather a rival for Kay's affections. The Snow Queen appears as Baroness Aurore, a tall, slim, elegant woman with white-gold hair and an ice-blue damask gown who makes Gerda feel frumpy and immature. She seduces Kay with her project of writing a book in which she "hopes to reveal the secret pattern of the universe" (27) and carries him off to northern Sweden as a research assistant. Motivated at first by jealousy and frustration, Gerda embarks on an adventure that takes her far beyond the safe confines of bourgeois society into a geographic and cultural "wilderness" in far northern Scandinavia, the region known as Sápmi that was as foreign to Andersen's readers as the sea kingdom of "The Little Mermaid."

Kernaghan devotes half the novel to the Sámi people, making a Sámi girl named Ritva, who is loosely based on Andersen's little robber girl, an equal partner in the narrative. Gerda's quest to find Kay unfolds in parallel to Ritva's quest to come to terms with the shamanistic powers she has inherited from her mother, making the comparison between the two young girls unavoidable. Rather than relying on the purity of her heart and the assistance of angels as Andersen's protagonist does, Kernaghan's Gerda requires Ritva's aid to reach the Snow Queen's palace and perform three impossible tasks in order to rescue Kay. By introducing the common folk tale tropes of threefold repetition and direct confrontation with an antagonist, Kernaghan transforms Andersen's story into more recognisable fairy tale shape, only to disrupt the associated expectation of an unproblematic happy ending. After rescuing Kay, Gerda finally realises that he does not reciprocate her love and she has to face the prospect of abandoning her dreams of bourgeois domesticity. Like Andersen's robber girl, Ritva strikes out on her own, but Gerda hesitates, torn between coaxing Kay into marriage or seeking her own fortune. This ambiguous, unresolved ending leaves the question open of how Gerda might best attain the happiness she desires but makes it clear that she cannot simply return to the domestic Biedermeier bliss of Andersen's tale. She must find a new way to relate to her community.

Published the same year as Kernaghan's novel, Francesca Lia Block's story "Ice" narrows the story's focus from a far-flung quest to an existential journey of self-discovery, embellished with allusions to details from Andersen's story. Block places three original protagonists – Gerda, who narrates the story, K, and the Snow Queen – into a love triangle that interrogates the benefits and costs of intimate relationships. Where Kernaghan's coming-of-age story grapples with gendered social expectations, the focus of Block's first-person narrative, from the first line – "she came that night like every girl's worst fear, dazzling frost star ice queen" – is the Snow Queen's dangerous sensuality and the threat she poses to the protagonists' relationship. The narrator realises as soon as the shining, sexually mature Snow Queen materialises in their usual hangout, "The Mirror," that she cannot compete with her. Instead, she surrenders her claim to K., and the vulnerability that physical and emotional intimacy carries with it: "She went straight for him and he couldn't fight her and I didn't hate him. I just vanished. I felt almost – relieved – because what I dreaded most in the whole world was going to happen and I wouldn't have to live with it anymore – the fear." (Block 2000, 201). Having invested her entire self in this relationship, however, with no other emotional support networks, the narrator fears that she is in danger of losing her own identity when she loses K.

Nevertheless, the narrator fights back and, improbably, wins, once she recognises that the battle between them is not physical but psychological. K. doesn't leave town physically, only mentally and emotionally, so the narrator has no cause to travel. However, as she assures the reader, "I would have ridden on a reindeer or the back of a bird, I would have gone to the North Pole" (Block 2000, 218). Since she doesn't live in a fairy tale but in the real world, she laments, "These are the things of stories and I couldn't do any of them." (219). Yet in the end, when the Snow Queen has gotten tired of K. and abandoned him in a frozen lump at the foot of her bed, the narrator finds the courage to confront her fears. She walks up to the Snow Queen's house, a white marble palace on a hill, and defies her rival, trusting in the power of selfless love to break evil spells. Despite the narrator's helpless awe of the Snow Queen and almost irresistible desire to "become what she was, no matter what it took," her tears melt K.'s frozen heart and wash away the shard of glass in his eye, and they kiss. He is rescued from the Snow Queen's clutches and the narrator is reunited with K. The ending is bittersweet, for the Snow Queen's irruption into the protagonists' lives has changed them irreparably, robbing them of the innocence of childhood's unfamiliarity with evil. The narrator concludes, "Once he and I were children, before this happened" (229), suggesting that although communities and families can be rebuilt, betrayal still leaves scars, and innocence once lost cannot be regained.

Finally, Karen Foxlee's novel, *Ophelia and the Marvelous Boy,* departs the farthest from Andersen's tale in the details of setting and characters, but its depiction of the restorative, unifying power of familial love as the core community of human relationships reinforces his suggestion that familial solidarity is the solution to the fragmentation of social bonds. Foxlee uses Andersen's story as a ghostly backdrop for her own, in which a young British girl named Ophelia Jane Worthington-Whittard undertakes to rescue a nameless, ageless boy from a secret prison room inside a museum in a "foreign city where it always snowed" (2014, 9), where her father has taken a job a few months after her mother's death from cancer. Unlike Andersen's quasi-sibling protagonists, Ophelia and her mysterious friend, whose name was "taken from [him] by a protectorate of wizards from the east, west, and middle to keep [him] safe" (14), did not grow up together but meet only after the boy has fallen into the clutches of the Snow Queen, who rules this faraway land. Her true nature is concealed from public view; she goes by the name Miss Kaminski and pretends to be the curator of the museum. Yet instead of rescuing the boy, Ophelia must save her sister Alice, who has been entranced by Miss Kaminski and is nearly sacrificed to sustain the Snow Queen's eternal youthfulness.

In Foxlee's novel, the Snow Queen embodies the divisive, distorting qualities of the devil's magic mirror in Andersen's tale. As one of the wizards who sends the marvelous boy on his quest explains: "The Snow Queen likes more than anything else to destroy good things. [...] She likes good things to become bad things, bad things to become sad things, sad things to become eternally frozen things." (2014, 20). Where Andersen's Snow Queen is content to kidnap a single boy and gradually entomb him in ice, Foxlee's Snow Queen poses a threat to society as a whole. She freezes everyone and everything around her, causing it to snow so much that it covers the "palace grounds, the once-green gardens, [...] the hills and the fields. [...] Whole villages simply disappeared. The lakes froze over, and then the sea. Children's faces grew thin and gray. Old ladies keeled over and froze in the streets" (2). Just as the threat the Snow Queen poses is more broadly framed as one facing the entire community, so too is the battle to defeat her more public, with a museum full of guests looking on as first Ophelia's father and then Ophelia herself fight not only for their own lives, but for the very fate of the world.

Unlike in most other adaptations, Foxlee's characters do not make a lonely journey away from civilisation, except for the "marvellous boy," whose mission in life to destroy the Snow Queen has led him into the human world from a magical realm, and they do not fight the Snow Queen alone. Ophelia is ultimately able to defeat the Snow Queen in battle only with the assistance of her father, her sister, and the ghost of her mother, who whispers, just at the moment when Ophelia is dueling with the Snow Queen on Christmas Eve, "Love is on your side." (2014, 224). After the Snow Queen's defeat and death, the marvellous boy is finally free to reclaim his name and re-join his own community, while Ophelia's formerly strained relationship with her sister Alice, who had been flattered by the Snow Queen's attentions and nearly sacrificed to the Snow Queen's vanity, is healed. Rather than simply affirming Ophelia's bravery and compassion, like Gerda's, Foxlee demonstrates the power of family ties and the strength of maternal love, even beyond the grave, to overcome both personal and societal challenges.

Each of these three literary re-imaginings of Andersen's "The Snow Queen" retains different parts of Andersen's original and transforms them into new creations. They vary in the way they depict the Snow Queen, the setting, and the scope of the protagonists' journey, but they share a common focus on the endangerment of community and the possibility of preserving or restoring it against the threat posed by the Snow Queen's embodiment of ambition, greed, vanity, and self-indulgence. By placing them in dialogue with each other, we can see how the stories respond to each other as well as to Andersen's text, challenging the Christian ideology underpinning the resolution of Andersen's story, shifting their narrative focus from the seductive allure of pure reason to that of physical perfection and power, and endorsing female empowerment, family solidarity, and rebellion against gender expectations as tools to resolve the crisis facing the community depicted within the text.

Conclusion

In both "The Little Mermaid" and "The Snow Queen" Hans Christian Andersen describes communities being fractured by interior and exterior pressures and requires his protagonists to engage with the challenges this situation creates. In "The Little Mermaid," his protagonist is both agent and victim of community fragmentation, as she abandons her community of origin because of its inability to meet her existential needs, as she fails to integrate into her community of choice that is blind to her worth, and as she is ultimately accepted into a third community, in which her value is determined neither by her physical appearance nor the ability to articulate her own desires, but by the desires of her heart, in particular her willingness to sacrifice herself for the sake of others. In "The Snow Queen," the underlying cause of the community deconstruction is external, represented by the mirror shards and the Snow Queen herself, but it is triggered by Kay's agentive choice to seek personal fulfilment outside his bourgeois home and resolved by Gerda's selfless determination to redeem him from the consequences of his own choices, at the cost of her own physical and emotional comfort.

Yet Andersen's readers are free to disagree with the resolutions he proposes, and as his stories have made their way into many other cultures' literary and cinematic traditions, the communities of readers around them have, in turn, generated webs of adaptations that engage with each other and Andersen over the question of community (de-)construction. It is in the interconnectedness of Andersen's stories and their adaptations, in the conversations and disagreements between them, that we see how deeply and influentially Andersen's stories have integrated themselves into the global community of stories that bind people and countries together. The many distinct transformations of "The Little Mermaid" and "The Snow Queen" examined in this chapter vary considerably in terms of setting, focus, style, and genre, but they each grapple with questions about community: What binds communities together, what tears them apart, how individuals can and should relate to communities that oppress or devalue them, and how to rebuild communities to be sources of strength and healing. While each adaptation reimagines Andersen's story in ways that resonate with the author's own priorities and concerns, the interpretative community they create together models the give and take of ideas and opinions that leads to true communication.

References

Andersen, Hans Christian. 1991. *Eventyr*. Edited by Johan de Mylius. København: Gyldendal.
Bakhtin, Mikhail. 1986. *Speech Genres and Other Late Essays*. Translated by Vern W. McGee. Austin: University of Texas Press.
Block, Francesca Lia. 2000. *The Rose and the Beast*. New York: Joanna Cotler Books.
Bruhn, Jørgen, Anne Gjelsvik, and Eirik Frisvold Hansen, eds. 2013. *Adaptation Studies: New Challenges, New Directions*. London: Bloomsbury.
Foxlee, Karen. 2014. *Ophelia and the Marvelous Boy*. New York: Knopf.
Fraser, Lucy. 2017. *The Pleasures of Metamorphosis. Japanese and English Fairy Tale Transformations of "The Little Mermaid."* Detroit: Wayne State University Press.
Hutcheon, Linda. 2013. *A Theory of Adaptation*. 2nd ed. London and New York: Routledge.
Kernaghan, Eileen. 2000. *The Snow Queen*. Saskatoon, Saskatchewan: Thistledown Press.
Lisitsa, Ellie. 2013. "The Four Horsemen: Contempt" [blog]. https://www.gottman.com/blog/the-four-horsemen-contempt.
Meyer, Marissa. 2016. *Stars Above: A Lunar Chronicles Collection*. New York: Feiwel and Friends.
Mitchison, Naomi. (1936) 2014. *The Fourth Pig*. Princeton, N.J.: Princeton University Press.
O'Neill, Louise. 2018. *The Surface Breaks: A Reimagining of The Little Mermaid*. London: Scholastic.
Oxfeldt, Elisabeth. 2009. *H.C. Andersen på film*. Odense: Syddansk Universitetsforlag.
Schaffert, Timothy. 2010. "The Mermaid in the Tree." In *My Mother, She Killed Me, My Father, He Ate Me*, edited by Kate Bernheimer, 171–199. New York: Penguin.

Notes

1. "Naar vi ere ved Enden af Historien, veed vi mere, end vi nu vide" (Andersen 1991, 61).
2. "som gjør sine Forældre Glæde og fortjener deres Kjærlighed" (Andersen 1991, 202).
3. "langt ude i Havet"; "mange Kirketaarne [stillet] ovenpaa hinanden" (Andersen 1991, 181).
4. "inde i den store By, hvor der ere saa mange Huse og Mennesker, saa der ikke bliver Plads nok til, at alle Folk kunne faa en lille Have, og hvor derfor de fleste maae lade sig nøie med Blomster i Urtepotter" (Andersen 1991, 62).
5. "at nede hos dem var dog allersmukkest, og der var man saa rart hjemme" (Andersen 1991, 185).

6 "havde den Egenskab, at alt Godt og Smukt, som speilede sig deri, svandt der sammen til næsten Ingenting, men hvad der ikke duede og tog sig ilde ude, det traadte ret frem og blev endnu værre" (Andersen 1991, 61).
7 "kunde man først see, [...] hvorledes Verden og Menneskene rigtigt saae ud" (Andersen 1991, 61).
8 "tilsidst var der ikke et Land eller et Menneske, uden at det havde været fordreiet deri" (Andersen 1991, 61).
9 "hundrede Millioner, Billioner og endnu flere Stykker"; "megen større Ulykke end før"; "hvert lille Speilgran havde beholdt samme Kræfter, som det hele Speil havde"; "da saae de Mennesker Alting forkeert, eller havde kun Øine for hvad der var galt ved en Ting" (Andersen 1991, 62).
10 "Han kunde snart tale og gaae efter alle Mennesker i hele Gaden. Alt, hvad der var aparte hos dem og ikke kjønt, det vidste Kay at gøre bag efter" (Andersen 1991, 66).
11 "glemt som en tung Drøm den kolde, tomme Herlighed hos Sneedronningen" (Andersen 1991, 90).
12 "tage Deel in Menneskenes evige Lykke" (Andersen 1991, 201).

Hans Christian Andersen and the Comic Art Community
The Strange Case of the Little Mermaid's New Clothes

Camilla Storskog
University of Milan

This chapter looks at the graphic novel Reflets d'écume *(Ange and Varanda 1994, 1995), a revisionist treatment of "The Little Mermaid" ("Den lille Havfrue," 1837) heavily relocating Hans Christian Andersen's iconic little mermaid. Arguing that the fairy tale is redone in a gothic mode, the analysis does not wish to achieve a comparative reading of fairy tale vs. graphic novel but rather aims to consider the latter as an interpretation of a classic, and on its own terms. Not only does the reframing call for a study of the graphic novel in relation to the Gothic, but also for a look at how the medium affordances of comics serve this particular reading. Considering adaptation as a form of translation, the methodology used draws on Roman Jakobson's (1987) notion of the 'dominant' and its employment in the field of translation studies, then combines with Julia Round's (2014) exploration of the connections between comics and Gothic, and lastly with Thierry Groensteen's (1999) semiotic approach to graphic narratives.*

In the opening remarks to the volume *Hans Christian Andersen and the Uncanny* (*H.C. Andersen og det uhyggelige*) (Bøggild, Grum-Schwensen and Thomsen 2015), a collection of articles exploring manifestations of the uncanny in Andersen's production, the editors observe that many translators of Andersen have taken great liberties with the original fairy tales, producing revisionist versions judged more "suitable" for the young readers that the author was, in their minds, addressing:

> Translators have often taken special liberties in the translation of Andersen; because he has been considered as a writer for children they have granted themselves a special license to reformulate and change his texts in order to address the readership, an audience of children speaking the target language, as flawlessly as possible. (9)[1]

As a consequence, more often than not, the editors conclude, the international Andersen comes across as "a tamed, domesticated, and harmless ditto" (Bøggild, Grum-Schwensen, and Thomsen 2015, 10)[2], and his narrative is rendered void of any unsettling qualities. In her analysis of a selection of cinematographic transpositions of the fairy tales, *Hans Christian Andersen's Fairy Tales on Film (H.C. Andersens eventyr på film)*, Elisabeth Oxfeldt likewise points out that Andersen's own efforts and personal strategies to suit his storytelling to a dual readership of both children and adults seem to have been overlooked in many adaptations for the screen (2009, 23–24).

Although the taming of Hans Christian Andersen is a common activity also among comic art creators dealing with intermedial translations of the fairy tales, this chapter will look at one particular case proving that alternative approaches do exist. *Reflets d'écume (Seafoam reflections;* vol. I, *Naïade [Naiad]*, Ange and Varanda 1994, and vol. II, *Noyade [Drowning]*, Ange and Varanda 1995), a graphic novel in two volumes scripted by Anne and Gérard Guéro (Ange) with artwork by Alberto Varanda, reads the terrifying core of Andersen's tale of the little mermaid through a magnifying glass and shows its potential as a gothic narrative aimed at an adult readership. *Reflets d'écume* drags the reader into a gloomy graphic universe contained in black gridding where gothic tropes and imagery abound: there are complotting patriarchal tyrants and a protagonist, Louise D'Escandras, playing the role both of the innocent nun and of the female victim; there are evil representatives of the clergy, a wicked bishop and nun in disguise, characterised by the absence of reason, decency, and morality; there are scenarios of entrapment and suffering such as hedge mazes and underground torture chambers and a setting which is very far from Andersen's palace with its white marble, precious textiles, sparkling fountains and glass dome letting the sunshine in. In its place we have a decaying medieval castle with a candle-lit room covered in cobwebs where young children are ruthlessly murdered. While showing the little mermaid around his abode, the Prince turns to his mute guest with the following words: "You would be surprised at the number of little boys of royal descent who have passed away in a foolish manner, suffocating in their breakfast so that a cousin, an uncle, or a brother could succeed to the throne" (Ange and Varanda 1994, 21)[3] – a statement indicating that the child-directed content of Andersen's fairy tale has been lost in transposition.

In contrast to the global tendency in the intermedial appropriation of Andersen's heritage, the graphic novel creators catch hold of Hans Christian Andersen's nightside and reach out to that adult readership so often ignored in processes of adaptation. Let us see how.

Methodological Approach[4]

In the volume *La Transécriture. Pour une théorie de l'adaptation: littérature, cinéma, bande dessinée, théâtre, clip*, André Gaudreault and Thierry Groensteen introduce the term 'transécriture,' coined to avoid comparative readings measuring transpositions against their source texts in terms of a preoccupation with 'fidelity' or 'distance' between the two. By focusing on the very essence of the adapter's transmedial variation, the two scholars foreground what they call the "icon" of the text:

> every reading of a text, every unique reading of a text, produces in the reader's mind what one could call an 'icon' of the text [...] it is this icon of the text that the adapter will adapt by putting it through the 'mill' of another medium. (Gaudreault 1998, 269)[5]

Elements such as the outline of the plot or the character gallery, if maintained in the 'transécriture,' are instead indicated with the term 'loan' (Gaudreault 1998, 269: "emprunt"). As suggested in the conclusions to the volume (Groensteen 1998, 273), the strategy for studying these 'loans' contemplates a range of different textual levels with the aim of investigating, for example, the 'fabula' (aspects including, but not limited to, variations in narrative structure, time and place, characters), the 'discourse' (how the adapter's interpretation of the source text might be influenced by the cultural, social, historical, or ideological climate in which the new version is born), or the 'medium' (how these loans, when transferred to a different context, depend on formal solutions proper to the new medium).

Is the neologism 'transécriture' preferable to words such as 'adaptation' or 'transposition'? Although a new terminology does not, on its own, change the way we look at transmedial variations on a source text, Gaudreault and Groensteen's idea that transécritures reincarnate, in a different form, what their creators see as the dominant 'icon' of the adapted text seems appealing to me as it resonates with the idea of adaptation as a form of translation. As a matter of fact, what Groensteen and Gaudreault formulate as the 'icon' of the source text draws close to the idea of the 'dominant,' which has migrated from the Russian Formalist school to the field of translation studies thanks to mediators such as Roman Jakobson, Peeter Torop, and Bruno Osimo. The conceptual device of the 'dominant' is best known through the lectures given by Jakobson, who, in 1935, spoke of the 'dominant' as "the focusing component of a work of art, it rules, determines, and transforms the remaining components." (Jakobson 1987, 41). In Jakobson's theorisation (41–42), the dominant is seen as an umbrella term able to host a wide range of textual aspects related, but not limited to, for instance, 'form' (rhyme, metre or intonation may constitute the 'dominant' in verse), 'function' (e.g., aesthetic or informative), and 'epoch' (different genres of art dominate different historical epochs). Thanks to its flexibility, the term has proved a useful tool in translation studies, where the prototext's lead device, as singled out in the translator's unique reading, guides the translation choices.[6]

With reference to the above-mentioned categories, I will proceed by bringing to the fore the way in which Ange and Varanda's intersemiotic translation subverts the telling of an old tale.[7] Of relevance in the transposition process is the authors' emphasis on the unsettling qualities in Andersen's text, expanded and intensified to the point of becoming the element – the 'icon' or 'dominant' – that specifies the new rendering and creates unity in the work: through the lens of a horrific gothic narrative, the 'fabula' – intended in a formalist sense as "the-events-as-they-happened" – of "The Little Mermaid" is rewritten in the graphic novel transposition. Thanks to the affordances of the 'medium' of comics this interpretation is enhanced and magnified to an extent where it even becomes splatter and risks losing hold of the subtleties in Andersen's handling of gothic terror.

The Little Mermaid's Gothic New Clothes

Readings of "The Little Mermaid" have taken many different interpretive directions. As Jacob Bøggild and Pernille Heegaard (1993) have observed in their work on the reception of the fairy tale and personal decoding of the text, biographical knowledge has brought critics to look at this fairy tale as a literary enactment of Hans Christian Andersen's personal traumas, while the final scene, in which the mermaid is lifted up from the abyss by the Daughters of Air, has been judged both an artistically misplaced act of compensation and an aesthetic failure, as well as an ending perfectly in line with the text's Christian message.[8] This much-debated final scene is completely discarded in *Reflets d'écume,* and, with it, the duality between the abyss of damnation and heavenly salvation is subverted. The little mermaid is instead lowered and confined (forever, it would seem) into an uncomfortable realm dense with less simplistic ambivalences: cross-contaminations not only of reality and fantasy but also of 'masculine' and 'feminine' occur as a male *ondin* appears in volume II to blur boundaries in a way that resonates with the gothic, "where monstrosity is associated with the copying, mirroring, or incursion of one gender form onto or into the other." (Kavka 2015, 211). In the mermaid's descent, one could argue, the text's circular structure is brought to perfection. Her return to the abyss at the end of this dark tale echoes the opening scene in which the newborn mermaid is thrown into the ocean, supposedly by her earthly mother. As Andersen's famous opening lines are quoted in French translation, the sombre hues characterising the two graphic albums turn transparent and fairy tale blue, even if it is just for an instant (fig. 1):

> Far out in the ocean the water is as blue as the petals of the loveliest cornflower, and as clear as the purest glass. But it is very deep too. It goes down deeper than any anchor rope will go, and many, many steeples would have to be stacked one on top of another to reach from the bottom to the surface of the sea. It is down there that the sea folk live. (Ange and Varanda 1994, 6) [9]

This is the only direct quotation from Andersen in the graphic novel. Elsewhere the reader's knowledge of the fairy tale plot is taken for granted: when the mermaid appears at the castle entrance as a mute

Fig. 1 Réflets d'écume – Naiade, par Alberto Varanda et Ange © 1994, Vents d'Ouest

two-legged young woman, only readers of Andersen will spot the intertextual reference to the sea witch, embedded in the puzzled Prince's question: "How did this happen? I will never know, I suppose. Are you mute from birth? Or has a witch stolen your tongue?" (Ange and Varanda 1994, 26).[10]

The team behind *Reflets d'écume* has transposed Andersen's tale by a shift of focus: from the underwater kingdom of the little mermaid the action is transferred to the medieval court of the Prince and to the realm of his adversary, King Lahr, and concentrates on complex political intrigues in a society devastated by the Inquisition. In this grotesque overwriting of the 'fabula,' the little mermaid saves a drunkard of a Prince who falls overboard while spending a night on his ship in the company of prostitutes. He then gets back to the castle in time for his own funeral, arranged by unreliable relatives and conspiring courtiers and celebrated in a gothic cathedral by a vicious bishop. In a plot against the Prince, the Duchess of Valès misleads him into believing that it was her niece, the novice Louise D'Escandras, who saved him from death by water. As it is discovered that Louise is carrying an heir, the bishop, now allied with King Lahr in the East, plans to kill the girl. Within this plot of political intrigues, the mute and eerie love-struck little mermaid who is found on the shore, is nothing but a ghostly presence. Being a mermaid, she is banned by the Inquisition as a demonic creature alongside witches, vampires, werewolves, and the sexually depraved, and fears for her life and mental sanity as the townspeople are being persecuted, tortured in the dungeons, and burned on pyres because of their inability to reveal what satanic rituals they use to evoke sea creatures. As the second volume comes to a close with the words "to be continued" ("à suivre"), King Lahr is making plans to profit from the disorders on the rivalling territory and overthrow young Prince Louis, heir to the throne after his father's mysterious death.[11]

As the abovementioned ingredients reveal, horror and fear – at times present in the shape of bloodshed and violence – are defining features of *Reflets d'écume*. The revelling in an imagery of gore and rage, as well as appearances such as the zombie-like combatants involved in a sword fight (fig. 2) have little to do with what instances of suspense there are to be found in Andersen's text. Although there are fearful episodes in "The Little Mermaid" incorporating elements

Fig. 2 *Réflets d'écume – Noyade*, par Alberto Varanda et Ange © 1995, Vents d'Ouest

of nightmarish atrocity, Andersen is bravely criss-crossing the line between a concrete display of horrifying elements and the suggestion of an atmosphere of dread. In the central scene of the fairy tale which sees the little mermaid approaching the witch den in the forest there are skeletons, black blood spilling out of the witch's chest, and snake-like creatures reaching out for the girl making fear a tangible experience, but there are also obscure details calling forth an almost supernatural kind of dread as the narration accounts for the witch's telepathic qualities and insists on the sense of irresolvability and entrapment connected to the demonic pact:

> She reached a large muddy clearing in the forest, where big fat water snakes slithered about, showing their foul yellowish bellies. In the middle of this clearing was a house built of the bones of shipwrecked men [...]. [...] "I know exactly what you want," said the sea witch. "It is very foolish of you, but just the same you shall have your way, for it will bring you to grief, my proud princess." [...] "Once you have taken a human form, you can never be a mermaid again. You can never come back through the waters to your sisters, or to your father's palace. And if you do not win the love of the Prince so completely that for your sake he forgets his father and mother, cleaves to you with his every thought and his whole heart, and lets the priest join your hands in marriage, then you will win no immortal soul. If he marries someone else, your heart will break on the very next morning, and you will become foam of the sea." [...] Then she pricked herself in the chest and let her black blood splash into the caldron. Steam swirled up from it, in such ghastly shapes that anyone would have been terrified by them.[12]

With reference to Ann Radcliffe's reflection on the two schools of gothic writing, Andersen's register can be said to span from uncensored 'horror' to suggestive 'terror' and back again. In the essay "On the Supernatural in Poetry," published posthumously in 1826, Radcliffe explained 'terror' as a narrative mode suggesting dread and obscurity though leaving the visualisation of these categories to the imagination of the reader. By contrast, 'horror' is characterised by graphic detail. Building on Radcliffe's distinction, an authority within gothic scholarship such as Devendra Varma has efficiently clarified the difference between 'terror' and 'horror' as the gap between "the smell of death and the stumbling against a corpse." (1966, 130).

Although *Reflets d'écume* offers no equivalent to the little mermaid's encounter with the witch, the examination of Andersen's skillful juxtaposition of atrocious elements, on the one hand, and anxiety and suspense on the other, serves to take account of what can be seen as the shortcomings of the graphic narrative. In a prevalently visual medium such as the graphic novel, the display of splatter and violence comes easy and is – if compared to the instances of gothic terror in Andersen's tale – driven to excess as it is unambiguously sprawled out on the page to be contemplated in frightening detail.

Medium-specific Analysis

In an attempt to go beyond the examination of a cast and a setting exploiting standard gothic tropes to create an atmosphere of horror and decay, we will turn our attention to how the medium affordances of comics are used to signal the gothic overwriting of Hans Christian Andersen's tale. Visual strategies concerning space (both domestic and outdoor) persuasively render the sense of entrapment of the imperilled heroine Louise D'Escandras, and enhance her psychodrama. The pages visualising Louise as she reveals her pregnancy (the consequence of a rape) to her maid, make use of nightmarish changes in perspective to create a feeling of vertigo, while heavy curtains and dark, labyrinthine, castle corridors entrancingly represent her imprisonment (Ange and Varanda 1994, 31-32). In volume II, suiting the action to the word and the word to the image, young and innocent Louise is led into a hedge maze accompanied by the ambassador's words: "A woman should not take part in games of power but be content with her role as wife and mother… […]. A wise philosophy in times of trouble" (Ange and Varanda 1995, 15).[13] The maze also articulates the Prince's blind descent into folly as he gets lost in its tortuous pathways and in his own subjective universe, where he is the only one to catch glimpses of the mermaid in red (16).

While the portrayal of Louise D'Escandras resonates with the standard interpretation of the gothic heroine as an oppressed victim, the representation of the little mermaid emphasises the uncanny turn the original tale has taken in the graphic rewriting. The mermaid's presence in *Reflets d'écume* recalls and embodies the gothic concept of haunting from several perspectives: on an intertextual level she is the uncanny echo of Andersen's familiar fairy tale heroine; within

Fig. 3 Réflets d'écume – Naiade, par Alberto Varanda et Ange © 1994, Vents d'Ouest

the narrative universe of the graphic novel she is both a repressed creature belonging to a pagan past and a revenant ghost persecuting the Prince and causing his mental and physical breakdown. Through the visualisation of water and sea foam that unexpectedly materialise to torment the characters, the grip of the past is suggested, and the mermaid is reminded of whom she really is: an unwanted presence who has gone underwater but surfaces time and time again. On several occasions (Ange and Varanda 1994, 19–20, 23, 40), the panels are submerged by water masses and the colouring changes to indicate that there is a psychic relocation from the castle's domestic space to a supernatural underwater world. As the little mermaid overhears a conversation and learns that the Prince is marrying Louise D'Escandras, she is touched by reflections of light and transferred to a surreal abyss where anonymous voices are urging her to kill the Prince (40; fig. 3). In addition to functioning as an explicit reference to the title of the albums, this recurring detail of the water, and the play of light on it, resonates with Julia Round's view on the use of braiding, a concept we will shortly take a closer look at, within the graphic Gothic. In this context, according to Round, the technique of braiding corresponds to "a haunting, an echo of something previously existent in the story." (2014, part 2, chapter 3: *Haunted Places*).

In comic art studies the notion of 'braiding' is, as a rule, used to describe a form of visual alliteration, or rhyme, through which the graphic artist connects single panels, or details in panels, within the narrative with each other, and is commonly founded "on the remarkable resurgence of an iconic motif." (Groensteen 2007, 152).[14] As Groensteen clarifies in his addendum (Groensteen 2015) to the chapter on the art of 'tressage' in *Système de la bande dessinée* (Groensteen 1999, 171–186), connections are established 'in praesentia,' when details in different panels within the single page relate and reappear, or 'in absentia,' when visual aspects in one panel communicate with those in other panels on distant pages. While on a first level braiding, just like verse rhymes, can be seen as a decorative repeating pattern creating coherence and unity in a graphic narrative, on a higher level it also tells about the relation of a portion of a work with respect to the work in its entirety, and creates meaning by giving special emphasis to a certain element or by visualising how episodes, even if thematically, spatially, or chronologically distant, tie up with each other. In addition, Groensteen (2015) also suggests that instances of braiding can be hierarchically ordered depending, for example, on the number of elements connected and their extension in the narrative. Regardless of the different lines of action that have brought the narration to this point, certain forms of repetition that occur in *Reflets d'écume* I and II decoratively chain the two albums to each other: the title page of *Noyade* is scattered with bloodstains, mindful of the gory battle taking place at the end of *Naïade*; the image of the Prince quite literally drowning in his madness on the following page echoes that of the mermaid in her dreamed underwater world which introduces *Naïade* and tells of his mad obsession with the sea creature; both volumes open and close with similar settings (a sombre seascape and a desolate shore), and with the same motif (sea-foam reflections). However, on other occasions the artist's use of braiding works, instead, as a dialogue with sematic consequences. By selecting a few examples I will look at what braiding can tell us about the medium affordances of the graphic novel and scrutinise how visual codes are used, in combination with verbal messages, to help to build up an eerie atmosphere and communicate the true nature of ambiguous characters.

A full moon shadowed by clouds is a frequently recurring element throughout the two volumes of *Reflets d'écume*. It is the first element to appear on the opening page of the first volume and its presence surrealistically accompanies most scenes of the narrative.[15] The moon is also framed within a panel of its own, thus inviting the reader to stop and contemplate its importance. The constant replication of the full moon is a highly effective strategy to underscore the gloomy, eerie atmosphere in which the transposition is cast, and works together with other elements, like character enunciations or image combinations, to create the desired mood. By having one of the characters metafictionally comment on its ghostly omnipresence (1995, 33; "but isn't the full moon a pagan symbol?")[16], by inserting the full-moon panel into sequences alternating the moon and the characters, as in volume 2, page 32, where close-ups of the unreliable counsellor are accompanied by the image of the moon, or on page 33, where panels representing the vicious bishop and one of his victims are positioned in a sequence concluded with the moon, or by visualising the moon beclouded by the flapping wings of nightmarish ravens (1995, 28), Ange and Varanda play on the visual codes of the Gothic. In the same way the draughtsman makes clever use of the archetypical black cat by having it appear and re-appear intermittently throughout the work (1994, 25-26 and 1995, 16).

Just like braiding, the grid organising the layout of the comics' page can express both function and ornamentation. In Round's analysis of the parallels between the gothic trope of the crypt and the use and function of gridding in comics (2014, part two, chapter 5: *Revenant Readers, the Crypt and the Archive*), the scholar notes that both spaces contain events and moments that are not fully revealed to readers and characters. Not only is the gridding black throughout both albums of *Reflets d'écume* but it is also, on occasion, smeared with blood (Ange and Varanda 1994, 10, 28, 36; see also fig. 2). The bloodstains around the panel framing a close-up of the bishop (10, 28) seem to emphasise the wickedness of this character by foreshadowing the evil deeds of which he will prove capable a few pages later (36). If the bleeding gutter can be seen as an indication pointing to the bishop's devilish nature, this is made explicit as the blood extends to his speech bubbles, especially to the ones connecting his victims. On this page (fig. 4), the potential of the medium is put on display as the bishop's statement "I know what shapes his [the devil's] servants take" (28)[17] is combined with the bishop's own shadow cast on the wall, visualising the true embodiment of the dark powers.

A final structural interference with the narrative modes of the Gothic concerns the possibilities exploited by the comics medium to break down the page layout in order to represent simultaneous episodes. Just like the gothic machinery in literary texts experiments with

Fig. 4 Réflets d'écume – Naiade, par Alberto Varanda et Ange © 1994, Vents d'Ouest

narrative layers and transposes the standard trope of the labyrinth on a structural level by working with multiple perspectives, numerous narrators introducing their own subjective worlds, stories within stories, dreams and nightmares, letters, manuscripts, and footnotes, comics can make use of its medium specific qualities to visualise this complexity. On the subject of simultaneity, Round writes: "A gothic structure is thus apparent in comics, as the narrative is presented in a non-linear manner where all moments co-exist on the page." (Round 2014, part 2, chapter 3: *Haunted Places*). An emblematic example taken from volume II (Ange and Varanda 1995, 44–45) showcases four episodes simultaneously on a double page spread: witches being burned in public, the Prince drowning in his madness, the mermaid at little Prince Louis's bedside, and Louise D'Escandras confronting her aunt, the Duchess of Valès.

Conclusions

By considering intermedial adaptation as a translational activity I have recurred to Roman Jakobson's notion of the 'dominant' to analyse the metamorphosis that Hans Christian Andersen's tale of the little mermaid undergoes in its transposition from fairy tale to graphic novel. Measured against the child-friendly little mermaid in revisitations and visualisations such as Walt Disney's animation, Ange and Varanda's gothic ditto comes across as a welcome counter-narrative to the global trend, generally encountered in translations of Hans Christian Andersen, looking to tame and sanitise the author, as pointed out by those scholars who have attempted to shine a light on the obscure and nuanced complexity of the original fairy tales. I have explored the rewriting of the 'fabula' with special attention to how persisting tropes from the gothic tradition are rendered with the medium affordances of comics. I have argued that formal and compositional choices made by the comics' creators conspire with the thematic concentration on gruesome intrigues and gothic archetypes to create an atmosphere of haunting, folly, horror, and decay. By making use of the technique of braiding to create an eerie atmosphere and by profiting from the gutter between panels as a space containing hidden secrets and messages, the graphic novel creates meaning by recurring to strategies proper to the comics' medium. The graphic gothic mermaid thus offers an original take on a many-times-told tale, and the comics' creators must be appreciated for drawing out the odd and uneasy 'adult' Andersen. However, their falling back on a set of pre-established, archetypal gothic props, and at times on horror and gore, risks standing in the way of detecting the subtler terror at display in Andersen's "The Little Mermaid."

References

Andersen, Hans Christian. 1963-90. "Den lille Havfrue." In vol. 1 of *H.C. Andersens Eventyr*, edited by Erik Dal, 87–106. København: Det Danske Sprog- og Litteraturselskab/Reitzel.

Ange, and Alberto Varanda. 1994. *Reflets d'écume*, I: *Naïade*. Gatineau (QC): Vents D'Ouest.

Ange, and Alberto Varanda. 1995. *Reflets d'écume*, II: *Noyade*. Gatineau (QC): Vents D'Ouest.

Bøggild, Jacob, Ane Grum-Schwensen, and Thorsten Bøgh Thomsen, eds. 2015. *H.C. Andersen og det uhyggelige*. Odense: Syddansk Universitetsforlag.

Bøggild, Jacob, and Pernille Heegaard. 1993. "H.C. Andersens 'Den lille Havfrue' – om tvistigheder og tvetydigheder." In *Andersen og Verden. Indlæg fra den Første Internationale H.C. Andersen-Konference 25.-31. august 1991*, edited by Johan de Mylius, Aage Jørgensen, and Viggo Hjørnager Pedersen, 311–320. Odense: H.C. Andersen-Centret/Odense Universitetsforlag. http://andersen.sdu.dk/forskning/konference/tekst.html?id=9708.

Gaudreault, André. 1998. "Variations sur une problématique." In *La Transécriture. Pour une théorie de l'adaptation. Littérature, cinéma, bande dessinée, théâtre, clip*, edited by André Gaudreault and Thierry Groensteen, 267–271. Montréal-Angoulême: Nota-Bene/CNBDI.

Gaudreault, André, and Thierry Groensteen, eds. 1998. *La Transécriture. Pour une théorie de l'adaptation. Littérature, cinéma, bande dessinée, théâtre, clip*. Montréal-Angoulême: Nota-Bene/CNBDI.

Groensteen, Thierry. 1998. "Le Processus adaptatif (tentative de recapitulation raisonnée)." In *La Transécriture. Pour une théorie de l'adaptation. Littérature, cinéma, bande dessinée, théâtre, clip*, edited by André Gaudreault and Thierry Groensteen, 273–277. Montréal-Angoulême: Nota-Bene/CNBDI.

Groensteen, Thierry. 1999. *Système de la bande dessinée*. Paris: PUF.

Groensteen, Thierry. 2007. *The System of Comics*. Translated by Bart Beaty and Nick Ngyuen. Jackson, MS: University Press of Mississippi.

Groensteen, Thierry. 2015. "Précisions sur l'art du tressage." Accessed 22 May 2018. https:// www.editionsdelan2.com/groensteen/spip.php?article58.

Groensteen, Thierry. 2016. "The Art of Braiding: A Clarification." *European Comic Art* 9 (1): 88–98.

Groensteen, Thierry. 2017. "Mer om sammanflätning i serier." Translated by Roza Ghalehdar. In *De tecknade seriernas språk. Uttryck och form*, edited by David Gedin, 93–102. Nacka: Gedin & Balzamo förlag.

Jakobson, Roman. 1987. "The Dominant." In *Language in Literature*, edited by Krystyna Pomorska and Stephen Rudy, 41–46. Cambridge, MA: Belknap Press of Harvard University Press.

Kavka, Misha. 2015. "The Gothic on Screen." In *The Cambridge Companion* to *Gothic Fiction*, edited by Jerrold E. Hogle, 209–228. Cambridge: Cambridge University Press.

Oxfeldt, Elisabeth. 2009. *H.C. Andersens eventyr på film*. Odense: Syddansk Universitetsforlag.

Round, Julia. 2014. *Gothic in Comics and Graphic Novels: A Critical Approach*. Jefferson, NC: McFarland.

Storskog, Camilla. 2012. "Myth as an Interpretive Paradigm of Reality: Strindberg's and Göranson's *Inferno*." *AION* XXII (1–2): 147–172.

Storskog, Camilla. 2016a. "*Bianca in Persona* – Guido Crepax läser Ingmar Bergman." *Bild & Bubbla*, no. 206: 60–70.

Storskog, Camilla. 2016b. "Historien som fick leva om sitt liv. Guido Crepax serieversion av Karen Blixens *Den udødelige Historie*." In *Litteratur inter artes. Nordisk litteratur i samspill med andre kunstarter*, edited by Unni Langås and Karen Sanders, 321–344. Kristiansand: Portal forlag.

Storskog, Camilla. 2017a. "Millennial gothic: On Runberg, Homs and Carot's graphic novel adaptation of Stieg Larsson's Millennium trilogy." *Journal of Graphic Novels and Comics* 8 (6): 533–549. http://dx.doi.org/10.1080/21504857.2017.1370002.

Storskog, Camilla. 2017b. "Topelius i serieformat. Interikonicitet som visuell berättarstrategi i Bovils *Fältskärns berättelser*." In *De tecknade seriernas språk. Uttryck och form*, edited by David Gedin, 140–164. Nacka: Gedin & Balzamo förlag.

Storskog, Camilla. 2018. "Stripping H.C. Andersen. Peter Madsen's *Historien om en mor* (or, what a graphic novel adaptation can do that its literary source cannot)." *European Journal of Scandinavian Studies*, 48 (2): 303–318.

Sütiste, Elin, Maria Lotman, and Kristiina Lotman. 2016. "'The Translator Must...': On the Estonian Translation Poetics of the 20th Century." *Interlitteraria* 21 (1): 17–34.

Torop, Peeter. 1997. "The Position of Translation in Translation Studies." In *Translation – Acquisition – Use. AFinLA Yearbook*, edited by A. Mauranen and T. Puurtinen, 23–40. Jyväskylä: Publications de l'Association Finlandaise de Linguistique Appliquée, 55.

Varma, Devendra. 1966. *The Gothic Flame: Being a History of the Gothic Novel in England*. New York, NY: Russell and Russell.

Notes

1 "[O]versættere [har] ofte taget sig særlige friheder ved oversættelsen af Andersen, fordi man har opfattet ham som en forfatter for børn og derfor har ment at have en særlig licens til at omformulere og ændre teksterne, således at de så lydefrit som muligt har kunnet tale til målgruppen: målsprogets publikum af børn." Unless otherwise indicated, all translations are my own (except from references to the fairy tales where I use Hersholt's translation).

2 "en afrettet, domesticeret og uskyldiggjort ditto."

3 "Le nombre de petits garçons de lignée royale qui s'éteignent bêtement, étouffés par

	leur petit déjeuner, pour qu'un cousin, oncle, frère accède plus facilement au trône... vous seriez surprise!"
4	The reflection on Hans Christian Andersen's place within the community of comics creators relates to a broader research project dealing with comic art adaptations of Scandinavian classics, which has led me to explore transpositions from the early 1940s to the present day and to single case studies dealing with adaptations based on the works of authors such as August Strindberg, Ingmar Bergman, Karen Blixen, Stieg Larsson, Zacharias Topelius, and Hans Christian Andersen (Storskog 2012, 2016a, 2016b, 2017a, 2017b, 2018). The methodological approach adopted in the present analysis of Ange and Varanda's rewriting of "The Little Mermaid" therefore relies on a reading strategy developed during the course of the research project, best reported in Storskog 2017a and 2018, from where the following description of method is taken. It departs from the term 'transécriture' (Gaudreault and Groensteen 1998), and merges with Roman Jakobson's concept of the 'dominant' as the focusing component of a work of art.
5	"chaque lecture d'un texte, chaque lecture singulière, produi[t] dans l'esprit du lecteur ce que l'on pourrait appeler un 'icone' du texte et [...] ce serait cet icone du texte que l'adapteur adapter[a], le faisant passer dans la 'moulinette' d'un autre média."
6	Applying Jakobson's concept within the field of translation studies, Elin Sütiste, Maria Lotman, and Kristiina Lotman (2016, 18) draw attention to the shift in its usage: "while for formalists and Jakobson dominant is rather an objective quality of a text, which determines it and holds its structure together, then in accordance with [a] poststructuralist approach the dominant of a reader and hence also that of a translator can be completely different from the author's intended dominant."
7	'Intersemiotic' or 'extratextual' translation is, in Peeter Torop's definition (1997, 28), "the transfer of a text written in a natural language by means of verbal and nonverbal codes into another text."
8	Cf. www.andersen.sdu.dk/forskning/konference/tekst.html?id=9708. Accessed 24 May 2018. In the introductory presentation of critical studies dedicated to "Den lille Havfrue," Bøggild and Heegaard discuss interpretations based on psychoanalytic and biographical approaches as well as readings founded on Structuralism and New Criticism that have appeared throughout the twentieth century.
9	"Loin en mer, l'eau est bleue comme les petals du plus beau bleuet, et claire comme le verre le plus pur, mais elle est profonde, trop profonde pour qu'aucune ancre puisse en atteindre le fond. Il faudrait poser un grand nombre de tours d'église les unes sur les autres pour monter du fond à la surface. C'est là, en bas, que des ondins ont leur demeure."
10	"Comment est-ce arrivé? Je ne le saurai jamais, j'imagine. Êtes-vous muette de naissance? Ou une sorcière vous a-t-elle volé votre langue?"
11	In spite of this ending, no sequence to the second album has hitherto been published.
12	"Nu kom hun til en stor slimet Plads i Skoven, hvor store, fede Vandsnoge baltrede sig og viste deres stygge hvidgule Bug. Midt paa Pladsen var reist et Huus af strandede Menneskers hvide Been [...]. [...] 'Jeg veed nok, hvad du vil!' sagde Havhexen, 'det er dumt gjort af dig! alligevel skal du faae din Villie, for den vil bringe dig i Ulykke, min deilige Prindsesse.' [...] 'naar du først har faaet menneskelig Skikkelse, da kan du aldrig mere blive en Havfrue igjen! du kan aldrig stige ned igjennem Vandet til dine Søstre og til din Faders Slot, og vinder du ikke Prindsens Kjærlighed, saa han for dig glemmer Fader og Moder, hænger ved dig med sin hele Tanke og lader Præsten lægge Eders Hænder i hinanden, saa at I blive Mand og Kone, da faaer du ingen udødelig Sjæl! den første Morgen efter at han er gift med en anden, da maa dit Hjerte briste, og du bliver Skum paa Vandet.' [...] nu ridsede hun sig selv i Brystet og lod sit sorte Blod dryppe derned, Dampen gjorde de forunderligste Skikkelser, saa man maatte blive angest og bange." (Andersen 1963, 98–100).

13 "La femme ne doit point prendre part aux jeux de pouvoirs. Se contenter d'être épouse et mère... [...]. Un sage philosophie quand les temps sont troublés."
14 Thierry Groensteen first elaborated the notion of 'braiding' (tressage) in his work *Système de la bande dessinée* (1999; *The System of Comics*, Groensteen 2007). In order to clarify the concept and follow up on the discussion that arose in the wake of *Système de la bande dessinée*, he published the article "Précision sur l'art du tressage" (Groensteen 2015), also available in English (Groensteen 2016), as well as in a Swedish translation (Groensteen 2017).
15 See for example Ange and Varanda 1994, 5, 29, 33, 35, 45, 47, 48, and Ange and Varanda 1995, 28, 30, 32, 33, 41.
16 "mais la pleine lune n'est-elle pas un symbole païen?"
17 "Je sais, moi, les formes que prennent ses serviteurs [du demon]."

War Veterans and Communal Guilt
Hans Christian Andersen's "The Tinder Box" and "The Steadfast Tin Soldier" in Contemporary Scandinavian Cinema and TV

Elisabeth Oxfeldt
University of Oslo

The main claim of this chapter is that with "The Tinder Box" ("Fyrtøjet," 1835) and "The Steadfast Tin Soldier," (Den standhaftige Tinsoldat," 1838) Hans Christian Andersen created two modern fairy tale war veteran figures that still serve as significant archetypes reflecting and shaping how Scandinavians imagine war veterans and their reintegration into community in the new millennium. I advance this claim by comparing the veteran figures in two contemporary audio-visual narratives about Scandinavian soldiers returning from the war in Afghanistan with those of Andersen's tales: The Norwegian TV-series; Nobel, Peace at Any Cost (Nobel - fred for enhver pris, 2016), *and the Danish feature film* Walk with Me (De standhaftige, 2016).

"There came a soldier marching down the high road-*one, two! one, two!* He had his knapsack on his back and his sword at his side as he came home from the wars." Hans Christian Andersen embarks on his career as a fairy tale writer in 1835 with the image of a lone soldier returning home from war in "The Tinder Box" ("Fyrtøiet," 1835). Three years later, in 1838, Andersen published "The Steadfast Tin Soldier" ("Den standhaftige Tinsoldat," 1838). This time, he introduced his soldier with a focus on camaraderie and brotherhood: "There were once five-and-twenty tin soldiers. They were all brothers, born of the same old tin spoon. They shouldered their muskets and looked straight ahead of them, splendid in their uniforms, all red and blue." Yet, this soldier, too, we are soon to discover, is marked as different and is thus given the status of a loner since "the tin was short, so he had only one leg." Whereas the tinderbox soldier is "every inch a soldier," the steadfast tin soldier is marked by his missing inches. One way of reading these tales is to consider them tales of war veterans. One soldier returns from the war physically intact; the other represents the veteran amputee. Both struggle to become integrated into their local communities.

In terms of psychologist Abraham Maslow's pyramid of human needs, the tales thus operate mainly at the level of psychological needs, above that of basic needs, and below that of self-fulfilment needs.[1] First among psychological needs are "belongingness and love needs," and then "esteem needs" (Maslow 1987, 20–21).[2] Andersen's tales are melodramatic with plots driven by the question of how the lone soldier will become reintegrated into his local community through a romantic relationship with a significant other who fulfils his needs for love and esteem (i.e. a princess or a princess-like figure such as the ballerina who lives in a castle). The question, in other words, is highly pertinent to war veterans: How are the returned soldiers to become loved and esteemed members of the communities for which they have fought?

The main claim of this chapter is that with the tinderbox soldier and the steadfast tin soldier, Andersen created two modern fairy tale war veteran figures that still serve as significant archetypes reflecting and shaping how Scandinavians imagine war veterans and their reintegration into community in the new millennium.[3] I will advance this claim by comparing the veteran figures in two contemporary audio-visual narratives about Scandinavian soldiers returning from the war in Afghanistan with those of Andersen's tales. First, I will turn to the Norwegian TV-series *Nobel – fred for enhver pris* (2016; *Nobel – Peace at Any Cost*) directed by Per-Olav Sørensen, which includes both veteran types in the figures of the protagonist and his best friend. I will then turn to Swedish-American director Lisa Ohlin's *Walk with Me (De standhaftige*, 2016), a Danish post-Afghanistan film that clearly establishes an intertextual link to Andersen's fairy tale universe through its title.[4]

Before analysing the audio-visual narratives, however, I will further contextualise and delineate Andersen's two fairy tale veterans as well as the contemporary narratives. My emphasis will be on how they all serve as modern narratives negotiating and possibly alleviating communal anxiety, guilt, and discomfort surrounding the homecoming of psychologically and physically injured soldiers. They do so at a time, I argue, when people see its successful accomplishment as the responsibility of an entire community, i.e. the nation.

Historical Background

Andersen lived through a series of wars. In the 1800s, Denmark most notably engaged in the Napoleonic Wars (1800-1813), the English Wars (1801 and 1807-14), the First Schleswig War (1848-50), and the Second War of Schleswig in 1864. On a personal level, Andersen's father served during the Napoleonic Wars in 1813, and as a student at Copenhagen University, Andersen himself served as corporal in the King's Life Guard (Kongens livkorps). In his autobiography, Andersen notes the great impression a Spanish soldier made on him when he lifted up the then three-year-old Andersen, danced around with him, cried, and kissed him (1996, 1: 31). Soldiers and veterans must have been quite visible in public and private, and Andersen responded to this throughout his life with songs, poems, drama, and fairy tales. Examples are the poem "The Soldier" ("Soldaten") written in 1829, the comedy *A Real Soldier: Dramatic Situation in Rhymed Verses with Songs and Choir in One Act* (*En rigtig Soldat. Dramatisk Situation paa rimede Vers med Sange og Chor i een Act,* 1838), and *Patriotic Poems during the War* (*Fædrelandske Vers og Sange under Krigen,* 1851).[5]

As a generation of soldiers having participated in the Second War of Schleswig (1864) passed away, the war veteran as a once common figure in the Danish public presumably vanished as Denmark did not participate as a combatant in any wars for over 100 years. This, however, changed in 1992 when Denmark decided to contribute to the NATO-forces in Bosnia.[6] On its mission in former Yugoslavia, Denmark suffered three casualties and many soldiers were wounded (unprofor.dk 2018). These Danish losses multiplied manifold in subsequent wars. Between 2002 and 2014, 8.600 Danish troops were deployed to Afghanistan, 43 died, and several hundred were physically and mentally wounded, (Veteranalliancen 2018; iCasualties: Operation Enduring Freedom 2018). In fact, Denmark suffered the heaviest losses per capita while also maintaining the highest level of public support among the troop-contributing nations to the International Security Assistance Force (ISAF) mission in Afghanistan (Jakobsen and Ringsmose 2015, 212).[7] In Norway, almost 10.000 women and men have contributed to international operations between 2002 and 2018 (Jakobsen 2018). The country has suffered ten deaths in the Afghanistan War, and at least 48 injured soldiers (iCasualties: Operation Enduring Freedom 2018; Håndlykken and Johansen 2011). Polls indicate that Norwegians have been slightly less positive to sending soldiers to Afghanistan than the Danes, but that support has been high during periods of Norwegian casualties, as when four Norwegian soldiers were killed by a landmine in June 2010.[8]

The positive Danish attitude has been particularly puzzling, given the nation's post-World War II reputation as a pacifist society (Daugbjerg and Sørensen 2017, 1–2). In this chapter, however, I argue that the positive attitude expressed should be regarded in conjunction with the cultural and aesthetic counter-narratives produced, indicating a darker side, pertaining to the anxiety and guilt evoked by the confrontation with dead and injured returned soldiers. We find the returned soldier for instance in various TV-series and films.

What, then, is the connection between the fates of real-life contemporary soldiers and their cultural and aesthetic representations? My claim is that fictional narratives with happy endings may serve a guilt-alleviating function on behalf of a community, and that the communal war and veteran imaginary is expressed through cultural products that are shaped not only by contemporary realities, but also by a common cultural and mythic heritage evolving over time. This is also a point of departure for Klaus Rothstein's study, *The Year of the Soldier (Soldatens år,* 2014), in which he catalogues the imprint the Afghanistan War has left on Danish literature and culture at large. One of Rothstein's main discoveries is that Danish literature about the wars in Afghanistan and Iraq focuses on psychology and interpersonal relations, i.e. the psychological needs depicted in the middle of Maslow's pyramid with which Andersen's tales are also concerned. A popular motif, according to Rothstein, is the returned soldier: "No novelist has chosen to write about the wars as a part of Danish history in a way that can be described as anything but stories of individual destiny about the deployed troops and their mental traumas that make impossible their post-deployment reintegration." (Rothstein 2014, 102, my translation). The same pertains to films, argues Rothstein, implying that what is needed is not a repetitive focus on psychological issues, but rather a political critique of war. I, nevertheless, find it significant that authors, filmmakers, and audiences are so concerned with the reintegration of veterans. It points to a social problem for which a community of readers needs narratives to reinforce and express a desire for justice and more specifically that veterans must be healed of their mental traumas, respected, and reintegrated into their communities.

On a formal level we find this desire for an official policy and civic culture of welcoming returned soldiers institutionalised in Denmark in 2009 and 2010 through the implementation of a national Flag Day, a newly invented tradition of veteran homecoming parades, and an overall national veteran policy with the aim of recognising the veterans in the best way, helping them "reestablish an everyday life and rebuild social relations" (Sørensen and Pedersen 2012, 31–32). Similarly, the Norwegian government implemented an annual Veteran's Day in 2010 in addition to the Norwegian Armed Forces' medal ceremonies and a Memorial Day, all serving to involve an entire society in honouring and recognising veterans and their families (Regjeringen.no 2010).

The national imaginary does not, of course, exist in isolation, and depictions of contemporary Scandinavian war veterans are often influenced by American cinema after the Vietnam War.[9] Yet, Rothstein, I find, is also correct in identifying a specifically Scandinavian literary historical tradition in contemporary depictions of veterans. Turning to Danish(-Norwegian) literature he finds that Jeppe from Ludvig Holberg's comedy *Jeppe on the Hill (Jeppe paa Bjerget*, 1722) may be the first returned soldier suffering from what today would be called post-traumatic stress disorder (PTSD). That is why Jeppe drinks, and Holberg's portrait remains relevant for today's literary depictions of soldiers returning from Afghanistan (Rothstein 2014, 22–23). The next author Rothstein mentions is Hans Christian Andersen and his "At the Soldier's Homecoming in 1864" ("Ved Soldatens Hjemkomst i 1864"). While Rothstein emphasises this poem written explicitly to honour the veterans of 1864, my claim is that in terms of providing archetypes for how we currently conceive of returned soldiers, Andersen's two tales, "The Tinder Box" and "The Steadfast Tin Soldier" cover the most relevant spectrum as they provide us with tales heavy in symbolism that express and may alleviate a communal sense of fear, guilt, and anxiety vis-à-vis the veteran soldier who struggles mentally upon his homecoming.

"The Tinder Box"

"The Tinder Box" has been read as a story about a happy-go-lucky Aladdin-type (Mylius 2004, 47), but also psychoanalytically as a story about deep, repressed energy, represented by the three dogs that the soldier has to confront and the power of which he eventually unleashes on society.[10] In such psychoanalytical readings, facing these brute forces has been understood on a general individual level as part of a Jungian individuation process and on a socio-political level as a democratic revolt against an oppressive King and patriarch – in the name of both gender and class equality (Værum 1992, 52).[11]

It should, however, also, be understood more specifically on the level of the war veteran suffering PTSD. In such a context, the soldier becomes a social liability in both senses of that word: Society is liable for the veteran's PTSD, and the veteran, in turn, is a threat to the stability of the society. This threat to an existing social order could be for better or worse, leading for instance to a terrorist attack or a democratic revolution. When the people in "The Tinder Box" finally shout out: "Soldier, be our King and marry the pretty Princess," we know that they have good reason to fear the power and rage of the soldier who has the dogs rip the judges and councillors apart, throw them high in the air, and let them fall down "broken to bits." Yet, their cry ultimately appears to be a sign that they, the people, have gained a voice, which they use to grant the soldier both power and recognition as their representative. This interpretation of the ending as happy is strengthened by the fact that the princess is so decisively on the side of the soldier. She has been unhappy about being kept in isolation at the castle away from the people. At the end of the tale we are told that she is "pleased" to marry the soldier.

"The Tinder Box" starts on a positive note with the soldier being met by a witch who offers him an opportunity to become rich. He has to go on a quest, confronting increasingly frightful scenarios (in the shape of the three dogs), trust the power of a checkered apron to control the dogs, fetch a tinderbox for the witch, and in return stuff his own pockets full of gold. In Jungian readings, the dogs have been interpreted as the soldier's repressed sides – his fears and demons – that he has to confront to become a full human being. In the context of war, however, we may also think of this passage through subterranean rooms of horror as reflecting his war experiences, which he has lived through once in reality and subsequently confronts repeatedly through involuntary memory flashes in the form of nightmares, etc. "Oh, what a horrible sight to see!" exclaims the narrator as the soldier faces the biggest dog. The fact that he needs a female-coded object (an apron) to confront the dogs (his inner terrors) shows that the path to recovery goes through domestication, in the sense of becoming reintegrated into his original community through female attachment.

The soldier is furthermore met with acknowledgment as the witch praises the soldier, complimenting his strength and virility, even if it is for self-serving purposes.[12] Yet, a theme of class difference also emerges as part of the tale as other people inform the soldier that the king harbours a fear of, and seeks to prevent, the princess' marrying "a common soldier." The soldier, we may conclude, remains subject to class oppression. Since his basic needs are fulfilled from the very beginning of the tale, the rest of the story can be devoted to his pursuit of psychological fulfilment in the form of love, social integration, and esteem.

Given that the witch grants the soldier a fortune, one would think he would be grateful for her welcome upon his homecoming. Yet, instead of simply giving her the tinderbox, he questions her: "If you don't tell me what you are going to do with it, I will draw my sword and cut off your head." "No," said the witch. The soldier immediately cut off her head, and there she lay on the ground." The soldier's cool and rather unmotivated decapitation of the witch has startled readers since the tale's publication in 1838, and in our context his violent behaviour may be interpreted as symptomatic of PTSD.

In the above-mentioned psychoanalytical readings of the tale, the witch becomes a maternal figure. In this role she inhibits the hero's powers and decapitating her is – psychologically speaking – a way of cutting the umbilical cord. In doing this, the soldier rids himself of a mother fixation and vacates her space as an object of desire so that he may mature into a grown man and marry a new female object of desire (Jensen 1993, 65; cf. Værum 1992, 54).

In a reading emphasising the soldier as a veteran suffering from PTSD, I would, however, suggest that the attachment the soldier ruptures (the witch in fact ties a rope around him before he climbs down the hollow tree trunk) is one to the king or the mother country for whom he has fought. The witch sends him on a mission comparable to that of war. In order to avoid a pattern of repetition, he has to free himself from authority figures that urge him to devote himself to warfare. He needs, in other words, to convert from "battlemind" to "homemind," as anthropologists Birgitte Refslund Sørensen and Thomas Pedersen term it (cf. Sørensen and Pedersen 2012, 34).

Overall, the encounter with the witch gives the soldier power, not only in the form of money, but also in the form of magic (the tinderbox). This magic may be understood as representing a burning desire of a community (of readers) for justice, and for the soldier's attaining love and esteem upon his return from war.

"The Steadfast Tin Soldier"

With "The Steadfast Tin Soldier" we get an entirely different type of soldier. Strictly speaking, he is simply a toy, but he represents a disabled figure, and towards the end of the tale, a veteran amputee, seeking a community of peers. He falls in love with a ballerina whom he thinks is also missing a leg. A little black bogey, a jack-in-the-box troll, warns him: "Tin soldier, will you please keep your eyes to yourself?" Psychologically speaking, the troll could represent the soldier's Freudian superego, a chastising Lutheran God, or a sense of guilt, shame, and bad conscience directed at his erotic desire. It tells him not to look at the erotic object, the ballerina, (especially not from below) and foresees some sort of punishment if he does. It could however also be an inner voice telling him that as a veteran amputee he is not worthy of the princess, of a full (sex)life, and of communal integration.

The next day what appears to be a random gust of wind blows him out the window and into the gutter. Causal connections and attributions are playfully presented as open and ambivalent in the tale. The eviction could be the punishment the troll has foreseen, it could just be an accident, or it could, perhaps, be a type of self-inflicted punishment as the soldier's desperate sense of loneliness instills in him the desire to leave his community. In any case, the soldier ends up put to the test on a journey of Biblical dimensions (like Jonas, he is swallowed by a fish). The passage in many ways resembles a journey of war and torture (especially water torture and bouts of isolation in the dark). He appears to be in a foreign country where he has to show his passport, and he is for instance confronted with "a roar that would frighten the bravest of us." The steadfast tin soldier is, however, brave and regardless of what he is subjected to, he "stood as steady as ever" and keeps quiet. The story is full of humour and irony – of course a tin soldier cannot move, talk, blink, or cry, and all the things that appear great and frightening to him, are small to human beings. The discrepancy becomes a source of laughter. Still, the story also allows for a serious reading, and one can concur that the soldier indeed proves that he is "remarkable," as the narrator promises us from the outset of the tale.

This fish ends up in the kitchen of the house where the soldier was first unwrapped as a birthday present, and he is reunited with his "brothers," the other toys, and the ballerina. At this point, he may be regarded as the returned soldier who has left his community for combat and now returns.

Things take a new turn, however, as the boy grabs the soldier and throws him into the oven. Again, urged by the narrator's suggestion that the troll could be behind this event, we may apply a psychological interpretation and read this as an expression of the soldier's self-destructive drive, or as his erotic desire being ignited by the sight of the ballerina. It burns him up, and by yet another twist of events it also burns up the ballerina as a draft blows her into the oven, too. All that is left behind is a tin heart into which he has been melted and the spangle the ballerina wore, which is burned black as coal.

In sum, Hans Christian Andersen has left us with two archetypical soldiers who – in today's world – may be interpreted as the traumatised soldier suffering from PTSD and thus possessing a dark side that may have dangerous consequences not just to himself, but also to his community. He is full of rage and violence and may go berserk when triggered in that direction. He may, however, also confront his demons – his inner dogs – and move on to a happy, integrated life of heterosexual domesticity. On the other hand, we have the less violent, physically injured soldier who represents the soldier returning from war as an amputee. His violence is directed inwards as he becomes self-destructive rather than violent towards his surroundings.

Both tales negotiate how veterans struggle to become reintegrated into their community. A key ingredient in this struggle is entering into a romantic relationship with a woman who will heal the soldier's mental or physical injuries by conferring upon him love and social esteem. In "The Tinder Box" this narrative of integration is fulfilled, and a community of readers may feel relieved and rejoice at a happy outcome of justice and recognition. "The Steadfast Tin Soldier" ends on a more bittersweet note. The ballerina does not pay the soldier due attention. The desire of the soldier (and the reader) is for them to be united, yet when they are united in the oven, they do not survive. Poetic justice is attained only as her legacy is a burnt spangle – a sign of vanity – whereas his is a tin heart, a token of steadfastness, devotion, love and esteem, not unlike that conferred upon soldiers who have served their countries in the form of a medal.[13]

Nobel – Peace at Any Cost

An example of a contemporary Scandinavian audio-visual narrative containing both types of veterans is the critically acclaimed series *Nobel* (2016), based on Norwegian participation in the Afghanistan War.[14] Lieutenant Erling Riiser (Aksel Hennie) is the ticking-bomb tinderbox soldier, while his colleague Lieutenant Jon Petter Hals (Anders Danielsen Lie) becomes more of a steadfast-tin-soldier type. Having stepped on a mine, he becomes an amputee veteran – a double amputee, even. He furthermore becomes a metaphorical amputee tragically in love not with a ballerina, but with the only character played by a Dane, namely the army translator Adella (Danica Čurčič).

Nobel is an eight-episode long war drama and political thriller centering on Lieutenant Erling Riiser, married to Johanne Riiser (Tuva Novotny) who works as the Foreign Minister's Chief of Staff. As suggested by the title, the series critically explores a series of paradoxes pertaining to Norway's status as a nation of peace. Pronounced variously as the adjective "noble" (in Norwegian spelled "nobel") and the last name Nobel (made famous by Alfred B. Nobel and his legacy of prizes),[15] it captures present-day tensions surrounding notions of how to act nobly in a global setting – showing superiority of character, ideals, and morals.[16] The alignment of *Nobel* and Norway captures how the nation combines hard military power and soft diplomacy, contributing with troops or "peace-keeping forces," to Afghanistan as well as humanitarian aid projects (NORAD)[17] while the politically independent Norwegian Nobel Peace Prize committee awards its annual prize, often in a controversial manner.

The complexity of hard and soft diplomacy is furthermore captured in the Riiser marriage, which may be read as an allegory for Norwegian foreign policy. Erling represents the military, war, and violence while Johanne represents development aid (NORAD) and peace negotiations. Their marriage is increasingly strained, not least due to Johanne's naïve view of both her husband's and her own involvement in Afghanistan. Johanne, who ends up representing the average Norwegian citizen in this regard, is shocked to learn that her sniper husband has killed children in Afghanistan, and finds it difficult to accept that Erling's involvement in the war is not contained in Afghanistan, but becomes part of his life – and hence their life – in Norway, too.[18] A final blow to Johanne is when she discovers that the one person she thought had noble intentions in Afghanistan and whose development project of establishing apple orchards in Afghanistan ("Fruit for Life") she has done everything to promote, also turns out to be corrupt. As reviewer John Doyle puts it: "Part of the texture of *Nobel* is a questioning of what's truly dangerous these days – outright war or diplomatic manoeuvres to gain access to natural resources?" (Doyle 2016).

In terms of Andersen's returned soldier types, Erling, as stated above, is the tinderbox type. Upon his return to Norway, he is also asked to carry out a dangerous domestic mission, putting him in contact with violent forces. The message is not delivered by a witch, but through a brief text message instructing Erling to assassinate Sharif Zamani (Atheer Adel). Sharif is an Afghan landowner with ties to the Taliban who has arrived in Oslo presumably to execute an honour killing of his Afghan wife, whom Norwegian soldiers have smuggled out of Afghanistan in an effort to bring her to safety. Erling immediately stabs Sharif to death. As viewers, however, we are left wondering – along with Erling – what drove him: Who instructed him to kill? Moreover, it seems possible that Erling is suffering from PTSD and acts on impulses in his own imagination. If this is so, it would be a case of the traumatised veteran becoming a liability to the nation.

In the end, we find out that the culprit is Rolf (Hallvard Holmen), an idealist who views Sharif as the main obstacle for his development project called "Oil for Development" and who has hacked the phone of Brigadier Ekeberg (Dennis Storhøi), the Head of Armed Forces' Special Command. Motivated by "the Norwegian way" – by the ideology of eliminating poverty by having the Afghans sign a contract stipulating that the oil in Afghanistan belongs to the people – he sets in motion an illegal act. He wants peace "at any cost" and turns into a criminal with murder on his conscience. Yet, considering that *Nobel* is a story about Norway, we realise that Rolf is simply one of several figures representing the dark side of Norwegian idealism, humanitarianism, and peace negotiating efforts. The army and the soldiers may well be the brutal "dogs," but those in possession of the proverbial tinderbox – those relying on and employing its forces – are all connected to Norwegian foreign policy. What the series exposes is a system of checks and balances between institutions such as the foreign ministry, the press, and the Nobel Peace Prize committee, all of which ultimately rely on military power and violence to promote peace.

In terms of gender, Andersen's tales suggest that the way to social integration goes through love and marriage. The tinderbox soldier uses his power over the dogs to have the princess furtively brought to his bed at nighttime. *Her* feminine beauty and *his* virility make them a good match: "The soldier couldn't keep from kissing her, because he was every inch a soldier." Far from feeling violated, the princess, as mentioned above, feels liberated from the confines of her father's castle, and ends up his happy wife: "The Princess came out of the copper castle to be Queen, and that suited her exactly."

In *Nobel*, the question of love and marriage on the one hand, and female and sexual liberation on the other, pertains to Erling and Johanne, but also to the allegorical dimension suggested by the Norway-Afghanistan relationship. In the first case, we see a heteronormative distribution of masculinity and femininity, of raw force and domestication. Erling represents tough Norwegian military forces; Johanne represents soft, domesticating forces. They have undergone extreme challenges to their marriage but are in the end happily reunited – they need each other to be complete, just as Norway evidently needs 'masculine' and 'feminine' forces for its foreign policy to be complete. In a final scene Johanne turns to Erling, and the two of them walk away from the camera, holding hands. Despite the violence in which he has participated abroad and at home, Erling is safely and lovingly reintegrated into his family and community.

As a tinderbox story about a social revolution pertaining to the liberation of women as well as the people more generally, *Nobel* is also about Norway's relationship to Afghanistan. In this regard, Afghanistan is personified by Sharif's wife and cousin Wasima Zamani (Ayesha Wolasmal) who, like Andersen's princess in "The Tinder Box," is furtively removed from an oppressive patriarch by soldiers. She, too, ends up happy within a new social order.

Hence, the major themes of "The Tinder Box" are adapted to a contemporary tale about Norway and Afghanistan. Erling, like Andersen's returned soldier, faces his inner demons and traumatic flashbacks,[19] avoids jail and prosecution, and seemingly reestablishes a happy marriage with Johanne. On a greater socio-political level, elements of Norwegian foreign policy have been, as Andersen might have put it, "tossed up," symbolically and literally speaking, with some of them, such as the foreign minister, "broken to bits."

In contrast, the experience of Jon Petter is that of the steadfast tin soldier. While in Afghanistan, he and army translator Adella are lovers. Adella wants to continue their relationship when they return to Norway, but for Jon Petter this is no longer a viable option. "I will never again undress in front of a woman," he tells Erling. Like the steadfast tin soldier, he experiences a troll voice (an inner voice) telling him that he should not gaze erotically at his object of desire. As an amputee we sense that he will end up sacrificing his love and "burn up," figuratively. Yet, in several ways Jon Petter regains his masculine, military identity. Like the steadfast tin soldier, he is a figure of integrity. When the troop is exposed in the media for having shot at a group of Afghans without first having identified their weapons, the Norwegian military succeeds in reasserting their reputation and sense of honour by having Jon Petter represent them on national televised news. Jon Petter, at first, is reluctant to appear on television as "the nation's cripple" ("nasjonalkrøpling"). Yet, when given the opportunity of being reinstated in the army and thus maintaining his military and masculine sense of identity and belonging (being one of the brotherhood of soldiers), he acquiesces. Confronted by journalists, he thoughtfully and persistently argues for the integrity of the Special Forces while questioning the war politics of the Norwegian government as well as the ethics of the press. Hence, Jon Petter once more earns his uniform and identity as a Norwegian soldier through his loyalty and steadfastness, this time in a verbal battle. Presumably the fact that he is allowed to remain part of his brotherhood and thus maintain a sense of military identity, contributes to his sense of masculinity vis-à-vis the opposite sex as well. As feminist literary scholar Jette Lundbo Levy has argued, tales like "The Steadfast Tin Soldier" thematise gender and power relations. They do so in complex ways in which the amputee soldier is crippled, emasculated, and feminised. Yet, as Levy points out, his materiality weighs in on the scale of masculine traits (Levy 1998, 262). Jon Petter similarly gets to show the nation what he and his fellow soldiers are made of.

In a final scene with the two ex-lovers, he allows Adella to help him work out even though it involves her touching his stumps, he invites her out for dinner, and as she pushes him out the gym in his wheelchair, he is able to joke about the situation, suggesting that they stop by the handicap toilet for a quickie. Evidently Jon Petter is able to silence the voice telling him he is not worthy of erotic love, and Adella, unlike Andersen's ballerina, is made of substance. She is not a vain paper figure, but a female member of the military "brotherhood." She has always paid Jon Petter due attention, and she still seems receptive to his wishes for an erotic union. The story ends on a tentatively happy note as Jon Petter, too, seems on his way to social integration as a loved and esteemed returned soldier.

De standhaftige

As suggested by its title, *De standhaftige* (*Walk with Me*, 2016), Lisa Ohlin's film is partly inspired by Andersen's tale. I write partly, since the main source of inspiration, revealed in the closing titles, is the Danish Wounded Warriors Project at the Royal Danish Ballet. The project started in 2009 when severely wounded soldiers returned from Afghanistan. Two dancers at the Royal Ballet volunteered to train physically and psychologically wounded soldiers through Pilates – which gave Ohlin the idea for a harsh, but ultimately romantic film, about a wounded veteran and a ballerina. She and Karina Dam wrote the script, which for a long time had the working title *Ballon* (*Balloon*), referring to a ballerina's lightness and ability to seemingly soar through the air.[20] In the film, this type of jumping serves as the ballerina's main source of motivation for hard training, she explains. Thus, her ballerina quality of lightness – as we know it from Andersen's tale – is also emphasised in this film where we find out that she lacks an overall sense of grounding. She seems to have no family, save an aunt who is dying from cancer. She is single, lacks trust in others, and is fearful of commitment.

The year is 2009. Thomas (Mikkel Boe Følsgaard) steps on a landmine in the Helmand province. He loses both legs and is sent home to Rigshospitalet (Denmark's national hospital). At the hospital's rehabilitation centre he works hard to be able to walk on prosthetic legs so that he may return to Afghanistan and continue fighting the Taliban – he thinks. At Rigshospitalet we also encounter Sofie (Cecilie Lassen). Sofie regularly visits her cancer-stricken aunt (Karen-Lise

Mynster) who has to use the rehabilitation room too. One day Sofie watches Thomas' struggle and with her dance expertise suggests how he can train muscles he was not even aware he had. The film uses cross-cutting to show what the two protagonists have in common – their focus on legwork, their killer instinct and perseverance, as well as a sense of loneliness – and eventually brings them together so that their two stories become one.

In terms of Andersen's soldier types, Thomas is a mixture of the tinderbox soldier and the steadfast tin soldier. Like the former, he is full of rage, capable of hurting people, of attracting friends, but also of losing them. In Thomas' case it is his own fault (to the extent that PTSD can be called his own fault). It is not that he, like Andersen's soldier, gains and loses riches, making him more or less attractive company, but that he loses his temper and screams at people – this goes for his friends and family as well as his girlfriend. Eventually, he isolates himself in his new apartment for days on end, plays war games on an Xbox, drinks alcohol, loads a gun, points it momentarily at himself, suggesting thoughts of suicide, and then points it at what appears to be an intruder on his balcony. He shoots a hole in the window, coming close to injuring Sofie who turns out to have called him on the phone and rung his doorbell in vain. She has finally resorted to climbing up to his balcony. In that sense she becomes Andersen's troll or gust of wind that tries to get Thomas to exit his abode through the window.

The film furthermore contains the water motif that we recognise from "The Steadfast Tin Soldier," a motif that commonly signifies a change of identity and rebirth (e.g. baptism). Sofie comes – like the gust of wind – to fetch Thomas through his balcony glass door. When he ignores her and keeps playing video games, she forcefully pushes him outside in his wheelchair so that he can get some fresh air and a new perspective on things. Yet, as he continues his fierce protesting, she gets so angry that she shoves him into the canal running next to his apartment building. Not unlike the steadfast tin soldier, Thomas is helpless and about to drown without his legs. Sofie has to jump in and save him and bring him back to the apartment. The identity theme from Andersen's tale in which the soldier on his journey through water is asked to show his identity papers, is given a new twist by Sofie calling him an amoeba, Danish slang for a feeble person.[21] Thomas has lost his resolve, integrity, and steadfastness, all of which Sofie earlier recognised and supported. From the onset, Sofie has regarded Thomas as a soldier returning to Afghanistan. She calls him "soldier," and promises that "before I am done with you, you will be able to walk all the way to Helmand yourself."[22]

Regarding the witch and her decapitation, the theme of a mother fixation is directed at mother figures in a way that combines the individual and the social level. There is, in other words, a strong connection between the mother and the motherland. As in "The Tinder Box," Thomas immediately encounters a female figure upon his return to Denmark. This is indeed his mother (Petrine Agger) sitting next to his girlfriend (Silja Eriksen Jensen) by his bedside as he wakes up in Rigshospitalet. Both are stereotypically Danish, blue-eyed, blonde women (as opposed to a dark-haired, dark-eyed Sofie) seeking to domesticate him and keep him away from the war. At least that is the way Thomas sees it. Thomas crudely sums it up as a matter of "war or sex" ("krig eller fisse"). And he is convinced that his mother does all she can to prevent him from being a soldier: "If it was up to my mother, we would just have to stay at home." When he receives an official letter concerning early retirement, he suspects that his mother has requested it, disregarding the fact that, as he exclaims, "I am a soldier!" As a housewarming gift, his mother gives him a potted orchid. Thomas sees this as yet another sign of maternal attachment and his mother's disregard of his soldier identity and plan of returning to Afghanistan.[23] He has no intention of further nourishing, or to be nourished by, his relationship to his mother – who, clearly hurt, vanishes from the plot after this scene.[24]

The film ends on a happy note with Thomas and Sofie entering into a serious relationship. By then, the film has taken several turns. Sofie who is also internationally oriented has tried her luck in New York, but it did not work out. Thomas has found work at a library and appears to have got over his war traumas. His colleagues are also his friends. One day, Sofie shows up to see him. They go for a walk and with a low-intensity, upbeat song on the soundtrack, they hug and kiss passionately. This is a time of new beginnings. You could say that Thomas leaves behind his soldier "brothers" and enters a new community of peers.

Hence, several aspects of the film's plot, characters, and theme line up with "The Steadfast Tin Soldier:" The attraction between characters that are opposite but also similar; gender roles and the questioning of feminine and masculine traits as they pertain to disability, steadfastness, sexuality, and commitment; the dangerous journey through water, and the return "home." Like *Nobel*, *De standhaftige* is an example of what Rothstein calls "stories of individual destiny about the deployed troops and their mental traumas that make impossible their post-deployment reintegration." (Rothstein 2014, 102, my translation). My point, however, is that the films show precisely the opposite – that in the end their reintegration does become possible.

Wishful Thinking?

As indicated earlier, some narratives gain mythical status and provide the framework for how people interpret their lives. As circumstances change, the myths, too, are rewritten and adapted to capture contemporary situations. Many of Andersen's tales were already such adaptations. Their staying power, it seems, resides in the way they resituate these myths in modernity – in verbal, situational, aesthetic, and thematic terms that we recognise – also in a late modern, globalised world. As furthermore mentioned in the introduction, Danes especially, have been surprisingly positive about participating in the Afghanistan War, despite a relatively high number of casualties. In trying to understand this, sociologists have investigated how popular opinion is influenced by "elite discourses," such as political and bureaucratic discourses (Jakobsen and Ringsmose 2015). By focusing on Andersen, this chapter has sought to complement such studies, by highlighting the discourses of popular culture, including contemporary film and TV, as well as more deep-seated narratives based on folk tales, art tales, and archetypes that may explain how Danes and Norwegians interpret and cope with the traumas of war and returned soldiers.

My main point has been to explore how Andersen's two art tale soldiers provide a framework for how we might understand the literal as well as the literary figure of the returned soldier. In audio-visual narratives like *Nobel*, they appear as two distinct characters, while in *De standhaftige*, the focus is on the steadfast tin soldier, who is nevertheless given a significant dose of tinderbox soldier traits. This allows for a happy ending, but also, I would maintain, for an investigation into the dark forces determining wars and soldier behaviour.

Hence, while one may politically support sending one's soldiers off to war, popular fiction indicates a growing concern with the successful reintegration of the veteran soldier. The fact that the contemporary narratives end on a happy note with the soldiers attaining their erotic objects of desire, camaraderie, as well as public esteem, may be seen as reflecting the desire of a community that feels responsible for the fate of their soldiers. One senses that the narratives are vested with the 'magic power' to alleviate a sense of anxiety and guilt vis-à-vis veterans, yet whether they also somehow prove valuable to the veterans themselves remains an open question.

References

Andersen, Hans Christian. 1996. *Mit Livs Eventyr*. 2 vols. København: Gyldendal.
Bugge, Stella. 2010. "Meningsmåling: Norge bør ut av Afghanistan." *VG*, August 8.
Daugbjerg, Mads and Birgitte Refslund Sørensen. 2017. "Becoming a Warring Nation: The Danish 'Military Moment' and Its Repercussions." *Critical Military Studies* 3(1): 1–6.
Doyle, John. 2016. "If you like Nordic noir, watch *Nobel – Peace at Any Price*." *The Globe and Mail*, December 14. https://www.theglobeandmail.com/arts/television/john-doyle-if-you-like-nordic-noir-watch-nobel-peace-at-any-price/article33322344/
Grimm, Jacob and Wilhelm. 2008. "The Blue Light," translated by D. L. Ashliman. https://www.pitt.edu/~dash/grimm116.html
Håndlykken, Tora Bakke and Marianne Johansen. 2011. "Forsvaret har ikke oversikt – men VG avslører: 48 norske soldater skadet i Afghanistan." *VG*, January 3.
iCasualties: Operation Enduring Freedom. 2018. "Coalition Deaths by Nationality." Accessed September 17 2018. http://icasualties.org/OEF/Nationality.aspx?hndQry=Denmark and http://icasualties.org/OEF/Nationality.aspx?hndQry=Norway
Jakobsen, Peter Viggo and Jens Ringsmose. 2015. "In Denmark, Afghanistan is Worth Dying For: How Public Support for the War was Maintained in the Face of Mounting Casualites and Elusive Success." *Cooperation and Conflict* 50(2): 211–227.
Jakobsen, Siw Ellen. 2018. "Afghanistan-veteranen: En soldat uten krig." *Forskning.no*, March 6. https://forskning.no/krig-og-fred-ny/afghanistan-veteranen-en-soldat-uten-krig/284679
Jensen, Jørgen Bonde. 1993. *H.C. Andersen og genrebilledet*. København: Babette.
Kofod, Else Marie. 1989. *De vilde svaner og andre folkeeventyr. Sidestykker til syv af H.C. Andersens eventyr*. København: Forlaget Folkeminder ApS.
Levy, Jette Lundbo. 1998. "Om ting der går i stykker. Ekelöf og Andersen."

Edda 1998(3): 259–268.

Lévy-Strauss, Claude. (1978) 2005. *Myth and Meaning*. London/New York: Routledge.

Maslow, Abraham H. 1987. *Motivation and Personality*. 3rd ed. Revised by Robert Frager, James Fadiman, Cynthia McReynolds, and Ruth Cox. New York: Harper Collins.

Mylius, Johan de. 2004. *Forvandlingens pris. H.C. Andersen og hans eventyr*. København: Høst & Søn.

NTB. 2008. "Flere skeptiske til norsk tilstedeværelse i Afghanistan." *Dagbladet*, July 17.

Ohlin, Lisa. 2016. *De standhaftige*. Asta Film.

Oxfeldt, Elisabeth. 2018. "White Guilt and Racial Imagery in Annette K. Olesen's *Little Soldier*." *Journal of Aesthetics and Culture* 10(2): 15–24. doi:10.1080/20004214.2017.1404890.

Regjeringen.no. 2010. "Egen dag for å hedre veteraner." December 2. https://www.regjeringen.no/no/aktuelt/egen-dag-for-a-hedre-veteraner/id627135

Rothstein, Klaus. 2014. *Soldatens år. Afghanistan-krigen i dansk litteratur og kultur*. København: Tiderne Skifter.

Sim, Gerald. 2011. "A Gray Zone between Documentary and Fiction: Interview with Janus Metz." *Film Quarterly* 65(1): 17–24.

Stéfansson, Finn. 2009. "Arketyper." In *Symbolleksikon*. København: Gyldendal. http://denstoredanske.dk/Symbolleksikon/Litterære_typer_og_figurer/arketyper

Sørensen, Birgitte Refslund and Thomas Pedersen. 2012. "Hjemkomstparader for danske soldater: Ceremoniel fejring af krigeren og den krigsførende nation." *Slagmark*, no. 63: 31–48.

Sørensen, Per Olav. 2016. *Nobel – Peace at Any Cost*. Oslo: Monster Entertainment.

Unprofor.dk. 2018. "Danmarks deltagelse i borgerkrigen i Jugoslavien." Accessed September 17 2018. http://www.unprofor.dk/unprofor/danmarks-deltagelse

Veteranalliancen. 2018. "Hvor mange har været udsendt?" Accessed September 17 2018. https://veteranalliancen.wordpress.com/fakta/hvor-mange-har-vaeret-udsendt-2

Værum, Peter. 1992. *Frøer og farisæere. Om eventyr og evangelium – set i lyset af Jung*. København: Klitrose.

Notes

1 Compared to Andersen's art tales, folktales seem to a greater extent to be governed by the protagonist's fulfilment of basic needs, e.g. "The Blue Light." This tale is about a soldier who returns wounded from war and is met by a King who tells him "there will be no more money for you, because wages are only for those who earn them" (Grimm 2008). Basic needs consist of physiological needs and safety needs, and the self-actualization need (ranging above both basic and psychological needs) pertains to excelling at something one feels individually "fitted for" (Maslow 1987, 15, 18, 22).

2   Maslow mentions soldiers in particular as "pushed into an unwonted brotherliness and intimacy by their common external danger, and who may stick together throughout a lifetime," and adds: "Any good society must satisfy this need, one way or another, if it is to survive and be healthy" (Maslow 1987, 20).

3   The term "archetype" is derived from Jungian psychology and describes an inherited idea derived from the experience of mankind and present in the unconscious of the individual. Archetypal figures are universal symbols that can mediate opposites in the psyche, often found in fairy tales across cultures (cf. Stéfansson 2009). Similarly, "mythic figures" can be understood anthropologically (and psychologically) in light of Claude Lévy-Strauss, according to whom: "Myths get thought in man unbeknownst to him" (Lévy-Strauss [1978] 2005, "An Introduction").

4   I will use the Danish title throughout this chapter as a reminder of the intertextual link it establishes with Andersen's tale (a link that is lost in the English title). When I include a Norwegian text in this analysis, it is because Denmark and Norway have a shared cultural heritage. Until the early 1900s, Norwegians published their literature in Copenhagen and one speaks of a common Danish-Norwegian literary market (cf. Andersen's "The Rags" from 1868). In 1955, Norwegian Ivo Caprino made a puppet animation film version of "The Steadfast Tin Soldier," which premiered in Odense, Denmark, on the occasion of the official celebration of Andersen's 150th anniversary. This is just one of several examples of how Andersen's texts have remained part of a shared cultural heritage until the present day.

5   "En rigtig Soldat" is a light comedy in which a woman dresses in her cousin's soldier uniform and manages to scare off an enemy army of nine men. It is a playful, gender-reversing role in which the young, beautiful woman knows how to talk like a man, bang the drum, blow the trumpet, and yell out war commands. She is the title's "real soldier." In 1836 Andersen submitted the piece to The Royal Theatre, but it was rejected. In 1838 he published it as part of *Tre Digtninger*.

6   Another narrative of Danish war history would include Danish participation in World War II where, for instance, the Danish freedom fighters (frihedskæmpere) were greeted with homecoming parades upon the nation's liberation in 1945 (cf. Sørensen and Pedersen 2012, 32).

7   This is based on a national poll conducted in October 2011 (Jakobsen and Ringsmose 2015, 212).

8   Polls indicate that percentagewise, public Danish support (2006-2009 and 2011) has been in the high 40s (49% and 46%). Norwegian support (2008, 2010) has been in the high 30s and low-to-mid 40s (36%, 42%, 45%) (Jakobsen and Ringsmose 2015, 214; NTB 2008; Bugge 2010).

9   Janus Metz, for instance, has discussed how his documentary film *Armadillo* (2010) is heavily influenced by other war movies, including Francis Ford Coppola's *Apocalypse Now* (1979) (Sim 2011). Annette K. Olesen's *Lille soldat* (2008; *Little Soldier*) similarly opens up with a scene reminding viewers of *Apocalypse Now*, and then to a greater extent draws intertextually on the plot of Martin Scorsese's *Taxi Driver* (1976). For an analysis of *Lille soldat* as a Danish, postfeminist version of *Taxi Driver* in an age of globalisation, see Oxfeldt 2018.

10 "The Tinder Box" is generally regarded as Andersen's reworking of "Aladdin and the Magic Lamp" from *Arabian Nights* (Jensen 1993, 59). Other tales regarded as sources for "The Tinder Box" (and variations of "Aladdin and the Magic Lamp") are "The Blue Light" (which exists in 1815 and 1857 Grimm versions) and various Danish folk tales, including "Den trekantede Hat" and "Lyset og Staalmanden" (Kofod 1989, 29). According to Jensen there exists about a dozen folk tale versions of "The Tinder Box" (Jensen 1993, 67). Andersen himself has claimed that he heard this folk tale on Funen during his childhood.

11 While Danish theologian and minister Peter Værum's reading is overtly Jungian, I also consider Danish literary scholar and critic Jørgen Bonde Jensen's reading heavily

influenced by Jung, as he writes about maternal attachment, maturation through confrontation with one's "disgusting" desire, and overall sees folktales as providing us with a common unconscious and the immediate discharge of the primary processes of "unpleasant memory glimpses" (Jensen 1993, 65, 67).

12 The witch says: "What a fine sword you've got there, and what a big knapsack. Aren't you every inch a soldier!"
13 A 20th-century example of such a medal is the American Purple Heart granted to wounded or killed soldiers.
14 The series and its actors were nominated for, and won, several awards, among others: The 2017 Rose d'Or for best drama series and the 2016 Prix Europa for best European TV-film/mini-series. In Norway, the series was nominated for ten 2017 Gullrute-awards.
15 Alfred B. Nobel was the inventor of dynamite who bequeathed his fortune to institute the five Nobel Prizes, of which the Peace Prize was to be awarded by a Norwegian, rather than Swedish, committee.
16 The term is also used explicitly in relation to contemporary warfare in the series in which in episode 5, the American minister of defense talks about the U.S. starting a war for a noble cause.
17 NORAD is The Norwegian Agency for Development Cooperation.
18 Erling makes this point explicitly, claiming about Johanne: "I suppose she is like the rest of Norway's population" (all translations from the TV-series into English are mine).
19 He does so especially in episode 5 as he struggles with memories of the people he has killed.
20 As of September 18, 2018, Den danske ordbog online defined the term as referring to a ballet dancer's ability to perform floating movements.
21 She says: "You amoeba!" As of September 18, 2018, Den danske ordbog online states that an amoeba can refer to a physically and/or morally weak person. The water motif is used several times in the film to suggest changes in lives and identities. When her aunt dies, Sofie ritualistically throws her scarf into the ocean. After Sofie has first spent the night at Thomas' apartment, and woken up to find out he no longer has a girlfriend, and then immediately leaves to make it clear that she does not want a relationship, Thomas sits half naked in his wheelchair, looking at his reflection in a window covered by raindrops, clearly wondering who he is, how others see him, and who he may become.
22 All translations from the film into English are mine.
23 Turning to Jimmy, he exclaims: "What the fuck am I to do with an orchid? Bring it to Helmand?"
24 Sofie may be regarded as going through a variation of the same process. In her case, her aunt is her mother figure, albeit one who encourages her to leave her motherland, Denmark, and try her luck in New York. Sofie is not irritated with Ruth the way Thomas is irritated with his mother, but she nevertheless does not enter a long-term love relationship until Ruth has passed away, and she has given her international career a shot.

"I'll sing about those who are gay, and those who are sorrowful"
The Use of Hans Christian Andersen's Fairy Tales in Narrative Medicine

Anders Juhl Rasmussen and Anne-Marie Mai
University of Southern Denmark, Odense

The chapter presents and discusses how Hans Christian Andersen's fairy tales could be of use in courses in Narrative Medicine. The overall aim of the relatively new field Narrative Medicine is to develop doctors' narrative competence in listening to patients' illness narratives through close reading of literary texts and creative writing. The hypothesis is that the competence of reading a fictional narrative is similar to the competence of listening to an authentic patient narrative. Our aim in this chapter is to discuss how Andersen's fairy tales could be used in a course in medical education making the students more attentive to not only the complexity of narratives in the community of health care, but also the enchanting qualities of modern life. The selected tales, "The Teapot" ("Thepotten," 1864) and "The Nightingale," ("Nattergalen," 1843) touch upon disability, suffering, and healing.

Narrative Medicine

"It is not a set of symptoms that visit the doctor – it is a human being with a story of his or her own." This statement by one of the managers of Odense University Hospital, Kim Brixen, points directly to the importance of humanistic knowledge to health science, and to the importance of developing a "narrative competence" in medicine today (Brixen and Mai 2017, 9). Throughout the 20th century, medicine has become evidence based, quantitative evaluations have been preferred over qualitative evaluations, and medical research has focused on disease as a biological dysfunction rather than a disruption of a life story. Medical Humanities evolved around 1950 with the explicit ambition to counterbalance this dominating "un-human," but statistically successful approach in medicine.

The founder of the relatively new interdisciplinary field Narrative Medicine is Rita Charon, Columbia University. She is a professor of internal medicine and holds a PhD in English literature. She defined narrative medicine around 2000 as a subfield within medical humanities, and it is a rapidly growing international field of research and of teaching in medical schools. According to Charon, the overall aim of narrative medicine is to develop a narrative competence in listening to patients' illness narratives:

> A scientifically competent medicine alone cannot help a patient grapple with the loss of health and find meaning in illness and dying. Along with their growing scientific expertise, doctors need the expertise to listen to their patients, to understand as best they can the ordeals of illness, to honour the meaning of their patients' narratives of illness, and to be moved by what they behold so that they can act on their patients' behalf. (2006, 3)

Literature is a storehouse rich with stories about human suffering. By becoming familiar with rigorous methods of reading slowly and with attention to detail followed by an individual, personal writing, it is expected that medical students and health professionals will improve their curiosity about and understanding of patients' illnesses and life-situations. If the doctor is to be able to understand the experience of his or her patients, the doctor needs to understand their narratives – and what author would be better at teaching narrative medicine than Hans Christian Andersen who with wit, feeling and humour masters storytelling to such an extent that readers worldwide keep on returning to his fairy tales?

   As teachers of literature to medical first-year students and graduate students in health care at the University of Southern Denmark since 2016 we are reminded of the relevance of the elementary question: Why does one read literature in academic education? Not any kind of literature, but timeless literature, literature that speaks to the deepest needs and highest wishes of human beings. In this case the answer might be that literature can re-enchant our contemporary, disenchanted life controlled by technology, reason, and predictability. Narrative medicine and its explicit clinical goals of improving the ability to listen and communicate with empathy to all persons in the community of health care can perhaps help the study of literature to become more aware of its own usability for academic education and for ordinary readers of today.

Andersen's Fairy Tales and his own Suffering

When the issue of empathy is debated in and around medical education, it is often a question whether or not empathy can be learned. One position argues that empathy is inborn and a purely epistemological concept, another – more widely accepted – that it is primarily learned through childhood and can be both unlearned and (re)learned in adult life. Literary scholar Suzanne Keen defines "narrative empathy" as "the sharing of feeling and perspective-taking induced by reading, viewing, hearing, or imagining narratives of another's situation and condition." (2013). If an understanding of other people's perspectives can be cultivated through reading, Andersen's fairy tales offer a potential to practice this skill. A crucial aspect of empathy is applying a perspective other than your own and imagining narratives of another person's situation. The tales and stories of Andersen invite our readerly identification with children like Gerda in "The Snow Queen" ("Sneedronningen," 1845) or a struggling figure like the little mermaid. Even a Chinese Emperor or a narrating teapot invite to identification. When reading Andersen's fairy tales as an adult one is often reminded of the stories known from one's own childhood. Rereading the tales will always guarantee new insights in and new identifications with the old stories. If empathy is primarily learned in childhood, through – among other things – the stories adults tell and read to children, then a reading of Andersen's fairy tales in medical education could potentially enhance narrative empathy.

Andersen's fairy tales had a double audience from the very beginning. He published his first and second booklet *Fairy tales, told for children* (*Eventyr, fortalte for Børn,* 1835). Initially he aimed his fairy tales at children "while always remembering that Father and Mother often listen, and you must also give them something for their minds." (letter to B. S. Ingemann, November 20, 1843 [H.C. Andersen 1878, 2:

94]). But later Andersen did not regard children as a primary target audience. He changed the title and genre in 1844 to *New Fairy Tales* (*Nye Eventyr*), and yet again to *Stories* (*Historier*) in 1852. In 1858 a collection was titled *Tales and Stories* (*Eventyr og Historier*), which today is the most common genre indication of the whole collection of 156 pieces of prose writing. The critics' appraisal of Andersen's contribution to a favoured genre in the 19th century was changing from an attitude of dismissal to an international, overwhelming approval. Through this period, Andersen himself moved from retelling the old folk tales (to children), which he knew from his provincial childhood in Odense, to inventing his own artistic fairy tales about witches, trolls, princesses, kings, and Emperors as well as talking animals like a nightingale, and things like a teapot with a consciousness.

As his international success evolved, Andersen wrote about his own incredible life playing with the idea of his lifestory as an enchanted tale. According to literary scholar Paul V. Rubow this idea was inspired by Andersen's friend, the famous scientist Hans Christian Ørsted, who found that miraculous events do not exist outside of, but within the human realm (1927, 77–85). *The True Story of My Life* (*Mit Livs Eventyr uden Digtning*), which in its Danish title uses the word 'fairy tale,' was written in 1846 to accompany a German translation of his collected works. *The Fairy Tale of My Life* (*Mit Livs Eventyr*) was written in 1855 to accompany an edition of his collected works in Denmark, and this was actually his third autobiography. Before his first extended journey outside Denmark to Italy in 1832, he wrote his first autobiography. However, the manuscript was left unfinished with no title, and published posthumously in 1925. Andersen is known to have said that "the history of my life will be the best commentary on my work," and this is true to a certain extent.

In the context of illness, one will notice the description of the lunatic asylum in the beginning of all three autobiographies. This "medical gaze," as Michel Foucault (1973) coined the term in his genealogy of the modern medical clinic, can reveal something important in Andersen research. Andersen knew the asylum through his beloved grandmother who took care of the hospital's garden. Here quoted from *The Fairy Tale of My Life*:

> On one occasion, when the attendants were out of the way, I lay down upon the floor, and peeped through the crack of the door into one of these

cells. I saw within a lady almost naked, lying on her straw bed; her hair hung down over her shoulders, and she sang with a very beautiful voice. All at once she sprang up, and threw herself against the door where I lay; the little valve through which she received her food burst open; she stared down upon me, and stretched out her long arm towards me. I screamed for terror – I felt the tips of her fingers touching my clothes – I was half dead when the attendant came; and even in later years that sight and that feeling remained within my soul. (2000, 7)

This terrifying recollection of a mad woman from Andersen's childhood finds parallels in the images of witches and demons in his fairy tales; think, for example, of the Snow Queen, the Ice Maiden or *Satania infernalis* in "Auntie Toothache." Typically, the devil is depicted as a man, but in Andersen's fairy tales the devil is very often a woman. Andersen's grandfather became insane, he was nicknamed "Mad Anders" and became the target of poor children's public teasing. Andersen feared that he had inherited his insanity. The vision of the insane grandfather at The Graabrødre Hospital in Odense haunted him and reappears in his fictional as well as in his autobiographical writings (2000, 34–35).

In his own life, Andersen experienced several common physical illnesses, but no other Danish author has written about toothache as Andersen did in one of his last tales. The tale deals with the romantic idea that creativity has its offspring in suffering, and that without suffering there is no creativity. Andersen plays with this topic by letting a talented writer choose between heavy toothache and artistic inspiration. In his diaries, Andersen writes in December 1872 about a visit from his dentist who cleaned his artificial teeth and did nothing to his four decayed natural teeth (1871–77, 9:377).[1] When one reads autobiographies or letters from the 19th century, one realises how people were suffering from diseases that today could be easily cured or eased.

In November 1872 his last volume of fairy tales appeared, including "Auntie Toothache" ("Tante Tandpine") and "The Cripple" ("Krøblingen"), the last one about the healing power of reading fairy tales. Shortly afterwards, Andersen experienced the first symptoms of the liver cancer that was to kill him. From beginning to end Andersen's diaries are full of sensuous details. In his early years one can follow him on his adventurous travels to every corner of Europe; in his late years one reads how a deadly disease is acknowledged and unsuccessfully treated. A sentence like "Kjed af at leve og dog angest for at dø!" ("Unhappy with life and yet anxious to die!") illustrates Andersen's ambivalence in this time/period of his life (1871–77, 9:351). His own mother died as an alcoholic in Odense when Andersen was visiting Italy for the first time. In his diary, the few remarks about the death of his mother are surprisingly dry (1871–77, 1:253). Andersen scholar Johan de Mylius has suggested in one of his biographies, *H.C. Andersens liv. Dag for dag*, that Andersen also drank too much alcohol towards the last ten to fifteen years of his life in order to escape from frustration and boredom in Copenhagen (1998, 202–203).

Another medical aspect of Andersen's life is his well-confirmed hypochondriac nature. The historian Kurt Jacobsen and journalist Klaus Larsen have depicted Andersen as a "difficult patient" in *Woe and welfare: Doctors, health, and society through 200 years* (*Ve og velfærd. Læger, sundhed og samfund gennem 200 år*, 2007). Through readings of his diaries, they give examples of the nervous Andersen who more than most people feared becoming sick and dying when there was nothing in particular to fear. Andersen's notorious fear of being buried alive has become a popular myth: When he was travelling, he had a slip of paper on his chest at night saying "I am only apparently dead."

However, Andersen was also an unusually brave man when it came to travelling and seeking adventure. One can recall the courageous decision of travelling (with no return) to Copenhagen as a 14-year-old, not to mention all his travels in Europe. The fact that Andersen wrote the aforementioned autobiography before going to Italy for the first time illustrates that travelling was equally dangerous and costly in the 19th century. As Andersen (2000) self-consciously remarks at one point in his later autobiography, he was nervous and fearful when it came to minor things, but he was brave and courageous when facing major challenges. As a highly sensitive human being Andersen knew enough about the experience of illness to write about suffering and healing in his tales, and maybe he even wrote about illness to find relief from his own anxiety of dying.

Close Reading as Enchantment

Reading sophisticated and complex literary texts in a narrative medicine course like Hans Christian Andersen's fairy tales could invite medical and health care students to think deeply about their own and other's situations. The significance of these tales should be measured by their ability to provoke or inspire one to think differently about one's own existence, ethical responsibility, and historical life. Through the otherness of the literary text the reader is expected to achieve a new, fresh look at the world as well as at him- or herself.

The goal of narrative medicine is to educate better and more empathetic physicians. The fairy tales of Andersen need to be read with careful attention to fulfill this ambition. In literary studies this activity is called "close reading:" One reads every sentence closely and every word in the fairy tale, so that ideally no information will escape the reader's attention. All this information then has to be configured in an interpretation of the fairy tale. To configure details into a pattern of understanding is what literary scholars are trained to do. They do not prove that their close reading is correct, rather they convince others that it is reasonable – leaving it open, if other similarly convincing interpretations will exist now or in the future.

Charon has pleaded the case for close reading in medical education in the following way:

> Students trained in close reading have been known to apply it to diverse sorts of texts and thus to discover things they would not otherwise have noticed [...]. If close reading helps persons to discover things they would not otherwise have noticed, perhaps it might help clinicians to notice what their patients try to tell them. (Charon et al. 2017, 164-65)

Another physician Rishi Goyal, who is an associate professor of literature at Columbia University, has described the transference like this: "the ability to read a book, a poem or a short story is similar to the act of listening well, and by training in the one, reading and writing, you can improve the other, listening and acting." (Rasmussen 2017).

Having taught narrative medicine in recent years at the University of Southern Denmark, we believe that one can actually train medical students to closely read significant texts about illness, suffering, and dying. Possibly, the students can thereby achieve a competence of empathetic listening and understanding of their patients' narratives in the clinic. Simultaneously, a rare and vulnerable room for self-reflection on the students' own narratives of life and mortality is opened in the classroom. Our belief in this correlation between the teaching and clinical practice is informed and supported by recent qualitative evaluations of the outcome from courses in narrative medicine or medical humanities in medical education (Miller et al. 2014; Barber and Moreno-Leguizamon 2017; Graham et al. 2016).

In her *Uses of Literature* literary scholar Rita Felski suggests that close reading can be compared to "an intense and enigmatic pleasure," "intoxication rather than detachment," not far away "from the child's enchantment with a fairy tale." (2008, 51, 54). Felski refers to the sociologist Jane Bennett who argues in *The Enchantment of Modern Life* that an attention to the marvels of everyday life enhances the motivation for ethical action. According to Bennett, enchantment is "a mood of fullness, plenitude, or liveliness, a sense of having had one's nerves or circulation or concentration powers tuned up or recharged – a shot in the arm, a fleeting return to childlike excitement about life," and she finds this mood, for example, in the stories of Franz Kafka (2001, 6). Felski's thesis is that close reading can be considered a kind of enchantment, and that it matters exactly because "people turn to works of art ... to be taken out of themselves, to be pulled into an altered state of consciousness." (2008, 76). She asks if we can explore the affective and absorptive, the sensuous and somatic qualities of aesthetic experience without the experience of being enchanted.

If enchantment is inherent in close reading as such, it ought to be considered if the act of reading is more than a purely cognitive act as often supposed in literary criticism. To be taken out of oneself and into an absorption of a fairy tale, for example, is emotionally demanding and essential to the understanding of the text. While the close reading is often mostly analytical, creative writing is mostly a free space for personal experience. A way of motivating the close reading is to begin in the embodied observations from the reading experience.

When narrative medicine is successfully practiced – from a literary point of view, – the close reading of literary texts respects both the emotional attachment of reading and the rational detachment of analysing, though these two approaches are never clear-cut: One is also thinking while reading, and the feelings for characters do not disappear in the interpretive act. Ideally (and paradoxically so), attachment to and detachment from the text are distinct and intertwined in the act of a close reading.[2]

Practicing the analysis of form and narrative without taking notice of how the tale addresses the readers as embodied individuals in a group would likewise be a mistake. One is often surprised by the variation of sensibility by and community of a group of medical or health care students. If one student has experienced a recent tragedy in the family or in the clinical practice, this student will often become deeply moved by the tragedy of for example the little mermaid. This kind of affective reading is not more or less true, but it is certainly untrue to this particular reader's emotions not to let the student reflect upon them.

From a medical point of view, it is crucial that the medical students will learn how to be curious, to imagine and understand the experiences of the sick persons and their ordeals. Perhaps the experience of enchantment – in close reading and in the genre of the fairy tale – can help the medical students to cultivate empathy. Two short fairy tales will here serve as examples of how to closely read Andersen in a future narrative medicine course.

"The Teapot"

Andersen's fairy tale "The Teapot" ("Theepotten") was published in 1864. The tale is very short, only one page long. Nonetheless, it is sophisticated and complex – rather told to interpreting parents than to children. The narrative in the tale can be resumed in three parts: At the beginning the teapot is a proud object on the table with anthropomorphic qualities; it is "proud of being made of porcelain, proud of its long spout and its broad handle." However, the teapot is imperfect: its lid was cracked and riveted, but that part of the tale belongs to the past, before the fairy tale is told. The imperfection has taught the teapot to be modest: "And I also know my imperfections, and I realise that in that very knowledge is my humility and my modesty. We all have many defects, but then we also have virtues." The teapot's most valuable virtues are endurance and optimism.

The tale appears like a quasi-biography told by the teapot: "[...] it talked to itself about its past life." It can be argued that human beings tell stories of their lives to better understand themselves because identity is – according to philosopher Paul Ricoeur (1991) – narratively configured. What moves the story forwards halfway through to the second part is that the almost perfect teapot is broken by a delicate but awkward hand, and given to a poor woman. This woman uses the teapot as a pot for flowers. Thus, instead of carrying hot boiled water with Chinese tealeaves, it now carries earth and a flower bulb.

Even this new mode of existence is changed in the ending lines of the tale when the pot is deliberately broken into two and thrown into the yard as potsherds. In other words, the narrative traces the teapot's decline from the bourgeois table of Chinese tea to the yard of poor people. Andersen's personal story, as he told it in his autobiographies, was quite the opposite, and still, he knew better than the bourgeois authors in Copenhagen how to tackle his imperfections.

The literary qualities of this fairy tale, like so many of Andersen's tales, lie in its lively 'surface' of irony and many sincere layers. The narrator is not only ironic towards the bourgeoisie; there is also a meta-level where the text reflects on its own making: "the lid is not worth talking about; enough has been said about that" refers to what the bourgeois people say as well as what was said by the narrator in the beginning of the tale.

The anthropomorphic qualities of the teapot are revealed in the following quotes: "The Teapot lay in a faint on the floor," "They called me an invalid," and "They broke me in two – that really hurt." Keeping in mind that the teapot is dropped on the floor and deliberately broken into two parts, this could be read as a story of bodily disability. In the first paragraph the teapot is proud of its almost perfect body. In the second the pot is proud of its aim. Despite the disability of the teapot, it never mourns or pities itself. Even when it is broken into two parts, it finds pleasure in remembrance of its past life: "But I have my memory; *that* I can never lose!" "The Teapot" can be interpreted as an illness narrative about losing bodily perfection and recalling the rich story of a life.

The teapot has a realistic perspective on dramatic changes in life: "One is one thing and then becomes quite another." These changes are equally recognised in illness as well as in motherhood. One is one thing, a young woman, and then becomes quite another, a grown-up mother. Already the first sentence indicates this interpretation: "There was a proud Teapot, proud of being made of porcelain, proud of its long spout and its broad handle. It had something in front of it and behind it [...]." Isn't this a curvy and attractive young woman? This line of interpretation is supported by two additional quotes: "And the bulb lay in the earth, inside of me, and it became my heart, my living heart, a thing I never had before. There was life in me; there were power and might; my pulse beat." Could this be the pulse of an embryo? The tale continues: "I saw it, I bore it, and I forgot myself in its beauty. It is a blessing to forget oneself in others!"

These quotes point to something quite different than disability, they outline the narrative of becoming a mother and the pleasure of forgetting oneself in the unlimited care of the child. It is surprising that these two equally well supported interpretations are contradictory. Becoming disabled is what most of us fear, becoming a parent is what most of us hope for. What binds these interpretations together is a dramatic change in life.

The interpretation of the teapot could be extended with an interpretation of the change as even more dramatic than disability or motherhood, namely, a burial: "They put earth in me, and for a Teapot that's the same as being buried." In that case, the tale is more precisely about eternal life and religious belief: "Who put it there and gave it to me, I don't know; but it was planted there." The unnamed and maybe even unnamable is God who – echoing the Danish poet N.F.S. Grundtvig's hymn from 1817 – plants a bulb, a daffodil (en påskelilje), i.e. Jesus Christ (Grundtvig 1817).

An attentive close reading of this very short fairy tale with medical or health care students would reveal the hidden pattern in the narrative and could develop their sense of perspective-taking and imagination of other people's conditions. The tale is suddenly about something else than one initially thought. The hypothesis in narrative medicine is, as previously mentioned, that reading a written, fictional narrative is similar to listening to an oral, authentic narrative. Of course, the physician must know what symptoms to look for, and some medical tests are non-narrative facts. Medicine is indeed a practice that relies heavily on natural science, but interpretation is also a part of medical practice. Medicine cannot be a natural science because it has as its object human beings, and these beings use language and narratives to express, explain, and understand themselves. Reading "The Teapot" with medical students can potentially train them to pay attention to a complex narrative with hidden meanings, letting no single interpretation to dominate the other. According to Charon and Goyal, training an increased capacity for ambiguity in understanding a narrative can be useful in a clinical practice with complex illness narratives.

"The Nightingale"

Another fairy tale about human suffering and a will to overcome illness is "The Nightingale" ("Nattergalen"), published in 1844. Like "The Teapot" this tale is narrated by an ironic and playful narrator. It begins like this: "The Emperor of China is a Chinaman, as you most likely know, and everyone around him is a Chinaman too." Three times in the first sentence the recipient is told that people in China are Chinese. This redundancy invites a smile on the lips of the listener or reader, but it does more than that, and that is one of the reasons why Andersen's tales are great literature. It also prepares the recipient for a narrative about an Emperor, who does not know a little, grey bird in his empire, let alone in his garden, esteemed above all his wealth by all his visitors. Interpreted as a symbol, the narrator tells a tale about the paradox that most human beings do not know what is most important in their own lives. This is a paradox, as one would expect everyone to know what is important for him- or herself.

The narration is a bit longer and more complicated in this fairy tale than in the story of the teapot. However, this narrative can also be divided in three parts with a beginning, a middle, and an end. The first part tells us how the Chinese emperor is introduced to the nightingale and hears its enchanting song. In the second part the living nightingale is compared to a mechanical nightingale, and by consequence the first hides in nature again. Finally, in the third part the living nightingale comes back to sing for the severely ill Emperor, and the song of the nightingale offers solace and hope by means of which the Emperor regains his health.

Like the tale of the teapot, the tale of the nightingale criticises social hierarchies. Almost to the end, the Emperor is depicted as ignorant, not knowing about the precious nightingale in his own garden, and not knowing how to appreciate its song when offering the nightingale to wear his golden slipper around its neck. An offer that ridicules the court culture of an absolute monarch. The only appraisal which the nightingale seeks, is the tears of the Emperor. The Emperor's servants and royal squires are depicted as being even worse, for example when they mistake the moo of a cow or the croaking of a frog for the beautiful song of the nightingale. On the contrary, the beauty of the bird's song is recognised by the poor fisherman and the poor little girl in the kitchen. These poor people resemble the innocent child in "The

Emperor's New Clothes," who says what is in plain sight, and what the narrator has told the reader from the beginning, namely that the Emperor is being fooled by two swindlers.

Likewise, it is the poor fisherman who proves his intuitive sensibility to the nightingale's singing when he says that the mechanical bird sounds "very nearly the real thing, but not quite." Even though the fisherman cannot verbalise his critique, his ears are more attuned to singing than the so-called music master who writes a "twenty-five-volume book about the artificial bird. It was learned, long-winded, and full of hard Chinese words, yet everybody said they read and understood it, lest they show themselves stupid and would then have been punched in their stomachs." The narrator's sympathy is entirely with the poor and honest people; one could call it a defence for the social position of the child and the poor thereby underlining the strength and weakness of this position.

This fairy tale also calls attention to the healing power of art. Near the end of the tale the mechanical bird is broken after wear and tear. The watchmaker repairs it, but only well enough for it to have to be played sparingly because the cylinder pegs were worn out. Soon after this episode, but five years later in the narrated time, the Emperor falls ill, he could "hardly breathe. It was as if something were sitting on his chest." No royal physician is mentioned in this paragraph, which is a bit odd because the physician was mentioned when the mechanical bird was broken. The Emperor is all alone in his bed fighting with Death who is sitting on his chest. Out of the blue, the little nightingale comes to the window and sings the song that some years earlier had moved the Emperor to tears, and as the bird sings the Emperor falls into a sweet and refreshing slumber. When he wakes up, he is "restored and well" again. The nightingale and the Emperor have a final dialogue, and the Emperor accepts that his knowledge of the nightingale must be kept as a secret. This is of course a delicate paradox as in the beginning, because the reader learns about this secret as it is agreed on between the bird and the Emperor.

Interpreted as a symbol, the fairy tale is about the secret therapeutic power of nature itself and of the fairy tale as an art genre. Both nature and the fairy tale are accessible for everyone, from the poor, simple people to the rich Emperor of China. In his Jungian interpretation of Andersen's fairy tales, psychologist Eigil Nyborg has noticed that the nightingale's song in the old folk superstition could alleviate pain, bring healing to the sick, and to the dying a peaceful death (Nyborg 1962, 194). The tale is told in a few pages, as opposed to the lengthy works of the "music master," and with no difficult words. Fairy tales have their origin in ordinary peoples' lives and are their artistic heritage. Everyone can and should be able to understand the tales in their own way, and nobody has to pretend an understanding of them which cannot be explained fairly easily, although the tales always keep something as a secret between the narrator and the recipient.

The healing potential of art has been known since Aristotle's *Poetics* where the identification with the hero in the Greek tragedy makes possible a purification of the emotions, also called a catharsis. The nightingale tells the Emperor that its song intends to make him "happy and thoughtful," and that it sings about "those who are gay, and those who are sorrowful." This is in fact a neat description not only of this fairy tale but of all Andersen's tales. The question is here why and how does literature, and more narrowly fairy tales, heal the suffering human heart? A question like this is open enough for a writing prompt to medical students 'in the shadow of' a close and curious reading of "The Nightingale." The prompt could be formulated as "write about healing words," thereby opening the spectrum from words in literature to words in the clinical practice.

Another, and slightly more demanding, exercise would be to ask the students to cut in paper their emotional reaction to the fairy tale. It is no secret that Andersen himself made papercuts while he was telling his tales – and towards the end of his life read these tales to children and adults – mostly the bourgeoisie in Copenhagen after or before a dinner with the famous author. Andersen revealed a few remarks about his papercuts indicating them as being part of the same creative process as his writing.[3]

A cutting prompt could sound like this: "Cut out in paper what you heard in the fairy tale." These cuttings cannot be shared aloud as the reading of the writing prompts. They can instead be put on a wall, and the students can ask each other what the fellow student's papercut tells them, or what they wanted to express by their own papercut. Expression through words is only one way of expressing oneself creatively. The nightingale in the fairy tale expresses itself through both words and song, giving the song a healing power.

Conclusion

Reading fairy tales like "The Teapot" and "The Nightingale" or other explicit illness tales like "The Story of a Mother" ("Historien om en Moder," 1848), "Auntie Toothache" and "The Cripple" with medical and health care students could possibly train their narrative competences in taking others' perspectives – across social, religious and cultural differences. The hypothesis in narrative medicine that reading a written, fictional narrative is similar to listening to an oral, authentic patient narrative, and that training in reading strengthens the ability to listen, seems promising when dealing with fairy tales of Andersen.

As argued by literary scholar Kathryn Montgomery, medicine is not a natural science, it is rather a narratively structured practice relying on science, because medicine fundamentally is a care for human beings who use narratives to express, explain, and understand themselves (2005, 29–41). This critical, narrative stance and vision of a more holistic medicine is confirmed by Goyal:

> The physician's diagnosis depends heavily on the story he or she hears from the patient, since it relates to a temporal structure and a change of state (usually from health to sickness). A 'good' medical story (one that makes causal connections clear, includes relevant information and interests the listener) makes diagnosis easier by eliciting the physician's empathy. (2013, n.p.)

Sometimes, the patient does not tell the story the physician expects, and sometimes the physician does not listen carefully enough to the patient's story. Reading Andersen's short and complex tales can potentially train medical students to pay more attention to the complexity of illness narratives in the clinical practice, to imagine themselves in the shoes of another for a moment, and to understand and tolerate the many interpretable layers of these stories. The complexity of a whole person with a long story cannot be reduced to a single diagnosis and efficient treatment plan.

As a perspective, it should be mentioned that scholars at the University of Southern Denmark have recently tried to expand their research into assessing the impact of creative writing workshops for patients with chronic illnesses (Hansen, Rasmussen, and Zwisler 2018). Writing imaginatively and creatively together with other patients and guided by experienced authors of fiction seems to improve the participants' well-being. Living with a chronic illness often narrows the horizon of life to the specific illness. By giving these patients a unique chance to re-open their horizons through creative writing one can perhaps give access to an increased quality of life.

Andersen's stories about those who are happy and those who suffer could be read with patients as a framework for their own inventive writing. The stories would remind the patients of the rich and enchanted life we all live, if we, like Andersen, have the talent to use our (childlike) imagination and make meaning and tell stories in a supposedly disenchanted world. With the enchanting stories of a life, sometimes harsh, sometimes easy, and always complicated by love and hatred, one – as argued by Bennett – could possible re-enter the community of the living and telling humans and *not* be left alone with medical treatment, medical science and medical industry.

As mentioned, recent evaluations from courses in Narrative Medicine at Columbia University's and other Western medical schools suggest that reading and writing actually can make a difference. Especially the fairy tales of Andersen and the experience of enchantment in close reading could possibly help patients as well as students to cultivate the important skill of narrative empathy and build up embodied communities – with fellow patients and with fellow professionals. In the end, we are all facing the fear of dying.

There seems to be little doubt that what Foucault called a 'medical gaze' on Andersen's fairy tales would contribute with a new and enriching interpretation of these canonical texts. For many years psychologists and psychiatrists have been investigating the tales, and narrative medicine has in fact its roots in psychoanalysis. Now it could be time for literary scholars with a medical gaze to reveal new aspects of these seemingly timeless tales.

References

Andersen, Hans Christian. 1878. *Breve fra Hans Christian Andersen* [Letters from Hans Christian Andersen]. Edited by C. St. A. Bille and Nikolaj Bøgh. 2 vols. København: Reitzel.

Andersen, Hans Christian. 1971–77. *H.C. Andersens Dagbøger 1825-1875*. 12 vols. Compiled by Kåre Olsen and H. Topsøe-Jensen and edited by Helga Vang Lauridsen, Tue Gad, and Kirsten Weber. København: Det Danske Sprog- og Litteraturselskab/Gad.

Andersen, Hans Christian. (1871) 2000. *The Fairy Tale of My Life* [Danish original *Mit Livs Eventyr*, 1855]. New York, NY: Cooper Square Press.

Andersen, Jens. 2002. "Scissor Writing." Det Kongelige Bibliotek. http://wayback-01.kb.dk/wayback/20101108104614/http://www2.kb.dk/elib/mss/hcaklip/intro-en.htm.

Barber, Sarah, and Carlos J. Moreno-Leguizamon. 2017. "Can Narrative Medicine Education Contribute to the Delivery of Compassionate Care? A Review of the Literature," *BMJ Medical Humanities* 43(3): 199–203.

Bennett, Jane. 2001. *The Enchantment of Modern Life*. Princeton, NJ: Princeton University Press.

Brixen, Kim, and Anne-Marie Mai. 2017. "Forord." [Preface]. In *Læse, skrive og hele. Perspektiver på narrativ medicin* [Read, write, and heal: Perspectives at narrative medicine], edited by Anders Juhl Rasmussen, 9. Odense: Syddansk Universitetsforlag.

Charon, Rita. 2006. *Narrative Medicine: Honouring the Stories of Illness*. New York, NY: Oxford University Press.

Charon, Rita, Sayantani Dasgupta, Nellie Hermann, Craig Irvine, Eric Marcus, Edgar Rivera Colón, Danielle Spencer, and Maura Spiegel. 2017. *The Principles and Practice of Narrative Medicine*. New York, NY: Oxford University Press.

Felski, Rita. 2008. *Uses of Literature*. Malden, MA/Oxford, UK: Blackwell.

Felski, Rita. 2015. *The Limits of Critique*. Chicago, IL: University of Chicago Press.

Foucault, Michel. 1973. *The Birth of the Clinic: An Archaeology of Medical Perception* [French original 1963]. New York, NY: Pantheon Books.

Goyal, Rishi. 2013. "Narration in Medicine." In *The living handbook of narratology*, edited by Peter Hühn et al., paragraph 6. Hamburg: Hamburg University. http://www.lhn.uni-hamburg.de/article/narration-medicine.

Graham, Jeremy, Lauren M. Benson, Judy Swanson, Darryl Potyk, Kenn Daratha, and Ken Roberts. 2016. "Medical Humanities Coursework Is Associated with Greater Measured Empathy in Medical Students." *The American Journal of Medicine* 129 (12): 1334–1337.

Grundtvig, Nikolai Frederik Severin. 1817. "Paaske-Lilien" [The Daffodil]. *Danne-Virke* 2: 291–325.

Hansen, Helle Ploug, Anders Juhl Rasmussen, and Ann-Dorthe Zwisler. 2018. "Skrivning som heling? De første danske erfaringer med skrivning som del af rehabilitering" [Writing as healing? The first Danish experiences with writing as part of rehabilitation]. *Månedsskrift for Almen Praksis* (May): 359–366.

Jacobsen, Kurt and Klaus Larsen. 2007. *Ve og velfærd. Læger, sundhed og samfund gennem 200 år* [Woe and welfare: Doctors, health, and society through 200 years]. København: Lindhardt og Ringhof.

Keen, Suzanne. 2013. "Narrative Empathy." In *The living handbook of narratology*, edited by Peter Hühn et al., paragraph 2. Hamburg: Hamburg University. hup.sub.uni-hamburg.de/lhn/index.php?title=NarrativeEmpathy&oldid=2044.

Miller, Eliza, Dorene Balmer, Nellie Hermann, Gillian Graham, and Rita Charon. 2014. "Sounding Narrative Medicine. Studying Students' Professional Identity Development at Columbia University College of Physicians and Surgeons." *Academic Medicine* 89 (2): 335–342.

Montgomery, Kathryn. 2005. *How Doctors Think*. New York: Oxford University Press.

Mylius, Johan de. 1998. *H.C. Andersens liv. Dag for dag* [The life of Hans Christian Andersen: Day by day]. København: Aschehoug.

Nyborg, Eigil. 1962. *Den indre linie i H.C. Andersens eventyr. En psykologisk studie* [The inner line in Hans Christian Andersen's fairy tales: A psychological study]. København: Gyldendal.

Rasmussen, Anders Juhl. 2017. "What does it mean to listen, and how can it be learned?" *BMJ Medical Humanities* [blog]. http://blogs.bmj.com/medical-humanities/2017/04/04/long-read-what-does-it-mean-to-listen-and-how-can-it-be-learned.

Ricoeur, Paul. 1991. "Narrative Identity." *Philosophy Today* 35(1): 73–81.

Rubow, Paul V. 1927. *H.C. Andersens Eventyr*. København: Levin og Munksgaard.

Notes

1. We refer to and quote from the Danish edition in our translation.
2. In The Limits of Critique Rita Felski investigates the distinction between attachment and detachment in the act of reading literature, especially in "Context Stinks!" (2015: 151–185).
3. "In Andersen's papercuts you see/ His poetry!/ A medley of diverting treasures/ All done with scissors" and "From Andersen's scissors/ A fairy tale sprang forth./ You were given the papercut;/ You are kindly critic!" ["Det hele er Andersen poesi/ i klipperi!/ Broget, løjerligt alleslags, alt med en saks!" og "Fra H.C. Andersens saks/ sprang et eventyr straks/ Du klipningen fik,/ Du er den milde kritik!"], jf. J. Andersen 2002.

Hans Christian Andersen's Literary Imagination Interpreted and Reconstructed in China
A Semiotic Reading

Ye Rulan
Fudan University, Shanghai

As an important carrier of cultural values and human spirit, literature contributes to the forming and reforming of culture and motivates cross-cultural communication that may generate cultural resonance. Hans Christian Andersen's fairy tales constitute a complex semiotic system that plays a dynamic role in connecting the past and present, the young and the old, and people who speak various languages and live in different social and cultural systems. In China, the alchemy of Andersen's literary imagination has motivated readers to respond to the values conveyed in the signs and symbols, and to interpret and recontextualise them with the impulse of the time and space. A semiotic analysis of Andersen signs in China demonstrates how the acceptance, interpretation and recontextualisation of the signs have empowered Chinese readers positively.

Hans Christian Andersen's fairy tales, with their prominent semiotic significance in the value of life and the essential beauty of the soul and love, has brought to different cultures his system of value and belief that has stimulated intertexual literary creation with his fairy tales as the inner semiotic core. The condensation of his fairy tales into signs has ensured the timeless vitality and boundless energy of his literary imagination till now. The fairy tale world formulated and constructed by Andersen is a powerful generator of semiosis (sign process, i.e. the production and interpretation of linguistic and visual signs) not only because of his incorporation of paper cutting – the visual art representations of his literary thoughts – operating as a kind of ritual atonement into the fabric of storytelling, but also because he created fairy tale characters that have all become the signs and symbols which signify in a semiotically profound way a view of life, of soul, of spirit, and are essential to the communication of ideas to readers. The semiotic abundance of his fairy tales builds up a dynamic world with a plurality of connotations around his works. The world brings itself to the reader/interpreter as open and promises future perceptions and meaning-makings.

The stories as a complex of the imagined huddle people together from different cultural backgrounds and various fields over a shared interest in the writer's literary imagination, and over shared values and beliefs. On the one hand, his fairy tales are old stories, but antiquity has an appeal in itself. Now they present a mythical or total effect that opens a door to the other world, and if we pass through, if only for a moment, we stand outside our own time and world. On the other hand, his fairy tales live because of a passion of imagination, which houses both the possible and impossible, and has the well-perceived infinitude of the potential and interpretive expansion of the fairy tales.

In China, the semiotic interpretation of Andersen's fairy tales as the emblem of purity, passion and perseverance has moulded Andersen into a moral benchmark with which one may do self-examinations and make self-improvement. Besides, the stories constitute a system of signs with great openness for interpretation, integration and re-contextualisation. A Hans Christian Andersen's fairy tale, for instance "The Little Mermaid" ("Den lille Havfrue," 1837), can become so agglomerated in the recipient's mind that the title alone is able to evoke in one's mind a cluster of objects: a self-immolating female image, abiding and altruistic love, sacrifice and suffering, pain and endurance, etc. That is to say, the sign that the title denotes carries with it all that is implied in the words and sentences that have been woven into the text. The same can be demonstrated by signs such as "The Emperor's New Clothes" ("Keiserens nye Klæder," 1837), "The Little Match Girl" ("Den lille Pige med Svovlstikkerne," 1848), "The Steadfast Tin Soldier" ("Den standhaftige Tinsoldat," 1838) and "The Ugly Duckling" ("Den grimme Ælling," 1844), to name but a few, all of which have within themselves the capability of unfolding into a series of signs that constitute a more complex meaning-making. A semiotic approach is to be used to analyse Andersen's signs in China to explicate that the process of the interpretation of the meaning of signs from the perspective of Chinese readers in the specific Chinese social and cultural contexts is also a process of generating new signs that contribute to the enrichment of the original Andersen signs. Moreover, it's a dynamic transcultural and transhistorical interaction that fosters a transition to better cultural or social values.

A Semiotic Approach

The American philosopher Charles S. Peirce proposed the definition of sign as "a First which stands in such a genuine triadic relation to a Second, called its *Object*, as to be capable of determining a Third, called its *Interpretant*, to assume the same triadic relation to its Object in which it stands to itself to the same Object." (1955, 99–100). Peirce's triadic approach provides a better interpretation than the signifier-signified dyad as it underlines the role of a sign's interpretant, which connects the sign's observable representamen and its signified object and actually becomes a new sign that generates new interpretants. For the study of literature, semiotics as a pragmatic approach offers an extensive perspective of interpreting, contextualising, reconstructing and re-contextualising literary signs that are capable of engendering infinite sign processes and stimulating meaning-making, each of which cannot be isolated from another. Floyd Merrell points out the importance of minds, which he calls semiotic agents, in the activation of Peirce's Firstness, Secondness, and Thirdness/representamen (sign)-object-interpretant triads.

Merrell expounds that it's the semiotic indeterminacy "at the heart of the *vagueness* and *generality*, the *inconsistency* and *incompleteness*, and the *overdetermination* and *underdetermination* of any and all signs" that guarantees the vitality of signs and their meaning. He further elaborates that meaning exists everywhere although it may be indiscernible, as it is "in the interrelations of the sign interaction incessantly being played out on the stage of semiosis." Therefore, "meaning" is taken as a plural rather than singular concept.

> Meaning does not emerge through some specifiable contact between people and people, and between people and language, and language and the

world, but rather, it is the very process of emergence, the emergence of everything that is in the world, our 'semiotic world'.

Moreover, in the process of our conscious searching for meaning of a sign in the semiotic process, the meaning has already turned into another sign when we embark on the search. The dynamic interaction and interrelatedness between signs and meanings shows that semiotics "is about meaning engendered when signs are in their act of becoming signs, a becoming that includes sign interpreters as participating agents in the very semiosis process of becoming" (1997, ix–x).

A sign either denotes or connotes something to a person in some respect or capacity. It is through representation that signs are identified, and it is through interpretation that signs are communicated. A sign is not a sign with meaning generating capability unless it gets translated into another sign, whether it be symbolic, iconic, emotional or any other type. According to Peirce, interpretation is a translation of a sign into a feeling, an effort of another sign or signs and the general role of interpretation is "to make the text understandable, and probable, by establishing it as part of an argument that is part of a discourse;" in this respect, "thought (as well as the self), being in itself essentially of the nature of a sign, [...] must grow in incessant new and higher translations." (1934, 594). As soon as one interprets a sign, he becomes part of it during the time of that interpretation.

Literature deals with the elements of the sign system of language – words and sentences, and words and sentences are an innate part of representation. The literary texts, with their interpretable strings or configurations, call for the involvement of their readers to interpret the verbal signs and the cooperation of them to generate meanings. As the major executors of interpretation, the readers play an indispensable role in the generative process of the text. In the sign process, there is no ruling point of view, which also includes the author's, and different perspectives are equally justifiable and rich in potential. Furthermore, sign reception and interpretation within a specific cultural context cannot be achieved without sign interpreters, who are also interpretants, and their efforts to integrate the signs into the semiotic systems that they are familiar with, because no text is read, understood and interpreted without the involvement of the readers' personal experiences in their particular cultural context. Apart from what is denoted and explicitly presented in the signs, the readers come up with frames of interpretations on the ground of their knowledge base and it is up to them to choose which codes to apply for the intertexual interpretations.

Andersen-texts as a Semiotic Universe

Hans Christian Andersen's fairy tales have emerged as a semiotic universe that transcends the boundary of culture and social context since they were introduced to China at the beginning of the 20th century. The reception of Andersen's works, their impact upon the Chinese readers and the use we make of them are closely related to our interpretations that are grounded in the Chinese cultural and social sign systems. The cultural and the social mechanism construct a sign's various interpretants. Culture, as has been stated by Anthony Giddens, "consists of the values the members of a given group hold, the norms they follow, and the material goods they create." (1989, 310). In the establishment of the values and the norms, and the creation of the material goods, literature has an essential part, because literature "draws from and participates in the construction of culture as a way of life, a system of values and beliefs, and in turn, it affects culture as a creative, representational practice." (King 1991, 2). But the intervention of literature in the construction and reconstruction of culture can't be achieved without the existence of a kind of cultural community in which the participants, i.e. both the writers and the readers, are engaged in a dynamic intersubjective world of discourse. In the collaboration-driven communities, the readers are not merely the recipients of the contents, they interpret the contents within their own cultural context and contribute to the enrichment of the contents. Moreover, such communities allow transcultural and transhistorical interactions. In *Basics in Semiotics* John Deely interprets such interaction as "a virtual semiosis," which refers to a series of interactions at the level of our awareness that "provides an actual pathway through time whereby it is possible that what happened long ago might be partially understood" (1990, 96), and from this perspective, Andersen's fairy tales can be regarded as a mosaic of traces from the past that generates shared values in a cultural community during the readers' interactive conceptual journeys with the stories.

As for the social significance, literature provides integrative or subversive signs for readers to compare and evaluate their own values, beliefs and norms of society in the process of interpretation. Paul Thibault argues that the social semiotic conceptual framework has to do with "the systems of meaning making resources" and is related to how the resources are used in "texts and social occasions of discourse" and the textual meanings that are "made, remade, imposed, contested, and changed from one textual production or social occasion of discourse to another" in and through the social practices of the social formations. He points out that "regular and systematic copatternings of textual meaning relations and their associated meaning-making practices function in ways that enact, maintain, reproduce, and change the social semiotic system." (1991, 6). As a significant meaning-making resource, Andersen's fairy tales have been a cradle for textual productions in the Chinese social semiotic system that serve to plant moral ideals and transvalue the old moral values.

This semiotic universe of Andersen-texts constitutes a flexible type of conglomerate that endows the signs with transindividual and transhistorical attributes. Their constitution of signs as purity, passion and perseverance in China allows Chinese readers to be connected to it both culturally and socially, to create in themselves an intermediate space where the texts' universe neither verily belongs to them nor is quite beyond them, and to journey into their own desire and unleash their inner creative energy.

The Semiotic Universe Interpreted

The integration and recontextualisation of Andersen's fairy tales in China shows the capacity of the fairy tales to register their meaningful values in different social backgrounds and cultures, and to participate in the shaping and reformation of values and beliefs. Andersen's fairy tales have a strong permeability and a sense of fluidity in time and space. This fluidity can always find expression in the perfect integration of the fairy tale signs with the interpreters' world, and such integration of bodily experience and fairy tale signs as a result of the contextual interpretation of them is well demonstrated in the peotic creations of Gu Cheng (顾城, 1956–93), one of China's finest and fervently loved modern romantic poets. Known as a "fairy tale poet," he devoted his whole life to the construction in his poetry of a fairy tale world full of warmth and tenderness, of goodness and beauty. He came of age during the Chinese Cultural Revolution (1966–76), during which a large number of innocent intellectuals were persecuted, and his famous two-line poem "The dark night gave me black eyes, But I use them to seek the light" that is titled "A Generation" (《一代人》, 1979) is considered an accurate representation of the younger generation's struggling in the Cultural Revolution to seek knowledge and future. When Gu Cheng felt lost in his searching for the value of existence and the way to achieve his dream, he found light in Hans Christian Andersen, a transindividual and transhistorical sign that he interpreted in his poetic lines, generating interpretants based on the particular social and cultural experience he had in his youth. Andersen as a sign first appeared in "To Hans Christian Andersen" (《给安徒生》), a poem he created in 1979:

To Hans Christian Andersen
The golden quicksand
Drowned your fairy tales
Together with my
Innocent smile and tears

I believe
All are seeds
Only through burial
Can they enjoy vitality

When I'm back
My hair has turned snowy white
While the desert has turned into
An emerald world

I would like to rest here
Among the flowers and dews
And retrieve
The lost emotions of my childhood.
(1995, 53)

Gu Cheng interpreted the semiotic world of Hans Christian Andersen as transhistorical by putting his mind into it in the first place. Having lived through the darkness and injustice of reality in his youth, he felt a strong sense of frustration in the cruel and ruthless adult world.

Nevertheless, he gained an emotional state of consciousness from Andersen in which the vibrancy, innocence, purity, and excitement of childhood can be experienced again. In "The Puppet-show Man" ("Marionetspilleren," 1851) Andersen wrote, "The whole world is a series of miracles [...] but we're so used to them we call them everyday things." Andersen mediates between Gu Cheng's bodily experience of a cultural "desert" and his aspiration of an "emerald world," bringing him out of the ordinariness to rediscover the miracles in life during the dark age of the Cultural Revolution. According to Merrell, an interpretant is not about "a sign in any raw, unmediated present, but of a sign of the next moment, which, by the time it has become a sign for some interpreter, has been mediated." Though a sign can be determined by relations between the components of the sign, it is its relation to the interpretant that generates meaning to the person. Accordingly, a sign "demands that it be interpreted in (translated into) another sign." (1997, 11).

Gu Cheng's restless heart was consoled in his effort to interpret Andersen's fairy tale signs because they force meaning into existence. All insurmountable barriers yield to his literary imagination: distance, darkness, and death itself are transcended by his fairy tale world. "To Hans Christian Andersen" presents Andersen as a semiotic model that conceptualises how the intellectuals of that generation could create meaning on the bumpy journey out of the desert that had suppressed the minds. One can feel how the historical and cultural forces have moulded the sign in this poem. By referring to Andersen, Gu Cheng articulated his cognitive position which did not accord with the conventional epistemological stance of his time and conceived a world with fresh dynamism and liveliness that the real world of political suppression was devoid of.

A year later Gu Cheng wrote another poem titled "For Hans Christian Andersen, My esteemed teacher" (《给我的尊师安徒生》, 1980):

For Hans Christian Andersen, My Esteemed Teacher
Both Andersen and I used to be clumsy carpenters.
You pushed the woodworking hand plan,
As if you sailed a canoe
On the smooth sea,
Drifting gently …
The wood shavings spread out like waves,

And vanished over the horizon;
The wood grains were the undulant verses,
Sending the greetings of time.
There were no banners,
No gold or silver, nor colourful silks,
But no emperor around the world
Was ever richer than you.
You carried a heavenly world,
Along with the balloons of flowers and dreams,
To your harbour
Of pure childlike innocence.
(1995, 67)

In this poem one sees Andersen as a transindividual sign that strikes a chord in Gu Cheng, and by addressing Andersen as "my esteemed teacher," Gu Cheng revealed his interpretation of this sign as iconic. Throughout the poetic lines he conversed with Andersen, and in Andersen he saw himself as the interpretant. Jørgen Dines Johansen called such a transindividual subjectivity "an anthropological constant" that "represents existential situations and problems that are constant in our species and hence of continuing interest and relevance, or, to put it in an old-fashioned way, are concerned with the universally human." (2002, 385).

In 1981 Gu Cheng wrote four poems dedicated to Hans Christian Andersen's four fairy tales "The Little Mermaid," "The Steadfast Tin Soldier," "Thumbelina," and "The Ugly Duckling:"

The Little Mermaid
In order to stand and live like humans,
You bore the hellish torments.
For the everlasting love and happiness of others,
You'd rather choose to dissolve into foams before dawn.

The Steadfast Tin Soldier
You walked your path steadfastly,
Regardless of abandonment, engulfment or banishment.
No one can ever change your posture as a soldier,
Except the fireplace with the heat of love.

Thumbelina
So dainty and delicate,
Ever the gentle breeze dared to seize you.
I extol the perpetual unrestrained love
That eventually led you into the kingdom of flowers.

The Ugly Duckling
Covered with the crude feathers of ducklings
You had the heart of a swan.
When your body and soul are unified,
You have never forgotten your original appearance.
(1995, 159)

In this collection of four poems, Gu Cheng articulated his interpretation of the semiotic significance of Andersen's fairy tale characters by having dialogic interactions with them. He integrated and contextualised the fairy tale characters into a set of signs denoting the virtues and values that were cherished by the Chinese of his time: the cultivation of a pure soul and an altruistic spirit, the building of passion and perseverance. Besides, the sequence of the four poems maps out Gu Cheng's belief that a pure and beautiful soul will eventually experience nirvana and attain immortality. He interpreted the little mermaid and the tin soldier with the symbolic significance of a pure and sincere soul for which death is not the destination of a life, but a path to nirvana, the kingdom of flowers that embraced Thumbelina. Such a journey of achieving nirvana after death is like the transformation of the ugly duckling. Andersen wrote in the fairy tale:

> Being born in a duck yard does not matter, if only you are hatched from a swan's egg. [...] He did not know what this was all about. He felt so very happy, but he wasn't at all proud, for a good heart never grows proud. He thought about how he had been persecuted and scorned, and now he heard them all call him the most beautiful of all beautiful birds.

Gu Cheng knew "what this was all about," and expressed his view that a noble soul will always remain true to his nature. The four poems, with Andersen's fairy tales as the pre-text, evoke mental images and emotions, and generate the processes of aesthetic semiosis. Gu Cheng's contextualised interpretations of what the fairy tale signs actively facilitate the realisation of the texts in China.

The Semiotic Universe Reconstructed

Andersen-texts are always characterised by semantic indeterminacy that indicate a certain degree of flexibility of the interpretation of its meaning that is not explicitly specified, and thus encourage the high involvement of the readers in generating alternative meanings in a semiotic system that is socially and culturally different from the source texts. In this case, interpretation is "a dialectic of discovery, integration, and rejection" (Johansen 2002, 364) and the recontextualisation of the text in this interpretation process is a reconstruction that produces representations of its own cultural or social meaning.

"The Emperor's New Clothes" ends with the Emperor walking "more proudly than ever, as his noblemen held high the train that wasn't there at all," which, for the Chinese readers, is semantically ambiguous, as they read it with the expectation of the realisation of context-dependent social implications. The image of the Emperor walking more proudly than ever is inconsistent with what is required for the moral construction in the Chinese context. Therefore "What happened afterwards?" is a frequently asked question, and consequently the fairy tale has turned into a pre-text for the Chinese readers to generate new stories that have more specific social functions in China. Various sequels to it are created, reflecting the distinctive social and cultural characteristics of the time. Ye Shengtao (叶圣陶, 1894–1988), the father of Chinese fairy tales, created a sequel that was contextualised in a situation-specific way. The story was first published in the 1970s in his famous fairy tale collection entitled "The Scarecrow" (《稻草人》).

Ye Shengtao started the story with a brief summary of Hans Christian Andersen's "The Emperor's New Clothes," and then posed the question: "What happened after that? Hans Christian Andersen didn't go further. Well, actually, a lot more occurred afterwards." His recontextualisation presented a tyrant who put a bold face on his people and refused to admit the truth that he hadn't anything on. As the procession went on, the officials tried every effort to hold back their laughters, but there were even louder cries and laughs from the crowd.

The irritated tyrant claimed that these new clothes would be his sole outfit and immediately laid down the law that anyone that laughs at the emperor would be sentenced to death. Since then everyone acted warily, out of fear that they might lose their life. But there were always unfortunate people. His favourite concubine was killed simply because she heedlessly blurted out the word "chest" instead of "clothes" when she saw the wine spilling out of the emperor's mouth onto his body when they were drinking together. A scholarly official lost his life because he murmured his wish not to see the emperor anymore when he tendered his resignation to him. On seeing the death of so many, a well-intentioned elderly official decided to do something to change the situation. He implied to the emperor by saying that the clothes looked old and wornout with the intention of persuading him to make a change. But the emperor thought otherwise and insisted that these magical clothes would remain new forever. As a result, the poor old man was sent to prison. Nevertheless, the emperor enjoyed no peace at all. As there were always jeers from here and there, he put an even crueler law in force, demanding that no one should make any sound when he was present. An old man plucked up the courage and humbly said to the emperor, "It's a felony to laugh at our emperor. But please, please don't deprive us of the freedom to talk and laugh." The emperor dismissed his request. Since then, whenever the emperor was out on the street, everyone would run away home and lock up the door. But the emperor had a suspicious mind. He stopped and listened carefully, and was furious to hear whispers behind the doors. He demanded the soldiers to crack open the doors and kill them. However, when the soldiers broke into the houses, all the people, instead of escaping this time, darted towards the emperor and pinched him together. They shouted: "Tear away your clothes of vanity." All the soldiers, instead of protecting the emperor, joined the crowd and laughed, and the story ended with the emperor helplessly collapsing on the ground (Ye Shengtao 2013, 13–19).

Ye Shengtao retained the title of Andersen's fairy tale for his articulation of the emperor's story, which yields a strong contextual relation with the Andersen pre-text that enacts the intertextual communication in a structured system of social occasion. The communicative practice is not a static or abstract process of production, but "a critical intervention directed toward the exposing, challenging, and changing of those social meaning-making practices that function to conceal and to maintain illegitimate and repressive relations of power and domination in the social order." (Bernstein 1982, 320–321). Ye Shengtao integrated the social agent of the long and dark decade of the Chinese Cultural revolution (1966–76), and great social and political turmoil of the time he bitterly experienced in his old age into the reconstruction and recontextualisation of Andersen's fairy tale. This has a great critical potential, "whereby social agents can intervene in, challenge, and change social meaning making practices, conceived as models of social action." (Silverman and Torode 1980, 340). It also shows the potential of those who are not yet voiced to have their social concerns voiced. Moreover, as J.R.R. Tolkien elaborated in his essay "On Fairy-Stories" (1947, 58-59): "if written with art, the prime value of fairy-stories will simply be that value which, as literature, they share with other literary forms. But fairy-stories offer also, in a peculiar degree or mode, these things: Fantasy, Recovery, Escape, Consolation." Ye Shengtao's narrative hints at a fantasy within, how people were suppressed and were deprived of their right to voice their opinions during the dark decade, and the happy ending of the story creates a fantasy for people who suffered mistreatment and gives consolation to all that had struggled for freedom and democracy in that decade. His attempt to re-envision the fairy tale serves not only the purpose of reinterpreting what the fairy tale represents, but the purpose of figuring out what it can do to his contemporaries.

There are many other versions of the sequel to this fairy tale that are more recently created in the virtual community on the Baidu[1] online forum. One of them, integrating the element of science fiction, describes how the desperate emperor is cheated again by two other swindlers who declare themselves to be from the 26th century and introduce a new-tech material that is woven by light, mixing the story with high-tech elements in today's world. The swindlers claim that although transparent in appearance, it can be painted with colours that can be erased with great ease and be replaced by other colours at any time. This recontextualisation ends with the emperor having to endure the ugliness of the terribly colour-stained skin. In another version tinged with the element of detective story, the swindlers are caught with the help of the little child who uttered the truth in Andersen's tale and the emperor is finally enlightened by the letter from the child and becomes fully committed to his people. In this version the new imaginative fabric joins some of the oldest to present a positive outlook for the readers. There is an important connection here in which literary imagination and cultural enrichment are close friends. There is a transgressive power in the literary imagination, in other words, it expands the concept of the real, replacing absence with presence, and superseding presence with newness. Besides, it offers to the mind a vision of how things could be, and therefore, people can be motivated to think out of the box, and encouraged to challenge the prevalent norms and values, and participate in the construction of wider cultural and social contexts.

Conclusion

By a semiotic approach, the chapter expounds that the acceptance of Andersen's fairy tales as signs of purity, passion and perseverance, and the re-envisioning and remoulding of Andersen signs to achieve integration and acculturation in a specific cultural or social context is a process of empowerment for both the Chinese readers and Andersen's fairy tales. Consequently, the fairy tales find their added value in the space beyond the value endowed by Andersen, a space where ideas are surpassed.

Chinese readers of Andersen's fairy tales may well transcend time and space to interact with Andersen's stories and produce their interpretations and recontexualisations from diversified angles and perspectives of the literary signs they receive in the texts. The signs the readers get, the different interpretations they provide, and the contextualisation and recontextualisation they proceed with in varied semiotic processes, all contribute to building a culture of continuous improvement. As the interpretation of signs is a participatory process, Andersen's fairy tales are continuously rejuvenated and injected with new vitality in China. In such an intersubjective interaction, Andersen and his fairy tales are not only the trace of past practice, but a dialogic process in the here and now. The continuous parallel between contemporaneity and antiquity not only brings fresh air to the fairy tales, but also provides rich nutrients and inspirations to the readers.

Andersen wrote in his autobiography *The True Story of My life* that he met a a good fairy in his childhood who said to him "Choose now thy own course through life, and the object for which thou wilt strive, and then, according to the development of thy mind, and as reason requires, I will guide and defend thee to its attainment." (2016, 2–3).

This is exactly what this semiotic romantic has done. His fairy tales and readers beyond his time and space are like the möbius strip, apparently two-sided, but always interrelated and intertwined: continuous and never ending. And the two sides are always in conversation on the way. We hear Andersen's fairy tales from many years ago, but as we listen, we begin to feel an intimacy and immediacy of that long ago moment so that Andersen is very much present with us during the storytelling, guiding the way and consoling the souls. But he doesn't have the only take on a sign or symbol, he takes the readers worldwide on a journey through his fairy tale semiotic system to enrich their understanding of the signs he invites them to consider. Readers can use their own collateral experience to add to the meaning and signification of what Andersen brings to the conversation. And it is, of course, in such a conversation that Andersen's literary imagination continues to be enlivened and empowered.

References

Andersen, Hans Christian. 2016. *The True Story of My Life: A Sketch*. Translated by Mary Howitt. CreateSpace Independent Publishing Platform.

Bernstein, Basil. 1982. "Codes, modalities and the process of cultural reproduction: A model." In *Cultural and Economic Reproduction in Education: Essays on Class, Ideology and the State*, edited by Michael W. Apple, 304–355. London and Boston: Routledge & Kegan Paul.

Deely, John. 1990. *Basics in Semiotics*. Bloomington: Indiana University Press.

Giddens, Anthony. 1989. *Sociology*. Cambridge: Polity Press.

Gu Cheng. 1995. *Complete Works of Gu Cheng* (《顾城诗全编》). Shanghai: Joint Publishing House.

Johansen, Jørgen Dines. 2002. *Literary Discourse: A Semiotic-Pragmatic Approach to Literature*. Toronto: University of Toronto Press.

King, Anthony D., ed. 1991. *Culture, Globalisation and the World System: Contemporary Conditions for the Representation of Identity*. London: Macmillan.

Merrell, Floyd. 1997. *Peirce, Signs, and Meaning*. Toronto: University of Toronto Press.

Peirce, Charles Sanders. 1934. *Pragmatism and Pragmaticism*. Edited by Charles Hartshorne and Paul Weiss. Vol. 5 of *The Collected Papers of Charles Sanders Peirce*, edited by Charles Hartshorne, Paul Weiss, and Arthur W. Burks. Cambridge, MA: Harvard University Press. 1931–58.

Peirce, Charles Sanders. 1955. "Logic and Semiotic: The Theory of Signs." In *Philosophical Writings of Peirce*, edited by Justus Buchler, 98–119. New York: Dove Publications.

Said, Edward. 1994. *Culture and Imperialism.* London: Vintage.
Silverman, David, and Brain Torode. 1980. *The Material Word: Some Theories of Language and Its Limits.* London/Boston: Routledge & Kegan Paul.
Thibault, Paul J. 1991. *Social Semiotics as Praxis: Text, Social Meaning Making, and Nabokov's Ada.* Minneapolis, MN: University of Minnesota Press.
Tolkien, J. R. R. 1947. "On Fairy Stories." In *Essays Presented to Charles Williams,* compiled by C. S. Lewis, 38-89. Oxford: Oxford University Press.
Ye Shengtao. 2013. *The Scarecrow: Collected works of Ye Shengtao* (《稻草人：叶圣陶作品菁华集》). Hunan: Hunan Literature and Art Publishing House.

Notes

1 https://zhidao.baidu.com/question/562304976116640244.html. Baidu Zhidao (百度知道) is a Baidu-search-engine-based online interactive knowledge sharing platform.

Performing Fairy Tales
Possibilities of Practicing Difference in the Museum

Henrik Lübker
Odense City Museums

Together with the exhibition design firm Event Communications Japanese starachitect Kengo Kuma has won the bid to rebuild the existing Hans Christian Andersen Museum from the ground up – in doing so transforming the biographical museum into a 'house of fairy tales.' However, in an Andersenian world, objects, plants, animals and stories show signs of agency and struggle for self-determination. They are not willingly reduced to traditional static museum objects – nor should they be. This chapter discusses how the performative strategies of Andersen's fairy tales can inform and question key museological concepts and practice, thereby opening for new ways of experiencing difference through adapting and staging such strategies as a foundation for the phenomenological experience of visiting an exhibition. As such, the chapter highlights the democratic potential of both Andersen's fairy tales and the museum as communal sites, which not only includes difference thematically, but produces it through form.

When Hans Christian Andersen published his first collection of fairy tales in 1835 critics were alarmed by the lack of formative qualities and moral lessons in the stories (Anonymous 1836, 13). Instead of handing down lessons, explicating the meaning of the story or the world for the reader, Andersen seemed to do quite the opposite in his fairy tales, playing on forms of textual doubleness that counteracted and frustrated any attempt to establish a final, meaningful moral lesson when turning that last page. In this way, his fairy tales are performative – they both say *and* do something (Lübker and Bøggild, forthcoming) – and instead of providing answers the fairy tales provoke questions for the readers to ponder over themselves.

In this chapter the possibilities of using Andersen's fairy tales and the challenge of representing their performative aspects to shed new light on the nature of the museum and its democratic potential will be explored. By utilising ways in which the fairy tales both create and disrupt the meaning-making of the reader as a lens, key concepts of the museum exhibition – the exhibition space, museum text, and the role of objects – are revisited and analysed in dialogue with museological, educational and phenomenological positions. By doing this, the chapter argues that Andersen's fairy tales hold performative power, which, when adapted to the exhibition space, has the potential to create a unique democratic and communal experience, not just by embracing individual difference as an institution, but also by confronting the emancipated, powerful individual with difference, with otherness. To achieve this requires a new form of museology. Just as Andersen's fairy tales frustrate and counteract meaningfulness before it solidifies, the museum must do the same: Challenging the visitor to reflect upon and engage with the world anew by destabilising fixed notions, reading history against the grain, inciting new questions, creating wonder and inspiring utopian reimagination.

The Emancipated Visitor

Looking at how ICOM, The International Council of Museums, presents and understands the communicative relationship between institution and visitor in their description of key museological concepts, the museum as an institution seems almost juxtaposed to the fairy tale world of questions and fantasy, stressing transmission and unilateral assimilation of knowledge (Desvallées and Mairesse 2018, 30). Such ideas about the relationship between subject and institution in which the subject is rendered completely passive have historically been challenged by, for example, the ecomuseums of the 1970s and the emergence of New Museology in the late 1980s (Vergo 1989). By embracing participatory practices and focusing on visitors' knowledge production, the idea has been to reform the museum into a democratic, communal institution, thereby empowering people (Vergo

1989, 3; Simon 2010, ii-iii). However, putting the visitor instead of the institution at the centre of things tends to merely reverse the hierarchy rather than to dissolve it altogether (Lübker 2016).

This hierarchical understanding of the relationship between institution and visitor seems to have been presupposed in both classical museology and New Museology, yet it is not without problems. Firstly, the communicative practice of exhibitions may historically have been hierarchical in one way or the other, but as a phenomenological space – as a meeting ground between visitor, material objects, and scenography – exhibitions challenge notions of hierarchy, explication and mere assimilation regardless of the intent of the curator, the institution, or even the visitor. Secondly, the rendering of the visitor as someone who passively assimilates knowledge hardly holds true irrespective of the communication design. This is something philosopher Jacques Ranciére has already pointed to in his writings on the juxtaposition between actor and spectator at the theatre:

> The spectator also acts, like the pupil or scholar. She observes, selects, compares, interprets. She links what she sees to a host of other things that she has seen on other stages, in other kinds of place. She composes her own poem with the elements of the poem before her. She participates in the performance by refashioning it in her own way […]. (2011, 13)

Never someone to be emancipated by the doings of the institution, the visitor, the recipient, is powerful and free from the very beginning. Hans-Thies Lehman explores this as well in his seminal book *Postdramatic Theatre* (2006), examining a new form of theatre, which has left behind the idea of the stage as a site in which actors and director try to transfer some original, hidden meaning from the manuscript to the audience passively watching. In such a theatre "the stage is the beginning and point of departure, not a site for transcription or copying." (32). Stressing the immediacy of perception, aesthetic experience and performance over representation and meaning, this form of postdramatic theatre emphasises the shared experience of the here and now. As such it disregards any traditional dichotomy between actor and spectator, active and passive, acknowledging instead whatever happens as a shared creation. Something similar is happening in Andersen's fairy tale universe. Just as a play is bound to linear time, so is a story or a fairy tale. However, like postdramatic theatre, Andersen's fairy tales do not necessarily lead us anywhere, but rather at the end leave us ever questioning the moral lesson or meaning or even the veracity of the tale. For example, "The Princess on the Pea" ("Prindsessen paa Ærten," 1835) ends by stating that "there, that's a true story," leaving it up to the reader do decide whether it was a *true* story or a true *story*. This way, Andersen's fairy tale universe is defined by ambiguity, doubleness and the flattening of hierarchy, leading Klaus P. Mortensen to describe it as "not static, centred, but constantly expanding, escaping all centredness" (2007, 288, my translation).

As a stage, as the meeting point between reader and text, Andersen's fairy tale universe is therefore not democratic because it embraces and includes the viewer. Contrarily, it is so because it actively rejects and works against both its own linearity, and the desire of the reader to reach an end, a finality of meaning. The fairy tales thrive on the tension between apparent opposed meanings of a tale which both incite interpretations and at the same time question the veracity of such interpretations and prompt the reader to consider them anew. By Andersen's frequent use of unreliable narration, romantic irony, play on words and so forth the fairy tales insist on a position of decentredness or in-betweenness at their very centre.

It is precisely this focus on the in-between which is also at play when museologist Barbara Kirshenblatt-Gimblett redescribes museums as a "force field between subject and object" defined by its gaps:

> The disjointed world brought into the museum, its pieces arranged in space, is defined by gaps (gaps in the record, gaps in the collection, gaps in the narrative) and by leaps (intuitive leaps, poetic leaps, leaps of faith). The gaps, the air between things, are not simply voids. They are openings. (2004, 2)

Kirshenblatt-Gimblett points to the fact that the representational mode of the museum is fundamentally underdetermined leaving plenty of gaps for the visitor's interpretation. This is something Lehmann has also described when it comes to the theatre image and literature. Unlike for example film or photographs the less dense reproduction of reality exhibits a lot of gaps, thereby allowing both intention and interpretation (Lehmann 2006, 116; Adorno 1974, 142). Arguably, the gaps are an even more definitive trait of the museum than of literature or theatre, since museum objects (at least in cultural history museums) are exhibited as metonymical representations of an underlying totality. As such it is the very absence of that reality that is brought to fore by the object. Also, whereas literature and theatre bind the reader or spectator to a progressive linear experience, the visitor at a museum is free to create his or her own linearity, stressing the interpretation and imagination of the individual visitor. Kirshenblatt-Gimblett thus presents a completely different understanding of the communicative possibilities of the museum than the transmission model previously mentioned (Desvallées and Mairesse 2018, 30). Looking at the formal and phenomenological aspects of the exhibition space, the defining trait of the museum might not be understood by the passive assimilation of knowledge but by the mobility and activity of the visitor (Kirshenblatt-Gimblett 2004, 4). Ultimately, the exhibition space is there at the disposal of the visitor to be navigated and interpreted. For Kirshenblatt-Gimblett however, this marks not merely a shift from an institutionally induced knowledge transmission to the knowledge production of the visitor, but also a shift from the real to the imaginative. It allows not only for the institution to *represent* utopia, but more importantly, the exhibition space becomes a site for the visitor actively "practising it as a way of imagining it" (1). Following this understanding of the exhibition site it seems as if the visitor is almost omnipotent in his or her shaping of meaning by filling gaps to recreate the world in his or her own individual utopian image.

However, whereas Kirshenblatt-Gimblett seems to almost revel in the utopian possibility of a site where everything can be undone and remade by the imagination of the God-like visitor, to properly represent the performative aspects of Andersen's fairy tales and unleash the democratic potential of the exhibition site something else is needed. By shattering the illusion of make-believe, clearly stressing the artificiality of the tales, by challenging the linear progression of a narrative's promise of meaning, Andersen keeps the reader in a state of openness – engaged in a dialogue with the world rather than roaming freely above it. Likewise, the exhibition site must combat synthesis – by striving to become a place of in-between where meaning is never entirely settled, always under negotiation, and therefore a place where the visitor is a subject in a continuous dialogue with the world around him or her. In the museum, he or she is just as susceptible to an undoing or reconfiguration of the 'I.' He or she too is not only shaping the world but is also being shaped by it.

The Performativity of the Gaze

By focusing on key words like the journey, play, and transformation the development of the new Hans Christian Andersen Museum has had the aim of creating a *Gesamtkunstwerk* in which architecture and exhibition form a phenomenological experience of Andersen's fairy tale universe. Since this universe is more a performative doing rather than a passive being, this is also reflected in the spatialisation of content and architecture. Already when entering the garden surrounding the future museum the design constantly shifts between creating smaller spaces by using hedges as envelopments and opening up sight lines. For the visitor exploring the garden it is thus an experience of continually shifting relations between the visitor and his or her surroundings. Whereas the sight lines empower the visitor's understanding of space and thereby allow the visitor to be in control, the hedges of the smaller enveloped spaces do the opposite. They tower above the visitor to a height of up to 6 meters, cutting off the vision and making the visitor diminutive in comparison. The manipulation of the landscape plane creates a similar effect by blurring the line between below and above ground, questioning even what ground is. In this way, already before entering the exhibition or even the museum, there's a play going on in which opposites start to dissolve and spill over their own borders, intertwining to the point where categorial distinctions give way and present themselves as questions rather than answers.

The exhibition itself is devised into three main sections – the author, the fairy tales and legacy – forming an overarching narrative, which is meant to go from our rational and well-known reality into the unreality of the fairy tales and back to our world in the last part of the exhibition focusing on Andersen's birthplace as a memorial site. The overarching narrative thus forms a typical home-away-from-home structure. In this case the logic behind the progression through the exhibition is that the man gives birth to the fairy tales which create his legacy and thereby give birth to the museum visit. Following this, the journey through the exhibition also mimics such a form of empowering of the visitor: At the beginning of the exhibition it is clearly the voices of the institution that are given the most space, but as the journey progresses into the realm of fairy tales it becomes more of a dialogue between visitor and fairy tales, and when the journey ends at the actual birthplace the voice of the institution falls silent, giving way to the individual feelings and experience of each visitor.

However, the individual scenes of the journey consist of many more departures than homecomings and thus frustrate the meaning-making process of the visitor by challenging set notions, raising questions while providing few answers.

Upon entering the exhibition, the first part is dedicated to Andersen but instead of treating it as a traditional biographical exhibition presenting the facts of his life, the museum plays with the idea that Andersen is an author narrating his own life through his writings – among these his three different autobiographies – which tell quite different stories. Andersen does not present facts – he performs and presents himself in certain ways to make the recipient see him in a certain light. In this way the biographical realm is not so much about telling the story of a person as it is about elucidating the process of becoming a person through the act of storytelling, of narrating one's own life. On a slowly descending ramp Andersen presents the visitor with select and idealised scenes from his life in a linear chronology thereby forming a narrative. But such an idealised narrative is at the same time questioned and destabilised as the visitor goes along. Firstly, this is done architecturally by manipulating light in ways that make the experience of space unreal – for example by filtering daylight from outside through hedges and glass. Secondly, every now and then one side of the ramp expands into thematic sections, which question and contrasts with the idealised narrative of Andersen. By doing this the museum explores the narrative, the biographical, and also the complexity of Andersen, by opening up multiple perspectives on the same events. The thematic section about "Love" for example tells quite a different story than Andersen himself does. Whereas Andersen often told the story that the reason for his failures in love was his poor financial situation, the objects relating to his different love interests question this, instead revealing a story in which his failures at love are just as much lucky escapes as tragedies. Instead of just being a story of loneliness and failure, "Love" also becomes a story of lability – of a love that goes wherever it will, but never dares to settle down or truly manifest itself as a relation. In this way the museum is widening the gaps in an otherwise linear and idealised narrative, creating a spatial encounter between contrasting perspectives that not only force the visitor to navigate the space and construct his own narrative, but also challenge any attempt at synthesis and thereby highlight that such narratives ultimately are constructions: Any narrative is created only by abandoning other perspectives that are just as valid.

The linear, chronological route down the ramp naturally comes to an end, with old age and fame, with death, but the promise of knowledge and wisdom implied in such a journey eludes both the visitor and Andersen. As Klaus P. Mortensen (2007) has noted, Andersen has an uncanny ability to present himself, to narrate himself, in ways that make himself visible to the other. But although the biographical realm shows how Andersen does this (as we all do), it also highlights the vulnerability of being exposed to the gaze of the other. We make ourselves and are made in the gaze of the other. This is never clearer than in this final section of the biographical descent, "Reflections," where Andersen is fragmented by the multiple perspectives of a communal murmur, constructing him both as a person and phenomenon, and thereby also deconstructing his own singular narrative. Stressing the relation between seeing and being seen, the gaze of the visitor is also returned since all the showcases are made of mirrors. As such the descent down the biographical realm does not add up to a meaningful whole or a final fixed narrative, and as the story reaches its end visitors are left with the double experience of both the creative power and vulnerability of being a subject – and with those final words of Andersen somehow marking a fitting end to his own fairy tale: "I know nothing at all." (1971–77, 10:482, my translation).

By challenging fixed notions and allowing for a multitude of voices and viewpoints a gap is opened which calls for continual self-reflection and interpretation. Arguably, this is a precise experience of both the radically contingent subject of modernity as well as of Hans Christian Andersen: As a "nowhere man" coming into being by the very positioning of himself to be seen and thus also to be defined by an exterior gaze (Mortensen 2007, 10). Philosopher Edmund Husserl has described such play between seeing and being seen as a form of exteriorisation in which the subject becomes self-conscious through seeing itself from the point of the other (1973, 175). Such an exteriorised subject, who is able to reflect upon his or her relation to the world, is fundamentally destabilised (Sartre 1956, 282), being caught in the in-between of positions, continually in a process of becoming, of the reformulation of self and its connection to its surroundings. The contrasting narratives, different ways of seeing the world, and the play between seeing and being seen are ways in which the museum strengthens the experience of the other and thereby also the experience of difference.

Spatialised Encounters

In the biographical realm the museum presents Andersen through existential rather than historical themes, thereby stressing the relevance of his story to visitors today. Likewise, the realm of fairy tales centres on twelve of the most iconic and well-known tales which are given scale so they form a world of their own that the visitor walks into and is immersed by. Unlike the linear progression of the biographical realm, here the visitor is free to roam and explore. The fairy tale realm thus empowers the visitor both by the mode through which it encourages visitors to experience the space and through its seemingly well-known fairy tale content. However, following Andersen's own strategies, the fairy tales do not always behave as expected.

One of the most important principles in developing the strategies for representing the fairy tales has been to stage the fundamental tensions and ambiguities of the fairy tales instead of providing an authoritative interpretation of them. As Andersen often highlights the fairy tales as constructions, thereby establishing a play between words as both content and material that challenge the stories as conveyers of meaning and truth, so we, as readers, immerse ourselves in the rich imagination of Andersen, only to be thrown back out of the fantasy whenever Andersen shatters the illusion. The fairy tales invite hermeneutic interpretation yet work against any final synthesis. By doing this, they are an act of opening up, a performative relation between text and reader, where the usual and well-known is made special and begs to be seen anew. To create this spatially means exploring the performative relationships as they appear in the fairy tales. The staging of the fairy tales has therefore been structured on contradictions and ambivalence, on emptying central signs of their content while giving weight to the understated, on making ambivalence and doubleness tangible to make visible the playfulness inherent in each of the fairy tales. One notable way of doing this is by striving for material authenticity at all times. This means that the museum wishes to represent Andersen in ways that do not give privilege to the content side, but rather establish a play between the material and what the material represents, thereby highlighting the world of Andersen as both realistic and constructed at the same time.

The staging of "The Little Mermaid" ("Den lille Havfrue," 1837) is an example of how architecture and scenography come together to create a spatial experience of the fairy tale. From the garden above you can see through a small pool of water into the fairy tale realm below. Likewise, from below you can see a cut-out of the sky through the pool of water. At the same time the pool of water acts as a filter: Combined with the light from above, the water creates a ripple effect on the walls which emphasises the experience of being submerged. As such the scenography always presents itself as a unique encounter between visitor and fairy tale. The story is never told in completely the same way – the meeting between visitor and fairy tale is always new since the light from outside changes during the day and the season. And because the pool is enveloped by a mirroring of the hedges above ground the eyes of the visitor are naturally drawn upwards, following the vertical axis from under water to ground to air. In the under water space, the little mermaid is absent and as such the space becomes an empty stage for the longing gaze of the visitor. By doing this it is no longer a representation of the story of the little mermaid but an architectural and scenographical performance which allows visitors to experience the longing and absence of the little mermaid spatially. Such a shift is supported by various readings of the fairy tale, stressing it as performative in the way that it engages and frustrates the meaning-making production of the reader (Bøggild 2012, 96–97), thereby becoming a form of "delayed death" in which longing and hope has not yet given in to that end all stories must come to (Møller 1995). Following this, the fairy tale spills over its borders in its postponement of its own end. Longing vibrates long after the last words have been read due to its open-ended conclusion pointing towards uncertainty which also is embodied in the original Danish text's final utterance: the em dash. In such a reading, the fairy tale is just as much a story of the reader's longing for meaning and closure as it is a story of the longing of the mermaid, and thereby, by keeping the longing alive beyond the borders of the text, the linear narrative with its promise of meaning and finality transforms into the spatial relation in which text and reader are dialectically entwined in the process of becoming.

"The Little Match Girl" ("Den lille Pige med Svovlstikkerne," 1848) is also concerned with endings and meaning. While many people regard it as a form of social realism showing Andersen's empathy for the poor, the fairy tale is, however, more about the reader or viewer than it is about the plight of those who are down and out – and not in the simple moralistic sense that we should give more to beggars. Firstly, the description of the reality for the little match girl is presented as hyperbole, pointing almost to the text as a construction rather than realism. Secondly, the descriptions are systematic in their portrayal of her sorry life from top to bottom, outside to inside. Bareheaded and having lost her shoes (which were too big in the first place) she has nothing to shield herself from the cold. And while it is cold outside, going home would be even worse: At home the roof is no shield against the wind and she also gets beaten. Andersen thus strips her of everything and isolates her. Thirdly, there amidst ultimate despair, the otherwise empathetic narrator suddenly takes delight in the beauty of it all, performing the role of an almost sadistic voyeur:

> Shivering with cold and hunger, she crept along, a picture of misery, poor little girl! The snowflakes fell on her long fair hair, which hung in pretty curls over her neck, *but certainly she did not think of such things*. In all the windows lights were shining, and there was a wonderful smell of roast goose, for it was New Year's Eve. Yes, she thought of that! (in italics: my translation of a sentence omitted by Hersholt)

Much more than being social realism "The Little Match Girl" points to the pleasures of seeing – in particular seeing someone or reading about someone worse off than yourself. It was exactly as one such pleasurable activity it became a popular tale to read out loud by the fireplace in the homes of the middle class in the last half of the 19th century (Lützen 1998, 120). Just as Andersen critically points to the fact that there is delight in the image of misery, the museum also wants to stress this aspect of the tale rather than its popularity as a tearjerker. In the museum's staging the visitor becomes the active part, since it is his or her desire for the narrative to continue which drives it onwards. By actively turning the pages, "lighting matches," the visitor triggers the story onwards to its end, thereby being complicit in the misery and untimely death of both story and the match girl.

Whereas the biographical realm was very much a deconstruction of linear narrative performed by the museum, the fairy tale realm is based on the immanent tensions of the fairy tales. Thereby, the museum withdraws somewhat in order to stage the complexity of the tales in an adequate manner for the fairy tales to be performed. In the final area, "Legacy," which consists of buildings from the old museum, the memorial hall and birthplace, the museum withdraws even further in order to create a space of contemplation in which the previous experiences can be reflected upon. As sites of remembrance, both the memorial hall and the birthplace are ultimately empty. They are there to be filled by the feelings and reflections of the visitors. Following this, the birthplace is stripped back to its most authentic state presenting the actual room he was born in as nothing but a humble shell, thereby juxtaposing the humble beginnings with the richness of his life and work.

Performance Text

The museum text is perhaps where the ideology of the museum's mode of communication is most clearly expressed through form. This is because the museum text is both a way to frame content and to direct the gaze of the visitor. Museum text is thus distancing because it is saying something about something other than itself. As a consequence, text places, the visitor on the outside of the scene or object it points to, severing the bodily connection between the visitor and object and the text directs the gaze of the visitor towards the object in a certain manner, thereby trying to control the relationship between the two. This leads not only to the museum as a learning environment based on transmission, but also to institutions perpetuating class structures in society rather than democratic community. By being told of objects, scenes, places, and life the visitor "learns" his or her place in society, as stressed by the definition of museal communication mentioned at the beginning of this chapter.

This is something Jacques Rancière points to in *The Ignorant Schoolmaster*. Just as he challenged the idea of the visitor or spectator as a passive recipient of institutionally transmitted messages, he also challenges the idea of transmission and explication. Explication, he says, is as a subtle and perverse form of oppression because to explain something to someone "is first of all to show him he cannot understand it by himself." (1991, 6). By explaining and interpreting the world for the visitor, a museum strips the visitors of their right to interpret their own reality. In such a structure the visitor remains forever less competent, less knowledgeable, since whatever knowledge the visitor attains has been granted through explication by another. Although attempts have been made to challenge such a textual praxis allowing visitor imagination to come more into play (Ekarv 1991), museum texts as a genre remains – even in their best versions – a generic, but effective, way to talk *about* and tell *of* something rather than it is a way to talk *as* something.

To avoid both explication and the distancing of text, the museum has explored new ways of communicating to create something Andersenian rather than reproducing the voice of an authoritarian museum. By treating text as material objects, they become set pieces rather than something external to the different fairy tale scenes. For example, in staging "Clumsy Hans" ("Klods-Hans," 1855), text is presented in the form of a tabloid newspaper, in "The Snow Queen" ("Sneedronningen," 1845) they are shattered words on the floor, and in "The Princess and the Pea" (Prindsessen paa Ærten," 1835) they are in the form of lengthy traditional museum text panels ironically claiming expert knowledge and truth when *explaining* how it is feasible that a princess really can feel a pea through twenty mattresses. Also, by employing new audio-technology it is possible to create a binaural experience in which voices are not an accompanying and distancing overlay to the spatial experience but embedded therein. By doing so it is also possible to emphasise the unique oral and tonal qualities of Andersen's writing and play through the different ways Andersen creates distance and intimacy, for example using humour and irony. Furthermore, it allows the museum to create a world in which a multitude of voices are present just as it is in Andersen's fairy tales. Objects come alive and speak offering often contrasting perspectives to the narrated voice of Andersen – each claiming truth. As such, the museum gives credence to the idea of polyphony rather than singular authoritarian communication. Thus, by offering conflicting perspectives, by being spatialised and embedded in the scenography on the same level as an object, a showcase or a set piece, text becomes something more than a vessel for content. It becomes a system of signs that is "more presence than representation, more shared than communicated experience, more process than product, more manifestation than signification, more energetic impulse than information." (Lehmann 2006, 85). Therefore, the significance of text does not as much reside in the supposed meaning it conveys but in its performative aspects. The same, I would argue, is true in Andersen's fairy tales. In "Thumbelina" ("Tommelise," 1835) for example, the whole fairy tale and proposed meaningfulness stems from a point of absence of meaning – from the incomprehensible "Chirp, chirp! Chirp, chirp!" of the once dead swallow. Following this, the fairy tale maintains a balance between representing something and being essentially 'bird singing:' An experience of the expressiveness and performance of something different than yourself but not something from which you can derive final meaning. In the same manner, it is through its act of making something visible, through the spatial distribution of unique voices, the call-response dialogue and deconstruction of these voices, the expressiveness and tonal qualities that text becomes a sensuous bodily experience in the museum.

Beyond Objecthood

A museum is a strange place for an object. It is through the collections and objects put on display that the foundation of a museum is laid, yet the museum is never truly the object's home. By placing objects in museums, they are severed from their social reality and thereby reduced to a mere semblance of an object. They become representations, metonymies, and the story of museums is therefore much more the story of man's power to displace, to hoard objects into the treasure holds called museums than it is a story of the objects themselves. Museum practice thereby inscribes meaning in objects by depriving the objects of their own meaningfulness. The museum becomes a celebration of man's ability to amass, manipulate, create and control objects and materials. Instead of widening perspectives, multiplying stories, displaying plurality, museums become the history of man presented as a form of inescapable fate in which the narrative of western society and the present as the pinnacle of civilisation is popularised (Witcomb 2007, 107).

The world view presented by Andersen in his fairy tales is, however, remarkably different. Having an eye for the stories of that which is overlooked, forgotten or disregarded, Andersen paints a world in which a plethora of voices intermingle – each with their own trajectory. Objects, plants, animals and stories all show signs of agency and struggle for self-determination. This struggle arises from the tension between their desire to escape objecthood while at the same time being defined by it. Defined by traits stemming from their biology, the material they are made of or the function they are given, their horizon seems limited and materially bound – for peas in a pod the whole world is green. Following this they are caught up in their own trajectories, unable to change paths and free themselves from their materiality. Although they exist in relation to their surroundings, as objects they can see nothing else other than their own story and therefore often come across as both petty and narrowminded. In this sense the multivocal world of Andersen is not one of dialogue but of miscommunication: filled with radically different voices which ultimately fail to truly relate to each other. Consider for example "The Sweethearts" ("Kjærestefolkene," 1844) who are so defined by their different respective natures that a relationship is impossible – the top can do nothing other than touch the ground since spinning is its primary function whereas the ball can do nothing but jump. One world is vertical and the other horizontal – but where their paths cross is the site of the fairy tale since this is the place where an irreconcilable difference emerges.

Such fairy tales have been likened to (Thomsen 2017, 57) what philosopher Jane Bennett has defined as assemblages: "[...] ad hoc groupings of diverse elements, of vibrant materials of all sorts. Assemblages are living, throbbing confederations that are able to function despite the persistent presence of energies that confound them from within." (2010, 24–25). But where Bennett's vital materialism sees such assemblages as a positive manifestation of "thing-power" and talks about them in terms of "a productive power on their own" (3), I remain more skeptical of their supposed quasi-agency. Andersen's fairy tales may display an abundance of assemblages and may show plenty of objects resisting reduction to a mere product of human intentionality, but they are never truly able to escape their own objecthood and so present themselves as something in themselves.

Again "Thumbelina" is a notable example of this. Thumbelina is searching for a meaningful relation in which the other sees and recognises her as a person instead of just a function of the desire of others. She wishes to transcend her own objecthood. At the end of the fairy tale Thumbelina seems to transcend her dehumanising identity when she is named Maya, thus apparently escaping the confines of her own materiality as something that defines her. But such a happy ending is only achieved by transporting Thumbelina into a magical place beyond the known world, where rules of nature do not apply – it is from such a utopian world that the swallow has carried its story to the ear of the teller of fairy tales. The unreal quality of the happy ending thus reverses the notion of transcending objecthood into its opposite: it becomes a story about the implausibility of freeing yourself from the material constraints you are determined and bound by.

In Andersen's world objects may strive for autonomy and claim to be something more than just objects, but they can only do so in a manner that objectifies them. The fairy tales are therefore characterised by a fundamental doubleness. On one hand, the fairy tales do not so much express thing-power as mourn their inability to truly achieve such a thing. On the other hand, they fail gloriously in a way that may not coalesce into a final meaningful whole, but that displays a semiotic abundance and take delight in performativity, creation, and playfulness as they fall apart. Following this, Bennett's ideas of object agency and thing-power has potential if it is seen as a form of play-pretend rather than ontological truth, allowing the museum to let the different voices of objects come to the fore, not merely as a form of mourning, but also as a playful celebration of difference and multi-vocality. Instead of focusing on their impossibility, a new materialist perspective allows the museum to play, recognise and not least stage human participation in a shared, vital materiality (2010, 14).

Therefore, in the new museum, objects are staged in a way where they are not willingly reduced to traditional static museum objects or employed as tools in a story by Andersen. On the contrary, they disrupt and defamiliarise, they protest and answer back. They do not merely want to be objects put on display for others and are no longer representations, metonymies, pointing to an underlying meaningful whole. Instead, focus shifts from what they represent to how they represent it – from being a vessel for content to displaying agency in themselves. They do this by highlighting the materiality they are bound by and offering contrasting perspectives. As such notions of hierarchy and meaning are destabilised since there is no privileged point of view, each perspective is isolated in its own limited vision and defined by its own materiality. Self-absorbed and petty, they are unable to see past their own noses. In this way, pen and inkstand keep quarreling even when on display in the museum. As a matter of fact, maybe they refuse to even share the same showcase, each making their own case for why they should be the centre of attention. One of Andersen's travelling passports may be out travelling, and is not there to be seen at all, while other objects can deem themselves too important to be shown to the visitor for more than five minutes in an hour (which is also a way of dealing with conservation issues for the museum) while others may be completely self-absorbed like the flowers in the flower garden in "The Snow Queen:" "I can see myself! I can see myself! Oh, how sweet is my own fragrance!" Others again dream of transforming themselves. The poem wants to be read aloud or sung to the sweetheart it was meant for instead of being put in a book. The papercuts want to be more than motions frozen in time. The museum stages those dreams, those voices.

Visiting Unfamiliarity: Concluding Remarks

This chapter has examined how the museum exhibition as phenomenological space can work together with strategies of performativity in Andersen's fairy tales to inform new ways of thinking and unleashing the democratic potential of the museum. By developing a scenography inspired by the play between form and content in Andersen's fairy tales, the new Hans Christian Andersen Museum does not tell of things or explicate scenes or meanings. Instead, it becomes a series of situations in which the visitor is confronted with his or her own place and role in the world. When the visitor explores the familiar but is suddenly confronted with the unreality of what they thought they knew, the illusion is shattered and immersion disrupted. Meaning ascribed to the phenomenological experience is questioned, thereby creating an exteriorisation of the subject shifting focus from experiencing the world to reflecting on experiencing the world. As such, the process of exteriorisation through immersion and disruption is a form of destabilised "eccentric" (ex-centric) thinking which allows the dialectical relation between subject and other to emerge (Biesta 2016, 147), permitting visitors to "experience the disorientation that is necessary to understanding just how the world looks different to someone else." (Disch 1996, 157).

The new museum, as well as Andersen's fairy tales, is such a place of disorientation, calling the visitor or the reader into question, asking him or her to consider yet again what it means to be in a world full of others. In this sense, the true democratic potential of both Andersen's tales and the exhibition as a phenomenological experience resides in the ways they stage and perform an experience of that which is different to oneself. Concerned neither with maintaining the museum institution as authority nor with homogenising difference into sameness through inclusive and participatory practices, such a form of museology is exploring the museum as a performative site of wonder and questions – as both a practicing and a production of difference.

References

Adorno, Theodor W. 1974. *Minima Moralia: Reflections from a Damaged Life*. Translated by E. F. N. Jephcott. London: New Left Books.

Andersen, Hans Christian. 1837. Letter from Hans Christian Andersen to Henriette Hanck, November 25. http://andersen.sdu.dk/brevbase/brev.html?bid=1084 (the letter is kept at the museum H.C. Andersens Hus).

Andersen, Hans Christian. 1971–77. *H.C. Andersens Dagbøger 1825-1875*. 12 vols. Compiled by Kåre Olsen and H. Topsøe-Jensen and edited by Helga Vang Lauridsen, Tue Gad, and Kirsten Weber. København: Det Danske Sprog- og Litteraturselskab/Gad.

Anonymous. 1836. "Eventyr, Fortalte for Børn." Review of *Eventyr, Fortalte for Børn*, by Hans Christian Andersen. *Dansk Literatur-Tidende* 1: 10–14. https://books.google.dk/books?id=QnIUAAAAYAAJ.

Bennett, Jane. 2010. *Vibrant Matter: A Political Ecology of Things*. Durham: Duke University Press.

Bøggild, Jacob. 2012. *Svævende stasis. Arabesk og allegori i H.C. Andersens eventyr og historier*. Hellerup: Forlaget Spring.

Biesta, Gert. 2016. "Reconciling Ourselves to Reality: Arendt, Education and the Challenge of Being at Home in the World." *Journal of Educational Administration and History* 48 (2): 183–192. doi:10.1080/00220620.2016.1144580.

Desvallées, André, and François Mairesse. 2010. *Key Concepts of Museology*. Paris: Armand Collin. http://icom.museum/fileadmin/user_upload/pdf/Key_Concepts_of_Museology/Museologie_Anglais_BD.pdf.

Disch, Lisa Jane. 1996. *Hannah Arendt and the Limits of Philosophy*. Ithaca, NY: Cornell University Press.

Ekarv, Margareta, Elisabet Olofsson, and Bjørn Ed. 1991. *Smaka på orden. Om texter i utställningar*. Stockholm: Carlssons.

Husserl, Edmund. 1973. *Zur Phänomenologie der Intersubjektivität*. Den Haag: Martinus Nijhoff.

Kirshenblatt-Gimblett, Barbara. 2004. "The Museum: A Refuge for Utopian Thought." Accessed 18 January 2018. http://www.nyu.edu/classes/bkg/web/museutopia.pdf. In German in *Die Unruhe der Kultur. Potentiale des Utopischen*, translated by Frank Born, edited by Jörn Rüsen, Michael Fehr, and Annelie Ramsbrock, 187–196. Weilerswist: Velbrück Wissenschaft.

Lehmann, Hans-Thies. 2006. *Postdramatic Theatre*. Translated by Karen Jürs-Munby. London: Routledge.

Lübker, Henrik. 2016. "Aliens and Auras: Towards a Critical Practice of Representing Difference." *The International Journal of the Inclusive Museum* 9 (3): 35–46.

Lübker, Henrik and Jacob Bøggild. Forthcoming. "Andersen's Method." In *HCA Education. Stories*, edited by Jens Thodberg Bertelsen and Johs. Nørregaard Frandsen. Aarhus: Systime.

Lützen, Karin. 2014. *Byen tæmmes. Kernefamilie, sociale reformer og velgørenhed i 1800-tallets København.* København: Hans Reitzels Forlag.

Møller, Hans Henrik. 1995. "Fraværets Tale." In *Det flydende spejl. Analyser af H.C. Andersens 'Den lille Havfrue,'* edited by Finn Barlby, 41–48. København: Dråben.

Mortersen, Klaus P. 2005. "Hjemløs." *Sprogforum*, no. 33: 10–13.

Mortensen, Klaus P. 2007. *Tilfældets poesi. H.C. Andersens forfatterskab.* København: Gyldendal.

Rancière, Jacques. 1991. *The Ignorant Schoolmaster: 'Five Lessons in Intellectual Emancipation.* Stanford, CA: Stanford University Press.

Rancière, Jacques. 2011. *The Emancipated Spectator.* Translated by Gregory Elliott. London: Verso.

Sartre, Jean-Paul. 1956. *Being and Nothingness.* Translated by Hazel Estella Barnes. New York: Philosophical Library.

Simon, Nina. 2010. *The Participatory Museum.* Santa Cruz: Museum 2.0.

Thomsen, Torsten Bøgh. 2017. "Vi har intet at hovmode os over. Den antiantropocentriske Andersen." *Passage. Tidsskrift for litteratur og kritik* 32 (77): 49–65.

Vergo, Peter. 1989. *The New Museology.* London: Reaktion.

Witcomb, Andrea. 2007. *Re-imagining the Museum: Beyond the Mausoleum.* London: Routledge.